Government
and the Sports Business

Studies in the Regulation of Economic Activity

Government and the Sports Business

ROGER G. NOLL, Editor

Papers prepared for a conference of experts,
with an introduction and summary

The Brookings Institution / *Washington, D.C.*

Library of Congress Cataloging in Publication Data:

Main entry under title:
Government and the sports business.

  (Studies in the regulation of economic activity)
  Includes bibliographical references.
  1. Sports and state—United States—Congresses.
2. Sports—United States—Congresses.   I. Noll,
Roger G., ed.   II. Series.
GV583.G68   1974   338.4'7'7960973   74-4371
ISBN 0-8157-6106-6
ISBN 0-8157-6105-8 (pbk.)

9 8 7 6 5 4 3 2 1

THE BROOKINGS INSTITUTION is an independent organization devoted to nonpartisan research, education, and publication in economics, government, foreign policy, and the social sciences generally. Its principal purposes are to aid in the development of sound public policies and to promote public understanding of issues of national importance.

The Institution was founded on December 8, 1927, to merge the activities of the Institute for Government Research, founded in 1916, the Institute of Economics, founded in 1922, and the Robert Brookings Graduate School of Economics and Government, founded in 1924.

The Board of Trustees is responsible for the general administration of the Institution, while the immediate direction of the policies, program, and staff is vested in the President, assisted by an advisory committee of the officers and staff. The by-laws of the Institution state, "It is the function of the Trustees to make possible the conduct of scientific research, and publication, under the most favorable conditions, and to safeguard the independence of the research staff in the pursuit of their studies and in the publication of the results of such studies. It is not a part of their function to determine, control, or influence the conduct of particular investigations or the conclusions reached."

The President bears final responsibility for the decision to publish a manuscript as a Brookings book or staff paper. In reaching his judgment on the competence, accuracy, and objectivity of each study, the President is advised by the director of the appropriate research program and weighs the views of a panel of expert outside readers who report to him in confidence on the quality of the work. Publication of a work signifies that it is deemed to be a competent treatment worthy of public consideration; such publication does not imply endorsement of conclusions or recommendations contained in the study.

The Institution maintains its position of neutrality on issues of public policy in order to safeguard the intellectual freedom of the staff. Hence interpretations or conclusions in Brookings publications should be understood to be solely those of the author or authors and should not be attributed to the Institution, to its trustees, officers, or other staff members, or to the organizations that support its research.

Foreword

PROFESSIONAL SPORTS LEAGUES employ an array of business practices that are unique among American industries. The most obvious are the restrictions on market competition imposed by leagues on their member teams—restrictions so important that the major assets of a sports enterprise are intangible, being the capitalized value of protected positions in the markets in which players are acquired and tickets and broadcasting rights are sold.

Government policy has played a crucial role in shaping the sports business. The limits to market competition imposed by leagues have been sanctioned by government, in several cases through the enactment of enabling legislation by Congress. Moreover, federal tax policy makes it possible to use ownership of a sports franchise as an effective shelter against income taxation; and local governments, in their attempts to lure and retain major-league teams, have provided playing facilities at rents significantly below costs.

This book analyzes the operation of professional team sports in the United States, with particular attention to the effects of government policy on the financial performance of teams. Its major purpose is to consider whether the peculiar requirement of sports—that teams must not differ too greatly in playing strength if popular interest in any team is to be maintained—demands the special status sports enjoy as compared with government policy toward other forms of business enterprise. The authors are not unanimous on what government policy toward sports should be, but they do concur on several important points: that uncertainty of outcome in sports contests is an important element in the financial success of teams, that restrictions on market competition do not equalize playing strengths of teams but do make teams more nearly equal financially, and that alternative institutional arrangements and government policies might be at least as effective as the present system in making sports contests more competitive.

Earlier versions of all but the last chapter of this book served as background papers for a conference of experts on the economics of sports held at the Brookings Institution in December 1971. The participants in that conference are listed on pages 433–34. While this book is not intended in any way to reflect their views, the conferees made comments and offered suggestions that led to substantial revision of all chapters. The authors are especially grateful to Bill Veeck, who, in addition to making numerous useful suggestions at the conference, was readily available to the authors for advice and assistance throughout the project. Other conferees who were a continuing and invaluable source of information and comment were Walter Oi, Edward F. Denison, Leonard Rapping, Lawrence Fleischer, Edward R. Garvey, and Philip Hochberg. Preparation of the paper by James Quirk and Mohamed El Hodiri was partially supported by a grant to the authors from the University of Kansas faculty research fund.

Roger G. Noll, a senior fellow in the Brookings Economic Studies program at the time of the conference, joined the faculty of the California Institute of Technology in the fall of 1973. He and the authors wish to thank Ralph Andreano, Lawrence Ritter, Barry R. Chiswick, Lowell E. Gallaway, Sherwin Rosen, Robert W. Peterson, Sheldon Cohen, Earl A. Thompson, and Edward Kelley, who criticized drafts; Norman Mauskopf, Dennis Noe, Susan Nelson, Richard Beatty, Roger Reynolds, Anthony Catanese, and Eden Yu, who provided research assistance; Evelyn P. Fisher, who checked the manuscript for accuracy; M. T. S. Tryon and Kathryn Breen, who provided secretarial support; Ellen A. Ash, who edited the manuscript; and Goddard W. Winterbottom, who prepared the index.

This volume is the eighth in the Brookings series of Studies in the Regulation of Economic Activity. The series presents the findings of a program of research focused on public policies toward business. The program is supported by a grant from the Ford Foundation and has been directed by Mr. Noll and Joseph A. Pechman, director of the Brookings Economic Studies program.

The views expressed in this book are solely those of the authors, and should not be attributed to the trustees, officers, or staff of the Brookings Institution or the Ford Foundation.

KERMIT GORDON
President

January 1974
Washington, D.C.

Contents

Tables

Figures

Government
and the Sports Business

CHAPTER ONE

The U.S. Team Sports Industry: An Introduction

ROGER G. NOLL

THE PROFESSIONAL SPORTS INDUSTRY provides a fascinating subject for students of the relationship between government and business. Virtually every major public policy toward business—antitrust, labor relations, taxation, even the constitutional prohibition against slavery—has a potentially significant application to sports.

The period since 1970 has been particularly rich in episodes within the sports business that raise important issues of public policy. Curt Flood launched and lost an antitrust suit against organized baseball. Two baseball umpires entered and lost a labor relations complaint that they had been discharged for attempting to form an umpires' union. Both football and baseball experienced their first league-wide player strikes. The two major professional football leagues completed a merger, then saw their revenues from the sale of television rights increase while their player costs, in the absence of interleague competition, declined. The two major professional basketball leagues, after several years of competition for players, petitioned Congress for an antitrust exemption to permit them to merge. The nation's capital found itself without a baseball team as the Senators' Minnesota-based owner shifted the franchise to Texas and both leagues, at least temporarily, turned down an appeal from local citizens and even from a committee of congressmen to let the city buy a replacement. In a repetition of the scenario enacted by the three other major professional sports in the past fifteen years, the fledgling World Hockey Association (WHA) was organized to compete—and, in all likelihood, eventually merge—with the highly successful National Hockey League (NHL). And in almost every major city in the country, lavish facilities costing tens of millions of dollars were being opened, constructed, or planned, more often than not at taxpayers' expense.

While these events were transforming the sports page of the American newspaper into a second financial section, sports fans and government officials alike could find little analytical or empirical information to help them form opinions on how public policy should respond to the chaotic business conditions in sports. As the bibliography at the end of this book shows, very little research has been done on the economics of sports and its public-policy implications; this book attempts to fill that void.

Many important aspects of the industry are not included in this book. The social implications of sports are not considered, and individual, as opposed to team, sports (bowling, golf, tennis) have been omitted, as have amateur sports; studies of these areas should properly constitute separate books. Also excluded, because of the unavailability of useful information, are investigations of gambling and concession operations. While all these topics may be as interesting and important as the issues examined here, the subject of this book is confined to the business practices of teams and leagues in the four major professional team sports.

This chapter provides an institutional, financial, and policy backdrop for the remainder of the book. First is a description of the operating rules of sports that are designed to prevent competition among teams for both players and customers. There follows a presentation of the available information on the profitability of teams in each of the four major sports. The chapter concludes with a summary of policy issues.

The Operation of Team Sports

A professional sports league is essentially a cartel, with the purpose of restricting competition and dividing markets among firms in the industry.[1] Each league has three types of restriction: one dealing with interteam competition for players, another with the location of league franchises, and a third with the sale of broadcasting rights.

1. The fact that leagues are cartels has no policy significance by itself. As sports entrepreneurs have long contended, restrictions on competition in business practices may be necessary in order to promote competition on the playing field. The validity of this contention is at the heart of the policy debate over the social justification for restrictive business practices in professional sports.

The Player Reservation System

The target of nearly all the antitrust cases in professional team sports has been the player reservation system, which limits competition among teams for players. This system includes rules governing the signing of new players, the promotion of players from minor to major leagues (of primary importance only in hockey and baseball), and the transfer of players from one major-league roster to another. These rules differ in detail from sport to sport, but their intention is everywhere the same—to limit, if not prevent, the competitive bidding among teams for the services of players.

THE RESERVE CLAUSE. The component of the player reservation system that receives the most public attention is the so-called reserve clause—that is, a clause in the contract of each player that assigns to a specific team the exclusive right to deal with him for his entire playing life. Technically, only baseball and hockey actually have a reserve clause. In these sports a player can change teams only if his current team grants another team the right to deal with him or releases him from the obligations of his contract. Football and basketball have rules that appear less restrictive than the reserve clause. In both sports a player may "play out his option" according to the provisions of the "option clause" in his contract.[2] The option clause states that a team has the exclusive right to retain a player's services, without his consent, for one year after the term of the contract has expired. If the player does not sign a new contract after his old one expires, his salary is 90 percent of what it was the previous year, and at the end of the year he is free to negotiate with other teams. Thus, under an option system the team has exclusive rights to deal with a player for only one year beyond the term of the contract, whereas under a reserve system the right is perpetual.

While in theory the option system gives the player more opportunity to decide for himself where he will play, in practice it is almost as restrictive as the reserve system. The most important reason for this is the "Rozelle rule," which provides that a team signing a player who has played out his option must indemnify the player's former team. The league commissioner

2. Again, to be technical, a basketball player's contract does not contain an actual option clause, but instead has a provision that is worded almost identically with baseball's reserve clause. The two basketball leagues simply interpret the clause as giving a team "option" rights instead of "reserve" rights.

has the authority, from which there is no appeal, to determine the amount of compensation, which can be in the form of any combination of rights to future draft choices or veteran players and cash payment deemed just by the commissioner.[3] A player who plays out his option thus sacrifices a substantial amount of current income for the risky proposition that he will get through the year uninjured and without loss of skill, and will then find another team willing to pay him a significantly higher salary—enough to compensate him for the loss of income and assumption of risk—despite the threat of a substantial indemnity payment if they sign him. It is not surprising that few players have played out their options and signed with new teams.

THE AGREEMENT NOT TO COMPETE. While reserve and option clauses receive the most public attention, they are not the most important component of the player reservation system. Clauses of personal service contracts that require an individual to work for a single enterprise for a long period of time have limited legal validity, as is demonstrated during periods of interleague competition, when a team that loses a player rarely succeeds in obtaining a judgment from the courts requiring him to fulfill his contract. For example, star players like Spencer Haywood in basketball and Bobby Hull in hockey have successfully switched leagues without completing the obligations of long-term contracts.

The key to the successful operation of the player reservation system is an agreement among the teams in a league not to compete for players. Each sport has an elaborate set of operating rules governing relations among teams, including prohibitions against negotiating with players whose rights are held by other teams. A team that contacts a player to determine if he might be interested in changing teams is guilty of "tampering" and can be severely punished by the league. The prohibition against tampering has two purposes. Obviously, it is designed to prevent interteam competition for players, but it also is said to maintain public confidence in the honesty of play. If a player were known to be negotiating with other teams and a misplay on his part led to a crucial defeat for his current team, the question could arise whether the player had intentionally committed the misplay or, at least, had been playing with something less than full dedication to victory. Sports entrepreneurs believe that there would be less public interest in professional sports if contests were re-

---

3. The two basketball leagues have proposed that after their merger they establish a system whereby a three-man committee, including a representative of the players association, would determine indemnity payments.

garded as "exhibitions" rather than "competitions"—that is, if the outcome were either predetermined or not the paramount concern of the teams.

During periods of interleague competition, the agreements not to compete within a league cease to be effective in preventing competitive bidding for players. When a new league is formed, the following sequence of events normally occurs. First, the financial strength of the new enterprise is tested during several years of increasingly intense competition for players, which causes player salaries to rise substantially. Eventually, the new league proves that its financial backing is adequate to survive the competition— and to cause financial losses to the established league. The second phase is then entered, during which the leagues negotiate a merger. To the fans, a merger means an interleague championship playoff and, in all sports but baseball, interleague play during the regular season. To the owners, a merger brings about an agreement among all teams in the sport to limit the competition for players. Thus, the reserve and option clauses, with their limited efficacy during interleague competition, become secure again through mutual agreement.

ACQUISITION OF NEW PLAYERS. The arrangements for the entry of new players into professional sports are similar to the rules governing competition for veterans. Each sport has a "drafting" system whereby teams select "free agents," that is, players who have yet to sign a professional contract. As presently constituted, the order of selection is roughly inversely related to the quality of the team.[4] Once a team drafts a player, it acquires exclusive rights to negotiate with him.[5] Again, the effectiveness of this system rests on an agreement among the teams to respect exclusive bargaining rights. During periods of interleague competition, however, two teams, one in each league, have legitimate negotiating rights to any given player, and they engage in competitive bidding for his services. Often this leads to a breakdown in the agreement not to compete *within* a league, since each league wants to prevent the other from signing the best new players. Some football and basketball players, for example, have

4. Priority in making draft choices is based on the standing of the teams in their leagues at the end of the season. Since leagues differ both in average team strength and in the distribution of strength among teams, the team ranked second or third from last in one league can actually be weaker than the last-ranked team in another, but the latter will receive a higher position in the selection order.

5. Depending on the sport, the exclusive rights can be permanent or of as short as six months' duration. Obviously, the shorter the term of the exclusive rights, the greater the bargaining strength of the player.

reportedly been signed by teams other than those holding their draft rights. Successful completion of a merger reinstates the effectiveness of a drafting system.

NONROSTER VETERAN PLAYERS. In all sports, teams have more players under exclusive contract than they normally have on their active rosters. For example, a baseball team can, for most of the season, carry only twenty-five players on its major-league roster, but it may have a total of forty players under exclusive contract; the fifteen extra men play for minor-league teams affiliated with the parent club. In football, although occasionally a nonroster player does play in the minor leagues, the seven nonroster players allowed to a team are usually placed on the "taxi squad" —a group of players that practices with the regular forty-man team but does not play in the games. In hockey, a team may have twenty-five players under contract, but normally only twenty are on the playing roster.[6] Thus, players with the greatest promise of developing major-league talent can be protected.

Two situations may arise in which teams might wish to compete for players even though a draft system or a reserve or option clause is in effect. First, a player who was not skilled enough to make the active roster of a team when originally signed to a professional contract may improve his skills over a period of several years until he becomes major-league material. Second, a player whose skills are not adequate to secure a position on one team may be acceptable to another. Each professional sport has provisions for limiting competition for these marginal players.

One such provision is the waiver rule. When a team gives up its exclusive rights to a player, the player does not at once become free to negotiate with all other teams. He must first "clear waivers," which means that each team in the league must have the opportunity to purchase from his old team, at a fixed price stated in league rules, exclusive rights to bargain with him. Even if he clears waivers, he may still not be free unless, as in baseball, he has played in the major leagues for several years or his team has already assigned him to the minor leagues the maximum permissible number of times.

Another important arrangement is the minor-league draft. In baseball and hockey, players not on the protected roster of major-league teams can be claimed by other teams at the end of each season. Furthermore, when

---

6. Hockey teams need not limit their playing rosters to fewer than the number of players under contract, but playing rosters rarely exceed twenty.

a team drafts a new player it must place him on the protected roster, thereby displacing a formerly protected player and making him available for drafting by other teams. This drafting procedure is, however, subject to important limitations. In baseball, a team cannot lose all of its unprotected players at once. And the payment exacted for a drafted player is $30,000 in hockey or $20,000 in baseball, which is a stiff price for a player who has not yet achieved major-league status.

While the veteran-player drafting procedures constitute a mechanism for circulating marginal players among teams, direct competition is discouraged. For example, a team that values a player more highly than his current team does may get the opportunity to draft him (and be obliged to compensate the team that loses him), but it is prevented from obtaining his services simply by offering him a higher salary or, if he is a minor-leaguer, by promising him a place on its major-league roster at his current salary.

The aggregate effect of all of the rules that limit competition for marginal players is more than just to prevent competitive bidding, although certainly they do achieve that as well. The other effect is to reduce the disparity in quality between the best and worst teams in a league. While a weak team that obtains rights to the rejects of championship teams is not likely to turn into a powerhouse, it probably will be stronger than if top-ranked teams were permitted to retain exclusive rights to an unlimited number of players. Whether the effect on competition is more far-reaching than this—that is, whether a system that prevents direct competition but permits drafting and acquisition through waivers actually produces more equally balanced sporting competition than a purely competitive system— is an unresolved controversy.[7]

Exclusive Marketing Rights

Just as league rules limit competition in the acquisition of players, so, too, do they limit competition in selling the product of the industry. Teams have three important sources of income: admissions, broadcasting, and concessions. In all three areas, teams are essentially monopolistic: for each sport, only one team in any city normally has the right to sell tickets to major-league professional contests, to offer broadcasts of contests, and to sell food, beverages, and souvenirs to those in attendance at its games.

7. See Chapters 2, 3, 10, and 12.

The rights to concessions are not covered by league rules and so are not treated in this book. Usually they are held either through contracts with stadium owners or because the team itself owns the stadium; teams then sell their concessions rights to catering companies through a competitive bidding process. The monopolies on contests and broadcasting in a particular sport do result from league rules and practices, and they raise important issues of public policy.

TEAM FRANCHISES. Each professional sport has rules governing the location of teams in the league. Although the rules vary among the leagues, the general effect is to prohibit a member team from locating in a city that another team has already designated as its home unless the latter gives its approval. Thus, each team has an exclusive right to sell admissions to major professional contests in the sport in its home territory.[8] Leagues also control the movement of existing franchises to cities without teams. A team wishing to relocate its franchise must obtain the approval of most of the other teams in its league (though the details differ from sport to sport). Established teams control the addition of new teams to the league by requiring not only that new teams pay multimillion-dollar fees to join the league, but also that they must locate in areas approved by the established teams.

As with the player reservation system, the exclusivity of franchise rights is threatened only by the emergence of interleague competition, and even this threat is minimal. The new football and basketball leagues that emerged in the 1960s failed, with the exception of the New York Jets of the American Football League, to survive the competition in the home cities of established teams. Two other teams, the Oakland Raiders and the New York Nets, survived competition with teams in the same metropolitan area but different cities. The World Hockey Association has attempted to challenge the National Hockey League in six cities, and its strongest franchise is presently in Boston. Perhaps the WHA will prove an exception to the general rule that new leagues can succeed only in new territory.

Whether the rules on franchising are legally enforceable is an interesting and debatable question. In the cases of the Milwaukee (now Atlanta) Braves and the Seattle Pilots (now Milwaukee Brewers), the courts have agreed that teams can move. But whether a team could be prevented from

8. The major exception to this generalization is in baseball, where a team in one league can locate in the home territory of a team in the other league as long as the stadiums are separated by five miles.

moving into an area already occupied by another team in the same sport, or, for that matter, from moving without receiving league approval, has never been tested in the courts, nor has a league's close control of expansion. Again, the key to the success of the franchising rules is the mutual agreement among teams, and even among those who seek to acquire teams, to abide by the decisions of the league. Regardless of the legal standing of the rules, they are effective as long as all concerned agree that the number of franchises should be limited and that teams should not compete for the same fans.

BROADCASTING RIGHTS. The limitations on competition in the broadcasting of games have two major features. First, rights to national broadcasts of games in each sport are controlled by the leagues. This situation resulted from legislation passed in the early 1960s that exempted sports from antitrust laws when teams in a sport combine to sell national broadcast rights.[9] Second, each team has exclusive rights to broadcast all home games that are not part of the league's national broadcasting package and to prevent the broadcast in its home territory of any game not in the package. Since all teams either have local monopolies or compete with only one other team in their sport, these rules create a local monopoly in broadcasting that can be more important to a team than league arrangements for national telecasts.[10] Teams may compete for broadcast rights outside of the home territory of any other team, but since nearly all large cities have teams in all sports, this competition is for a relatively limited market.

Conclusions

As the preceding discussion makes clear, professional sports leagues have a remarkably complex set of rules and practices that all but eliminate business competition among their members. The extent of the anticompetitive practices is made especially apparent by the contrast between normal operations and conditions during the occasional periods when a new league emerges, when, until one league fails or a merger is consummated, competition prevails. During these "wars," player salaries, espe-

9. P.L. 87-331, approved Sept. 30, 1961 (75 Stat. 732).
10. For all sports except football. A football team can sell radio rights for all games and television rights for exhibition games; television rights for regular-season and playoff games are sold only through the league. In the other sports, a team can televise as many games as it wants, as long as it does not infringe on any other team's local monopoly rights in broadcasting.

cially for rookies and superstars, are considerably higher, team profits appear to be much lower, and the number of major-league teams is greater. Only twice has the end of a period of competition not been accompanied by a reduction in the number of major-league teams: at the turn of the century, the American League "war" ended when the National League accepted its competitor as an equal; and, in the mid-1960s, the American Football League merged with the National Football League without the loss of any teams.

The other major consequence of competition is that formation of a new league has *always* meant that some owners in the new league will obtain major-league franchises when peace is restored. The Federal League (baseball), the All-America Conference (football), and the American League (basketball) all folded, and the Continental League (baseball) never even began to play, but in each instance at least one team owner in the new league obtained the franchise of a team in the old after the new enterprise had gone out of business. This consistent pattern bodes well for owners and fans of the WHA.

Profits

Rules limiting competition presumably raise revenues and lower costs for teams. An investigation of the profits of teams provides some basis for measuring the financial effectiveness of these restrictions.

In order to estimate the profitability of sports teams, two difficulties must be dealt with. The first is the general unavailability of data for either individual teams or entire leagues. A few teams are publicly held joint-stock corporations, and so release public annual reports. A few others have been willing to give some expense and revenue information to members of this research project, but only on a confidential basis. For most of the remaining teams, data could be collected only on official paid attendance, published ticket prices, broadcasting revenue, and rent payments (for teams playing in facilities owned by government organizations). Finally, some unaudited financial information was submitted as evidence in the Curt Flood case.[11] The profitability estimates reported herein are based upon this admittedly fragmentary information.

11. Arthur D. Little, Inc., "Economic Analyses of Certain Aspects of Organized Baseball" (prepared for defendants in *Curtis C. Flood* v. *Bowie K. Kuhn et al.*, 316 F. Supp. 271 [S.D.N.Y. 1970], n.d.; processed), and the transcript of the testimony in *Flood* v. *Kuhn*.

The second major difficulty in making profitability estimates is the conceptual one of devising a definition of profits that is uniform and analytically useful. In addition to the net revenues after taxes that appear on income statements of teams, the following items should be included in the calculation of profit:

1. The depreciation of the percentage of a franchise's purchase price that is attributed to the value of player contracts. As explained in Chapter 5, depreciation of the original cost of a team is taken not for the usual purpose of accumulating funds to replace an asset at the end of its useful life, but instead to provide, in a profitable enterprise, a nontaxable cash flow to the owners.

2. Some part of the salaries of administrative officers of the team. Since most professional sports teams are partnerships, sole proprietorships, or Subchapter-S corporations, any profits of the team are included in the total income of the owners and taxed at personal income tax rates. Consequently, the effect on the owners' after-tax income is identical whether they pay themselves salaries or dividends. As will be shown below, administrative costs tend to rise and fall with the fluctuating success of a team, which could indicate that owners—particularly majority owners in a more widely held corporation or partnership—in good years vote themselves profits in the form of salary increases.

3. Interest payments. The size of interest payments made by a team reflects the method used by the owners to raise capital: if a new owner puts up his own money to buy a franchise, he pays no interest; but if some of the money is borrowed, the lender has first claim on profits to the extent of the interest due him. Both interest paid and the team's net profits represent returns to the investors in the team, and hence both should be included in the total profit figure.

4. Stadium rentals. For the few teams that own their own stadiums, the rent they pay for use of the facilities may or may not be at the going market rate. The decision of the owners in such a case about how much rent one arm of the company should charge the other need not be related to the actual costs of operating the facility. If the rent a team pays differs from what would be charged another firm, that discrepancy should be included in the calculation of team profits. Most of the available information on rents is for teams playing in government-owned stadiums; as Chapter 9 shows, these rents are probably lower than the true cost of providing the facilities. Hence, though the following estimates may overstate the profits of teams that play in their own facilities, the error is probably

Table 1. Average Operating Statements of Basketball Teams, Fiscal Years 1970 and 1971[a]

Thousands of dollars

Item	American Basketball Association League average[b] 1970	1971	Typical teams, 1971[c] Weak	Medium	Strong	National Basketball Association League average[b] 1970	1971	Typical teams, 1971[c] Weak	Medium	Strong	Very strong	Recent expansion
Revenues	394	619	453	658	1,154	1,715	1,762	1,612	1,352	1,774	6,393	958
Game	n.a.	n.a.	337	540	1,018	n.a.	n.a.	1,133	1,027	1,225	5,691	n.a.
Broadcasting	n.a.	n.a.	0	40	32	n.a.	n.a.	365	314	404	n.a.	n.a.
Other	n.a.	n.a.	116	78	104	n.a.	n.a.	114	10	145	n.a.	n.a.
Direct costs	767	1,122	1,329	1,016	1,234	1,767	1,814	2,024	1,383	1,808	5,357	1,154
Player compensation	n.a.	n.a.	380	354	n.a.	n.a.	n.a.	632	616	933	n.a.	n.a.
Rent and other game	n.a.	n.a.	430	223	n.a.	n.a.	n.a.	806	429	397	n.a.	n.a.
General and administrative	n.a.	n.a.	318	395	n.a.	n.a.	n.a.	408	164	273	n.a.	n.a.
Promotion	n.a.	n.a.	201	44	n.a.	n.a.	n.a.	178	174	205	n.a.	n.a.
Operating income	-373	-503	-876	-358	-80	-52	-52	-412	-31	-34	1,036	-196
Other income	4	70	-11	0	-10	565[d]	54[d]	0	0	200	n.a.	260
Net income	-369	-433	-887	-358	-90	422	1	-412	-31	166	1,036	60
Other costs	96	140	279	168	42	268	434	18	153	927	0	1,607
Player depreciation	67[d]	108[d]	189	138	38	214	371	17	33	673	0	1,575
Interest	29[d]	32[d]	90	30	4	54[d]	63[d]	1	120	254	n.a.	32
Book profit[e]	-449	-593	-1,166	-526	-131	109	-438	-430	-184	-761	1,036	-1,543

Source: Calculated from the financial statements of professional basketball teams submitted to the Senate Antitrust and Monopoly Subcommittee. A complete presentation and analysis of these data can be found in "Statement by Roger G. Noll and Benjamin A. Okner," in *Professional Basketball*, Hearing before the Subcommittee on Antitrust and Monopoly of the Senate Committee on the Judiciary, 92 Cong. 2 sess. (1972), Pt. 2, pp. 1042–56 (Brookings Reprint 258). Figures are rounded.

n.a. Not available.

a. The fiscal years of the teams end at various times but usually include the previous playing season.

b. Based on a less than complete sample of teams, since some teams submitted too little information to make valid estimates possible.

c. Actual figures for teams considered typical. Data for most teams can be found in the Noll and Okner statement.

d. Average based on fewer teams than used for other items, since some teams did not show this item separately. Net income and book profit figures are not adjusted for incomplete data.

e. Book profit = net income minus other costs.

negligible, particularly since rents are a relatively small part of expenses for most teams. That several teams have freely chosen to build their own facilities rather than play in publicly owned ones bears this out. In a few cases, in fact, where rental payments are astronomical, they clearly represent, in large measure, profits.

The following estimates of profits refer exclusively to the situation in recent years. It is likely that, except for baseball, profits are now as high as they have ever been; particularly in basketball, owners may have sustained substantial losses during the postwar period, which are only now being recaptured. Nevertheless, the present is probably a better indication of the future than the past and therefore more relevant to future policy. It should be reemphasized that these figures are calculated on a basis that is intended to measure the long-term viability of teams, and are not necessarily those a team might actually use for tax or public relations purposes.

Basketball

Of the four major professional team sports, basketball is the least profitable. Most teams show book losses, but, because of the tax treatment of player depreciation, probably only the weakest teams do not have a positive cash flow.

FINANCIAL DATA. Many teams have rather large depreciation deductions, reflecting the decision of the owner, following acquisition or expansion, to depreciate most of the cost of the team over the expected career life of the players (see Table 1). The after-tax profit of a team depends heavily on such depreciation decisions and on the status of the team for tax purposes (do individual or corporation tax rates and rules apply?), so no estimate of after-tax profit is included.

Most teams either lose money or barely break even; a few make enormous profits. In fiscal 1971, nine of the fifteen National Basketball Association (NBA) teams submitting reports were profitable if player depreciation and interest expense are not deducted from income, but only one of the nine American Basketball Association (ABA) teams submitting reports was profitable by the same measure. One highly profitable team is the Milwaukee Bucks, a public corporation issuing public annual reports. Table 2 shows the Bucks' finances for its first three fiscal years of operation. Before acquiring Kareem Abdul-Jabbar, the team had accumulated losses of $415,000, losing $370,000 in 1968–69 alone while fielding one of the two very poor expansion teams then playing. Abdul-Jabbar's

Table 2. Operating Statements, Milwaukee Bucks, Fiscal Years 1969, 1970, and 1971[a]

Thousands of dollars

Item	1969	1970	1971
Revenues	863	2,166	3,072
Game	615	1,755	2,198
Exhibition	27	155	141
League	547	1,399	1,785
Playoff[b]	41	201	272
Broadcasting	166	301	481
Regular season	146	263	452
Playoff	20	38	29
Other	81	110	393
Interest	0	123	177
Miscellaneous	81	−13	31
Basketball camp	0	0	185
Direct costs	1,061	1,425	2,219
Team and game	664	920	1,408
Sales	151	145	} 693
General and administrative	246	359	
Basketball camp	0	0	118
Gross income	−198	741	852
Other costs	174	446	72
Player depreciation	174	98	98
Loss averaging	0	348	−26
Carryover	0	211	0
Deferred	0	137	−26
Taxable income	−372	295	780

Sources: Milwaukee Professional Sports and Services, Inc., *1971 Annual Report* and *1970 Annual Report.* Figures are rounded.

a. Fiscal year ends on May 31.

b. Net of league share and direct costs.

first season, 1969–70, produced a profit of about $300,000; in 1970–71, when a second superstar (Oscar Robertson) was added to the team, profits rose to almost $800,000 as the team won the league championship. Actually, total profits for the 1970–71 season were probably even higher, as reflected in the $200,000 increase in the elusive "general and administrative" expense item.[12] Table 3 shows the Bucks' profits for fiscal years

12. Selling costs alone could not account for the huge increase in the sum of sales and general costs shown in the 1971 financial statement. Nearly all teams for which information is available spent several hundred thousand dollars less than the Bucks on these items.

1970 and 1971 as a percent of total investment; the profit rate is about twice the average for American corporations. The Bucks are not, however, the most profitable franchise in basketball. Both the New York Knicks and the Los Angeles Lakers draw many more fans, and the Knicks charge much higher prices. The profits of the Knicks, including the amounts finally attributed to the team's parent corporation through rent and concession income, are at least $2.5 million annually, and perhaps substantially more.

The wide disparity in the financial performance of teams has two sources. Most important is the exclusive territorial right given to each team. The teams in the most lucrative markets—New York, Los Angeles, Chicago, and a few others—are immune from competition, no matter how great the demand for professional basketball in their home cities. This situation, of course, exists in all sports.

The other factor contributing to divergent financial health is the gate-sharing arrangement. In basketball, as in hockey, the home team keeps

Table 3. Summary of Return on Investment, Milwaukee Bucks, Fiscal Years 1970 and 1971

Thousands of dollars

Item	September 1, 1969 to May 31, 1970[a]	June 1, 1970 to May 31, 1971
Total investment through fiscal 1969	2,491	2,491
Less accumulated player depreciation	272	370
Depreciated investment	2,219	2,121
Gross income	793	852
As percent of total investment	31.8	34.2
Less player depreciation	98	98
Less tax liability[b]	160	390
Gross income after depreciation, before tax	695	754
As percent of depreciated investment	31.3	35.6
Gross after-tax income, before depreciation	633	462
As percent of total investment	25.4	18.5
Net income	535	364
As percent of depreciated investment	24.1	17.2

Source: Milwaukee Professional Sports and Services, Inc., *1971 Annual Report* and *1970 Prospectus*. Figures are rounded.

a. Fiscal year was changed from period ending Aug. 31 in 1969 to period ending May 31 in 1970.

b. Fifty percent of taxable income.

virtually all of the gate receipts, so that teams from cities with poor attendance do not benefit from the enormous crowds that attend their away games in the biggest cities. Consequently, basketball and hockey teams in smaller cities have less chance of financial success than baseball or football teams, where the visiting team receives some share of the gate (for baseball, 20 percent in the American League and about 10 percent in the National League; for football, 40 percent).

PLAYER COSTS AND THE CASE FOR MERGER. The two basketball leagues defended their request for legislation permitting their merger by arguing that competition for players was undermining the financial health of the sport. While player costs were high in basketball, they were not the most important cause of rising expenditures in the years when competition emerged. Table 4 shows the sources of cost increases in the period 1968–71 for the ABA and NBA teams that provided disaggregated cost data for at least two fiscal years. Because the data are based on a relatively small sample, definitive conclusions are not warranted; the results, however, are still striking. For the ABA, in all but one of the four periods for which data were available, the increase in other costs was approximately double the increase in player compensation. Furthermore, the period based on the largest number of teams (six of a total of eleven) shows the greatest differential between player and other costs.

The NBA data reveal a pattern similar to that found for the ABA: player compensation accounts for less than half the cost increases these teams have experienced during the period of interleague competition.

These data suggest that a merger of the two leagues would not reduce player costs sufficiently to alter the viability of the financially weak teams. Table 5 lists total player compensation and measures of profit for the seven ABA teams that provided sufficiently disaggregated data for 1971 to make meaningful comparisons possible; it shows that player salaries are consistently dwarfed by book losses. Even if player salaries fell to zero, the aggregate book loss would still be $2 million. When interest and depreciation are subtracted from book loss (leaving net return), losses still exceed player costs by about $100,000 per team. Interestingly enough, if total salaries for these teams fell by *half* this amount, the average annual salary would be under $20,000, which is the minimum salary permitted in the NBA through an agreement (concluded November 15, 1972) with the players' association. Quite obviously, such a drastic reduction in salaries is completely unrealistic. And even if salaries could be cut by 100 percent, the annual losses, measured by net return, of the three most

Table 4. Aggregate Player and Operating Costs[a] of Basketball Teams, Fiscal Years 1968–71

Thousands of dollars

Number of teams reporting[b] and cost item	1968	1969	1970	1971	Increase
American Basketball Association					
4 teams					
Player compensation	375	n.a.	n.a.	1,558	1,183
Other operating costs	1,127	n.a.	n.a.	3,438	2,311
5 teams					
Player compensation	n.a.	933	1,272	n.a.	339
Other operating costs	n.a.	2,019	2,352	n.a.	333
6 teams					
Player compensation	n.a.	1,117	n.a.	2,161	1,044
Other operating costs	n.a.	2,627	n.a.	4,936	2,309
5 teams					
Player compensation	n.a.	n.a.	1,228	1,878	650
Other operating costs	n.a.	n.a.	2,461	3,880	1,419
National Basketball Association					
6 teams					
Player compensation	1,938	n.a.	3,444	n.a.	1,506
Other operating costs	3,918	n.a.	5,670	n.a.	1,752
5 teams					
Player compensation	n.a.	n.a.	2,756	3,224	468
Other operating costs	n.a.	n.a.	4,003	4,519	516

Source: Same as Table 1.

n.a. Not available.

a. Player compensation costs include fringe benefits and bonuses; other operating costs exclude player depreciation and interest.

b. Includes only those teams—a total of eight in the ABA and six in the NBA—that supplied disaggregated cost data for each period.

unprofitable franchises shown in the table would still equal or exceed $500,000.

Baseball

Baseball is substantially healthier than basketball, in terms of both the average profitability of teams and the even distribution of operating profits within the sport. Table 6 shows the revenues, costs, and profits of four

Table 5. Player Compensation and Profits of Selected American Basketball Association Teams, Fiscal Year 1971

Thousands of dollars

Team[a]	Player compensation	Book profit	Net return[b]
A1	382	−1,117	−1,118
A2	380	−1,165	−887
A3	221	−766	−716
A5	320	−100	209
A8	354	−526	−358
A9	561	−466	−175
A10	263	−269	−4
Total	2,481	−4,409	−3,049

Source: See Table 1.
a. Team symbols, used to maintain anonymity, are consistent with those used in the Noll and Okner "Statement" cited in the Table 1 source.
b. Net return = book profit plus interest and depreciation.

teams, the reported profitability of all twenty-four teams offered as evidence in the Curt Flood case, and estimates of the extremes within the sport.

For numerous reasons, the baseball-wide averages reported in the table probably underestimate the profitability of the sport. For example, the Baltimore Orioles showed an after-tax profit in 1969 that was about $500,000 larger than the reported average, despite the fact that in 1969 their reported total revenues (including playoff revenues) were roughly average and, because they employed several star players and were consistent winners, their payroll was almost certainly larger than average.

The average profit figure is undoubtedly much depressed by the few teams with heavy depreciation and interest expenses. It is highly likely, furthermore, that the unaudited financial data presented in *Flood* v. *Kuhn* were not prepared according to consistent accounting practices, since many different teams were involved. Three cost items, in particular, appear to have been treated in a manner that would tend to reduce profit estimates.

First, while the costs of acquiring players are included, either as direct costs or, if the team amortizes player acquisition costs, as part of player depreciation, the revenue from sales of player contracts is not. This means that when a player's contract changes hands it appears as a cost for the team that buys it but not as an offsetting revenue for the team that sells it.[13] Since roughly forty trades involving cash were reported during 1969, this is not a negligible omission.[14]

Second, part of the true profitability of a team may be hidden in administrative costs. Between 1966 and 1969, sales, general, and administrative costs, taken together, increased by about one-third, or around $250,000 per team; miscellaneous expenses showed the next largest increase, about $150,000 per team.[15] Since this period saw increasing public concern over the effects of competition in sports—the emergence of the ABA and the merger of the football leagues occurred during these years—baseball teams may well have decided that it was politic to transfer some profits to essentially equivalent cost items, such as salaries and amenities for owners.[16] It is also possible, of course, that other items may account for the growth of the heterogeneous "general and administration" category; professional fees, for instance, especially legal costs, are known to be rising for all sports teams. Nevertheless, it is reasonable to assume that some owners choose to draw executive salaries while others do not, and these salaries would have to be accounted for in arriving at a correct estimate of the profitability of a team and in making valid interteam comparisons.

Third, interest charges, here included as costs, should properly be excluded since they are actually part of the return to capital. Interest charges can form an enormous percentage of the costs of a newly purchased team. For example, of the $10 million cost of the Montreal Expos, an expansion team, at least $4.5 million was obtained through borrowing, indicating that the team probably pays several hundred thousand dollars a year in interest.[17] Similarly, $6 million of the $8.3 million paid for the Washington Senators in 1968 was financed by loans.

13. See testimony of John Clark, Jr., *Flood* v. *Kuhn*, p. 1710 of the trial transcript.

14. *Official Basesball Guide for 1970* (Sporting News, 1970), pp. 369–73.

15. Arthur D. Little, Inc., "Economic Analyses of Certain Aspects of Organized Baseball."

16. The data for the Atlanta Braves show the same correlation between administrative costs and playing success exhibited by the Bucks. In 1969, when Atlanta won the National League's Western Division championship, administrative costs were 25 percent higher than in the next, less successful, season. The "sportsman" owned Cubs, on the other hand, did not experience this cost rise in 1969, when they were enormously profitable and nearly won the title in the National League's Eastern Division.

17. Testimony of John McHale, *Flood* v. *Kuhn*, pp. 1310–11, 1326–29 of the trial transcript.

Table 6. Operating Statements of Baseball Teams, Fiscal Years 1969 and 1970

Thousands of dollars

Item	Atlanta Braves 1969	Atlanta Braves 1970	Baltimore Orioles 1969	Baltimore Orioles 1970	Chicago Cubs 1969	Chicago Cubs 1970	Washington Senators 1969	Washington Senators 1970	Baseball-wide average, 1969	Estimates, 1970 Most successful team	Estimates, 1970 Least successful team
Revenues											
Game	5,238[a]	4,248	2,499	2,624	3,339	3,471	2,659	2,614	3,199	6,000	1,700
Broadcasting	972	1,080	1,866	1,962	1,077	1,252	613	700	1,422	2,000	750
Other	601	337	871[b]	895[b]	859	872	484	447	606	750	350
Playoff	n.a.	0			0	0	0	0	...	...	...
Total	6,811	5,664	5,236	5,481	5,274	5,594	3,755	3,760	5,227	8,750	2,800
Costs											
Player development[c]	1,328	1,314	1,446	1,265	1,371	1,596	721	870	1,317	1,800	700
Player depreciation	680	567	3,260[e]	3,550[e]	0	0	1,680	1,962	445	0	500
Team[d]	1,723	1,864			1,491	1,785	1,335	1,557	1,072	2,000	700
Game	1,048	904			979	1,103	751	822	1,192	1,200	800
General and administrative	774	621			524	730	933	1,097	1,004	750	400
Sales	271	233					287	321		300	100
Miscellaneous[f]	215	−32					*	8	371	150	100

Income taxes	425	73	298	321	n.a.[g]	n.a.[g]	0	0	150[h]	1,475	0
Total	6,464	5,544	5,003	5,136	4,365	5,215	5,708	6,638	5,549	7,675	3,300
Profits											
Before tax	772	193	530	666	909	380	−1,952	−2,877	−172	2,550	−500
After tax	347	120	232	345	n.a.[g]	n.a.[g]	−1,952	−2,877	−322	1,075	−500
Cash flow[i]	1,199	799	300	420	900	380	−211	−211	123	1,075	0

Sources: Atlanta, Baltimore, Chicago, and Washington data, from relevant annual reports of the teams to stockholders; baseball-wide average, calculated from testimony and supporting documents in *Curtis C. Flood v. Bowie K. Kuhn et al.*, 316 F. Supp. 271 (S.D.N.Y. 1970); estimates for most and least successful teams made on the basis of six teams: most successful—Dodgers, Mets, and Reds; least successful—Indians, White Sox, and Padres. Since none of the sources fully explains the procedures followed in assigning costs and revenues to categories, data are not strictly comparable (see testimony of John Clark, Jr., *Flood v. Kuhn*, pp. 1710–12 of the trial transcript). Figures are rounded.

n.a. Not available.

a. Includes playoff.

b. In the Orioles' financial report, this item is listed as "other income and expenses (net)"; but the status of this item in pennant and nonpennant years, together with the statement elsewhere in the report that the profitability of the team is due entirely to the league championship playoff and the World Series, points to the conclusion that playoff revenues account for nearly all of this item.

c. Primarily minor-league subsidy and scouting expenses.

d. Includes player compensation.

e. The Orioles do not list player depreciation separately; however, elsewhere in the report the book value of contracts eligible for depreciation is listed at approximately $380,000. Assuming a five-year period of amortization, this gives about $75,000 a year.

f. Interest income recorded as a negative expense.

g. Deductions (amount not specified) for federal and state income taxes, as well as fees from the rental of Wrigley Field for football games, are included in the broadcast revenues item.

h. Calculated on the basis of the similarity of total revenues in this column to those of the Orioles in 1969. Since about half of all teams include a depreciation item, the average income tax figure is assumed to be about half that of the Orioles.

i. The net cash flow is the sum of after-tax profits, interest, and player depreciation. In most cases, however, including the figures for the baseball-wide average, interest expenses could not be estimated, so the true cash flow is larger than shown. In addition, for purposes of calculating liability for income taxation, book losses can be used to offset income earned in other activities, as discussed in Chapter 5. An estimate of the tax reductions resulting from these book losses is not given here.

* Less than $500.

For these and other reasons, baseball profits (including interest and owner salaries) are probably a few hundred thousand dollars per team higher than reported in the Flood case. This does not, however, alter the basic financial picture of the sport: most teams are profitable, but not enormously so; very few teams actually lose money.

Only a few baseball teams reap true monopoly rewards, and even these probably do not do as well as the healthiest basketball franchise. The most profitable baseball teams are the Dodgers and the Mets, each of which consistently draws around two million fans. While little information is available about either team, it is unlikely that their profits are as high as the Knicks', despite the significantly more robust financial health of their sport. The principal reason for this is the gate-sharing arrangement prevalent in baseball. If the Mets could keep 100 percent of the Shea Stadium gate, their pretax profits would be roughly $300,000 greater. At the other end of the scale, such a gate-sharing arrangement would cost a team like the Indians about $200,000 a year in net revenues. If the estimated profits in Table 6 are roughly accurate, it is only the gate-splitting arrangement that keeps the shakiest baseball teams financially viable. An interesting aspect of the financial situation of baseball is the overwhelming dominance of the National League: in 1970, the six presumably most profitable franchises were all in the senior circuit.

Football

Football finances are a more closely guarded secret than baseball and basketball data. Aside from the one publicly held team, the New England Patriots, only one other team, the Philadelphia Eagles, has revealed audited financial data, and this only in connection with a bankruptcy case.[18] A few teams have confidentially provided members of this research project with some information on various cost and revenue items.

The profitability of football franchises is estimated in Table 7. The public information available for the Patriots and the Eagles provides some interesting hard data. First, the Patriots were, until 1971, the least successful team at the gate; in 1970 they drew nearly fifteen thousand fewer fans per game than the next-ranking team. But they have shown profits since the American Football League (AFL)–National Football League

---

18. Jerry Wolman, former owner of the Eagles, was involved in bankruptcy proceedings in late 1967.

Table 7. Operating Statements of Football Teams, Fiscal Years 1968 and 1970

Thousands of dollars

	New England Patriots, 1970	Philadelphia Eagles, 1968	Estimates, 1970		
Item			Average team, AFC	Good team, NFC	Most successful team, NFC
Revenues					
Game[a]	n.a.	2,911	2,500	2,900	3,800
Broadcasting	n.a.	1,299	1,750	1,950	2,000
Other	n.a.	269	250	350	400
Total	3,700	4,478	4,500	5,200	6,200
Costs					
Game	905	} 2,930	900	1,000	1,100
Team	2,230		2,300	2,600	2,800
General and administrative	228	983	250	300	300
Interest	109	120	100	100	100
Taxes[b]	8	24	50	50	50
Miscellaneous	14	57	50	50	50
Total	3,493	4,114	3,650	4,100	4,400
Operating income	207	364	850	1,100	1,800
Other income[c]	286[d]	220[e]	156[f]	220[e]	220[e]
Other costs[g]	220[e]	...	200	...	...
Profits[h]	273	584	806	1,320	2,020

Sources: Patriots' data, " The Eleventh Annual Report of the Boston Patriots of the American Football Conference of the NFL" (1971), Exhibit B; Eagles' data, calculated from the preliminary eleven-month financial report included in the Securities and Exchange Commission registration form of Jerry Wolman Enterprises, Inc. (Registration 2-29555, filed March 14, 1969) (eleven-month figures are prorated to twelve months, based on other information in the statement, unless complete twelve-month data occur elsewhere in the statement); estimates for the categories of average, good (would include Atlanta, Detroit, Green Bay, New Orleans, San Francisco, and Washington, plus the old AFL teams of Cincinnati and Miami), and most successful (would include Cleveland, Dallas, Los Angeles, and the New York Giants, plus Oakland and the New York Jets from the old AFL) teams, based on Patriots' and Eagles' annual income statements, adjusted for the differences in attendance, prices, and average player salaries reported in Chapters 4 and 6. Data include pre- and postseason games (with the exception of the Super Bowl, as it is assumed that none of the teams got that far in the playoffs). Figures are rounded.

n.a. Not available.

a. Includes the team's share of the gate at away games and excludes admissions tax and payments to visiting teams and the league for home games.

b. Does not include federal income tax because of loss carryovers from premerger operations. All teams except the Patriots are private corporations (usually Subchapter-S as defined in the U.S. Internal Revenue Code) or partnerships, so that tax liability depends on the other income of the owners. All profit calculations, therefore, exclude federal tax treatment (with net franchise and player sales being considered a capital gain). Since nearly all AFC teams probably had large tax losses prior to merger, tax liabilities of these teams are likely to be low.

c. Includes revenues from player sales, expansion, and merger.

d. Sale of player contracts, franchise, and television privileges.

e. The Eagles reported receiving this amount in 1968, and the Patriots reported paying the NFL amortization on $2 million over twenty years at 6.5 percent interest for the merger and $562,500 over ten years at 6.5 percent for AFL expansion. $220,000 amortization is used in the estimates for the good and most successful teams.

f. The Patriots reported $156,250 as the annual amortized payment from Cincinnati and Miami for league expansions. This figure is used in the estimate for the average team.

g. Estimated merger payment.

h. Before federal income tax, but after other taxes.

(NFL) merger, even though they were required to pay indemnities to the National Football Conference (NFC) teams in consequence. Second, the Eagles appear to be a roughly average NFC team in attendance and gate receipts. They failed to realize the profits shown in the table only because they made more than $1.5 million in uncollectable loans to their former owner. A comparison with the "good" NFC team estimates for 1970 suggests that the 1969 merger probably caused the Eagles' pretax profits for that year to reach about $1 million, based on an estimated $750,000 rise in revenues (from increased broadcasting income) and static costs (rising costs elsewhere offsetting declining player costs).

The most striking feature to be observed in Table 7 is the relatively small disparity in profitability among the teams. As with baseball, an important source of this relative financial equality is the revenue-sharing arrangements. The teams split broadcasting revenues almost equally, and gate receipts are divided 60–40. With a 100–0 gate split, as in basketball, the profit extremes would have widened: in 1970, for example, the Patriots would have had about $300,000 less revenue, putting them in the red; while a highly successful team would have received about $500,000 more. Football teams also show relatively small differences in total attendance figures. The most successful teams draw about twice as many fans as the least successful, in contrast to baseball, where the ratio is about four to one, and basketball, where it is seven to one. An important question is whether football's differential is intrinsic to the sport, or whether it results from operating practices that could be adopted by other sports.

Hockey

Unfortunately, very few data on the financial operations of hockey are available. None of the teams issues public statements, and only one voluntarily offered confidential information. Furthermore, only one publicly owned arena agreed to provide information about rental agreements. For some teams, not even average ticket prices could be calculated, for they refused to provide complete information on season-ticket prices. Relatively complete financial information is available for only one team, the Boston Bruins, whose annual reports are part of the record of the lawsuits that ensued when Derek Sanderson and Gerry Cheevers left the Bruins to play in the WHA. The available data are shown in Table 8, but it should be noted that the profit estimates are necessarily subject to substantial uncertainty.

Table 8. Operating Statements of Hockey Teams, Fiscal Years 1970, 1971, and 1973

Thousands of dollars

Item	Boston Bruins		Estimates for World Hockey Association teams, 1973[a]			Estimates for National Hockey League teams, 1973[b]		
	1970	1971	Weak	Aver-age	Best	Below aver-age	Aver-age	"Big five"
Revenues								
Game	3,196	3,605	250	700	1,500	2,000	3,450	4,600
Broadcasting	407	565	75	100	175	400	550	700
Player sales[c]	1,076	108	0	0	0	0	0	250
Other	2	105	25	50	125	100	150	250
Total	4,681	4,383	350	850	1,800	2,500	4,150	5,800
Costs								
Team	644	764	500	600	650	750	1,000	1,250
Game	754	670	450	500	550	500	600	700
General and adminis- trative	318	313	150	175	200	200	225	250
Player development	95	99	0	0	0	100	100	100
Sales and publicity	48	49	75	100	100	100	75	50
Player depreciation[d]	87	98	0	0	0	1,000	1,000	0
Rent	1,028	1,177	75	125	300	350	750	950
Total	2,974	3,170	1,250	1,500	1,800	3,000	3,750	3,300
Profits								
Pretax	1,707	1,213	−900	−650	0	−500	400	2,500
Operating[e]	1,794	1,311	−900	−650	0	500	1,400	2,500

Sources: Bruins' data, from evidence submitted in *Boston Professional Hockey Association* v. *Derek Sanderson*, U.S.D.C. Mass., C.A. 72-2490C (1972). The data have been rearranged to make this table consistent with those for the other sports. Income and costs of the parent corporation that are unrelated to hockey have been excluded, and the after-tax income is the estimated share of hockey operations in the larger total. The Bruins receive no concessions income, since concessions are handled by the parent corporation. WHA and NHL data, estimated by author.

a. Of the twelve WHA teams in 1972–73, Ottawa and Alberta fall into the "weak" category and New England and Quebec into the "best" category; the remaining eight teams, with average attendance ranging from 4,000 to 5,600 per game, comprise the "average" category. Average teams are assumed to make the first round of playoffs, while best teams are assumed to make the second round.

b. The NHL had sixteen teams in 1972–73. The "below average" column depicts a hypothetical team that averages about eleven thousand fans per game, considerably more than the attendance of the California Golden Seals, by far the weakest franchise in the NHL. This category includes the New York Islanders, Pittsburgh, Atlanta, Detroit, and Los Angeles. The "big five" teams—New York, Chicago, Toronto, St. Louis, and Montreal—draw around seventeen thousand fans per game. The "average" teams attract around fifteen thousand per game and include Buffalo, Boston, Vancouver, Minnesota, and Philadelphia. Estimates include first-round playoff revenues for average teams, second-round revenues for the "big five."

c. These figures include expansion fees paid to the Bruins and estimated for the most successful NHL teams; however, in practice a larger number of teams will share in expansion revenues. Other player sales are assumed to equal the amortization of purchased player contracts (shown as a cost), so that, except for depreciation of the initial purchase price of a team (see note d), player sales and player depreciation are both entered as zero in the estimates.

d. Player depreciation is assumed to be zero except for amortization of the cost of player contracts in the purchase price of a franchise. Since expansion franchises in the NHL currently cost over $6 million, it is assumed that newly purchased teams amortize $5 million in player contracts over five years in equal installments of $1 million. The "below average" and "average" categories include this depreciation expense, and hence these columns are not representative of teams that have not been recently purchased. The pretax profits of such teams would be $1 million more.

e. Excludes player depreciation.

The game revenues in the table are calculated from the estimates of average ticket price and reported attendance for league games summarized below:

	WHA			NHL		
Item	Weak	Average	Best	Below average	Average	"Big five"
Regular-season games						
Attendance per game	2,500	4,500	7,250	11,000	14,500	17,500
Average ticket price						
(dollars)	2.50	3.25	4.00	4.50	5.50	5.50
Playoff games						
Number of games	0	3	8	0	3	8
Attendance per game	...	8,000	10,000	...	15,000	17,500
Average ticket price						
(dollars)	...	4.00	4.50	...	5.50	5.50
Total gate receipts						
(thousands of						
dollars)	250	681	1,520	1,980	3,438	4,620

The average ticket price is the key assumption made here, and these figures are, if anything, conservative; WHA prices are certain to be higher than those charged by the best minor leagues, which average $3.07 in the American Hockey League and $2.47 in the Western Hockey League.[19]

NHL attendance varies from four thousand per game in Oakland and about ten thousand in Los Angeles to seventeen thousand per game in New York, Chicago, Toronto, and Montreal, and over eighteen thousand in St. Louis. Average ticket price varies between $4 and $6, with the more popular teams generally charging higher prices. Thus, ticket revenues in the NHL probably range from around $600,000 in Oakland to nearly $5 million in New York,[20] all of which goes to the home team.

Attendance figures for the WHA are much lower than for the NHL, with nearly all teams averaging four to five thousand fans per game. WHA teams, especially the less successful ones, practiced widespread ticket discounting in their first year. Thus, the two teams with the lowest attendance probably had revenues from ticket sales of under $300,000, and perhaps much less, while the most successful teams probably collected $1.5 to $2 million (including playoffs).

19. See *Philadelphia World Hockey Club, Inc.* v. *Philadelphia Hockey Club, Inc.*, U.S.D.C. Eastern Pa., C.A. 72-1902 (1972), Exhibit P-71.

20. New York has a slightly lower average attendance than St. Louis but apparently much higher prices.

Other income in the NHL is assumed to be comparable to that of football or successful basketball teams drawing about the same number of fans a season. For established teams, this includes an average of about $250,000 a year from the sale of players to new teams. When Vancouver and Buffalo joined the league in the 1969–70 season, expansion revenues were about $1 million apiece for the established NHL teams. The league expanded again with the inclusion of Atlanta and the New York Islanders in 1972–73. Expansion is expected to continue, with the addition of two teams every three or four years. Income in the NHL is also boosted by the standard clause in players' contracts that gives the team the right to share in a player's endorsement fees.

Other revenues in the WHA are likely to be rather small. Unlike the NHL, the endorsement income of star WHA players is not shared by the team unless the endorsement is arranged by its agent. And, although the WHA has obtained a national broadcasting contract that calls for a minimum of five games to be televised by CBS, the broadcast revenues of most teams are probably quite small—certainly under $100,000 a year in most cases.

From the relatively complete data submitted in the hockey antitrust suits, much can be inferred about hockey costs. In 1970–71, the Boston Bruins paid roughly one-third of their gate receipts in rent, which is substantially higher than the rental formulas reported by publicly owned arenas but consistent with the rents of teams that play in arenas belonging to their owners; the Bruins are a wholly owned subsidiary of the Boston Garden–Arena Corporation. The excess of this rent over the normal rental fee of about 20 percent of the gate should probably be regarded as profits for the team, regardless of how it is accounted for by a firm that owns both team and arena.

The Bruins paid salaries to players and coaches of approximately $37,000 per person in fiscal 1971.[21] This was far higher than the league average, because the Bruins were defending Eastern Division champions in that year.[22] The season before, the average Bruin salary had been approximately $5,000 less. In both seasons for which data are available, the Bruins spent slightly under $100,000 on player development and an

21. A hockey team has nineteen or twenty players and a coach.

22. The 1971–72 NHL average was reportedly $24,000. See *Philadelphia World Hockey Club, Inc.* v. *Philadelphia Hockey Club, Inc.*, U.S.D.C. Eastern Pa., C.A. 72-1661, Opinion (Nov. 8, 1972), p. 14. In 1972–73, the average was reported to be $40,000 (*Washington Post*, March 1, 1973).

approximately equal amount on player depreciation. Since the original cost of the franchise was not being depreciated, this represents an amortized cost of contracts purchased from other professional and amateur teams and was offset by a roughly equal revenue from sales of contracts, not including revenues from league expansion. The team also spent over $300,000 on general and administrative costs, including approximately $65,000 in salaries to top corporate officials. These salaries are excluded from estimates for the other teams, since they are not separable conceptually from profits, as explained above. Finally, miscellaneous costs, including sales, travel, and equipment, totaled around $750,000. For a team less successful than the Bruins, the figure would probably be very similar, with higher selling costs for a team less assured of selling out virtually every game being balanced by lower costs associated with the games.

Hockey, with its system of awarding all gate receipts to the home team, resembles basketball in that team profits vary greatly. But hockey is significantly healthier financially than basketball, for most of the NHL teams, including several expansion teams, are doing exceedingly well. Some teams may even challenge the NBA's Knicks for first place among all sports teams in total profits. Furthermore, several hockey teams are in the super profitable category, which, perhaps, explains the formation of the WHA. The California Golden Seals are probably the only unprofitable franchise in the NHL. According to their owner, Charles Finley, the Seals lost about $1 million in 1972–73,[23] which is essentially what could be predicted on the basis of the above estimates.[24] The next worst NHL franchise, the Los Angeles Kings, probably shows a small profit, assuming that the rent it pays to its parent corporation is on the order of 20 percent of the gate.

The financial condition of the WHA appears shaky, with all but two teams probably losing between $300,000 and $1 million in the 1972–73 season, but these figures by themselves are deceiving. It must be remembered that the cost of a franchise in the NHL is over $6 million, so that

23. *Washington Post,* Jan. 5, 1973.

24. In addition to gate receipts of $600,000, the Seals probably receive about $275,000 in broadcast revenues and $25,000 from other sources. Their costs can be assumed to be quite similar to those estimated for a "below average" NHL team, except that they probably pay less rent. Since Finley was in his third year of ownership in 1972–73, he was probably taking some depreciation on the original price of player contracts, so his book loss would be significantly in excess of $1 million.

if most WHA teams earn profits after five years of operations, the losses sustained in their early years would constitute a much smaller cost of entering the hockey business than the alternative of buying a team in the established league. Furthermore, a couple of the teams in the WHA were already at or near profitability in 1972–73, which is very unusual in the first year of a new league.

The enormous increase in the number of professional hockey teams, which began in the late 1960s through NHL expansion and has continued with the formation of the WHA, seems to have a much sounder economic justification than the growth in basketball that preceded it. With almost all of its sixteen teams operating well in the black, the NHL in 1973 was almost as healthy as the National Football League. Furthermore, most of the expansion teams are doing well, including those in relatively small metropolitan areas, such as Atlanta, Buffalo, and Vancouver. According to the Boston Garden–Arena Corporation's 1971–72 financial report, even the Bruins' minor-league teams, the Boston Braves and the Oklahoma City Blazers, showed pretax profits of $350,000 and $25,000, respectively. All these factors point to a bright future for the WHA, if it can convince fans that it is of major-league status. This seems likely, considering that the most successful WHA franchise, the New England Whalers, is located in Boston, also home of two other profitable teams, the Bruins of the NHL and the Braves of the American Hockey League. The situation of the WHA in 1973 is much more reminiscent of the American Football League in 1959 than the American Basketball Association in 1967; so there is reason to suppose that the WHA, perhaps with attrition of some members, will survive long enough to force the NHL into interleague play and, to the extent permitted by Congress and the courts, eventually merger.

Policy Issues

Most of the policy debate surrounding the team sports industry concerns the extent to which anticompetitive practices—and the profits they create—are necessary to the operation of a league.

A key issue is whether the player reservation system leads to more stable operations and a game that is more attractive to the fans. Attacks by players and new leagues against player reservation, and attempts by competing leagues to obtain a legal merger, periodically refocus the attention of the courts, the Congress, and the public on the question of whether sports is so special an industry that it needs to monopsonize its principal input, athletes. Resolution of this issue requires examination of sports on two levels: the theory of league operations, which is examined in Chapters 2 and 3; and the empirical factors affecting attendance at games, which is the topic of Chapter 4.

Another important factor affecting team profits, which has only recently received much public attention, is the tax treatment of sports. The practice of capitalizing and depreciating players as if they were physical assets has become a tax advantage that has attracted a new type of owner to sports and significantly affected the structure and operation of leagues. These issues are examined in Chapter 5.

Especially since the formation of active player unions in the mid-1960s, public attention has also been directed toward discontent among players with the reserve clause and other restrictions on their behavior, as well as with the racial attitudes of owners. The impact of collective bargaining in sports—what it means to owners, players, and fans, and the extent to which it can overcome the effects of monopsonization of the player market by the owners—is discussed in Chapter 6. The special problem of discrimination is examined in Chapter 7, which investigates practices in baseball a generation after its color line was broken.

Broadcasting policy is another issue that has been the subject of repeated public debate. The major leagues in the various sports have succeeded in obtaining congressional approval for pooled offerings of national broadcasting packages and have used blackouts and territorial limitations to prevent competition for local rights. As with competition in the player market, owners argue that competition in broadcasting will destroy professional sports; certainly vigorous competition between minor-league games and national telecasts of the major leagues did all but destroy the former, especially in baseball. Chapter 8 treats these and other public policy issues related to the sale of broadcast rights.

Local government has become involved in policy making toward sports enterprises by financing the construction of playing facilities in most of the nation's large cities. These stadiums rarely recover their costs, and the subsidies that local governments provide through renting them below cost are a major component in the profits of many teams. Subsidized sports facilities are usually justified on the grounds that they benefit the city by generating increased business and public relations. Chapter 9 examines local government policy at each stage of the history of a stadium—when the decision to build is made, when the facility is operating and has a large debt to be repaid, and when the debt has been fully amortized.

The possible institutional arrangements that might respond adequately to the problems of sports operations have been given little serious attention. Only one arrangement has been in use in the recent past. Each sport is run by a commissioner and a committee of owners, who attempt to keep their sport profitable and competitive (on the playing field). Owing to its antitrust exemption, baseball has had the greatest freedom to develop a cartel organization, and its long history provides material for a study of the effectiveness of this kind of operation. Chapter 10 examines the baseball cartel during the twentieth century to see how it has responded to numerous challenges to its profits and the public's confidence in its product, and to determine whether the interests of players, fans, and owners are served as well by this particular arrangement as they might be by other alternatives.

The chief instrument of policy that has been used against professional sports is antitrust action. Chapter 11 reviews the history of antitrust in sports, and then discusses antitrust precedents established in other industries that might apply to team sports. The chapter further examines whether the current system of relying on antitrust suits to keep in check the practices of the otherwise unregulated sports industry is likely to have a significant effect on anticompetitive practices.

A proposal radically to reconstruct the operation of sports has been offered by Senator Marlow W. Cook of Kentucky. He suggests that a federal regulatory commission be established to oversee sports operations, thus creating an important role for the federal government in the formulation of operating rules and policies. Chapter 12 examines this proposal on two levels: first, what kinds of changes in the operating rules of sports might make the industry more competitive on the field *and* in the marketplace without risking its destruction? and second, what performance might be expected from a federal sports commission, based on the experience of federal regulation in other industries? In providing answers to these questions, Chapter 12 draws upon the findings of the other chapters of this book and constitutes a summary of their policy implications.

This book offers no uniform, final judgment on what the long-term effects of business competition in sports would be. The historical record is investigated for evidence bearing on this issue, and our understanding of the institutional details is greatly enriched thereby. Opinions differ among the authors on the implications of the various analyses presented in this book. All would agree, however, that restrictive practices do not primarily serve to control the differences in quality among teams within a league. None finds any evidence that these practices actually equalize playing competition, while all find that they have important effects on the economics of sports—on the total income of all participants in the sports business, and on the distribution of income among them.

CHAPTER TWO

The Economic Theory of a Professional Sports League

JAMES QUIRK *and* MOHAMED EL HODIRI

THIS CHAPTER applies economic theory to the analysis of the business operations of a professional sports league.[1] Special emphasis is given to the implications of the player reservation system—the rules structure for the distribution of playing strengths among the teams in a league—since partisans of professional sports claim that this system is essential to the goal of "equalizing competitive playing strengths" among teams.

Owners of professional sports teams have argued that without the player reservation system big-city franchises would acquire the bulk of the playing talent in a league, leading to an imbalance of playing strengths that might result in the destruction of the league itself. But imbalance problems persist even if a strong player reservation system is in force, since the reserve clause gives franchises with low drawing potential an incentive to sell their star players to higher drawing-potential franchises, which can afford to pay a higher price for them. The player reservation system simply gives this payment to the team rather than the player.

The Theoretical Model[2]

Consider a league possessing a monopoly with respect to its sport[3] and operating under a rules structure incorporating the provisions described

---

1. The results presented here are extensions of those reported in an earlier paper, Mohamed El Hodiri and James Quirk, "An Economic Model of a Professional Sports League," *Journal of Political Economy,* Vol. 79 (November–December 1971), pp. 1302–19, which in turn was stimulated by the pioneering work of Simon Rottenberg (see "The Baseball Players' Labor Market," ibid., Vol. 64 [June 1956], pp. 242–58).

2. A mathematical statement of the model is given in Appendix A.

3. By postulating the monopolistic character of the league, the problems discussed in Chapter 3 are obviated. As is pointed out there, the league can maintain its monopoly position only so long as it keeps playing skills at a level high enough to discourage the birth of "outlaw" leagues.

in detail in Chapter 1. Briefly, these include: (1) exclusive franchise rights in specified geographic areas; (2) the reserve clause, under which a player belongs to the team owning his contract until he retires or his contract is sold to another team in the league; (3) a drafting procedure making new talent available to teams on the basis of reverse order of finish; (4) a gate-sharing arrangement specifying fixed percentages of receipts to be allocated to the home and away teams; (5) equal sharing of national television revenues by all teams in the league, with local revenues being assigned solely to the home team.

Elements of the Model

Associated with each player is a certain amount of playing skills. The playing skills of a team are assumed to be the sum of the playing skills of its players.[4] Under the league's decentralized operation, each franchise owner, who is assumed to know with certainty the number of units of playing skills possessed by each player, makes decisions about the number of units of existing skills to buy or sell in the market for player contracts and about the number of units of new skills to purchase in the draft, subject to the reverse-order-of-finish provision of the drafting procedure. It is assumed that playing skills depreciate at an exponential rate, so that replacements are continuously needed simply to maintain the existing stock. Trades of players for players are not considered here, but they can be viewed either as simultaneous purchases and sales of player contracts or as transactions designed to enable a franchise to attain the best possible mix of complementary skills. Also omitted are problems associated with training new talent.[5]

Associated with the stock of playing skills is the level of salary and related costs for the team. No attempt is made to solve the bilateral monopoly problem involved in wage determination;[6] instead, the wage rate per unit of playing skills is accepted as given by each franchise owner and is assumed to be the same for all teams, a simplification that might understate

---

4. This assumption bypasses the complexities associated with the diverse skills of players and the interrelationships of players and positions on a team, but may be justified on the grounds that we are concerned here mainly with the financial aspect of professional sports. For an extension of the model in which an attempt is made to capture certain of these aspects of team sports, see Appendix A, pp. 71–76.

5. But see the discussion in Appendix A, p. 71.

6. Discussed in Chapter 6.

the costs of big-city teams relative to smaller-city teams. Total costs of a team consist of salary and related costs (equal to the number of units of playing skills possessed by the team times the "wage rate" per unit, this rate being the same for all teams); bonus costs for new players acquired in the draft (equal to the bonus payment per unit of new playing skills times the number of such units acquired in the draft); and costs of acquiring player contracts in the existing playing skills market (equal to the number of units of playing skills purchased times the price per unit). It is assumed that franchise owners take as given the bonus payment per unit of new skills and the price per unit of existing playing skills, the former being lower than the latter. Furthermore, arbitrage operations are assumed to ensure that each team pays the same bonus per unit of new skills and the same price per unit of existing skills.

The revenue of a team consists of gate receipts from home and away games, plus television revenues, plus income derived from the sale of player contracts. Each team is assumed to play a home and away schedule with each other team in the league, with the home team receiving a specified fraction of the gate. Gate receipts depend on the drawing potential of the area in which the home team is located and on the probability that the home team will win the game. The probability that team i will defeat team j is given by the ratio of team i's stock of playing skills to the total for teams i and j. Gate receipts for each team are assumed to increase with an increase in the probability of the home team's winning up to some level of probability between ½ and 1, and to decrease thereafter. While gate receipts follow the same general pattern for every team, the higher the drawing potential of a franchise, the greater the gate receipts associated with every level of probability of the home team's winning. Television revenues are divided into national broadcasts, with equal shares for all teams, and local broadcasts, for which all revenues are allocated to the home team. Local receipts are assumed to be positively related to the playing strength of a team and to the drawing potential of the team's location, while national receipts for the league are predetermined.

Franchise owners are assumed to be motivated solely by profits from the operation of their franchises, and capital markets are assumed to be perfect, so that each owner can borrow as much as he wishes at the going market rate of interest. Thus each franchise owner is assumed to act so as to maximize the discounted present value of net cash flows from the operation of his franchise, using the market rate of interest as the discount rate.

The particular complication that arises in the analysis of a professional sports league, even using the simplifying assumptions incorporated into the model described above, is that, although each team has direct control over its own stock of playing skills, its revenue and its access to new players depend upon the stocks of playing skills held by the other teams in the league.[7] This leads to externalities in the operation of the team. Technically, the joint decision problem faced by the teams in a league can be characterized as an *n*-person non-zero-sum differential game. Unfortunately, no general method has been devised for "solving" such games; in fact, even the notion of a "solution" to such games is itself ambiguous. Our approach is to postulate the existence, at each point in time, of an "equilibrium" of the league, defined as follows: an equilibrium occurs if, when each team maximizes discounted net cash flows in the expectation that certain choices will be made by other teams, these expectations are in fact realized; and when choices in the aggregate result in the clearing of markets both for existing player contracts and for contracts of newly recruited players. While strategic behavior is not taken into account in this notion of a "solution" to the joint decision problem, choices made by teams do reflect their presumed effects on the stocks of playing skills of other teams.

The analysis of the model of a professional sports league is thus carried out under the assumption that at each point in time the league is in equilibrium. Because the long-run implications of the rules structure are of primary concern here, attention is focused on the special case where the league is in a *steady state equilibrium*, that is, a situation in which the stock of playing skills of each team remains fixed over time, with newly recruited players replacing those lost through depreciation of skills.

The following conclusions can be drawn from the model.[8] In an ongoing professional sports league, with franchises in locations representing marketing areas of varying drawing potential and with franchise owners motivated solely by profit considerations, the distribution of playing strengths within the league tends toward a state in which:

1. Franchises located in areas with high drawing potential have stronger teams than franchises in low drawing-potential areas.

2. On balance, franchises in low drawing-potential areas sell players to franchises in high drawing-potential areas.

---

7. The implications of this fact are explored more fully in Chapter 3.
8. The mathematical derivations of these conclusions are given in Appendix A.

3. If local television revenues are ignored, the distribution of playing strengths among teams is independent of the gate-sharing arrangements, which, instead, determine the level of player salaries and bonuses and the purchase price of player contracts.

4. The home team's gate share must exceed 50 percent in order for a steady state situation to exist, and the higher the home team's gate share, the higher the costs of players and the smaller the chance of survival for franchises in low drawing-potential areas.

5. The higher the share of television and radio revenues accruing to the home team, the higher the costs of players and the smaller the chance of survival for low drawing-potential franchises.

6. The distribution of playing strengths is the same as it would be if the league were operated as a syndicate with central control over the allocation of players among teams.

7. The speed of convergence to an equilibrium, given an arbitrary initial allocation of players among teams, is greater the fewer the teams in the league and the shorter the average playing lifetime of players.

8. Equalization of playing strengths among teams can be achieved only by eliminating the sale of player contracts among teams or by assigning franchise rights so as to equalize drawing potential rather than on the basis of geographic area.

Implications of the Model

These conclusions follow directly from the assumptions of profit maximization and the existence of an equilibrium at each point in time. Consider the decision problem facing any given franchise owner. Taking into account only revenue from games played at his home stadium, the owner will wish to field a team that is stronger than the league average but not too strong, since revenues fall if the probability of winning is too high, reflecting the loss of public interest in contests that lack uncertainty of outcome. But even before the point of declining revenues is reached, cost considerations act to limit the owner's incentive to strengthen his club. In order to field a strong team, the owner has to incur costs associated with buying additional units of playing skills and with paying player salaries, and in fact the profit-maximizing owner will add additional units of playing skills only to the point where the last unit acquired adds as much to revenue as it does to cost. In other words, players are added to the point where marginal revenue equals marginal cost.

The relevant measure of the marginal cost of acquiring an additional unit of playing skills is the discounted present value of the added costs associated with the unit. This in turn is equal to the purchase price of the unit plus the discounted present value of wages paid over the life of the unit plus the discounted present value of profits forgone because the team's drafting priority is lowered by the addition of playing skills. In equilibrium, these forgone profits are given by the decrease in the number of units that can be drafted times the difference between the price of a unit in the existing player market and the bonus paid per unit in the draft. All franchises are assumed to pay the same wage cost per unit and the same prices in the existing player market and the draft. It is further assumed that the addition of a unit of skills reduces by the same amount the number of units that a team can draft, regardless of its priority. Under these assumptions, the marginal cost of acquiring an additional unit of playing skills is the same for every team, whatever its playing strength.

The marginal revenue associated with adding an additional unit of playing skills equals the increase in local television revenue plus the increase in home gate receipts times the home team's share less the decrease in away game receipts times the visiting team's share. When team i acquires a unit of playing skills from team j in the market for existing player contracts, this increases the probability that team i will beat team j (and all other teams); hence it raises gate receipts at team i's home stadium and lowers gate receipts at team j's home stadium (particularly for games involving i and j). Both effects must be taken into account by the franchise owner in determining the marginal revenue of an additional unit of playing skills.

In equilibrium, adding a unit of playing skills to either team results in the same increase in home gate receipts, wherever the game is played.[9]

9. For example, consider a case where only two teams are involved (formal treatment of the general case of an n-team league is given in Appendix A). Suppose team j sells one unit of playing skills to team i. Let α denote the home team's share of the gate, with $1 - \alpha$ being the visiting team's share. Let ΔR^i denote the increase in the discounted present value of team i's home gate receipts and let ΔR^j denote the decrease in the discounted present value of team j's home gate receipts. Suppose, for simplicity, that there is no effect on either team's local television revenues. Then marginal revenue to team i for the additional unit of playing skills acquired from team j is

$$\alpha\Delta R^i - (1 - \alpha)\Delta R^j.$$

Similarly, the decrease in revenue for team j is

$$\alpha\Delta R^j - (1 - \alpha)\Delta R^i.$$

Sales between the teams will stop when the last unit sold by team j causes marginal

This situation is consistent with an equality of playing strengths for the two teams only if they are located in areas with equal drawing potential; if team i is in an area with higher drawing potential than team j, it must have a larger stock of playing skills to achieve the same result. Profit maximization and market clearing thus imply that big cities have strong teams and small cities have weak teams, as asserted above.

The distribution of playing strengths that satisfies the equilibrium condition is independent of the particular values chosen for the shares of gate receipts going to each team; whatever the gate-sharing arrangement, the distribution of strengths among teams in a steady state equilibrium will always be the same, with the stronger teams being located in the areas with higher drawing potential. The gate-sharing arrangement is not a variable of the model; it is one of the business rules of the league decided upon by the franchise owners. However, under the condition that marginal revenue equals marginal cost, an increase in the home team's share must be accompanied by an increase in the cost per unit of playing skills (wages and/or bonuses and/or price on the existing market) if equilibrium is to be maintained. The intuitive reason for this is that the higher the home team's share, the more revenue depends upon success at home games, so that demand for players is an increasing function of the home team's share. With higher home team shares, profits for the league as a whole fall because of increased player costs; however, there is a redistribution of income to teams located in high drawing-potential areas at the expense of teams located in low drawing-potential areas. It follows that the higher the home team's share, the less chance small-city franchises have for survival. Since equilibrium at a steady state can occur only if all franchises are profitable, the higher the home team's share, the less chance there is that an equilibrium steady state for the league can persist.[10]

If the sale of player contracts were prohibited, the drafting procedure

---

revenue to equal marginal cost for team i; similarly, the last unit sold by team j will cause the decrease in its revenue to equal the resulting decrease in its costs. But, under the assumptions about prices of player contracts and drafting rules, the decrease in team j's costs is the same as the marginal cost to team i. Hence, when the teams are in equilibrium, the last unit sold by team j to team i satisfies the condition

$$\alpha \Delta R^i - (1 - \alpha) \Delta R^j = \alpha \Delta R^j - (1 - \alpha) \Delta R^i,$$

or

$$\Delta R^i = \Delta R^j.$$

10. Certain of these conclusions must be modified slightly when local television revenues are taken into account. See Appendix A, pp. 60–69.

would guarantee equalization of playing strengths among teams at a steady state, since weak teams are given preferential access to newly recruited talent. Under the present rules structure, the draft operates instead as a funnel through which newly drafted players (or their experienced equivalents) flow into big-city franchises through player sales by weak franchises. The draft performs a twofold function: first, by limiting competition for newly recruited players, it reduces the cost to the entire league of such players; second, by providing preferential treatment to the weak franchises, it distributes a disproportionate share of this cost saving to the small-city franchises, thus increasing their chance of survival. The draft does not, however, lead to equalization of playing strengths.

Finally, if the league were operated as a syndicate rather than under a decentralized system, then for any level of wage and bonus costs the syndicate would allocate players among teams so as to maximize the discounted present value of revenue for the league. But this implies that marginal revenues are equal for all teams; hence the distribution that would emerge under syndicated control of the league is the same as the equilibrium that exists under decentralized management of franchises.

Qualifications to the Model

These theoretical conclusions are derived from an admittedly simplified model of a professional sports league. Some qualifications to that model must be taken into account in applying it to the operation of existing leagues.

First, details of the rules structure assumed for the model differ among the leagues. In baseball, the reserve clause operates rigidly, as it did in the National Hockey League (NHL) before the emergence of the World Hockey Association (WHA). In football, the National Football League (NFL) permits players to play out their option subject to the Rozelle rule, which requires a team signing a player who has played out his option to indemnify his former team. In basketball, both leagues now apparently function under a version of the NFL's option clause; and in hockey, though the WHA has no reserve clause, players are subject to a "secondary draft" that limits movement among teams. Home–visitor gate-sharing arrangements range from the 100–0 arrangement in hockey and basketball to 80–20 in baseball and 60–40 in football. Monopolistic league structures control baseball and football; in basketball, the American Basketball Association (ABA) and National Basketball Association (NBA) are still occasional competitors while awaiting congressional approval of a merger agreement; and in hockey, the WHA is at sword's point with the NHL after signing some sixty players from NHL reserve lists in 1972. These and other differences in rules structures among the sports affect the applicability of the theoretical conclusions of this paper, but of more importance is the questionable realism of some fundamental elements of the model.

The model assumes that decision making by franchise owners is decentralized, with each team operating independently. And in fact, leagues in each of the sports have rules prohibiting pooling agreements among teams and ownership of or substantial interest in more than one team in a league by the same individual or group. However, these rules are not always enforced. For a period of time in the 1950s, for example, a group headed by James D. Norris owned the Chicago Black Hawks and controlled the Madison Square Garden Corporation, which in turn owned the New York Rangers, while Norris's half-sisters and half-brother owned the Detroit Red Wings. The Norris family thus controlled three of the six teams then playing in the NHL.[11] In the late 1890s, the Baltimore and Brooklyn franchises of the National League (NL) were owned by the same group, which transferred virtually all the star players from Baltimore to Brooklyn when Baltimore failed to draw well. At about the same time, the Cleveland and St. Louis teams in the NL were also jointly owned, with St. Louis being favored, leading to such a fall in attendance at Cleveland that a number of "home" games were played on the road.[12] More recently, charges of conflict of interest have been raised concerning the links between the Kansas City Athletics and the New York Yankees in the 1950s, as well as the sale of the Yankees to the Columbia Broadcasting System in 1964, which led to a congressional investigation.[13] An even more recent example of pooling of interests has occurred in the WHA, where the owners of the twelve franchises contributed equally to a fund of $1 million paid as a bonus to Bobby Hull when he signed with the Winnipeg WHA franchise,

11. *Organized Professional Team Sports,* Hearings before the Antitrust Subcommittee of the House Committee on the Judiciary, 85 Cong. 1 sess. (1957), Pt. 3, pp. 2965 ff.

12. *Organized Baseball,* Report of the Subcommittee on Study of Monopoly Power of the House Committee on the Judiciary, H. Rept. 2002, 82 Cong. 2 sess. (1952), p. 38.

13. *Professional Sports Antitrust Bill—1965,* Hearings before the Subcommittee on Antitrust and Monopoly of the Senate Committee on the Judiciary, 89 Cong. 1 sess. (1965).

thus agreeing to strengthen one team at the expense of the others in order to increase public acceptance of the league.[14] To the extent that such activities conflict with decentralized profit maximization, the conclusions of the theoretical model must be correspondingly modified.

The assumption that the actions of franchise owners are motivated solely by profits from operation of their franchises is admittedly somewhat unrealistic. Owning a major-league franchise carries with it prestige and publicity, and a wealthy owner might view it simply as a type of consumption; for such a "sportsman"-owner, winning games rather than making money might be the motivating factor. For an owner engaged in other businesses, the publicity and prestige of being a franchise owner might engender profits in his other enterprises. The classic case of a sportsman-owner is Thomas A. Yawkey of the Boston Red Sox, who is often cited as an illustration of the fact that spending money on a team does not necessarily buy success.[15] Philip K. Wrigley of the Chicago Cubs, Joan W. Payson of the New York Mets, and Ewing Kauffman of the Kansas City Royals have been similarly characterized. (That not all wealthy owners have ignored profitability is illustrated by Jacob Ruppert and, later, Dan Topping of the New York Yankees.)

At the other extreme from the sportsman-owner is the franchise owner whose resources are so limited that he finds it difficult to compete with his wealthy competitors in the market for players. In the American League (AL), the Chicago White Sox, with the second largest drawing potential in the league, went thirty-nine years without a pennant under the ownership of the Comiskey family, which derived essentially all of its income from its baseball holdings. The lack of funds for farm club operations and bonus competition for new players was a major factor in the White Sox' lack of success on the field. In the NL, the Philadelphia Phillies were notorious during the twenties and thirties as a club teetering on the brink of ruin, saved only by selling players to other clubs. The owners of the Phillies had no independent sources of wealth, and finally the club went bankrupt and was taken over by the league in the early forties. These examples illustrate that the perfect capital market postulated in the theoretical model is not always realistic; credit limitations applying to some but not

14. *Philadelphia World Hockey Club, Inc.* v. *Philadelphia Hockey Club, Inc.,* U.S.D.C. Eastern Pa., C.A. 72-1661, Opinion (Nov. 8, 1972), p. 64.

15. Success is measured in terms of pennants won. However, the Yawkey money was certainly the major factor in improving the quality of the Red Sox. Prior to Yawkey's purchase of the team, its won-lost record was .359 (1922–32); after his purchase, it was .522 (1933–70). Average finish improved from 7.66 (in an eight-team league) to 4.39, during the same periods.

all franchises might well result in a distortion of the condition of equilibrium under which marginal revenues are equated among franchises.

Some owners who were not wealthy have managed to assemble championship teams, but they have often responded to adversity by selling their best players, in accordance with the profit-maximization hypothesis. Connie Mack, like Charles Comiskey, earned his living from his franchise. His Philadelphia Athletics included several great teams, especially those of 1909–14, which won four pennants, and the pennant winners of 1929, 1930, and 1931, sometimes regarded as the greatest teams in the history of baseball. After both of these periods of pennants and high profits, attendance began to fall, and Mack, in essence, sold his teams and began again from scratch. Clark Griffith's Washington Senators, which represented his major source of income, are a similar case. After the pennant-winning year of 1933, many players—including Griffith's son-in-law—were sold.

The conclusions derived from the model posit steady state conditions in which franchises are fixed in location and earning rates of return that justify continued operations. In fact, each of the major professional sports leagues has gone through extended periods of expansion, contraction, and movement of franchises. Perhaps the best example of franchise stability occurs in baseball between 1903 and 1953, when the two leagues consisted of the same sixteen teams in the same locations. Since 1953, there have been ten franchise moves and the creation of eight expansion franchises. Hockey experienced a comparable period of stability between 1943 and 1967, when the NHL consisted of the same six teams. Since 1967, the NHL has added ten expansion franchises and the WHA has created an additional twelve franchises. Compared to its early history, the NFL achieved a rather stable position with the beginning of divisional play in 1933; but since that time expansion, incorporation in 1950 of several franchises from the All-America Conference, and the emergence of the American Football League (AFL) have altered the franchise list. In basketball, the NBA has had a fluctuating list of franchises for most of its history. The changes that have occurred in the location of franchises in the four major sports are summarized in Appendix B.

The creation, movement, and abandonment of franchises reflect dynamic elements in the development of a viable league structure that are not taken into account in the model. Prominent among such elements are changes in the size and distribution of population, technological advances, competition from existing or potential rival leagues, and, of central importance, drawing potential. The early history of almost every league is characterized by the movement of franchises away from smaller towns as public acceptance of the league grows. This pattern is the dynamic counterpart of the static proposition that low drawing-potential franchises cannot support strong teams; under dynamic conditions, an alternative to selling players is to move the franchise. In the context of the static model, this might be interpreted as selling *all* (rather than some) players to a higher drawing-potential franchise when profits at the existing location are inadequate for continued operation. The classic exception to this generalization is the Green Bay Packers of the NFL. It is of interest to note that Green Bay is one of the rare nonprofit enterprises in professional sports; it is also relevant, of course, that the Packers play in a league with gate- and television-sharing arrangements that are the most favorable to weak franchises of any in professional sports.

Much of the change in franchise locations over the past twenty to thirty years represents the expansion of leagues from regional to national organizations, made possible by dependable air transportation and by the growth of population centers on the West Coast. In contrast, potential competition accounts for the moves of baseball teams into Minnesota and New York City (triggered by the plans announced for the Continental League) and, recently, the NHL expansion into Long Island in response to the new WHA franchise planned for that area, a franchise that subsequently moved to New York City and then to New Jersey. The game of musical chairs that the baseball leagues have been playing with small-city franchises over the past decade (in and out of Kansas City, Milwaukee, Seattle, and so forth) indicates that in a league's maturity, drawing potential is again a primary factor in the movement of franchises, as it was in an earlier period. Unfortunately, analysis of franchise movement is beyond the scope of the static model of this chapter.

Because of the simplified nature of the model, other postulates are subject to qualification as well. For example, the gate receipts function is based on the assumption that what is being sold is strictly "competition on the playing field," a product unique to sports. This formulation neglects such elements as the entertainment value of the game, the effect of traditional rivalries, intertemporal correlations of gate receipts, and the like.[16]

---

16. Bill Veeck has pointed out in conversation that the product of professional sports is somewhat more ephemeral than competition and prefers to call it "dreams" to reflect the intense identification of fans with a team and its players. Since this attitude affects owners as well as fans, it could act as a major inhibiting factor in the sale (or trade) of players, especially stars.

There is also no place in the model for the truly innovative entrepreneur who can change the institutional structure of a sport. The prime example, of course, is Branch Rickey, whose development of the farm system in the 1920s enabled a small-town franchise, the St. Louis Cardinals, to dominate the recruitment and training of players for over a decade. Similarly, Bill Veeck's promotional activities at Cleveland, St. Louis, and Chicago revolutionized the marketing strategies of all professional sports; he is also responsible for opening the door to franchise moves in baseball and for discovering the tax-avoidance possibilities of franchise ownership, both with lasting results. If the number of franchises were very large, the impact of such innovators might be overwhelmed by the aggregate; but sports leagues involve only a few franchises, so the distortions introduced by innovators cannot be easily eliminated from the data.

Theoretical Predictions versus the Historical Record

The basic theoretical conclusion of this chapter is that high drawing-potential franchises have strong teams and low drawing-potential franchises have weak teams. For most sports this can be translated roughly as the statement that big cities have winning teams and small cities have losing teams. This section examines the evidence from league histories in each of the major sports to determine the validity of this proposition. Many kinds of data might be useful, but here only the relationships between population and percentage of games won, franchises abandoned or moved, and championships won are considered.

Population and Team Strength

In Tables 1 through 4, which deal with percentages of games won and population, periods during which franchise locations were relatively stable have been chosen, so that the situation postulated in the theoretical model is roughly approximated. Thus, expansion teams and teams with less than ten years' history have been excluded from the rank ordering. Table 1, however, presents baseball data both for the period of stable franchise locations and for a longer period that includes younger expansion teams. Data for the NL begin in 1900, with its reorganization into an eight-team league, while the AL data begin in 1903, with the end of the AL-NL war. As indicated by the rank correlation coefficients, population rank and percent

Table 1. Years in League and Correlations of Average Won-Lost Percentages with City Population Rankings, Baseball Teams, 1900–70

Location of team or correlation item	Years in league	Period I[a]			Period II[b]		
		Popu-lation rank[c]	Average won-lost		Popu-lation rank[c]	Average won-lost	
			Per-centage	Rank		Per-centage	Rank
American League							
Veteran teams							
New York	68	1	57.3	1	1	57.2	1
Chicago	68	2	49.3	5	2	50.4	6
Detroit	68	3	51.7	3	3	51.9	5
Philadelphia	52	4	47.8	6	4	47.5	8
Cleveland	68	5	52.6	2	5	52.7	3
Boston	68	6	50.9	4	6	50.0	7
St. Louis	51	7	42.7	8	9	42.7	10
Washington (Senators I)	58	8	47.5	7	7	46.6	9
Baltimore	17	...	...	...	8	52.7	3
Minnesota	10	...	...	...	10	54.9	2
Kansas City (Athletics)	13	...	...	...	11	40.4	11
Oakland	3	...	...	...	...	53.3	...
Expansion teams							
Washington (Senators II)	10	...	...	...	...	42.0	...
California	10	...	...	...	...	47.7	...
Kansas City (Royals)	2	...	...	...	...	41.4	...
Seattle	1	...	...	...	...	39.5	...
Milwaukee	1	...	...	...	...	40.1	...
Rank correlation							
1903–53	0.67[d]						
1903–70	0.39[d]						
Excluding Minnesota	0.57[e]						
National League							
Veteran teams							
New York (Giants)	58	1+	55.8	1	2	55.1	3
Brooklyn	58	1+	50.2	5	2	51.2	8
Chicago	71	3	54.1	2	4	51.9	6
Pittsburgh	71	4	53.6	3	6	52.4	5
Philadelphia	71	5	43.2	8	7	44.3	10
Boston	53	6	43.8	7	8	43.8	11
Cincinnati	71	7	48.1	6	9	49.3	9
St. Louis	71	8	51.6	4	10	51.8	7
Los Angeles	13	...	...	...	1	54.1	4
San Francisco	13	...	...	...	5	55.4	2

Table 1. Continued

Location of team or correlation item	Years in league	Period I[a] Popu-lation rank[c]	Period I[a] Average won-lost Per-centage	Period I[a] Average won-lost Rank	Period II[b] Popu-lation rank[c]	Period II[b] Average won-lost Per-centage	Period II[b] Average won-lost Rank
Milwaukee	13	...	...	...	11	56.3	1
Atlanta	5	...	...	...	...	50.9	...
Expansion teams							
Houston	9	...	...	...	...	43.4	;..
New York (Mets)	9	...	...	...	...	39.6	...
San Diego	2	...	...	...	...	35.5	...
Montreal	2	...	...	...	...	38.6	...
Rank correlation							
1900–52 0.46[d]	0.46[d]						
Excluding St. Louis	0.66[d]						
1900–70 0.18[d]							
Excluding Milwaukee	0.67[e]						

Sources: Population, U.S. Bureau of the Census, *Statistical Abstract of the United States*, relevant years; won-lost percentages and years in league through 1969, Hy Turkin and S. C. Thompson, *The Official Encyclopedia of Baseball* (5th ed. rev., A. S. Barnes, 1970); 1970, *The World Almanac and Book of Facts, 1971* (Newspaper Enterprise Association, 1970), pp. 872–77.

a. For the American League, 1903–53; for the National League, 1900–52.

b. For the American League, 1903–70; for the National League, 1900–70.

c. Based on average population during the period, adjusted for the number of baseball teams in the metropolitan area.

d. Not significant at the 5 percent level.

e. Significant at the 5 percent level.

won rank are positively related in both leagues during the period of stable franchise location, though the positive correlation, because of the small number of observations, fails the usual significance tests. To indicate the extent of the "Rickey effect," the rank correlation for the NL is computed both including and excluding St. Louis. Because of franchise moves and expansion, problems arise when making comparisons within the longer periods. The short histories of Minnesota and Milwaukee introduce distorting factors, so rank correlations are computed both including and excluding them. These teams represent the major exceptions in baseball history to the thesis of this chapter, that low drawing-potential areas produce weak teams.

The second test of the model's conclusions is an investigation of franchise shifts. The following baseball teams have moved: AL—St. Louis,

Philadelphia, Washington (twice), Kansas City, and Seattle; NL—New York, Brooklyn, Milwaukee, and Boston. Five of these are small-city teams—St. Louis, Kansas City, Seattle, Milwaukee, and Washington—while the remainder are in the larger cities. (The move of the Brooklyn franchise, it should be noted, was not due to lack of success either on the field or at the gate.) These data indicate the nature of the problem in "supporting a losing team"; from 1903 to 1970, every AL team with a losing record moved its franchise. Finally, using pennants won as a measure of success, the record shows that in the AL the four largest cities won forty-nine out of sixty-eight pennants; and in the NL the four largest cities won forty-one out of seventy.[17] Generally speaking, baseball data are consistent with the conclusion that big-city teams are strong and small-city teams are weak, although there are several exceptions to this general rule.

Table 2 presents data for the NFL, beginning with the first year of divisional play and ending with the reorganization of the league into the American and National Conferences. The rank correlation for games won and population is negative when both teams in two-franchise cities are included and is positive but low when these teams (either abandoned or moved during the period) are excluded. The low value of the coefficient is accounted for in part by Green Bay, as the alternative computation indicates. As a nonprofit enterprise, this team presumably operates under quite different constraints and with quite different objectives than other teams do.

The period covered by the data saw a number of franchise relocations, abandonments, and expansions. Franchises moved or abandoned during the history of the NFL include the following: pre-1933—Buffalo, Akron, Canton, Dayton, Rock Island, Pottsville, Rochester, Columbus, Toledo, Racine, Milwaukee, Marion, Hammond, Hartford, Louisville, Evansville, Duluth, Frankford, Kenosha, Providence, Stapleton, Cleveland, New York (Yankees), Detroit, Boston, Cincinnati, Brooklyn, Los Angeles, Kansas City, and Minneapolis; 1933–72—Portsmouth, Cleveland, Chicago Cardinals, Baltimore, Dallas, Boston (in 1936 and in 1948), Brooklyn, New York Yanks, and New York Bulldogs. This list clearly indicates the difficulty of survival for two classes of teams: small-city franchises and "second" franchises in large cities.

The record of divisional championships in the NFL (1933–67) is con-

17. Both of these proportions differ significantly (at the 5 percent level) from a probability of ½, which would be the share of these teams if pennants were evenly distributed among teams.

Table 2. Years in League and Correlation of Average Won-Lost Percentages with City Population Rankings, National Football League Teams, 1933–68[a]

Location of team or correlation item	Years in league	Population rank[b]	Average won-lost Percentage	Average won-lost Rank
Team				
New York	36	1+	60.2	3
Brooklyn	12	1+	39.0	12
Chicago Bears	36	3+	66.3	1
Chicago Cardinals	27	3+	32.1	13
Los Angeles	23	5	53.5	6
Philadelphia	36	6	43.6	10
Detroit	35	7	50.9	7
San Francisco	19	8	49.7	8
Pittsburgh	35	9	39.2	11
Cleveland	27	10	62.6	2
Baltimore	17	11	57.6	4
Washington	32	12	48.1	9
Green Bay	36	13	57.2	5

Rank correlation, −0.14[c]

Excluding Brooklyn and Chicago Cardinals, 0.22[c]
Also excluding Green Bay, 0.34[c]

Sources: Won-lost percentages, Roger Treat, *The Official Encyclopedia of Football* (8th ed. rev., A. S. Barnes, 1970); other data, see Table 1.
a. Includes only teams that were in the league for more than ten years.
b. Based on average population during the period.
c. Not significant at the 5 percent level.

sistent with the conclusion that big cities tend to have strong teams. The four largest cities in the league accounted for thirty-three out of seventy-two divisional titles for the period, with the other nine teams over ten years old (including the Chicago Cardinals and Brooklyn) accounting for thirty-seven.[18]

Data for basketball are shown in Table 3, beginning with the organization of the present NBA in the 1946–47 season and continuing to the beginning of the recent wave of expansion in 1968. The rank correlation between population and won-lost record is barely positive. The period covered was one of great franchise instability; indeed, it is difficult to identify any lengthy period when changes in the NBA franchise list did

18. Significantly different at the 5 percent level from an equal probability of winning.

not occur. Between 1947 and 1972, the following franchises were moved or abandoned: Washington, Providence, Toronto, Cleveland, Detroit, Pittsburgh, Philadelphia, St. Louis (twice), Baltimore, Chicago (twice), Rochester, Minneapolis, Fort Wayne, Indianapolis, Syracuse, Anderson, Tri-Cities, Sheboygan, Waterloo, Denver, Milwaukee, Cincinnati, and San Diego. Most of these are clearly small-city franchises relative to the more or less permanent teams of New York, Boston, Philadelphia, Detroit, and Los Angeles. Finally, the record of league championships shows the top three teams in population rank (1947–68) winning thirteen out of twenty-two championships, with the remaining four long-term clubs accounting for nine.

Table 4 indicates the large negative correlation between population rank and percent won rank in the NHL. The data begin in 1939, when the Montreal Maroons left the league; except for the abandonment of the New York Americans franchise in 1942, franchise locations were stable during the entire period. The lack of agreement between population rank and percent won rank is due to the known inaccuracy of population as a measure of drawing potential in hockey, the national game of Canada and until recently a minor sport in the United States. The television receipts of

Table 3. Years in League and Correlation of Average Won-Lost Percentages with City Population Rankings, National Basketball Association Teams, 1947–68[a]

Location of team or correlation item	Years in league	Population rank[b]	Average won-lost	
			Percentage	Rank
Team				
New York	22	1	47.3	5
Philadelphia	21	2	53.7	4
Boston	22	3	62.7	1
St. Louis	14	4	55.4	2
Baltimore	16	5	36.4	7
Minneapolis	13	6	55.0	3
Cincinnati	16	7	46.3	6
Rank correlation, 0.25[c]				

Sources: Won-lost percentages and years in league, *National Basketball Association Official Guide for 1970–71* (Sporting News, 1970); other data, see Table 1.

a. Includes only teams that were in the league for more than ten years.

b. Based on average population during the period, adjusted for the number of basketball teams in the metropolitan area.

c. Not significant at the 5 percent level.

Table 4. Years in League and Correlation of Average Won-Lost Percentages with City Population Rankings, National Hockey League, 1939–67[a]

Location of team or correlation item	Years in league	Population rank[b]	Average won-lost	
			Percentage[c]	Rank
Team				
New York	29	1	41.8	6
Chicago	29	2	44.1	5
Detroit	29	3	56.4	2
Boston	29	4	45.7	4
Montreal	29	5	60.3	1
Toronto	29	6	54.4	3
Rank correlation, -0.71[d]				

Source: Robert A. Styer, *The Encyclopedia of Hockey* (A. S. Barnes, 1970), pp. 74–127.

a. Includes only teams that were in the league for more than ten years.

b. Based on average population during the period, adjusted for the number of hockey teams in the metropolitan area.

c. Excludes ties. When ties are included, the percentages are New York, 43.2; Chicago, 44.3; Detroit, 55.3; Boston, 46.1; Montreal, 58.5; and Toronto, 53.6, with a rank correlation coefficient of -0.71, not significant at the 1 percent level.

d. Not significant at the 1 percent level.

hockey for the 1967–68 season illustrate this: Montreal and Toronto shared $1.5 million in receipts, compared with $2.3 million shared by the other four original NHL teams.[19] Of the twenty-nine Stanley Cup championships during the period, Montreal and Toronto took twenty, with nine being shared among the other four teams in the league. That four of the twelve original WHA franchises were assigned to Canadian cities, all significantly smaller in population than the American cities in the league, is indicative of Canada's higher drawing potential.

The data presented in Tables 1 through 4, supplemented by the history of abandonment of small-town franchises and the record of championships won in the various sports, offer some evidence of the correspondance between drawing potential and playing strength. The small number of franchises and the limited time spans cause difficulties in analyzing the data, but a fair appraisal would indicate clearly that small-city teams have had little, if any, chance of surviving in professional sports; that high drawing-potential areas get more than their share of championships; and that per-

19. *Broadcasting*, Vol. 79 (Oct. 9, 1967), pp. 60–61.

cent won–population comparisons, while tending to support the proposition, are not conclusive.

Player Sales and Team Strength

The theoretical model predicts that big-city franchises will acquire strong teams through purchase of players from small-city teams. It is generally difficult to obtain data on the volume of player sales in any sport. The best information available is that collected in the 1950s by the House Subcommittee on Study of Monopoly Power on acquisition costs of player contracts in baseball for the years 1929, 1933, 1939, 1943, 1946, and 1950. These data are summarized in Table 5 and are compared with population rank and percent won rank.

Acquisition costs are an ambiguous measure of the tendency for weak teams to sell players to strong teams, since they include bonuses paid to new players and purchases of players from the minor leagues as well as purchases of players from other major-league clubs. With this qualification, the data indicate strong positive correlation between the strength of an AL team and its payment for players, excluding the well-known acquisitions made by Thomas A. Yawkey for the Red Sox. The NL data are particularly striking: if Rickey's teams, the Cardinals and the Dodgers, are included, the rank correlation is negative; but if they are excluded, a strong positive correlation between acquisition costs and percentage of games won emerges.

How important an element in profitability was the sale of players during the period covered by Table 5? Data that would provide a complete answer to this question are not available, but an indication of the possible importance of player sales is given by the following hypothetical case. For the six years covered by the acquisition data, total expenditures in the AL were $2,584,000, or $323,000 per team; for the NL, the total is $3,846,000, or $481,000 per team. If very few interleague sales of players took place, these figures represent average team expenditures on bonuses and purchases from minor-league clubs. (Intraleague sales would, on average, be zero.) Further assuming that each team actually spends the league average on these items, then expenditures for intraleague purchases can be derived by subtracting $323,000 from each AL team's acquisition costs, as shown in Table 5, and subtracting $481,000 from each NL team's costs. We thus obtain the following hypothetical amounts spent for intraleague purchases of players in 1929, 1933, 1939, 1943, 1946, and 1950 in total.

American League		National League	
Team	Amount of intraleague purchases (thousands of dollars)	Team	Amount of intraleague purchases (thousands of dollars)
Boston	459	New York	586
New York	317	Chicago	367
Cleveland	150	Pittsburgh	138
Detroit	132	Cincinnati	− 17
Washington	− 125	Boston	− 107
Chicago	− 176	Philadelphia	− 126
Philadelphia	− 291	Brooklyn	− 165
St. Louis	− 466	St. Louis	− 678

A comparison can then be made between these hypothetical data and profits for the period 1920–50, as reported for each franchise in the House hearings, and shown in Table 6. Assuming that the average expenditure per year for the six years applies to the entire thirty years, the comparison between cumulative profits and hypothetical intraleague purchases of players is as follows:

Team	Cumulative profits (thousands of dollars)	Hypothetical net intraleague player purchases (thousands of dollars)
American League		
New York	8,497	1,585
Detroit	4,702	660
Cleveland	3,670	750
Washington	2,746	− 625
Chicago	1,347	− 880
Philadelphia	1,091	− 1,455
St. Louis	1,088	− 2,330
Boston	− 2,075	2,295
National League		
St. Louis	5,962	− 3,390
Brooklyn	3,944	− 825
Pittsburgh	3,213	690
Chicago	2,920	1,835
New York	2,892	2,930
Cincinnati	1,571	− 85
Philadelphia	− 13	− 630
Boston	− 295	− 535

Table 5. Correlation of Acquisition Costs of Player Contracts of Baseball Teams with Average Won-Lost Percentages and City Population Rankings, Selected Years, 1929–50[a]

Location of team or correlation item	Acquisition costs		Average won-lost		Population rank
	Amount (thousands of dollars)	Rank	Percentage	Rank	
American League					
Team					
Boston	782	1	50.8	4	6
New York	640	2	61.7	1	1
Cleveland	473	3	53.4	3	5
Detroit	455	4	53.7	2	3
Washington	198	5	48.1	5	8
Chicago	147	6	44.9	7	2
Philadelphia	32	7	45.1	6	4
St. Louis	−143	8	42.0	8	7

Rank correlation of acquisition costs with:

Average won-lost percentage	0.81[b]
Excluding Boston	0.93[c]
City population rank	0.22[d]

National League					
Team					
New York	1,067	1	52.4	4	1
Chicago	848	2	52.9	2	3
Pittsburgh	619	3	50.8	5	4
Cincinnati	464	4	46.3	6	7
Boston	374	5	46.3	6	6
Philadelphia	355	6	39.4	8	5
Brooklyn	316	7	52.9	2	1
St. Louis	−197	8	58.7	1	8

Rank correlation of acquisition costs with:

Average won-lost percentage	−0.13[d]
Excluding St. Louis and Brooklyn	0.89[b]
City population rank	0.42[d]

Sources: Acquisition costs, *Study of Monopoly Power*, Pt. 6, *Organized Baseball*, Hearings before the Subcommittee on Study of Monopoly Power of the House Committee on the Judiciary, 82 Cong. 1 sess. (1952), pp. 1606–09; other data, see Table 1.

a. Acquisition costs are the total for the years 1929, 1933, 1939, 1943, 1946, and 1950; won-lost percentages and population rankings are based on the entire period.

b. Significant at the 5 percent level.

c. Significant at the 1 percent level.

d. Not significant at the 5 percent level.

Table 6. Correlation of Cumulative Profits of Baseball Teams with City Population Rankings, 1920–50[a]

Location of team or correlation item	Cumulative profits		Population rank
	Amount (thousands of dollars)	Rank	
American League			
Team			
New York	8,497	1	1
Detroit	4,702	2	3
Cleveland	3,670	3	5
Washington	2,746	4	8
Chicago	1,347	5	2
Philadelphia	1,091	6	4
St. Louis	1,088	7	7
Boston	−2,075	8	6
Rank correlation, 0.54[b]			
National League			
Team			
St. Louis	5,962	1	8
Brooklyn	3,944	2	1
Pittsburgh	3,213	3	4
Chicago	2,920	4	3
New York	2,892	5	1
Cincinnati	1,571	6	7
Philadelphia	−13	7	5
Boston	−295	8	6
Rank correlation, 0.08[b]			
Excluding St. Louis, 0.64[b]			

Sources: Profits, *Organized Baseball*, House Hearings, pp. 1599–1600; other data, see Table 1.
a. Profits are the total for the period 1920–50; population rankings are based on the entire period.
b. Not significant at the 5 percent level.

These hypothetical comparisons suggest that player sales were responsible for the profits of Philadelphia and St. Louis (AL), for the small losses of Philadelphia and Boston (NL), and for roughly 60 percent of the profits of St. Louis (NL). In support of these hypothetical figures, actual data show that the St. Louis Browns (AL) received $1.3 million from player sales between 1947 and 1951, and that sales accounted for

Table 7. Sales and Trades of Players, Baseball, 1950, 1960, and 1970

Year and transaction	Number of transactions			
	Total	Interleague	American League	National League
1950				
Trades	7	0	4	3
Sales[a]	21	8	7	6
Total	28	8	11	9
1960				
Trades	32	13	12	7
Sales[a]	31	16	7	8
Total	63	29	19	15
1970				
Trades	51	21	16	14
Sales[a]	46	18	13	15
Total	97	39	29	29

Source: *Official Baseball Guide* (Sporting News, 1951, 1961, 1971).
a. Any transaction involving cash is treated as a sale.

an estimated 90 percent of the profits of the St. Louis Cardinals (NL) during the period 1922–41.[20]

Although it appears that sales of players were of critical importance in the business operations of baseball during the period covered by our data, it is now generally believed that sales of players for cash are much less common than in earlier years. Table 7 summarizes data on player transactions for selected years. The data show that trades are indeed tending to replace sales as a percentage of total transactions, but the number of sales actually increased between 1950 and 1970. Numbers of transactions are unfortunately the only data available; dollars amounts involved in sales, which would be of particular interest, are not published.

A limited amount of information about cash sales in the other major sports is available, although the quality of the data is far more uncertain than that for baseball. In football, twenty-seven transactions are listed for 1972 in the *NFL Guide,* all involving trades of players for players or of

20. *Organized Baseball,* H. Rept. 2002, p. 95.

players for draft choices.[21] Hockey data for 1971, derived from *The Hockey Register,* show sixty-three transactions other than intraleague drafts and waiver sales between NHL teams, of which twenty-seven were sales and thirty-six were trades. For the portion of 1972 (roughly through October) covered in the *Register,* thirty-nine transactions between NHL teams were recorded, involving twenty-four sales and fifteen trades.[22] Basketball data for the NBA give twenty-five transactions other than waivers in 1971, including sixteen trades and nine transactions involving cash.[23] These data suggest that cash sales probably play a smaller role in sports as a whole than the earlier baseball data would predict, and are no doubt partially accounted for by the possibility of a franchise move that was not available in baseball prior to 1952.[24]

Gate Sharing and Team Strength

One of the theoretical conclusions was that the distribution of playing strengths within a stable league is independent of the gate-sharing arrangement; instead, a high home-team gate share has the effect of raising player costs and reducing the probability of survival of the small-city franchise. Although comparisons among sports are at best only suggestive, it is worth noting that for the periods covered in the won-lost percent tables above, the two sports having a 100–0 gate-sharing arrangement had the following range between best and worst records: basketball, 1947–68, .627–.364; hockey, 1939–67, .603–.418. During the period of stable franchise locations, baseball, with an 80–20 gate-sharing arrangement, had best-worst ranges of .573–.427 (AL) and .558–.432 (NL). In the NFL, which has the most equal gate-sharing arrangement, the range is .663–.321. While the peculiarities of each sport might affect the relationship between the

21. *1972 National Football League Guide* (Sporting News, 1972). Whether this reflects a league policy to maintain confidentiality about the terms of transactions is not known.

22. *The Hockey Register, 1972–73* (Sporting News, 1972).

23. *National Basketball Association Official Guide for 1971–72* (Sporting News, 1971).

24. Before 1952, the rules of baseball required unanimous consent within the league to which the team belonged, and a majority vote by the other league, for a franchise move. Following 1952, only the team's own league had a voice (provided the new location had no other major-league team), with unanimous consent being later lowered to a three-fourths majority.

distribution of skills and percentage of games won, the data do not indicate that gate-sharing arrangements have any inherent equalizing effect.

Summary

The basic issue to which this chapter addresses itself is the problem of league balance in terms of the distribution of playing strengths. The data for the four professional team sports show that big-city teams tend to win significantly more league championships than small-city teams, except in hockey, where Canadian teams, traditionally the high drawing-potential franchises, have dominated Stanley Cup competition. They also show that small-city franchises tend to be abandoned or moved much more often than big-city franchises. With respect to percentages of games won, the data are more ambiguous; eliminating the Canadian teams in hockey and the second teams in two-franchise cities in football, all rank correlations with population are positive, but they are not sufficiently high to justify definite conclusions. What is clear is that nowhere in the data is there any indication that the present rules structure has resulted in a balancing of playing strengths among teams. The evidence points instead toward the conclusion that the rules structure of professional sports is relatively ineffective in balancing playing strengths, and that imbalance is due to the differences in the drawing potentials of franchises.

APPENDIX A: A Mathematical Model of a Sports League

Let I_t^i = the inventory of playing skills of team i at time t

x_t^{ij} = the number of units of playing skills purchased by team i at time t from team j

x_t^{iN} = the number of units of new playing skills drafted by team i at time t

b_t = the cost per unit of playing skills acquired by interteam sale at time t

b_t^N = bonus per unit of new playing skills acquired in the draft at time t

w_t = salary cost per unit of playing skills during the tth period

R_t^i = revenue from gate receipts and television of team i in period t

$R_t^{ij}(i)$ = gate receipts from games played between teams i and j at team i's home park in period t

T_t^i = television revenue of team i in period t

x_t^{NS} = supply of new playing skills available to be drafted at time t

$p_t^{ij} \equiv \dfrac{I_t^i}{I_t^i + I_t^j}$ = probability of team i winning in a game between teams i and j in period t

$I_t^T \equiv \sum\limits_{j=1}^{n} I_t^j$ = total inventory of playing skills in the league in period t

$M_t^i \equiv \dfrac{I_t^i}{I_t^T}$ = relative share of league playing strengths possessed by team i in period t

δ = market rate of interest per period

μ = percentage rate of depreciation per period.

The drafting procedure in the model is represented by

$$x_t^{iN} = g(M_{t-1}^i)x_t^{NS},$$

where g satisfies $g(1) = 0$, $0 < g(M^i) < 1$ for $0 < M^i < 1$ and $g'(M^i) < 0$ for $0 < M^i < 1$, with

$$\sum_{i=1}^{n} g(M^i) = 1.$$

In particular, g is represented by the linear function

$$g = \frac{1}{(n-1)}(1 - M_{t-1}^i).$$

Thus, each team faces the same drafting function, with greater team strength relative to the rest of the league reducing its access to new players.[25]

In the model of this section, players are not identified by age cohort; instead, the percentage rate of depreciation is assumed to be constant over time, independent of the ratio of recently drafted players to total playing stock. A later model discusses the cohort problem in an activity analysis framework in which the interrelationships among positions on a team are also taken into account.

---

25. To simplify analysis of the model, a team's order in the draft is assumed to be based on the amount of playing skills it possesses, rather than on its position in the ranking of teams by skills.

The revenue function for team i appears as follows:

$$R_t^i = \alpha \sum_{j \neq i} R_t^{ij}(i) + (1 - \alpha) \sum_{j \neq i} R_t^{ij}(j) + T_t^i,$$

where α, $0 \leq \alpha \leq 1$ is the home team's share of gate receipts. $R_t^{ij}(i)$ is taken to be a concave function of p_t^{ij}, attaining a regular maximum at some $\bar{p}_t^{ij} > \frac{1}{2}$. It is also assumed that $R_t^{ij}(i)$ is a function of a parameter A_t^i, representing the drawing potential of the area where team i's franchise is located, as measured, say, by population, per capita income, etc. In particular it is assumed that $R_t^{ij}(i)$ may be written as $f(p_t^{ij}:A_t^i)$ for each i, j with

$$[(\partial^2 f)/(\partial p_t^{ij} \partial A_t^i)] > 0 \text{ for } p_t^{ij} < \bar{p}_t^{ij}.$$

This assumption amounts to postulating that attendance and gate receipts at any stadium depend only on the relative strengths of the home and visiting teams rather than on the identity of the visiting team (thus excluding the effect of traditional rivalries) and further that all franchises are identical except for their drawing potential. These assumptions are somewhat restrictive, since if a team is really weak attendance will be highest at games involving the top-ranked opponents. However, taking account of such factors in the revenue function only reinforces the results derived below, so the simpler case will be used.

The term T_t^i, representing television and radio revenues for team i, is assumed to be of the form $T_t^i = F(M_t^i, A_t^i) + G$ with F concave in M_t^i and attaining a regular maximum at some $\bar{M}_t^i$, $(1/n) < \bar{M}_t^i < 1$, with

$$[(\partial^2 F)/(\partial M_t^i \partial A_t^i)] > 0 \text{ for } M_t^i < \bar{M}_t^i.$$

F represents receipts from local television and radio broadcasts, while G, which is fixed, represents receipts from national television contracts. For football, F is quite small, representing mainly sales of radio rights, while G is quite large. For baseball, the situation is reversed, with the bulk of the revenue coming from local broadcasts.

The first model considered is one in which training costs and time lags associated with drafted players are ignored.

The decision problem for the ith team is as follows:

$$\max \sum_{t=0}^{\infty} [R_t^i - w_t I_t^i - b_t \sum_j x_t^{ij} - b_t^N x_t^{iN}]/(1 + \delta)^t$$

subject to

$$I_t^j = (1 - \mu)I_{t-1}^j + \sum_k x_t^{jk} + x_t^{jN}, j = 1, \cdots, n.$$

Under the drafting procedure outlined above,

$$x_t^{jN} = [1 - (I_{t-1}^j)/(I_{t-1}^T)][1/(n-1)]x_t^{NS}.$$

Formulating the problem in this fashion implies that each team actually exercises its rights to drafted players, which in turn implies that the price of a unit of playing skills acquired in the draft is not larger than the price of a unit of playing skills acquired through purchase from another team; that is, $b_t^N \le b_t$ for every t.

Because the long-run effect of the institutional structure of professional sports on the relative playing strengths of teams is of particular interest, the stock of new talent available in the draft is assumed to be constant, that is, $x_t^{NS} = x^{NS}$ for every t. Under this assumption, the difference equation for I_t^j can be solved explicitly to obtain

$$I_t^j = I_0^j \prod_{s=0}^{t-1} a(s) + \frac{x^{NS}}{n-1}\sum_{s=0}^{t-1}\prod_{r=s}^{t-1} a(r) + \frac{x^{NS}}{n-1}$$

$$+ \sum_{s=1}^{t-1}\left(\sum_k x_s^{jk}\right)\prod_{r=s}^{t-1} a(r) + \sum_k x_t^{jk}$$

where

$$a(r) = \left\{1 - \mu - \frac{x^{NS}}{(n-1)I_r^T}\right\}, \qquad r = 0, 1, \cdots.$$

Team i thus must choose what sales (purchases) of players to (from) other teams in the league it will make, that is, must choose values of $x_t^{ij}, j \ne i, t = 0, 1, \cdots$. But, in an equilibrium situation, a choice by team i to sell a certain number of units of playing skills to team j must also involve the corresponding choice of team j to purchase the same number of units of playing skills from team i. As outlined above, an equilibrium of the model is a state in which team i regards sales to "third parties" by team j as given and chooses x_t^{ij} to maximize the discounted present value of net cash flows, with the following consistency conditions being satisfied:

(1) $x_t^{ij} = -x_t^{ji}$ for all i, j, t; that is, team i's optimal choices of player sales are consistent with the other teams' optimal choices of player purchases from team i.

(2) Let $x_t^{jk}(i)$ denote the level of sales by j to k ($j, k \ne i$) expected by team i in period t. Then $x_t^{jk}(i) = x_t^{jk}$ for every i, j, k ($j, k \ne i$) and for every t; that is, expectations about "third-party" sales are in fact realized.

An equilibrium of the model is said to occur when the choices of player sales made by all teams with the object of maximizing the discounted present value of net cash flows also satisfy (1) and (2) above. When equilibrium occurs, then condition (1) implies $\Sigma_i\Sigma_j x_t^{ij} = 0$ for every t, where $x_t^{ii} = 0$ for every i, t. Hence, we can solve explicitly for the time path of the total stock of playing strengths in the league, under the assumptions that $x_t^{NS} = x^{NS}$ for every t and equilibrium occurs for every t, obtaining

$$I_t^T = (x^{NS}/\mu) + (1 - \mu)^t\{I_0^T - (x^{NS}/\mu)\}.$$

Since $0 < \mu < 1$, $\lim_{t\to\infty} I_t^T = x^{NS}/\mu$, with I^T constant over time if and only if $I_0^T = x^{NS}/\mu$.

Returning to the profit maximization problem for team i, let L^i denote the Lagrangian, where L^i is defined by:

$$L^i = \sum_{t=0}^{\infty} \{[R_t^i - w_t I_t^i - b_t\Sigma x_t^{ij} - b_t^N x_t^{iN}]/(1 + \delta)^t$$

$$+ \sum_{j=1}^{n} \lambda_t^{ij}\left[I_t^j - I_0^j \prod_{s=0}^{t-1} a(s) - \frac{x^{NS}}{n-1}\left(1 + \sum_{s=0}^{t-1}\prod_{r=s}^{t-1} a(r)\right)\right.$$

$$\left. - \sum_{s=1}^{t-1}\left(\sum_k x_t^{jk}\right) \prod_{r=s}^{t-1} a(r) - \sum_k x_t^{jk}\right]\},$$

where λ_t^{ij} is the multiplier associated with the jth constraint at time t. Necessary conditions for a maximum at an equilibrium position are given by:

(i) $\dfrac{\partial L^i}{\partial I_t^i} = \left(\dfrac{\partial R_t^i}{\partial I_t^i} - w_t\right)/(1 + \delta)^t - b_{t+1}^N \dfrac{\partial x_{t+1}^{iN}}{\partial I_t^i}/(1 + \delta)^t + \lambda_t^{ii} = 0;$

(ii) $\dfrac{\partial L^i}{\partial I_t^j} = \dfrac{\partial R_t^i}{\partial I_t^j}/(1 + \delta)^t - b_{t+1}^N \dfrac{\partial x_{t+1}^{iN}}{\partial I_t^j}/(1 + \delta)^{t+1} + \lambda_t^{ij} = 0, j \neq i;$

(iii) $\dfrac{\partial L^i}{\partial x_t^{ij}} = -b_t/(1 + \delta)^t + \lambda_t^{ij} - \lambda_t^{ii} + \sum_{\tau=t+1}^{\infty} (\lambda_\tau^{ij} - \lambda_\tau^{ii}) \prod_{r=\tau}^{t-1} a(r) = 0, j \neq i;$

(iv) $I_t^j = I_0^j \prod_{s=0}^{t-1} a(s) + \dfrac{x^{NS}}{n-1}\left(1 + \sum_{s=0}^{t-1}\prod_{r=s}^{t-1} a(r)\right)$

$$+ \sum_{s=1}^{t-1}\left(\sum_k x_s^{jk}\right) \prod_{r=s}^{t-1} a(r) - \sum_k x_t^{jk}, j = 1, \cdots, n.$$

In the above formulation, each team is assumed to be an ongoing enterprise, so that it is profitable for each team to maintain a positive stock of playing skills at each point in time. Further, by the equilibrium assumption, $x_t^{jk} = -x_t^{kj}$ for every j, k. Define q_t^{ij} by $q_t^{ij} = (1+\delta)^t \lambda_t^{ij}$. Then conditions (i), (ii), and (iii) can be rewritten as:

(i') $\dfrac{\partial R_t^i}{\partial I_t^i} - w_t - \dfrac{b_{t+1}^N}{(1+\delta)} \dfrac{\partial x_{t+1}^{iN}}{\partial I_t^i} = -q_t^{ii};$

(ii') $\dfrac{\partial R_t^i}{\partial I_t^j} - \dfrac{b_{t+1}^N}{(1+\delta)} \dfrac{\partial x_{t+1}^{iN}}{\partial I_t^j} = -q_t^{ij}, j \neq i;$

(iii') $b_t = q_t^{ij} - q_t^{ii} + \displaystyle\sum_{\tau=t+1}^{\infty} (q_\tau^{ij} - q_\tau^{ii}) \prod_{r=t}^{\tau-1} a(r), j \neq i$, where

$$\frac{\partial x_{t+1}^{iN}}{\partial I_t^i} = \frac{x^{NS}}{n-1} \frac{I_t^i - I_t^T}{(I_t^T)^2}, \frac{\partial x_{t+1}^{iN}}{\partial I_t^j} = \frac{x^{NS}}{n-1} \frac{I_t^i}{(I_t^T)^2}.$$

Hence,

$$b_t = \frac{\partial R_t^i}{\partial I_t^i} - \frac{\partial R_t^i}{\partial I_t^j} + \sum_{\tau=t+1}^{\infty} \frac{\partial R_\tau^i}{\partial I_\tau^i} \prod_{r=t}^{\tau-1} a(r) + \frac{x^{NS}}{(1+\delta)(n-1)}.$$

$$\sum_{\tau=t+1}^{\infty} \frac{b_{\tau+1}^N}{I_\tau^T} \prod_{r+t}^{\tau-1} a(r) - w_t \sum_{\tau=t+1}^{\infty} \frac{b_{\tau+1}^N}{I_\tau^T} \prod_{r=t}^{\tau-1} a(r), j \neq i.$$

A steady state situation for the league is a set of profit-maximizing choices for all teams in the league such that an equilibrium occurs at each point in time and such that the following conditions obtain:

(1) $I_t^j = I^j$ for all t and for all j;
(2) $x_t^{jk} = x^{jk}$ for all t and for all j, k;
(3) $b_t = b, b_t^N = b^N$ for all t, and $w_t = w$ for all t.

Note that (1) implies that I^T is constant over time with $I^T = (x^{NS}/\mu)$, so that $a(t)$, defined earlier, may now be written as $a(t) = 1 - [n/(n-1)]\mu$ for all t, with $0 < a(t) < 1$ for $0 < \mu < [(n-1)/n]$. We postulate $\mu < [(n-1)/n]$.[26]

As an inspection of (i'), (ii'), and (iii') makes clear, at a steady state $q_t^{ij} = q^{ij}$ for every i, j, hence

$$b = (q^{ij} - q^{ii})\left(1 + \sum_{\tau=t+1}^{\infty} \prod_{r=t}^{\tau-1} \{1 - [n/(n-1)]\mu\}\right).$$

26. The rate of depreciation of playing skills varies widely among the sports; but even in football, which probably has the shortest average playing life, the rate of depreciation certainly does not exceed 0.5 (player half-life of less than two years), so that the assumption does not appear to be particularly restrictive.

From this it follows that $q^{ij} = q^{ik}$ for every j, $k \neq i$, hence denote q^{ij} by q^i. The first-order conditions evaluated at a steady state become:

$$\frac{\partial R^i}{\partial I^i} - w - \frac{b^N x^{NS}}{(1+\delta)(n-1)} \frac{I^i - I^T}{(I^T)^2} = -q^{ii}$$

and

$$\frac{\partial R^i}{\partial I^j} - \frac{b^N x^{NS}}{(1+\delta)(n-1)} \frac{I^i}{(I^T)^2} = -q^i, j \neq i,$$

together with

$$b = \frac{(q^i - q^{ii})(n-1)}{\mu n},$$

while

$$I^j = \frac{x^{NS}}{n\mu} + \frac{(n-1)}{\mu} \sum_k x^{jk} \, j \neq i.$$

Since $I^T = x^{NS}/\mu$, this implies $I^j \gtrless I^T/n$ if and only if $\sum_k x^{jk} \gtrless 0$. Thus the following proposition and corollary is obtained.

Proposition 1. At a steady state, every team of greater than average playing strength is a net purchaser of players from other teams and every team of less than average playing strength is a net seller of players to other teams.

Corollary. At a steady state, there is equalization of playing strengths among teams if and only if no sales of players take place among teams.

This raises, then, the fundamental issue of identifying the factors determining which teams in the league will possess greater than average stocks of playing strengths. To investigate this issue requires examination of the properties of the revenue functions of teams in the league. From the earlier discussion,

$$R^i = \alpha \sum_{j \neq i} R^{ij}(i) + (1 - \alpha) \sum_{j \neq i} R^{ij}(j) + T^i.$$

Hence,

$$\frac{\partial R^i}{\partial I^i} = \sum_{j \neq i} \left(\alpha \frac{\partial R^{ij}(i)}{\partial p^{ij}} - (1 - \alpha) \frac{\partial R^{ij}(j)}{\partial p^{ji}} \right) \frac{I^j}{(I^i + I^j)^2} + \frac{\partial T^i}{\partial M^i} \frac{I^T - I^i}{(I^T)^2}$$

and

$$\frac{\partial R^i}{\partial I^j} = \left(\alpha \frac{\partial R^{ij}(i)}{\partial p^{ij}} - (1 - \alpha) \frac{\partial R^{ij}(j)}{\partial p^{ji}} \right) \frac{-I^i}{(I^i + I^j)^2} + \frac{\partial T^i}{\partial M^i} \frac{-I^i}{(I^T)^2}.$$

The first-order conditions evaluated at a steady state imply that $\partial R^i/\partial I^j = \partial R^i/\partial I^k$ for all j, $k \neq i$, so that

$$\left(\frac{1}{(I^i + I^j)^2}\right)\left(\alpha \frac{\partial R^{ij}(i)}{\partial p^{ij}} - (1 - \alpha)\frac{\partial R^{ij}(i)}{\partial p^{ji}}\right)$$

$$= \left(\frac{1}{(I^i + I^k)^2}\right)\left(\alpha \frac{\partial R^{ik}(i)}{\partial p^{ik}} - (1 - \alpha)\frac{\partial R^{ik}(k)}{\partial p^{ki}}\right)$$

for every $j, k \neq i$. Denote this quantity by θ^i. From the first-order conditions,

$$\theta^i \sum_{j \neq i} I^j + \frac{\partial T^i}{\partial M^i}\left(\frac{I^T - I^i}{(I^T)^2}\right) + \theta^i I^i + \frac{\partial T^i}{\partial M^i}\frac{I^i}{(I^T)^2} - w$$

$$- b^N \frac{x^{NS}}{n - 1}\left(\frac{I^i - I^T}{(I^T)^2}\right) + \frac{b^N x^{NS}}{(1 + \delta)(n - 1)}\left(\frac{I^i}{(I^T)^2}\right) = \frac{n\mu b}{n - 1},$$

that is,

$$\theta^i I^T + \frac{\partial T^i}{\partial M^i}\frac{1}{I^T} = w + \frac{\mu}{n - 1}\left(b - \frac{b^N}{1 + \delta}\right) + \mu b.$$

Since this holds for $i = 1, \cdots, n$, it is also true that

$$\theta^i I^T + \frac{\partial T^i}{\partial M^i}\frac{1}{I^T} = \theta^j I^T + \frac{\partial T^j}{\partial M^j}\frac{1}{I^T}$$

for every i, j so that, in particular,

$$\frac{I^T}{(I^i + I^j)^2}\left(\alpha \frac{\partial R^{ij}(i)}{\partial p^{ij}} - (1 - \alpha)\frac{\partial R^{ij}(j)}{\partial p^{ji}}\right) + \frac{\partial T^i}{\partial M^i}\frac{1}{I^T}$$

$$= \frac{I^T}{(I^i + I^j)^2}\left(\alpha \frac{\partial R^{ij}(i)}{\partial p^{ji}} - (1 - \alpha)\frac{\partial R^{ij}(i)}{\partial p^{ij}}\right) + \frac{\partial T^j}{\partial M^j}\frac{1}{I^T},$$

that is,

$$\left(\frac{I^T}{I^i + I^j}\right)^2\left(\frac{\partial R^{ij}(i)}{\partial p^{ij}} - \frac{\partial R^{ij}(j)}{\partial p^{ji}}\right) = \left(\frac{\partial T^j}{\partial M^j} - \frac{\partial T^i}{\partial M^i}\right).$$

Because revenue depends only on the relative playing strengths of i and j (and the size of the market area), $R^{ij}(i)$ can be written as $R(i)$, and similarly for j, and the equation can be rewritten as

$$\left(\frac{I^T}{I^i + I^j}\right)^2\left(\frac{\partial R(i)}{\partial p^{ij}} - \frac{\partial R(j)}{\partial p^{ji}}\right) = \left(\frac{\partial T^j}{\partial M^j} - \frac{\partial T^i}{\partial M^i}\right).$$

Then, if there are no local television revenues, at a steady state

$$\frac{\partial R(i)}{\partial p^{ij}} = \frac{\partial R(j)}{\partial p^{ji}}.$$

If $A^i = A^j$ (teams i and j are located in areas of equal drawing potential), then setting $p^{ij} = p^{ji} = \frac{1}{2}$ would satisfy this condition, so that $I^i = I^j$. If $A^i > A^j$, then, because $\partial^2 R(i)/\partial p^{ij}\partial A^i > 0$ and because, by hypothesis, the functional forms for $R(i)$ and $R(j)$ are identical, I^i must be chosen larger than I^j to satisfy the condition $\partial R(i)/\partial p^{ij} = \partial R(j)/\partial p^{ji}$. Even when local television revenues are taken into account, the basic conclusion is unaltered, since again $A^i > A^j$ implies $I^i > I^j$; whether local television makes this result more or less pronounced depends on the sensitivity of the television revenue function compared to the gate receipts function. In any case, Proposition 2 is immediate.

Proposition 2. At a steady state, teams located in cities with higher drawing potential will have greater stocks of playing skills than teams located in smaller cities will.

Corollary. At a steady state, equalization of playing strengths occurs if and only if the drawing potential of each team in the league is equal.[27]

Because the home team's gate share differs so markedly among the four major sports, it is of interest to examine the effect of its size on the variables of the model. From the expressions given above,

$$\theta^i I^T + \frac{\partial T^i}{\partial M^i}\frac{1}{I^T} = w + \frac{\mu}{n-1}(b - b^N) + \mu b,$$

which implies

$$\alpha = \frac{(I^i + I^j)^2\left[w + \dfrac{\mu}{n-1}\left(b - \dfrac{b^N}{1+\delta} + \mu b - \dfrac{\partial T^i}{\partial M^i}\dfrac{1}{I^T}\right)\right] + \dfrac{\partial R(j)}{\partial p^{ji}}I^T}{I^T\left(\dfrac{\partial R(i)}{\partial p^{ij}} + \dfrac{\partial R(j)}{\partial p^{ji}}\right)}$$

for every $j \neq i$.

---

27. If wage rates differ among teams, Proposition 2 and its corollary must be revised. The appropriate condition (with no local television revenues) is given by

$$\frac{\partial R(i)}{\partial p^{ij}} - \frac{(I^i + I^j)^2}{I^T}w^i = \frac{\partial R(j)}{\partial p^{ji}} - \frac{(I^i + I^j)^2}{I^T}w^j$$

where w^i and w^j are the wage rates per unit of playing skills for teams i and j. To the extent that wage rates are higher in large cities, the difference in playing strengths between large- and small-city teams is reduced; and if the difference in wage rates were sufficiently great, one might even find that the small cities had larger stocks of playing skills than the large cities. (We are indebted to Walter Oi for raising this issue.) While, as noted earlier, there are few data on the difference in wage rates, the fact that when trades occur player salaries are continued at the same levels suggests that wage rates per unit of playing skills do not differ much among teams.

Note that, in establishing Proposition 2, the distribution of playing strengths was found to be independent of α.[28] Thus the value of α determines only the size of the expression

$$w + \frac{\mu}{n-1}\left(b - \frac{b^N}{1+\delta}\right) + \mu b;$$

the larger α is, the larger this expression is, reflecting either higher wages or higher costs of acquiring players. In effect, if the home team receives a larger share of the gate, its total revenues depend much more on its ability to win, since this increases its home revenues, than on its performance on the road, where its *in*ability to win increases its revenues. It can be shown that, at a steady state with no local television receipts, $\alpha > \frac{1}{2}$. This follows because

$$\alpha = \frac{(I^i + I^j)^2}{I^T\left(\dfrac{\partial R(i)}{\partial p^{ij}} + \dfrac{\partial R(j)}{\partial p^{ji}}\right)}\left[w + \frac{\mu}{n-1}\left(b - \frac{b^N}{1+\delta}\right) + \mu b\right] + \frac{\dfrac{\partial R(j)}{\partial p^{ji}}}{\dfrac{\partial R(j)}{\partial p^{ji}} + \dfrac{\partial R(i)}{\partial p^{ij}}}.$$

Since the last term $= \frac{1}{2}$ and the first term is positive, $\alpha > \frac{1}{2}$. This leads to the following result.

Proposition 3. At a steady state, the larger the home team's share of the gate, the higher are wages and/or the cost of players purchased from other teams; the distribution of playing strengths among teams is not affected. In particular, with no local television revenues, the home team's gate share must exceed 50 percent to sustain a steady state.

Corollary. The larger the home team's share of the gate, the smaller the total profits for teams in the league at a steady state.

A final issue to be explored is the convergence over time to a steady state.

From the first-order conditions,

$$b_t = (q_t^{ij} - q_t^{ii}) + \sum_{\tau=t+1}^{\infty} (q_\tau^{ij} - q_\tau^{ii}) \prod_{r=t}^{\tau-1} a(r),$$

hence

$$a(t)b_{t+1} = (q_{t+1}^{ij} - q_{t+1}^{ii})a(t) + a(t) \sum_{\tau=t+2}^{\infty} (q_\tau^{ij} - q_\tau^{ii}) \prod_{r=t+1}^{\tau-1} a(r),$$

28. This conclusion rests upon the assumption of an ongoing league with profitable franchises. The larger α is, the less chance there is that profits will be positive for small-city teams, hence the less chance of the existence of a steady state.

so that

$$b_t = (q_t^{ij} - q_t^{ii}) + a(t)b_{t+1}.$$

Suppose $b_t = b$ for all t; then

$$\lim_{t \to \infty} (q_t^{ij} - q_t^{ii}) = b[1 - \lim_{t \to \infty} a(t)] = b\frac{n\mu}{n-1}.$$

Since $q_t^{ij} - q_t^{ii}$ approaches its steady state value asymptotically, the distribution of playing strengths approaches its steady state value as well. This verifies the following:

Proposition 4. If the model attains an equilibrium at each point in time and if the cost of acquiring players from other teams is constant over time, then, given any initial distribution of playing strengths among teams, this distribution converges to the steady state distribution asymptotically.

To summarize: assuming the cost of acquiring players from other teams to be constant over time, the distribution of playing strengths converges to a steady state distribution in which teams located in high drawing-potential areas have large stocks of playing skills acquired through purchases of players from teams located in low drawing-potential areas. A team's share of gate receipts determines the cost of players, a high home-game share increasing the acquisition and wage costs of players. This shows that the reserve clause and drafting procedures do not eliminate the tendency of teams in large cities to dominate the league, since these equalizing procedures are offset by the ability of such teams to purchase players from other teams.

Suppose that the exchange of players for cash between teams were prohibited by agreement within the league. (Trades of players are viewed here as exchanges of equals for equals, and hence have no effect on the distribution of playing strengths.) Then the expression for I_t^j becomes:

$$I_t^j = (1 - \mu)I_{t-1}^j + x_t^{jN} = \left\{(1 - \mu) - \frac{x_t^{NS}}{(n-1)I_t^T}\right\}I_{t-1}^j + \frac{x_t^{NS}}{n-1}.$$

If $x_t^{NS} = x^{NS}$ for every t, then

$$I_t^j = I_0^j \prod_{s=0}^{t-1} a(s) + \frac{x^{NS}}{n-1}\left(1 + \sum_{s=0}^{t-1} \prod_{r=s}^{t-1} a(r)\right),$$

where

$$a(r) = \left\{(1 - \mu) - \frac{x^{NS}}{(n-1)I_r^T}\right\},$$

with

$$\lim_{t \to \infty} a(t) = \left\{ 1 - \frac{n\mu}{n-1} \right\},$$

so that $0 < \lim_{t \to \infty} a(t) < 1$. Hence,

$$I_t^j - I_t^k = (I_0^j - I_0^k) \prod_{s=0}^{t-1} a(s)$$

with

$$\lim_{t \to \infty} I_t^j = \frac{x^{NS}}{\mu n} \qquad \text{for } j = 1, \cdots, n.$$

This establishes the following:

Proposition 5. If the flow of new players is constant over time and if the sale of player contracts between teams is prohibited, then, whatever the initial distribution of playing strengths among teams, there is asymptotic convergence to an equalized distribution.

Corollary. The shorter the average playing lifetime (the larger is μ) and the fewer the number of teams in the league, the faster is the speed of convergence to equal playing strengths.

It should be remembered that this analysis is based on the assumption that every team in the league survives, that is, makes positive profits. Because increasing the home team's gate share raises costs for all teams in the league, it might well be that at high home-team gate share percentages the smaller franchises go out of existence. (This seems to be particularly true throughout basketball history.) It might also be the case that when sales of contracts are prohibited the weak franchises become unprofitable, so that subsidies by the league might be required to maintain them. An obvious way to replace the revenue earned by a team from player sales is to provide more equal gate and television revenue sharing, and such actions should certainly be considered complementary to any action to restrict sales of players.

Finally, consider the relationship between the steady state results achieved under decentralized control, as summarized in this section, and industry-wide profit maximization (syndicated control). Under centralized control (and assuming $x_t^{NS} = x^{NS}$ for all t), the maximization problem becomes:

$$\max \sum_{t=0}^{\infty} \left[\sum_{i=1}^{n} R_t^i - w I_t^T - b_t^N x^{NS} \right] / (1 + \delta)^t,$$

where

$$I_t^T = (1 - \mu) I_{t-1}^T + x^{NS}.$$

Taking w and b_t^N $(= b^N$ for all $t)$ as parameters and assuming a steady state $(I_t^T = x^{NS}/n\mu$ for all $t)$, the first-order conditions become:

$$\sum_{i=1}^{n} \frac{\partial R^i}{\partial I^j} = 0, j = 1, \cdots, n,$$

where, as before,

$$R^i = \alpha \sum_{k \neq i} R^{ik}(i) + (1 - \alpha) \sum_{k \neq i} R^{ik}(k) + T^i.$$

Since the gate-sharing arrangement is irrelevant to total industry revenue, take $\alpha = 1$ so that we may rewrite the first-order conditions as:

$$\sum_{i \neq j} \frac{I^i}{(I^i + I^j)^2} \left(\frac{\partial R(j)}{\partial p^{ji}} - \frac{\partial R(i)}{\partial p^{ij}} \right) - \sum_{i \neq j} \frac{\partial T^i}{\partial M^i} \frac{I^i}{(I^T)^2} + \frac{\partial T^i}{\partial M^j} \frac{(I^T - I^j)}{(I^T)^2}$$
$$= 0, j = 1, \cdots, n.$$

The comparable condition under decentralized control states is:

$$\frac{\partial R(j)}{\partial p^{ji}} - \frac{\partial R(i)}{\partial p^{ij}} = \frac{(I^i + I^j)^2}{(I^T)^2} \left(\frac{\partial T^i}{\partial M^i} - \frac{\partial T^j}{\partial M^j} \right), \qquad j \neq i.$$

Direct substitution verifies the following:

Proposition 6. The distribution of playing strengths achieved at a steady state under decentralized ownership and control of teams maximizes the discounted present value of net cash flows for the league as a whole, given that x^{NS}, w, and b^N are treated as parameters.

Of course, under syndicated operation of the league, the levels of bonuses and wages and the total stock of playing strengths for the league are variables, not parameters. Since in this formulation revenue depends on only the relative strengths of teams and not the absolute strengths, there is an incentive under syndicated operation to reduce the total stock of playing strengths and thus reduce costs. This leads to the development of competitive "outlaw" leagues, with ensuing bilateral monopoly problems that are beyond the scope of this chapter.[29] Suffice it to say that, at least in the short run, profits are less under decentralized control than under syndicated ownership, because of the monopsonistic character of the latter. This conclusion does not consider the problems of fan support for syndicated operation of a league, which might overwhelm all other considerations by lowering revenues.

29. See Chapter 3 for a discussion of interleague competition and the level of playing skills.

The basic elements of the model remain unchanged when training of players is taken into account. The introduction of training considerations (the maintenance of minor leagues, and so forth) produces a time lag in the stock-of-playing-skills function that reflects the period required before a drafted player is skilled enough to add to the team's playing strength; it also adds an additional cost to the net cash flow function, representing training costs for players in the training pool. Offsetting this additional cost would be a decrease in bonus payments for such relatively unskilled players. Because the method of analyzing a model that includes training factors is in most respects identical to that employed above, only the framework of such a model is given here, leaving as an exercise for the reader the verification of the results of the previous model.

Formally, let players drafted τ periods earlier enter the stock of playing skills at time t and let h_t denote the cost of training in period t, where

$$h_t = h\left(\sum_{r=t-\tau+1}^{t} x_r^{iN}\right),$$

with $h' > 0$. The maximization problem is:

$$\max \sum_{t=0}^{\infty} [R_t^i - wI_t^i - b_t^N x_t^{iN} - h_t]/(1 + \delta)^t$$

subject to

$$I_t^j = (1 - \mu)I^j + \sum_k x_t^{jk} + x_{t-\tau}^{iN}, \, j = 1, \cdots, n.$$

The same steady state results apply, assuming $x_t^{NS} = x^{NS}$ for all t, except that $b^N/(1 + \delta)$ in the analysis of the previous model is now replaced by

$$\frac{b^N}{(1 + \delta)} + h' \sum_{r=1}^{\tau+1} \frac{1}{(1 + \delta)^r},$$

which reflects the discounted present value of training costs as well as the bonus payment. Convergence results also still hold, so we may conclude that the introduction into the model of the training operations peculiar to baseball and hockey requires no essential modifications of the results already obtained.

Some Extensions of the Model

An interesting extension of the original model is to dispense with the assumptions that playing strength is homogeneous and that the objective of team owners is to maximize profits. In this model, a team is treated as a process or activity, with playing strengths a measure of the level of operation. At a given level of operation, various playing skills are required. Playing skills are functions of the relevant stocks of players of various types. The stock of players of a given type is determined by new drafts, trades or sales, and retirements. The owner is now treated as a "consumer," whose satisfaction depends on the probability of winning and on consumption of a composite commodity called "other goods." He is also assumed to derive income from nonsport sources. His objective is to maximize his total "discounted" utilities with a "discount rate" representing his time preferences, subject to the condition that the profits of the team and his own wealth are nonnegative.

Let $K^j(t, r, m)$ = the level of service of players, for team j at time t, of type r of vintage m; $r = 1, \cdots, R$; $m = 1, \cdots, M$

$K^j(t)$ = the $R \times M$ matrix with elements $K^j(t, r, m)$

$V^j(t, r, m)$ = the stock of players of type r of vintage m owned by team j at time t

$x^j(t, r, m)$ = players acquired by team j at time t of type r and vintage m

$\alpha^{ji}(t, r, m)$ = proportion of $V^j(t, r, m)$ sold by team j to team i at time t

$x^{jn}(t, r, m)$ = drafts by team j at time t of type r and vintage m

$x^{ij}(t, r, m)$ = purchases by team j at time t from team i of players of type r of vintage m

$C^j(t)$ = consumption of "other goods" by the owner of team j

$q(t)$ = the price of C

$y^j(t)$ = the nonsports income of the owner of team j

$W^j(t)$ = the wealth of the owner of team j, not including the team

$I^j(t)$ = the playing strength of team j

w = wage rate per unit of playing skill

$\pi^j(t)$ = net cash flow resulting from operating team j,

and the other symbols are as before.

Associated with a given stock of players is a stream of services starting at the time of purchases and ending with the time of retirement, that is, with $V^j(t, r, m)$ are associated $M + 1$ functions $g^j(\theta, r, m)$, $\theta = 0, \cdots, M$.

These functions reflect appreciation and/or depreciation in the playing ability of a player as a function of his age and experience. Hence,

$$K^j(t, r, m) = \sum_{\theta=0}^{M} g^j[\theta, r, m; V^j(t - \theta, r, m)],$$

where

$$V^j(t, r, m) = \sum_{\theta=0}^{M} \left[1 - \sum_{s=0}^{\theta-1} \sum_{i \neq j} \alpha^{ji}(t, r, m) \right] x^j(t - \theta, r, m),$$

and where

$$x^j(t, r, m) = x^{jN}(t, r, m) + \sum_{i \neq j} x^{ij}(t, r, m) + x^{jN}(t, r, m)$$

$$+ \sum_{i \neq j} \alpha^{ij}(t, r, m) V^i(t, r, m).$$

Since a team cannot sell more than all of its stock of players, α^{ij} must satisfy the following constraints:

$$\alpha^{ij} \geq 0, \quad \text{and} \quad \sum_{s=0}^{m} \sum_{j \neq i} \alpha^{ij}(s, r, m) \leq 1.$$

The playing strength of team j is given by:

$$P^j(t) = f^j(K^j(t), t).$$

Taking w, b, and b^N, as defined above, as $R \times M$ matrices, $\pi^j(t)$ can be written as:

$$\pi^j(t) = R^j(t) - \sum_r \sum_m w(t, r, m) V^j(t, r, m) - \sum_r \sum_m x^{jN}(t, r, m) b^N(t, r, m)$$

$$- \sum_{j \neq i} \sum_r \sum_m b(t, r, m) \alpha^{ji}(t, r, m) V^i(t, r, m)$$

$$+ \sum_{j \neq i} \sum_r \sum_m b(t, r, m) \alpha^{ij}(t, r, m) V^j(t, r, m).$$

The wealth of the owner is given by the difference equation:

$$W^j(t) - W^j(t - 1) = \pi^j(t) + y^j(t) - q(t)C(t).$$

Letting p_t^j denote the vector of probabilities of winning for team j, denote the owner's utility at time t by $U(C_t, p_t^j)$.

The problem is to maximize

$$\phi[\Sigma U^i(C_t^i, p_t^i)(1 + \rho)^{-t}, \Sigma \pi_t^i(1 + \delta)^{-t}],$$

where ρ is some positive rate of subjective discount, subject to the above constraints and to the constraints that (1) all variables are nonnegative, and (2) π and W are nonnegative. Where ϕ is independent of U, the problem is the same as in the original model. To show what happens when ϕ is independent of π_t, the model is specialized as follows: let C_t, y_t, and W_t remain unchanged; the change in wealth is given by

$$W^i_t - W^i_{t-1} = \delta W^i_{t-1} + \pi^i_t - \sigma C^i_t,$$

where δ is the rate of interest and σ is the "price level" of consumption. The problem thus is:

$$\max \sum_t U^i(p^i_t, C^i_t)(1 + \rho)^{-t},$$

subject to:

$$I^j_t - I^j_{t-1} = \sum_{j \neq k} x^{jk}_t + x^{jN}_t - \alpha I^j_{t-1}, \ \pi^i_t \geq 0, \ W^i_t \geq 0, \ C^i_t \geq 0, \ I^j_t \geq 0,$$

where α is now the rate of depreciation.

The previous propositions must now be modified. To indicate the direction of modification, and assuming that the optimum is interior, the necessary conditions for a maximum for both the original model and the present one can be derived as follows.

The relevant Lagrangian L^1 is:

$$L^1 = \sum_t U^i(p^i_t, C^i_t)(1 + \rho)^{-t}$$

$$+ \sum_t \mu^i_t[W^i_{t-1}(1 + \delta) - W^i_t + \pi^i_t - \sigma C^i_t]$$

$$+ \sum_j \sum_t \lambda^{ij}_t[I^j_{t-1}(1 - \alpha) - I^j_t + \sum_{j \neq k} x^{jk} + x^{jN}_t]$$

$$+ \sum_t \gamma^i_t \pi^i_t.$$

The first-order conditions, using the assumptions and conventions of the original model, are:

$$L^1_{I^i_t} = U^i_{p^{ij}} p^{ij}_{I^i_t}(1 + \rho)^{-t} - \lambda^{ij} + (1 - \alpha)\lambda^{ii}_{t+1}$$

$$+ \sum_j \lambda^{ij}_{t+1} x^{Nj}_{Ii} + \pi^i_{Ii}(\mu^i_t + \gamma^i_t) - b_N x^{iN}_{Ii}(\mu^i_{t+1} + \gamma^i_{t+1}) \leq 0$$

(where the partial derivative of Z with respect to s is denoted Z_s), and

$$L^1_{I^i_j} = U^i_{p^{ij}} p^{ij}_{I^j_i}(1 + \rho)^{-t} - \lambda^{ij} + (1 - \alpha)\lambda^{ij}_{t+1}$$

$$+ \sum_k \lambda^{ik}_{t+1} x^{Nk}_{Ij} + \pi^i_{Ii}(\mu^i_t + \gamma^i_t) - b_N x^i_{Ii}(\mu^i_{t+1} + \gamma^i_{t+1}) \leq 0.$$

$$L_{Wi}^1 = \mu_{t+1}^i(1+\delta) - \mu_t^i \le 0$$

$$L_{Ci}^1 = U_{Ci}^i(1+\rho)^{-t} - \sigma\mu_t^i \le 0$$

$$L_{xij}^1 = \lambda_t^{ii} - \lambda_t^{ij} - b\mu_t^i \le 0.$$

If an interior solution exists, these conditions hold as equations, with $\gamma_i^i = 0$. Eliminating the multipliers yields

$$U_{Ci}^i/U_{Ci+1}^i = \frac{1+\delta}{1+\rho}$$

$$(p_{Ii}^{ij} - p_{Ij}^{ij})U_{pij}^i = \frac{b}{\sigma}U_{Ci}^i - \left(\frac{1-\alpha}{1+\rho} + \frac{x^{sN}}{(n-1)I^T}\right)U_{Ci+1}^i\frac{b}{\sigma}$$

$$- (\pi_{Ii}^i - \pi_{Ij}^i)U_{Ci}^i/\sigma + b_Nx_{1i}^{iN}U_{Ci+1}^i/\sigma(1+\rho)$$

$$= \frac{U_{Ci}^i}{\sigma}(b - \pi_{Ii}^i + \pi_{Ij}^i)$$

$$- \frac{bU_{Ci+1}^i}{\sigma}\left(\frac{1-\alpha}{1+\rho} + \frac{x^{sN}}{(n-1)I^T} - \frac{b_N}{b(1+\rho)}(x_{Ii}^{iN} - x_{Ij}^{iN})\right).$$

Now, rewriting the first-order conditions for the original model,

$$L = \Sigma\pi_t^i(1+\delta)^{-t} + \sum_j\sum_t\lambda_t^{ij}[I_{t-1}^j(1-\alpha) - I_t^j + \sum_{j\ne k}x_t^{jk}\Sigma x_t^{jN}].$$

The necessary conditions for an interior solution are

$$\hat{L}_{Ii} = \pi_{Ii}^i(1+\delta)^{-t} - \lambda_t^{ii} + (1-\alpha)\lambda_{t+1}^{ij} + \sum_j\lambda_{t+1}^{ij}x_{Ii}^{Nj} - b_Nx_{Ii}^{iN}(1+\delta)^{-t} = 0$$

$$\hat{L}_{Ij} = \pi_{Ij}^i(1+\delta)^{-t} - \lambda_t^{ij} + (1-\alpha)\lambda_{t+1}^{ij} + \sum_k\lambda_{t+1}^{ik}x_{Ij}^{Nk} - b_Nx_{Ij}^{iN}(1+\delta)^{-t} = 0$$

$$\hat{L}_{xij} = \lambda_t^{ii} - \lambda_t^{ij} - b(1+\delta)^{-t}.$$

Eliminating the multipliers we have

$$(\pi_{Ii}^i - \pi_{Ij}^i) - b = (1-\alpha)\frac{b}{1+\delta} - \frac{x^{NS}}{(n-1)I^T}\frac{b}{1+\delta} + b_N(x_{Ii}^{iN} - x_{Ij}^{iN})$$

$$= b\left(1 - \frac{1-\alpha}{1+\delta} - \frac{x^{NS}}{(n-1)I^T(1+\delta)}\right) + b_N(x_{Ii}^{iN} - x_{Ij}^{iN}).$$

Comparison of the results of this model with those developed above indicates that Proposition 1 is no longer true, due to the fact that whether a team is a net purchaser or a net seller depends on the marginal utility of winning.

In general, once the utility function contains as an element the probability of winning as a source of satisfaction distinct from its effect on profits, any earlier assertions about the relationships between the distribution of playing strengths and the drawing potentials of franchises must be severely qualified. In principle, a sufficiently wealthy owner concerned with "winning at all costs" could attain his objective even if he owned a franchise in a small city, simply by spending enough money. In practice, this has not commonly happened, reflecting no doubt the more basic economic fact that wealthy individuals are rarely unconcerned about financial losses even when operating a "hobby"-type enterprise like a sports team. It might be conjectured that the major source of satisfaction to wealthy owners lies in producing winning teams through superior management skills rather than through the crass exercise of overwhelming purchasing power. If this were true, the actions of wealthy owners might not deviate substantially from those of profit-maximizing managers; the only essential difference might lie in the owner's superior ability to survive over a long period if he is sufficiently wealthy.

As typically happens when the assumption of profit maximization is abandoned, almost any conclusion may be rationalized by imputing sufficient strength to nonprofit motivating factors. The more restrictive original model has, in contrast, the virtue of predicting well-specified testable results that do not appear to be widely at variance with the empirical results reported in the body of the chapter.

APPENDIX B: Duration of Major-League Franchises

The following list shows the changes in franchise locations that occurred in the four major sports between 1900 and 1972. The left-hand column shows franchise location, the right-hand column, years at location.

Baseball[30]

American League (1903–53)

New York, Boston, Chicago, Cleveland, Detroit, St. Louis,
  Philadelphia, Washington   51

American League (1954–72)

New York, Boston, Chicago, Cleveland, Detroit, Baltimore   19

---

30. *The World Almanac and Book of Facts, 1973 Edition* (Newspaper Enterprise Association, 1972), p. 947.

Washington (two franchises)	18
Kansas City (two franchises)	17
Minnesota, Los Angeles–Anaheim	12
Oakland	5
Milwaukee	3
Seattle, Texas, Philadelphia	1

National League (1900–52)

New York, Brooklyn, St. Louis, Cincinnati, Pittsburgh, Boston, Philadelphia, Chicago	53

National League (1953–72)

St. Louis, Cincinnati, Pittsburgh, Philadelphia, Chicago	20
New York (two franchises)	16
Los Angeles, San Francisco	15
Milwaukee	13
Houston	11
Atlanta	7
Brooklyn	6
San Diego, Montreal	4

Football[31]

National Football League (1921–32)

Chicago Bears, Chicago Cardinals, Green Bay	12
Dayton	9
New York Giants, Frankford, Buffalo	8
Providence	7
Cleveland, Columbus, Akron	6
Duluth, Minneapolis, Canton, Rock Island, Rochester, Milwaukee, Hammond	5
Pottsville, Detroit, Stapleton, Brooklyn, Racine	4
Portsmouth, Kansas City, Louisville	3
New York Yankees, Boston, Toledo, Marion	2
Cincinnati, Hartford, Evansville, St. Louis, Kenosha, Los Angeles	1

National Football League (1933–68)

New York Giants, Green Bay, Chicago Bears, Philadelphia (two franchises)	36
Detroit, Pittsburgh	35

31. Roger Treat, *The Official Encyclopedia of Football* (8th ed. rev., A. S. Barnes, 1970).

Washington	32
Chicago Cardinals	28
Cleveland (two franchises)	27
Los Angeles	23
San Francisco	19
Baltimore (two franchises)	17
Brooklyn	12
Boston (two franchises), St. Louis, Dallas (two franchises)	9
Minnesota	8
Atlanta	3
New York Yankees, New Orleans, Cincinnati	2
Portsmouth, New York Bulldogs	1

American Football League (1960–68)

Houston, New York, Buffalo, Boston, Oakland, Denver	9
San Diego	8
Kansas City	6
Dallas, Miami	3
Los Angeles, Cincinnati	1

National Football League (1969–72)

| National Football Conference: New York Giants, Detroit, Minnesota, Dallas, Washington, Philadelphia, St. Louis, Green Bay, San Francisco, Los Angeles, Atlanta, New Orleans | 4 |
| American Football Conference: Miami, Baltimore, New York Jets, New England (formerly Boston), Buffalo, Cleveland, Pittsburgh, Houston, Cincinnati, Kansas City, Oakland, San Diego, Denver | 4 |

Basketball[32]

National Basketball Association (1947–56)

Philadelphia, New York, Boston	10
Rochester, Minneapolis, Fort Wayne	9
Syracuse	8
Baltimore	7
Indianapolis	5

32. *National Basketball Association Official Guide for 1972–73* (Sporting News, 1972); *1972–73 Official American Basketball Association Guide* (Sporting News, 1972).

Milwaukee, Washington, St. Louis	4
Chicago	3
Tri-Cities, Providence	2
Anderson, Sheboygan, Waterloo, Denver	1

National Basketball Association (1957–72)

New York, Boston, Detroit, Cincinnati	16
Philadelphia (two franchises)	15
Los Angeles	13
St. Louis	12
San Francisco	11
Baltimore	10
Chicago (two franchises)	9
Syracuse	7
Seattle	6
Milwaukee, Atlanta, Phoenix, San Diego	5
Minneapolis	4
Portland, Buffalo	3
Houston	2
Kansas City–Omaha	1

American Basketball Association (1967–72)

Indiana, Kentucky, Dallas, Denver	6
New York, Miami, Pittsburgh (two franchises)	5
Carolina, New Orleans	4
Virginia, Utah, Memphis, Minnesota (2 franchises), Houston, Oakland, Los Angeles	3
New Jersey, Anaheim, Washington	2
San Diego	1

Hockey[33]

National Hockey League (1922–66)

Montreal Canadiens, Toronto	45
Boston	43
New York Rangers, Chicago, Detroit	41
New York Americans	16
Montreal Maroons	14
Ottawa	13

33. Robert A. Styer, *The Encyclopedia of Hockey* (A. S. Barnes, 1970), pp. 46–125; *World Almanac,* various editions.

Pittsburgh	5
Hamilton	4
Brooklyn	1

National Hockey League (1967–72)

Montreal, Toronto, Boston, Detroit, New York Rangers, Chicago, California, Los Angeles, Philadelphia, Pittsburgh, St. Louis, Minnesota	6
Buffalo, Vancouver	3
New York Islanders, Atlanta	1

World Hockey Association (1972)

New England, New York, Philadelphia, Minnesota, Cleveland, Chicago, Los Angeles, Houston, Winnipeg, Alberta, Quebec, Ottawa	1

CHAPTER THREE

The Social Benefits of Restrictions on Team Quality

MICHAEL E. CANES

TEAM OWNERS have long argued that restrictive arrangements in sports are necessary to produce teams of comparable playing strength. They allege that without such arrangements wealthier teams would monopolize the best players, games would become one-sided, spectator interest would decline, and poorer teams would be driven out of business. On the other hand, some scholars have argued that restrictive rules such as the reserve system do not equalize playing strengths but serve only to monopsonize the market for player services.[1]

This chapter attempts to answer a number of questions raised in this debate. First, is the equalization of playing strengths a desirable social goal? Second, do current restrictive practices attain that goal? Third, what effect would a competitive market have on team quality? Fourth, do existing restrictive rules move team quality levels toward the social optimum? Fifth, what is the most efficient means of producing a socially optimal quality of play?

The answers to these questions have important policy implications, since public support should be given to the market arrangements that maximize social benefits. Arrangements other than open competition and the current set of restrictions are not examined in detail here, and it should be kept in mind that some other system might be preferable to either.

---

1. James Quirk and Mohamed El Hodiri in Chapter 2 of this book; Jay H. Topkis, "Monopoly in Professional Sports," *Yale Law Journal,* Vol. 58 (April 1949), pp. 691–712; Simon Rottenberg, "The Baseball Players' Labor Market," *Journal of Political Economy,* Vol. 64 (June 1956), pp. 242–58.

Restrictive Practices and the Public Interest

Existing restrictions on the movement of players among teams are justified on the grounds that they contribute to the equalization of playing strengths, and that this effect is in the public interest.[2] Both of these assumptions are of dubious validity.

Equal Team Strengths as a Policy Goal

The demand for sports contests in an area is related to many factors—population, per capita wealth, popularity of the sport, average ticket-price, availability of recreational substitutes, climate, and stadium comfort and accessibility, and the probability that the home team will win.[3] In addition, in most circumstances teams are probably "natural monopolies," in that there are economies of scale to greater attendance.[4] If team income reflects the value of its performance to spectators, and if the demand for winning teams differs among areas, some owners will have a greater incentive than others to build a strong team.

In such a case, a policy aimed at equalizing team strengths would transfer team quality from areas where winning is more valued to areas where it is less valued. Team owners can be viewed as "brokers," accepting "bids" for winning teams from residents of various areas, with higher bids resulting in higher winning percentages. A policy of equalizing team strengths would increase winning percentages in areas where consumers are willing to pay relatively less for a winning team and decrease winning percentages in areas where consumers are willing to pay relatively more. Since those who gain place lower value on increased wins than those who lose, *net* social benefits would be reduced. This conclusion raises doubts whether equality of team strengths is a desirable social goal.[5]

2. The restrictions are also defended on two other grounds: first, they are said to "maintain the integrity of the game" by promoting the confidence of fans that players are loyal to their current teams; and, second, by averting a bidding war for players, they make a greater number of cities economically viable as franchise sites.

3. For support for these assumptions, see Chapter 4.

4. A realistic assumption: the rules of a sport specify a minimum number of players on a team, and, for given costs of acquiring the services of players of a given quality, the cost per fan in attendance of producing a team is less the greater the number of tickets sold.

5. One argument for equalization of playing strengths is that since sports fans

The Distribution of Player Talent

Whether or not equality of team strengths is a desirable social goal, public support of existing restrictive practices rests on the presumption that they in fact achieve that goal. To test whether the most important of these arrangements—the reserve system, the free-agent draft, and the player draft—actually equalize the distribution of player talent among teams in a league, three types of data are used: (1) number of championships won by each team, (2) percentage of games won by championship teams,[6] and (3) repeat of championship wins. Comparisons are made between sports with and without a particular rule and within a sport before and after introduction of the rule. The empirical data are preceded by summaries of the theoretical conclusions[7] about whether the effect of the rules on player distribution differs from that of an open competitive market.

THE RESERVE SYSTEM. The reserve system gives teams exclusive rights to purchase their players' services for the next season; in practice, it ties nearly all players to teams for their playing lifetimes. It has been alleged that the system prevents "rich" teams from hiring players away from "poor" teams.[8] This argument can be refuted by a principle enunciated by R. H. Coase,[9] that, given "well-defined" property rights and the absence of costs of transacting, resources move toward their highest valued use. Under the reserve system, a team owner has rights to the player's future services. If the team for which he plays values the player's services more

---

prefer close intraleague races, organizational rules are beneficial if they close the gap between weak and strong teams. But if this contention were true, the public interest would coincide with team owners' interests, for owners of weak and strong teams would have an incentive to approach more closely the league average, in which case a policy of securing an equal distribution of player talent would be superfluous.

6. This criterion for the equalization of team strengths is given in *Organized Baseball,* Report of the Subcommittee on Study of Monopoly Power of the House Committee on the Judiciary, H. Rept. 2002, 82 Cong. 2 sess. (1952), p. 105, where it is stated that the reserve system adopted by the baseball industry in 1879 was responsible for lowering the winning percentages of championship teams. This claim is investigated below.

7. See Chapter 2 and Rottenberg, "The Baseball Players' Labor Market."

8. "The reserve rule, by giving each club exclusive right to enter new contracts with its players, inhibits the moneyed clubs from acquiring all of the best talent" (*Organized Baseball,* H. Rept. 2002, p. 105).

9. In "The Problem of Social Cost," *Journal of Law and Economics,* Vol. 3 (October 1960), pp. 1–44.

highly than any other team, no other team will be willing to pay enough for his services to induce his current team to sell his contract. If the player *is* more highly valued by another team, and if the costs of transferring the player's contract are slight, then it will be to the advantage of the team that values him most to buy his contract and of the team owning his contract to sell it. For example, if a player is worth $100,000 to Atlanta and $50,000 to San Francisco and he plays for Atlanta, San Francisco will not be willing to pay enough to secure his contract. If the player's contract is owned by San Francisco, it will pay both teams to transfer the contract to Atlanta at any price between $50,000 and $100,000. Thus, the reserve system theoretically affects the player market only in that it is the team that receives the price of a player transfer instead of the player himself.

The reserve system was secretly adopted in 1879 and first used in sports by the National League in 1880. At that time the system applied to the contracts of five players per team; in 1883, the number was raised to eleven, in 1885 to twelve, and in 1887 to fourteen. The season of 1880 is used here as the first in which the reserve system was operative.

The decade before 1880 can be divided into two periods, each having different institutional arrangements. Just when professional baseball originated is uncertain, but by 1868 newspapers were telling "of whole teams that were being paid for playing." In 1869 the Cincinnati Reds announced they were an all-salaried team. In 1871 the National Association of Professional Base Ball Players was formed, and in that year professional teams first participated in a championship tournament. Between 1871 and 1875 individuals could enter teams in annual tournaments simply by paying a ten-dollar fee,[10] and teams could be entered and withdrawn while the tournaments were in progress. Playing records of teams varied widely; for example, in a tournament in 1875, one team won one game and lost thirteen, another won two and lost forty-two, while the team winning the tournament won seventy-one games and lost but eight.[11] These statistics have been cited to defend the reserve rule as necessary to provide a more uniform distribution of player talent.[12] This inference does not take into account, however, the effect on competitive balance of other institutional changes. The reserve rule was instituted several years after the tournament

10. David Q. Voigt, *American Baseball*, Vol. 1: *From Gentlemen's Sport to the Commissioner System* (University of Oklahoma Press, 1966), Chaps. 2–4. The quotation is from p. 19.
11. Ibid., p. 51.
12. *Organized Baseball*, H. Rept. 2002, pp. 213–14.

Table 1. Won-Lost Records and Average Percentage of Games Won, Championship Baseball Teams, National League, 1876–87

Year	League champion	Won-lost record	Average percentage of games won
1876	Chicago	52–14	
1877	Boston	31–17	
1878	Boston	41–19	71.0
1879	Providence	55–23	
1880	Chicago	67–17	
1881	Chicago	56–28	
1882	Chicago	55–29	68.9
1883	Boston	63–35	
1884	Providence	84–28	
1885	Chicago	87–25	
1886	Chicago	90–34	72.0
1887	Detroit	79–45	

Source: *Information Please Almanac, Atlas and Yearbook, 1967* (Simon and Schuster, 1966), p. 835.

arrangement had been abandoned. In 1876 a group of team owners buried the old Association after forming the National League of Professional Base Ball Clubs. Important changes in the conduct and structure of major-league games were embodied in the league constitution. Entry to the league was restricted to teams from cities of more than 75,000 people, and established teams voted whether to allow a new team into the league. Teams refusing to play games already contracted for were threatened with expulsion.[13] Since the institutional framework of the sport between 1876 and 1879 was thus considerably different from that of the earlier period, these four years are a more valid basis for comparison with the period after the reserve system took effect. Table 1 shows that before the adoption of the reserve system three different teams (out of eight teams in 1876, six in 1877–78, and eight at the beginning of the 1879 season) won championships, one team won two consecutive championships, and the average percentage of games won by a championship team was 71.0.

In the four years after adoption of the reserve clause, two different teams won championships, one team won three consecutive championships, and the average winning percentage of a championship team fell

13. Voigt, *American Baseball,* pp. 64–65.

to 68.9. In the years 1884–87, during which the reserve system was extended to more and more players, three different teams won championships, one team won two consecutive championships, and the average winning percentage of a championship team rose to 72.0. None of these data support the hypothesis that the reserve clause equalizes team quality.[14] Only the 68.9 winning percentage for 1880–83 suggests at all that the reserve clause had an equalizing effect, and this is offset by the 72.0 winning percentage for 1884–87. In any event, if it is assumed that 71.0 is the expected percentage of games won by a championship team for the entire period, values of 68.9 or 72.0 fall well within the 0.95 confidence range for the numbers of games played. In short, there is no significant difference in the relative quality of championship teams for the three periods.

THE FREE-AGENT DRAFT. The free-agent draft involves a set of rules limiting bidding competition among teams for players who have not yet entered professional sports. This system could conceivably cause a different distribution of players than a competitive market would: since teams exercise draft rights in reverse order of their playing records, the draft should give weaker teams more opportunity for improvement than stronger ones. But, as demonstrated above, if the costs of transferring contracts are slight, players will ultimately be hired by teams that value their services most highly. The eventual distribution of players would thus be independent of the original distribution of rights. If contract transference costs are significant,[15] thereby reducing the extent of player sales, the reverse order of selection may promote some degree of team equality, assuming that the players chosen by weaker teams are significantly better athletes than players chosen by stronger teams. But an openly competitive market might produce a similar result. Suppose that a consistently winning team

14. Although two major leagues entered the baseball market during the years 1880–87, so few reserved players were affected that this factor is ignored. The first entrant, the American Association, signed only one player under reservation to a National League team before an agreement was formed with that league to respect one another's reserve clauses. The second entrant, the Union Association, signed only a handful of players from National League teams and went out of business after one year (*Organized Baseball,* H. Rept. 2002, pp. 26–29).

15. Transfer costs may be indirect. For example, fan support for teams that sell players may decrease greatly, while support for teams that buy players may increase only slightly. If so, team owners will be reluctant to sell players. But there have been instances of star baseball players' contracts being sold (see Chapter 2), and in Britain professional soccer player contracts are often exchanged for cash. Thus it is unlikely that noneconomic factors alone severely inhibit transference of player contracts.

becomes less appealing to its fans over a long period of time as winning becomes commonplace. The quantity of playing skills desired by a profit-maximizing team owner will then be less for a team that has won regularly in the past. Under these conditions, the free-agent draft and the competitive market produce essentially the same result.

The effects of the draft can be tested by comparing the distribution of talent among teams with and without its use. Baseball and hockey have only recently begun to use the draft, so the available data are not adequate to measure its long-term effects on those sports. Basketball has had a free-agent draft since the formation of the National Basketball Association after the Second World War, and football has used a free-agent draft since 1935,[16] but the period before use of the draft was too short to permit a useful comparison with later data.

Because of this lack of data, comparisons must be made between professional sports with and without free-agent drafts, and between college and professional leagues in the same sport. Unfortunately, comparisons between sports are not powerful tests of a single rule or practice because other factors undoubtedly influence the difference in team performance. Thus, even after adjustments for numbers of teams and games, the comparisons provide only broad indications of whether significant differences exist in the distribution of player talent between sports with and without free-agent drafts. Similarly, comparisons between college and professional leagues are unreliable because the two institutional frameworks are quite different.[17] Nevertheless, in one important way the two are similar: both colleges and professional teams attempt to make money from football and basketball teams.[18] An important difference is that colleges, unlike pro-

16. The history of football is similar to that of baseball. Teams were entered without restrictions in tournaments during the 1920s, and most teams formed in those years failed to survive. In 1933, team owners of the National Football League agreed to a set of institutional arrangements similar to those in use today.

17. For example, college players are "eligible" to play for only four years, whereas there are no restrictions on the career lengths of professionals. Unfortunately, it is not clear how this eligibility limitation affects the distribution of college player talent. Although it prevents particular groups of players from dominating a sport for very long, it also enhances the importance of persistent recruiting and can result in a less even distribution of talent if colleges have very different abilities to recruit.

18. For example, coaches are hired and fired on the basis of their ability to win games and thus attract spectators and alumni contributions; colleges actively compete for superior prospective athletes; a college that consistently loses money in football will withdraw from the sport, and so forth.

Table 2. Variance of Distribution of Major-League Championships,[a] Frequency of Successive Championship Wins, and Average Won-Lost Percentages, 1950–65

Sport, draft status, and league	Variance of championship distribution[b]	Percentage of years in which teams won successive championships	Average won-lost percentage of championship teams[c]
Basketball (draft)			
National Basketball Association[d]	8.50	53	68.4
Baseball (no draft)			
National League[d]	4.25	20	61.3
American League[d]	17.50	67	63.4
Football (draft)			
National Football League, Eastern Conference[e]	12.56	60	80.2
National Football League, Western Conference[e]	1.88	47	78.2
Hockey (no draft)			
National Hockey League[e]	11.88	60	69.1

Sources: *Information Please Almanac, 1967*, pp. 834–35, 844, 853; *The World Almanac and Book of Facts* (Newspaper Enterprise Association), yearly issues, 1951–66.

a. Champions are defined as teams with the highest won-lost percentages.

b. Calculated from the number of championships won by each team and the expected number per team over the period.

c. Percentage of wins out of total wins and losses (thus excluding ties in football and hockey).

d. Includes the eight teams operating during the entire period.

e. Includes the six teams operating during the entire period.

fessional teams, compete for prospective players.[19] Thus, if the free-agent draft significantly affects the distribution of player talent among teams, a comparison between college and professional leagues should indicate it.

Table 2 presents data for the four major professional team sports from 1950 to 1965. During this period the distribution of championships among National Basketball Association teams, which used a draft, has a lower variance than that of American League baseball teams, which did not; for all teams, the frequency with which teams won consecutive championships and the percentage of games won (excluding ties) exhibit no consistent relationship with the presence or absence of the free-agent draft.

19. Although the setting and enforcement of maximum wages by the National Collegiate Athletic Association restrains direct competition, colleges still compete through offers of trips for prospective athletes and their families, numbers of pretty girls on campus, lucrative summer jobs, quality of education, large publicity departments, free tutoring, expensive athletic facilities, and so forth.

In fact, championship teams in leagues without a draft had a lower average won-lost percentage than champions in leagues with a draft. It is possible, though not likely, that the larger number of games per season played by baseball and hockey teams explains the differences in winning percentages;[20] but, in any event, the data show no significant relation between the distribution of talent and the method of acquiring new players.

Table 3 presents football and basketball data for professional leagues and most major college conferences. Comparison of the data is distorted because each of the college conferences has more teams than the professional leagues, the effect of a larger number of teams being to reduce both the variance of the distribution of championships and the expected frequency of championship repeats. If the distribution of player talent were uniform among teams, an increase in league size from six to eight teams would reduce the variance of the distribution of championships by about 30 percent, and the expected frequency of championship repeats by about 45 percent.

As with the intersport comparisons, Table 3 provides no support for the view that the free-agent draft equalizes team strength. Only the won-lost percentage data suggest that the free-agent draft in professional leagues equalizes team strengths. But alternative explanations can probably account for the statistical differences. If all teams were of equal strength, the chance that a team would win a large fraction of its games is lower the more games the team must play. In both football and basketball, college teams play far fewer games than professional teams, thus possibly accounting for the lower won-lost percentages of their championship teams.[21]

20. For example, the average won-lost percentage in football is 79.2 and the average number of games twelve per season; the average percentage in hockey is 69.1 and the average number of games that do not end in ties fifty-seven per season. The won-lost percentage can be interpreted as the probability that a team will win a game, so that if the free-agent draft equalized team strengths in football, without the draft the probability that a championship team would win would be greater than 79.2 percent; but even if the true probability were as low as 79.2, the probability is only about 6 percent that a championship team would have a won-lost percentage as low as 69.1 in a fifty-game season. This means that, after adjustment for the number of games per season, the free-agent draft has no perceptible effect on a championship team's probability of winning.

21. The average winning percentages are: 85 for college basketball, 69 for professional basketball, 92 for college football, and 79 for professional football. The probability that a basketball team will win 85 percent of fifteen games or 69 percent of eighty games is less than 1 percent. Similarly, the probability that a football team will win 92 percent of six games is about 11 percent, and that it will win 79 percent of twelve games, about 7 percent.

Table 3. Variance of Distribution of Professional and College Football and Basketball League Championships,[a] Frequency of Successive Championship Wins, and Average Won-Lost Percentages, 1950–65[b]

Sport, draft status, and league	Variance of championship distribution[c]	Percentage of years in which teams won successive championships	Average won-lost percentage of championship teams[d]
Football			
Professional (draft)			
National Football League, Eastern Conference (6 teams)	12.56	60	80.0
National Football League, Western Conference (6 teams)	1.88	47	78.0
College (no draft)			
Southwest Conference (7 teams)	4.48	20	88.0
Big Ten (10 teams)	2.04	7	90.0
Atlantic Coast Conference (8 teams)	6.57	40	92.0
Pacific Eight (8 teams)	2.86	20	92.0
Big Eight (8 teams)	14.20	73	98.0
Skyline Conference (8 teams)	5.71	40	92.0
Basketball			
Professional (draft)			
National Basketball Association (8 teams)	8.50	67	69.3
College (no draft)			
Atlantic Coast Conference (8 teams)	7.14	47	84.4
Southwest Conference (8 teams)	0.86	27	81.2
Southeast Conference (12 teams)	6.79	27	90.6
Big Ten (10 teams)	3.15	53	86.7
Missouri Valley Conference (8 teams)	3.43	40	86.9
Big Eight (8 teams)	9.71	33	85.0
Mountain States Conference (8 teams)	6.57	40	83.5

Sources: *Ronald Encyclopedia of Football* (Ronald Press), *Ronald Encyclopedia of Basketball* (Ronald Press), and *World Almanac*, selected years.

a. Champions are defined as teams with the highest won-lost percentages.

b. Not all the college leagues listed operated between 1950 and 1965, so in some cases fifteen-year periods beginning in the late 1940s or early 1950s were used.

c. Calculated from the number of championships won by each team and the expected number per team over the period.

d. Percentage of wins out of total wins and losses (thus excluding ties in football).

THE PLAYER DRAFT. The player draft is an annual procedure in hockey and baseball whereby team owners can be required to exchange contracts of certain players, primarily minor leaguers, for previously stipulated amounts of money. It theoretically prevents teams from hoarding players and allows weaker teams to purchase players from stronger ones at a below-open-market price. With no costs for contract transfers, the player draft would simply redistribute wealth among team owners in increments equal to the differences between the market and draft prices of player contracts. If there are significant contract transfer costs, the extent to which this arrangement actually distributes playing talent more evenly depends on the costs to owners of avoiding the provisions of the draft by discovering which players should be protected from it and by estimating the abilities of players subject to the draft.

Effects of the player draft are tested here with data from the National Hockey League. Rules specifying a player draft were agreed to in September 1952 (first operative during the 1953–54 season) and have been in use since then. Table 4 shows the number of times each league team won the Stanley Cup during 1939–53 and 1954–67, before and after adoption of the draft.[22] A cursory inspection of the two distributions indicates that the draft has had little effect on the distribution of player talent. The effect of the player draft can also be tested by comparing the distribution of winners of the "league race" before and after introduction of the draft. These data follow the same pattern as those for the Stanley Cup race.

The draft fails by another measure as well. Between 1939 and 1953 the relative frequency of a team's winning Stanley Cups in consecutive years was 0.143; between 1954 and 1967 the relative frequency of successive wins was 0.615. Thus the player draft has decisively not reduced the chances that a team will win successive Stanley Cup championships.

A Model of a Team Sport Market

The preponderance of evidence indicates that restrictive league rules do not alter the distribution of player talent from what it would be in an open-market situation, but they may have another useful function. Their absence may encourage team owners to produce higher team quality than

22. During these years the same six teams competed for the Stanley Cup.

Table 4. Distribution of Stanley Cup Champions and National Hockey League Winners, 1939–53 and 1954–67

Team	1939–53	1954–67
Stanley Cup champions		
Toronto	6	4
Montreal	3	7
Detroit	3	2
Boston	2	0
New York	1	0
Chicago	0	1
National Hockey League winners		
Detroit	6	4
Montreal	4	8
Boston	3	0
Toronto	1	1
New York	1	0
Chicago	0	1

Sources: Stanley Cup data, *World Almanac, 1973*, p. 871; NHL winners, *World Almanac*, yearly issues, 1940–68.

is socially efficient. The model of a competitive sports market formulated below explains this argument.[23]

Quality Levels in a Competitive Market

The model assumes (1) that there are openly competitive markets for skilled players, (2) that profit-maximizing organizations are formed to produce "championship races" among teams, (3) that teams play both home and away games, and (4) that an individual team owner maximizes profits and possesses local monopoly power.[24]

The value to fans of a contest in a given location is assumed to be negatively related to the frequency of contests and positively related to the quality of play. Thus, the more games played per unit of time, the less the

23. A mathematical statement of the model appears in the Appendix to this chapter.

24. It is frequently noted that team owners derive benefits from a winning team and will sacrifice some profits to win more games. This assertion is not denied here; rather, an owner's demand to win is included in his valuation of his team, so that having a winner increases his net profits even though his financial receipts may be lower.

fan enjoyment of any one game; and the greater the skills of the teams,[25] the greater the fan enjoyment. Spectator enjoyment is further assumed to be related to the quality of play of *all* teams in a sport. That is, since spectators want teams located in their own areas to win, the demand for contests is positively related to the quality of the home team relative to the quality of all teams in the sport.[26]

The cost of a game is assumed to consist only of the cost of obtaining the two teams. The owner of a team takes as given the number of games and chooses the price of a ticket and the skill level of his team so as to maximize profits. Under these conditions, an owner will be induced to take account of how the use of more player skills will affect demand for both his home and away games, and hence his profits.[27] At home games, more skill will have two positive effects: consumers will pay more to see higher home team quality *and* to see higher home team quality relative to other teams. At away games, more skill will have both a positive and a

25. Team skills are the physical skills of players—how fast they run, how hard and accurately they throw or hit a ball, how high they jump—which are the combination of player efforts and complementary factors such as coaching, training facilities, and special foods. An appropriate index of skill would include measures of player running speed, strength, reflex action, and so forth.

26. This assertion is valid within the range of quality in which any rational team owner will try to operate. Fans apparently prefer to watch relatively evenly matched teams, so that there are diminishing and then negative returns to a team that is increasingly more skilled than its opponents. Although a team owner cannot directly control the average playing skills of opposing teams, he can control the skills of his own team, and if rational he will not operate in a region of negative returns to quality.

27. Since consumers actually pay for contests rather than quality, it is necessary to be more explicit about the nature of the demand for contests. A plausible assumption is that a consumer's marginal rate of substitution between money (command over all other goods) and team quality is equal to his marginal rate of substitution between money and contests that provide an increment of quality times the number of contests he attends. Thus,

$$\frac{\frac{\partial u}{\partial S}}{\frac{\partial u}{\partial M}} = B \frac{\partial}{\partial S} \left(\frac{\frac{\partial u}{\partial B}}{\frac{\partial u}{\partial M}} \right)$$

where B = number of ball games, M = money, and S = quality of play. Thus, a consumer's demand for contests will shift in response to a change in team quality in such a way that the incremental amount he will be willing to pay for contests will reflect the value he places on the change in quality. This assumption implies a utility function of the form $U = f(M) + Bg(S)$. Using the partial derivatives for games and quality, the marginal utility of viewing contests depends upon the quality of contests and the marginal utility of quality depends upon the number of contests attended.

negative effect: consumers will pay more to see higher visiting team quality but less because their own home team will have lower quality relative to other teams. The owner will increase the quality of his team until team revenue generated at home and away because of the last increment in quality exactly equals its costs.[28]

Because demand for contests in any area depends on the quality of the home team relative to the quality of all teams, the quality of any one team will affect demand at home contests of all other teams. For example, if one team improves its skills, demand for all games in which that team does not play will fall. Since the owner's profits are not affected by decreased demand for games in which his team does not play, he will not take such effects into account; that is, they will be external to the owner's cost and revenue calculations.[29] Under competitive conditions, this leads team owners to produce more team quality than is socially efficient. This will occur because owners will only take account of returns in their own teams' contests (the "private" returns) in calculating what levels of quality to provide, whereas calculations of social efficiency would take account of returns in *all* teams' contests (which, by conjecture, are less).[30]

28. Local monopoly power in the production of contests implies a divergence between price and marginal cost. The misallocation resulting from local monopoly is assumed to be independent of the misallocation resulting from competitive production of skill. The validity of this assumption rests on the functional form of the demand for contests (see note 30 below).

29. In economic terminology, the model assumes that an owner is compensated for his team's private marginal products only in its home and away contests, so that the effects of a quality change on returns in contests between other teams are external to the owner. These effects are *real* externalities because, by conjecture, there is a direct effect on the utility of fans at contests between other teams. Since the effects are negative, quality increases produce external diseconomies, while quality decreases produce external economies.

This formulation may apply to areas other than sports, as well. That is, there are certain types of products whose consumers are concerned with the quality not only of the units they consume, but also of those consumed by others; symphony orchestras and weapons come immediately to mind. However, the magnitude of externalities generated and the costs of controlling them vary widely among products. The sports industry is particularly interesting in that the magnitude of the externality appears to be significant, while costs of controlling it appear to be manageable.

30. Under the assumptions made above about consumer demand, local monopolies in the production of contests will not affect the production of team quality. A monopolist offering an increment in quality will receive from consumers an increment in price per unit that on the margin will be equated to the costs of producing the quality. The summed increments in price paid by consumers represent the value they place on a unit of quality, so that in equilibrium the marginal value of quality

Means of Producing Socially Efficient Team Quality

The external effects of team quality might be compensated for in several ways. Consumers in each area might organize to persuade producers to take account of the effect of quality levels on *all* consumers' enjoyment; the costs to consumers of such collaborative efforts are, however, probably prohibitive. Team owners might agree to compensate one another for revenue losses caused by "excessive" team quality, thus allowing each owner to adjust to the value that consumers in all areas place on a unit of quality. But this would require difficult decisions about which teams should be compensated and to what extent. Moreover, if not all team owners were party to the agreement, some could increase the quality of their teams and so displace the others, or could threaten to increase quality in order to be compensated not to do so.

A more efficient instrument to control and compensate for the external effects of quality would be a league that was designed to maximize the joint profits of member teams. In order to maximize joint profits, a league would need to have the power to choose both the number of games and the level of skill of the teams; team owners would control only ticket prices.[31]

A single, profit-maximizing league would consider the effect of an additional unit of quality in one team on contests involving other teams,[32] and therefore would field teams of lower quality than individual owners under competitive conditions would. If several leagues compete in a sport, each league will ignore the effects of additional quality on returns to teams in other leagues, which will lead again to socially excessive team quality. Hence, adequate control of external effects associated with quality will be achieved only if there is but one league in a sport.

---

to consumers is equal to its cost. Other plausible assumptions about consumer utility functions can be made, however, under which teams will produce less quality in a monopolized than in a competitive market; so it must be concluded that the conjectured externality and its effects may be, but are not necessarily, independent of the inefficiency of local monopoly.

31. If the cost to the league of an increment in skills is constant, or if the league can perfectly discriminate between sellers of skill, no monopsony misallocation will result from the league's choice of team skill level. Because playing skills cannot be physically separated from their sellers, with perfect information about reservation prices of players' skills a single league in a sport would be able to make perfect discriminations.

32. By implication, the resources used to produce team quality—coaching, scouting, training facilities, and so forth—are also overproduced under open competition.

The decrease in team quality caused by the establishment of a league will have several effects. It will cause both total costs and total revenues to decline, but revenues will decline by less, thus producing greater profits for the league. This in turn makes it possible for more teams to survive. Lower team quality will also cause fewer resources to be allocated to the production of skills and more to uses more highly valued by the public.

Evidence of Externalities Associated with Team Quality

The preceding theoretical arguments were based on the conjecture that demand for contests is positively related to the quality of the home team relative to that of all teams in the sport—that is, that externalities are associated with the production of team quality. Empirical evidence bearing on the following hypothesis will provide a test of the conjecture. If all teams in a league are known to decrease in quality by varying amounts, teams that decrease relatively less will rise in league standings. Similarly, if all league teams increase in quality by varying amounts, teams that increase relatively less will decline in league standings. In this situation, home demand for a team's contests will move in the opposite direction from known changes in its level of quality, thus reflecting the influence of other teams' quality levels.

Table 5 shows the changes in baseball attendance figures during the period surrounding the Second World War. During the war, players from every major-league baseball team entered the armed services. Team quality thus was undoubtedly greater before and after the war than during it, so that demand for contests could be expected to have decreased during the war and increased afterward. The data support the prediction of the hypothesis, that demand for home contests of teams whose quality increased relative to other teams (but still decreased absolutely) would increase in wartime, and demand for home contests of teams whose quality decreased relative to other teams (but still increased absolutely) would decrease in the postwar period.

Comparing first the prewar and wartime data, total attendance decreased during the war in both the National and American Leagues, but in both leagues, home attendance *increased* for teams whose winning percentages increased during the war. In other words, the wartime decline in these teams' quality was more than offset by the even greater decline in the quality of other teams. The comparison between wartime and postwar years is less forceful because attendance increased dramatically al-

Table 5. Changes in Baseball Attendance Figures, by League, 1938–49

Percent

League	*Prewar (1938–41)* *to* *wartime (1942–45)*	*Wartime (1942–45)* *to* *postwar (1946–49)*
Total attendance		
National League	−5.8	122.1
American League	−4.1	124.3
Total home attendance of teams whose winning percentages increased		
National League	6.9	132.7
American League	21.9	160.1
Total attendance of teams whose winning percentages decreased		
National League	−19.4	111.2
American League	−15.4	46.7

Source: *Study of Monopoly Power*, Pt. 6, *Organized Baseball*, Hearings before the Subcommittee on Study of Monopoly Power of the House Committee on the Judiciary, 82 Cong. 1 sess. (1952), pp. 1617–18, 1637–38.

most everywhere.[33] However, it is clear that teams whose winning percentages increased in the postwar period showed greater attendance gains than teams whose winning percentages declined.

A Measure of the Externalities Associated with Team Quality

A change in a team's league standing reflects a change in either the team's quality or the quality of other league teams. The greater the change in a team's standing, the less probable it is that changes in the absolute quality levels of other teams are the cause.[34] The following equations

33. Home attendance declined only for the St. Louis Browns in the postwar period. The Browns' aggregate winning percentage declined from 0.510 in 1942–45 to 0.386 in 1946–49.

34. Suppose there is probability p_1 that a team's one-place move in league standings is caused by a change in its own quality (p_1 the same for all teams and $0 < p_1 < 1$). Suppose also that the probability that a team's two-place move is caused by a change in its own quality is p_2, where $p_2 = p_1 \cdot p_1$. Then for an n-place move, $p_n = (p_1)^n$. If a team moves n places, the probability that the move is entirely due to changes in the qualities of *other* teams is:

$$p_1 \cdot p_2 \cdot p_3 \ldots p_n = p_1^{(1+2+\ldots+n)} = p_1^{\frac{n(n+1)}{2}}.$$

The larger n is, the greater the difference between probabilities p^n and $p^{\frac{n(n+1)}{2}}$.

express (in thousands) the statistical relationship between quality changes in baseball teams (indicated by changes of four or more places in major-league standings) and changes in season attendance, both for the team that changes its standing and for other teams in its league.[35] The figures in parentheses are *t*-statistics.

In all three equations the coefficient of X is statistically significant by conventional standards. In equation (1), the coefficient of the change in standings is significantly negative, so that a one-place rise in a team's league standing will decrease attendance at home games of other teams by about 53,400 spectators a season.[36] Since away game attendance of the team changing in quality is included in the dependent variable (total attendance in all other cities), the coefficient of quality underestimates the external effects of improved quality (that is, the effects that apply to the baseball industry at large but not to the team in question).

(1)
$$Y = -94.1 - 53.4X$$
$$(0.87) (2.4)$$
$$R^2 = 0.09; \text{ degrees of freedom} = 54,$$

where Y = annual change in attendance at league contests in cities other than the home city of the team changing its league standing

X = change of four or more places in a team's position in league standings.

To better estimate such effects, equation (2) shows changes in attendance only at contests not involving the team changing in quality. A one-place rise in a team's league standing decreases attendance at contests

---

35. Based on data for 1920–68 (excluding the war years) in *Study of Monopoly Power,* Pt. 6, *Organized Baseball,* Hearings before the Subcommittee on Study of Monopoly Power of the House Committee on the Judiciary, 82 Cong. 1 sess. (1952), pp. 1617–18; and *Information Please Almanac, Atlas and Yearbook* (Macmillan, Simon and Schuster), selected years (title varied). No attendance figures for teams' away games could be obtained for the pre-Second World War years. Changes in attendance at away and home contests for the years 1946–68 were therefore correlated, and the estimated relationship was assumed to obtain for the entire period. The correlation coefficient was 0.46; that is, for a change in attendance of 100 fans at home contests, a change in attendance at away contests of 46 is predicted. Given the size of the sample, 0.46 is significantly different from zero at the 0.95 level, and the true correlation lies between 0.06 and 0.72 within 95 percent confidence.

36. Since only changes of four or more places are used to produce this estimate, a more exact interpretation of the coefficient is that attendance declines by 53,400 per place-change for changes of four or more places. The argument assumes that the attendance effect bears the same relation to place changes for smaller changes in quality than are used to estimate the equation.

between all other league teams by 84,900 spectators a season. Some of this decrease in attendance can be attributed to fans choosing to see the away games of the team changing in quality instead of games involving other league teams, so that the magnitude of the external effect is actually somewhat less than 84,900 spectators a year. Since equation (1) provides an underestimate of the external effect of a quality change and equation (2) an overestimate, the magnitude of the effect lies between 53,400 and 84,900 fans a season; for simplicity, let the arithmetic average of these figures, 69,150, be the adjusted estimate of the external effect.[37]

$$(2) \qquad Y^1 = -64.2 - 84.9X$$
$$(0.63) \quad (4.0)$$
$$R^2 = 0.23; \text{ degrees of freedom} = 54,$$

where Y^1 = annual change in attendance at league contests not involving the team changing its league standing.

Equation (3) shows the combined change in attendance at home and away games of the team changing its league standing. According to the equation, a one-place rise in league standing will increase attendance by about 84,000 spectators a season. This equation thus provides an estimate of the private returns to a team that raises its quality level, assuming that owners receive the real value of their teams' services. Using the estimated external effect calculated above, the social returns of increased quality—that is, the difference between the gain of the team that improves and the losses of other teams—are roughly 18 percent of the private returns.

$$(3) \qquad Y'' = -6.8 + 84.4X$$
$$(0.20) \quad (11.8)$$
$$R^2 = 0.72; \text{ degrees of freedom} = 54,$$

where Y'' = annual change in attendance at home and away contests of team changing its league standing.

Restrictive Rules as Controls of Team Quality

The preceding analysis suggests a novel explanation for the restrictive rules imposed by sports leagues: they are instruments employed by profit-maximizing team owners to adjust the amount of quality of each team to

37. Since the methods used here take no account of possible changes in other leagues while one team changes in league standing, the formulae may underestimate the total external effect of a quality change.

what it would be if the individual owner compensated other owners for the effects of improving the quality of his team. According to this hypothesis, restrictive rules reduce team quality to about the same level as would obtain if external effects were compensated for.

The hypothesis that league rules produce a socially efficient level of team quality applies to a wider set of rules than alternative explanations. The idea that the rules function simply to prevent competition for players explains only the player reservation system. A monopsony hypothesis does not apply to rules covering television and gate receipt divisions among teams or the ranking of selection rights in the free-agent draft.[38] The present hypothesis does not deny that rules that reduce competition for players also serve to increase owners' profits; the important point is that these rules, as well as several practices that are not restrictive, also control and compensate for real external effects associated with team quality.

DIVISION OF GATE RECEIPTS. Every major sports league has a formula specifying percentages of gate receipts to be paid to home and visiting teams. The shares are identical for every regularly scheduled league contest during a playing season and are not changed for many years at a time. The effect of these fixed gate shares is to reduce incentives to produce higher team quality below their level in markets where receipts are awarded in accordance with playing skills.[39] Fixed percentage shares prevent a team owner from realizing the entire returns of higher quality; some of these returns are paid to other teams. For example, a formula awarding the home team 100 percent of gate receipts prevents a team owner from making a profit from providing higher team quality to away games. The 80–20 division used in baseball reduces the financial return to increased team skill at a rate of about 39 percent.[40] The reduction in the returns to skill due to a 100–0 split is 32 percent, and on a 60–40 split is 47 percent.

38. As shown above, none of these rules can be explained as a means to distribute player talent more evenly among teams, and some have the opposite effect. See also Michael E. Canes, "The Economics of Professional Sports" (Ph.D. thesis, University of California, Los Angeles, 1970), pp. 88 ff.

39. As, say, in the boxing industry, where gate shares often vary with the relative skills of competing fighters.

40. For every $1.00 increase in home game receipts resulting from higher team quality, there is a $0.46 increase in away game receipts (see p. 98, note 35). The revenue accruing to the improved team, given an 80–20 gate split, is then $0.80 \times \$1.00 + 0.20 \times \$0.46 = \$0.89$. Therefore, an owner whose team improves receives $\$0.89/\$1.46 \times 100 = 61$ percent of the additional receipts generated by his team's improved quality.

In all major leagues, team owners make payments to the league to compensate officers and umpires or referees. In addition to these payments, National Basketball Association teams contribute a percentage of gross gate receipts (currently 6 percent) to a fund held by the league office. League expenses are paid from the fund, and at the end of each season what remains is divided equally among the teams. This collection and redistribution results in a portion of a team owner's income being entirely unrelated to his team's quality, while a portion of costs is directly related to quality. Assuming that an owner can control his team's quality, this practice encourages a quality level lower than that in a market without such a redistribution.

DIVISION OF NATIONAL TELEVISION RECEIPTS. Team owners bargain collectively with television networks for the rights to nationally televised league contests.[41] Television receipts are divided equally among league teams, irrespective of the number of each team's contests televised or the relative quality of each team. Under this system, a team that produces higher quality in televised games receives only a small portion of the appropriate returns. If team owners can control quality, the amount of quality supplied will be smaller than under a system in which each team sells rights for its own games and receives all profits resulting from higher team quality.

THE PLAYER RESERVATION SYSTEM. The reserve or option clause, by preventing competitive bidding for players, reduces player salaries to less than the (private) value of player services.[42] That salaries are in fact below private values is evidenced by the sale of player contracts for positive sums by one owner to another. If players under contract always received a wage equal to the value of their services, a team owner would pay no premium for a player contract.[43]

41. In most sports, rights to local broadcasting of contests are sold by individual team owners.
42. That is, below their value to individual teams, as distinguished from their value to all consumers, which is lower.
43. Rottenberg, "The Baseball Players' Labor Market," pp. 253–54, cites an argument by Gary S. Becker that positive prices for major-league baseball players' contracts may represent a return to team owners from investment in information about which players qualify for the major leagues. For every player that makes it to the major leagues, several do not, and owners must invest resources to separate qualified from unqualified players; this argument suggests that all players taken together receive their marginal product. However, basketball and football teams, which spend much less to separate qualified from unqualified players, also sell player contracts.

In a market that allowed competitive bidding for amateurs, the reserve clause would not reduce a player's expected lifetime earnings, since owners would offer signing bonuses equal to the discounted value of the amount by which player reservation would depress future wages. But under the free-agent draft, a player can either sell his services to the team drafting him or refuse to enter the sport.[44] There is some room for bargaining between an owner and a drafted player, but, in general, the bargaining solution will produce bonuses between zero and an amount equal to the bonus that would result from competitive bidding. Thus, lifetime player earnings are less than those in a market without the reserve clause and free-agent draft.

If the supply of amateurs responds to changes in wages, the reduction of lifetime earnings under the restrictive rules implies that less skill will be offered. Fewer amateurs will attempt to develop the skills necessary to become professionals, and those who do become professionals will have devoted fewer resources (such as personal efforts, coaching, physical equipment, and so forth) to improving their skills.

For players already under contract, the reduction in earnings due to the reserve clause and free-agent draft has no effect on the amount of skill offered. Given the assumption that teams can perfectly discriminate among players, players will be paid exactly the amounts necessary to produce increases in skill. The player reservation system simply allots to teams the difference between the value to fans of player skills and the costs of producing such skills, whereas in a competitive market the players receive the sum.

THE PLAYER DRAFT. The player draft limits a team owner's rights to the future services of a player under contract to him, and therefore reduces his incentive to invest in the skills of such a player. Since the draft distributes rights to a player's future services to all owners, it would not reduce investment in total player quality if all owners could invest in player skills as cheaply collectively as individually. Presuming that collective investment is costlier than private, however, the draft reduces the level of player skills in the sports to which it applies, baseball and hockey.

THE WAIVER RULE. Major-league constitutions contain a "waiver rule," which restricts the sale of player contracts to teams outside the league. An owner wishing to make such a sale must first secure the agreement of each team owner in his league to relinquish his right to purchase the con-

44. With the exception of baseball, where a drafted player may refuse to sign a contract and become subject to the draft again later.

tract at a fixed price. By restricting opportunities to sell player contracts, the rule reduces the value to a team of signing a player, and hence the incentives to team owners to invest in player skills.

THE RANKING OF SELECTION RIGHTS. The free-agent and player drafts and the waiver rule contain provisions for the distribution of rights to select players. Such rights could be distributed among teams by auction; that would distribute rights to their highest valued user within the league. But leagues generally specify that teams select players in reverse order of their playing records.[45] If two teams have identical playing records, a coin is tossed to decide which has selection priority.

This ranking of selection rights reduces incentives to produce team quality in the following manner. A profit-maximizing owner with first selection rights will choose the player with the greatest net market value (after payment to the player).[46] Every other owner will use the same strategy in making selections from the remaining eligible players. The larger the choice of players, the greater the expected increase in an owner's profit from his selection; so that the earlier an owner selects a player, the greater his expected profit increment. Since order of selection is negatively related to team quality, the better the quality of an owner's team, the less his expected increase in profit. The team quality thus encouraged is lower than competitive bidding would produce.

TEAM PLAYER LIMITS. All major leagues specify a maximum number of players that a team may have under contract. In a market without a team player limit, a profit-maximizing team owner would contract for players until the value of a player were equal to the cost. So, if team quality is positively related to number of players, it is reduced by a player limit because, to some degree, owners are forced to substitute other, less efficient means of acquiring more player skills.

RESTRICTIONS ON AMATEUR CONTRACTS. The constitutions of the football and basketball leagues prohibit contracts with college players whose class has not graduated.[47] Hockey rules prohibit contracts with players

45. In baseball, the free-agent draft has two phases. The ranking of selection rights in the first is as described. The second phase applies to amateur players who refuse to sign with teams that have drafted them; selection rights to such players are distributed randomly among teams.
46. If exchange costs inhibit later exchange of player contracts, the owner will select the player with the greatest playing value to his team.
47. This arrangement has been ruled illegal under section 1 of the Sherman Act in *Denver Rockets* v. *All-Pro Management, Inc.*, 325 F. Supp. 1049 (C.D. Cal. 1971). See Chapter 11 for a discussion of the significance of this case.

younger than a specified age. Baseball teams may not purchase the services of players whose high school class has not graduated, college students who have not completed their sophomore year, and players with teams sponsored by the American Legion.[48] Such restrictions limit the number of "eligible" players at any point in time and hence reduce the possible levels of team quality.

RESTRICTIONS ON TRAINING. The National Football League restricts the amount of time that teams are allowed to practice. The National Basketball Association specifies an annual date on which practice may begin, and a baseball ruling stipulates that spring training can begin no earlier than March 1.[49] If effective, a rule restricting training time would reduce the quality of teams.

BONUS RULES. Team owners in all sports are prohibited from compensating players during a playing season for winning any one contest or series of contests. According to league constitutions, player rewards can be paid only at the season's end. Enforcement of such bonus rules, by preventing owners from using money incentives to induce players to win particular contests or series of contests, tends to reduce the amount of resources devoted to short-term production of skilled play. If players are sensitive to such incentives, the level of team quality will be reduced.

Summary

The supply of quality in a sport is composed of players and their skills. If the supply of skills were independent of player earnings, restrictive rules that reduce payments for skills would not reduce the amount of skills supplied, but would merely transfer income from players to producers and consumers of contests. Several reasonable conclusions can be drawn from the evidence that refute this hypothesis. Since amateur players devote effort to improving their skills, a reduction in potential earnings will reduce

48. *Organized Professional Team Sports,* Hearings before the Antitrust Subcommittee of the House Committee on the Judiciary, 85 Cong. 1 sess. (1957), Pt. 2, pp. 1591–92, and Pt. 3, p. 2580ab; see also J. C. H. Jones, "The Economics of the National Hockey League," *Canadian Journal of Economics,* Vol. 2 (February 1969), p. 19.

49. *Organized Professional Team Sports,* House Hearings, p. 2580y; *Organized Baseball,* Hearings, p. 1626; and personal communication from Fred Schaus, General Manager of the Los Angeles Lakers basketball team. The baseball rule does not seem to have been effective, and there have been reports of baseball owners agreeing to start spring training late in February in order to reduce costs (see *Cleveland Plain Dealer,* Aug. 6, 1971).

this effort. Also, since prospective players are free to choose occupations other than sport, lower player earnings will reduce the quantity of players supplied. Finally, there is indirect evidence that the skills of professional players respond positively to increased earnings.

Players with outstanding records reportedly receive much larger salaries than players with average or mediocre records, a situation not explained by the weak correlation between alternative opportunities and playing skills. Reported changes in player salaries are usually directly related to changes in quality of performance. Furthermore, in some sports player contracts contain incentive clauses, which relate wages to conditioning (weight, speed) or to indices of performance (yards gained, points scored). If player skills were completely independent of wages in a monopsonized market, team owners would have no reason to relate wages to performance or to insert incentive clauses in contracts. The positive response of player skill levels to wages means that restrictive rules that limit the rewards to players for increased skills serve to reduce the amount of skills produced, and hence team quality.

Conclusions

This chapter has applied to team sports the normative proposition that restrictive contractual arrangements among firms in an industry should be judged on the basis of their relative benefits and costs. By this measure, equalization of team strengths has been shown not to be a desirable social goal. Moreover, even if, as team owners claim, such a goal were desirable, the preponderance of theoretical and empirical evidence supports the conclusion that restrictive league rules, especially the player reservation system, have no significant effect on the distribution of player skill.

An alternative rationale for support of various restrictive rules is that, paradoxically, they may produce a level of team quality of greater net social benefit than an openly competitive market would. A model of a team sport market demonstrates that improvements in team quality have important external effects, which some restrictive arrangements—principally fixed shares of gate receipts, the reserve clause and free-agent draft, and the ranking of selection rights—may compensate for by generating less demand for team quality than an openly competitive market would. However, it is impossible to determine whether these and other restrictions analyzed are perfect offsets for the external effects.

The major policy conclusion of this chapter is that sports leagues must adopt some institutional mechanism to counteract the incentive to over-invest in team quality. The existing arrangements are, of course, only one among many alternatives, each of which has its own costs and secondary effects on league operations. Some modification of the existing system—such as a more nearly equal division of gate receipts among teams, combined with a less restrictive free-agent draft—might be more effective in providing the appropriate incentives to owners with regard to team quality. What is clear is that some such arrangements are necessary for achieving a quality of play that is economically efficient.

APPENDIX: A Mathematical Model of a Team Sport Market

Let N = the number of teams in the sport

S_i = an index of the skill of the team i

S_j = an index of the skill of the team j

$$(j = 1, \cdots, N; j \neq i)$$

S_o = the average skill of all teams in the sport, where

$$S_o = \frac{\sum_{j=1}^{N} S_j}{N}$$

B_i = the number of contests in city i per unit of time (here assumed to be one playing season).

By definition,

$$B_i = \sum_{\substack{j=1 \\ j \neq i}}^{N} B_{ij},$$

where B_{ij} is the number of games between teams i and j in city i per playing season.

The postulated arguments of consumer demand for contests are as follows:

(1.0) $$Q_d^{ij} = Q_d^{ij}(P_i, S_i, S_j, S_i/S_o, B_i),$$

where

Q_d^{ij} = the number of tickets demanded in city i for a contest between teams i and j (henceforth the first superscript will refer to the location of the contest as well as to a team)

P_i = average ticket price in city i.

Presuming that a contest is a normal good,

(1.1)
$$\frac{\partial Q_d^{ij}}{\partial P_i} < 0.$$

By hypothesis,

(1.2)
$$\frac{\partial Q_d^{ij}}{\partial B_i} < 0;$$

demand for any given contest decreases as the number of contests offered increases.

(1.3)
$$\frac{\partial Q_d^{ij}}{\partial S_i} > 0$$

and

(1.4)
$$\frac{\partial Q_d^{ij}}{\partial S_j} > 0;$$

demand is positively related to the skill of the home and visiting teams. Further,

(1.5)
$$\frac{\partial Q_d^{ij}}{\partial S_i / S_o} > 0;$$

demand is positively related to the relative skill of the home team within the range in which any rational team owner i will operate.[50] In the ith city S_i skill is supplied. Let $C(S_i)$ be the cost per game of this skill. The ith team plays B_i games at home and is the visiting team in B_i games; hence, the cost of S_i skill over a season is

(2.0)
$$2B_iC(S_i) = \sum_{\substack{j=1 \\ j \neq i}}^{N} 2B_{ij}C(S_i).$$

Then assume

(2.1)
$$\frac{\partial C}{\partial S_i} > 0;$$

the cost per game of skill increases with the amount of skill acquired.

The organization in the sport that produces championship races determines the number of games between each pair of teams; each team plays an equal number of games with every other team, half in the home city of

50. See p. 93, note 26.

each. To the organization, the number of games in area i between the ith and jth teams (B_{ij}) is a choice variable, whereas the price per ticket P_i and skill levels S_i and S_j are parameters. The organization's profit function for the season-long N–team race, Π_L, is

$$(3.0) \qquad \Pi_L = \sum_{i=1}^{N}\sum_{\substack{j=1\\j\neq1}}^{N} P_i B_{ij} Q_d^{ij} - \sum_{i=1}^{N}\sum_{\substack{j=1\\j\neq i}}^{N} 2B_{ij}C(S_i).$$

The organization maximizes Π_L by choice of B_{ij}. Necessary and sufficient conditions for such a maximum are

$$(3.1) \qquad \frac{\partial \Pi_L}{\partial B_{ij}} = \sum_{i=1}^{N}\sum_{\substack{j=1\\j\neq i}}^{N}\left[P_i Q_d^{ij} + P_i B_{ij}^* \frac{\partial Q_d^{ij}}{\partial B_{ij}} - 2C(S_i)\right] = 0$$

and

$$(3.2) \qquad \frac{\partial^2 \Pi_L}{\partial B_{ij}^2} = \sum_{i=1}^{N}\sum_{\substack{j=1\\j\neq i}}^{N}\left[2P_i \frac{\partial Q_d^{ij}}{B_{ij}} + B_{ij}^* P_i \frac{\partial^2 Q_d^{ij}}{\partial B_{ij}^2}\right] < 0,$$

where B_{ij}^* = the profit-maximizing number of games.

The owner of team i takes B_{ij}^* as a parameter, and chooses P_i and S_i so as to maximize profit. Assuming that the cost of a game is composed only of the cost of obtaining two skilled teams, and that owner i receives shares of gate receipts equal to the private marginal product of his team's quality in contests, the profit function of the ith team is

$$(4.0) \qquad \Pi_i = \sum_{\substack{j=1\\j\neq i}}^{N} P_i a_{ij}(S_i, S_j) B_{ij} Q_d^{ij}$$

$$+ \sum_{\substack{j=1\\j\neq i}}^{N} P_j b_{ij}(S_i, S_j) B_{ji} Q_d^{ji} - 2B_i C(S_i),$$

where

$a_{ij} = a_{ij}(S_i, S_j)$ = the share of gate receipts awarded team i for home games against team j

$b_{ji} = b_{ji}(S_i, S_j)$ = the share of gate receipts awarded team i for away games against team j.

Team owner i takes B_{ij} as given and maximizes equation (4.0) by choice of P_i and S_i. Necessary and sufficient conditions for such a maximum are

$$(4.1) \qquad \frac{\partial \Pi_i}{\partial P_i} = \sum_{\substack{j=1 \\ j \neq i}}^{N} a_{ij} B_{ij} \left[Q_d^{ij} + P_i^* \frac{\partial Q_d^{ij}}{\partial P_i} \right] = 0$$

$$(4.2) \qquad \frac{\partial^2 \Pi_i}{\partial P_i^2} = \sum_{\substack{j=1 \\ j \neq i}}^{N} 2 a_{ij} B_{ij} \frac{\partial Q_d^{ij}}{\partial P_i}$$

$$+ \sum_{\substack{j=1 \\ j \neq i}}^{N} a_{ij} B_{ij} \frac{\partial^2 Q_d^{ij}}{\partial P_i^2} < 0,$$

$$(4.3) \qquad \frac{\partial \Pi_i}{\partial S_i} = \sum_{\substack{j=1 \\ j \neq i}}^{N} P_i^* B_{ij} \left[a_{ij} \left(\frac{\partial Q_d^{ij}}{\partial S_i} + \frac{\partial Q_d^{ij}}{\partial S_i/S_o} \frac{\partial S_i/S_o}{\partial S_i} \right) \right.$$

$$\left. + Q_d^{ij} \frac{\partial a_{ij}}{\partial S_i} \right]$$

$$+ \sum_{\substack{j=1 \\ j \neq i}}^{N} P_j^* B_{ji} \left[b_{ji} \left(\frac{\partial Q_d^{ji}}{\partial S_i} + \frac{\partial Q_d^{ji}}{\partial S_j/S_o} \frac{\partial S_j/S_o}{\partial S_i} \right) \right.$$

$$\left. + Q_d^{ji} \frac{\partial b_{ji}}{\partial S_i} \right] - 2 B_i \frac{\partial C}{\partial S_i} = 0,$$

$$(4.4) \qquad \frac{\partial^2 \Pi_i}{\partial S_i^2} = \sum_{\substack{j=1 \\ j \neq i}}^{N} P_i^* B_{ij} \left[2 \frac{\partial a_{ij}}{\partial S_i} \left(\frac{\partial Q_d^{ij}}{\partial S_i} + \frac{\partial Q_d^{ij}}{\partial S_i/S_o} \frac{\partial S_i/S_o}{\partial S_i} \right) \right.$$

$$+ a_{ij} \frac{\partial}{\partial S_i} \left(\frac{\partial Q_d^{ij}}{\partial S_i} + \frac{\partial Q_d^{ij}}{\partial S_i/S_o} \frac{\partial S_i/S_o}{\partial S_i} \right)$$

$$\left. + Q_d^{ij} \frac{\partial^2 a_{ij}}{\partial S_i^2} \right]$$

$$+ \sum_{\substack{j=1 \\ j \neq i}}^{N} P_j B_{ji} \left[2 \frac{\partial b_{ji}}{\partial S_i} \left(\frac{\partial Q_d^{ji}}{\partial S_i} + \frac{\partial Q_d^{ji}}{\partial S_j/S_o} \frac{\partial S_j/S_o}{\partial S_i} \right) \right.$$

$$+ b_{ji} \frac{\partial}{\partial S_i} \left(\frac{\partial Q_d^{ij}}{\partial S_i} + \frac{\partial Q_d^{ji}}{\partial S_j/S_o} \frac{\partial S_j/S_o}{\partial S_i} \right)$$

$$\left. + Q_d^{ji} \right] - 2 B_i \frac{\partial^2 C}{\partial S_i^2} < 0,$$

where P_i^* = the profit-maximizing ticket price in area i.

The quality of the ith team will affect revenues at home contests of the

N–1 other teams. The marginal effect in city j of an increase in team i's skill is

$$(5.0) \quad B_{ji}P_j\left[\frac{\partial Q_d^{ji}}{\partial S_i} + \frac{\partial Q_d^{ji}}{\partial S_j/S_o}\frac{\partial S_j/S_o}{\partial S_i}\right] + \sum_{\substack{k=1 \\ k\neq i,j}}^{N} B_{ik}P_j \frac{\partial Q_d^{jk}}{\partial S_j/S_o}\frac{\partial S_j/S_o}{\partial S_i}$$

$$= B_{ji}P_j\left[\frac{\partial Q_d^{ji}}{\partial S_i} + \frac{\partial Q_d^{ji}}{\partial S_j/S_o}\frac{-S_j}{NS_o^2}\right] + \sum_{\substack{k=1 \\ k\neq j,i}}^{N} B_{jk}P_j \frac{\partial Q_d^{jk}}{\partial S_j/S_o}\left(\frac{-S_j}{NS_o^2}\right),$$

where

Q_d^{jk} = the quantity of tickets demanded for a contest between teams j and k in the jth city.

Since

$$\frac{\partial Q_d^{jk}}{\partial S_j/S_o} > 0$$

(by hypothesis) and

$$\frac{\partial S_j/S_o}{\partial S_i} = \frac{-S_j}{NS_o^2} < 0,$$

an increment in team i's skill will *decrease* revenues from contests in the jth city between team j and teams other than i. This may be partly due to substitution away from games between teams j and $k(k = 1, \cdots, N; k \neq i,j)$ and toward games between j and i, but by assertion the quality change exerts an additional effect on demand. Even when substitution is taken into account, the increment in team i's skill may *decrease* revenues from contests between teams i and j in city j. This depends upon the relative magnitude of

$$\frac{\partial Q_d^{ji}}{\partial S_i} > 0 \quad \text{and} \quad \frac{\partial Q_d^{ji}}{\partial S_j/S_o}\frac{\partial S_j/S_o}{\partial S_i} < 0.$$

Thus demand for *all* contests in city j may decrease with an increase in the skill of team i.

Suppose there are N cities in which contests are produced. If a socially efficient amount of skill is produced, then in equilibrium the sum of marginal values to consumers in the N cities of an increment of skill in team i is equal to its marginal cost. For N cities there are N equations expressing necessary conditions for the production of a socially efficient amount of skill in each city:

(6.0)
$$\sum_{j=2}^{N} P_i B_{ij} \left[\frac{\partial Q_d^{ij}}{\partial S_i} + \frac{\partial Q_d^{ij}}{\partial S_i/S_o} \frac{\partial S_i/S_o}{\partial S_i} \right]$$

$$+ \sum_{j=2}^{N} P_j B_{ji} \left[\frac{\partial Q_d^{ji}}{\partial S_i} + \frac{\partial Q_d^{ji}}{\partial S_i/S_o} \frac{\partial S_i/S_o}{\partial S_i} \right]$$

$$+ \sum_{j=2}^{N} \sum_{\substack{k=2 \\ k \neq j}}^{N} P_j B_{jk} \frac{\partial Q_d^{jk}}{\partial S_j/S_o} \frac{\partial S_j/S_o}{\partial S_i} - \sum_{j=2}^{N} 2 B_{ij} \frac{\partial C}{\partial S_i} = 0$$

$$\vdots$$

$$\sum_{j=1}^{N-1} P_N B_{Nj} \left[\frac{\partial Q_d^{Nj}}{\partial S_N} + \frac{\partial Q_d^{Nj}}{\partial S_N/S_o} \frac{\partial S_N/S_o}{\partial S_N} \right]$$

$$+ \sum_{j=1}^{N-1} P_j B_{ji} \left[\frac{\partial Q_d^{ji}}{\partial S_N} + \frac{\partial Q_d^{ji}}{\partial S_j/S_o} \frac{\partial S_j/S_o}{\partial S_N} \right]$$

$$+ \sum_{j=1}^{N-1} \sum_{\substack{k=1 \\ k \neq j}}^{N-1} P_j B_{jk} \frac{\partial Q_d^{jk}}{\partial S_j/S_o} \frac{\partial S_j/S_o}{\partial S_N} - \sum_{j=1}^{N-1} 2 B_{Nj} \frac{\partial C}{\partial S_N} = 0.$$

Now suppose a "league," which chooses both the number of games and the level of quality of the teams. The owner of team i, located in city i, takes these decisions as parameters, and chooses only the ticket prices he will charge.

Equation (4.0) suggests that the profit function of a league is

(7.0)
$$\Pi_L = \sum_{i=1}^{N} \sum_{\substack{j=1 \\ j \neq i}}^{N} P_i B_{ij} Q_d^{ij} - \sum_{i=1}^{N} \sum_{\substack{j=1 \\ j \neq i}}^{N} 2 B_{ij} C(S_i).$$

A necessary condition for profit maximization of the skills of team i is:

(7.1)
$$\frac{\partial \Pi_L}{\partial S_i} = \sum_{\substack{j=1 \\ j \neq i}}^{N} P_i \bar{B}_{ij} \left[\frac{\partial Q_d^{ij}}{\partial S_i} + \frac{\partial Q_d^{ij}}{\partial S_i/S_o} \frac{\partial \bar{S}_i/S_o}{\partial S_i} \right]$$

$$+ \sum_{\substack{j=1 \\ j \neq i}}^{N} P_j \bar{B}_{ji} \left[\frac{\partial Q_d^{ji}}{\partial S_i} + \frac{\partial Q_d^{ji}}{\partial S_j/S_o} \frac{\partial S_j/S_o}{\partial S_i} \right]$$

$$+ \sum_{\substack{j=1 \\ j \neq i}}^{N} \sum_{\substack{k=1 \\ k \neq i \\ k \neq j}}^{N} P_j \bar{B}_{jk} \frac{\partial Q_d^{jk}}{\partial S_j/S_o} \frac{\partial S_j/S_o}{\partial S_i} - \sum_{i=1}^{N} \sum_{\substack{j=1 \\ j \neq i}}^{N} 2 \bar{B}_{ij} \frac{\partial C}{\partial S_i} = 0,$$

where

$\bar{B}_{ij}\,(i,j = 1, \cdots, N; i \neq j)$ = the profit-maximizing number of games between each pair of teams

$\bar{S}_i$ = the profit-maximizing skill of team i.

In equilibrium the profitability to the league of producing an increment of quality in each of the N cities in which contests are produced is

(8.0)
$$\sum_{j=2}^{N} P_i B_{ij} \left[\frac{\partial Q_d^{ij}}{\partial S_i} + \frac{\partial Q_d^{ij}}{\partial S_i/S_o} \frac{\partial S_i/S_o}{\partial S_i} \right]$$

$$+ \sum_{j=2}^{N} P_j B_{ji} \left[\frac{\partial Q_d^{ji}}{\partial S_i} + \frac{\partial Q_d^{ji}}{\partial S_i/S_o} \frac{\partial S_i/S_o}{\partial S_i} \right]$$

$$+ \sum_{j=2}^{N} \sum_{\substack{k=2 \\ k \neq j}}^{N} P_j B_{jk} \frac{\partial Q_d^{jk}}{\partial S_j/S_o} \frac{\partial S_j/S_o}{\partial S_i} - \sum_{j=2}^{N} 2B_{ij} \frac{\partial C}{\partial S_i} = 0$$

$$\vdots$$

$$\sum_{j=1}^{N-1} P_N B_{Nj} \left[\frac{\partial Q_d^{Nj}}{\partial S_N} + \frac{\partial Q_d^{Nj}}{\partial S_N/S_o} \frac{\partial S_N/S_o}{\partial S_N} \right]$$

$$+ \sum_{j=1}^{N-1} P_j B_{jN} \left[\frac{\partial Q_d^{jN}}{\partial S_N} + \frac{\partial Q_d^{jN}}{\partial S_j/S_o} \frac{\partial S_j/S_o}{\partial S_N} \right]$$

$$+ \sum_{j=1}^{N} \sum_{\substack{k=1 \\ k \neq j}}^{N} P_j B_{jk} \frac{\partial Q_d^{jk}}{\partial S_j/S_o} \frac{\partial S_j/S_o}{\partial S_N} - \sum_{j=1}^{N} 2B_{Nj} \frac{\partial C}{\partial S_N} = 0,$$

where

$$\sum_{\substack{j=1 \\ j \neq i}}^{N} 2B_{ij} \frac{\partial C}{\partial S_i}$$

refers to the marginal wage per unit of skill paid by a perfectly discriminating monopsonist.[51]

The N equations of expression (8.0) are the same as those of expression (6.0); the league produces a socially efficient quantity of skill because it takes account of effects on demand in all N cities where contests are produced.

51. Perfect monopsony is assumed in order to concentrate on the league's recognition of revenue changes resulting from team quality levels.

The previously established first-order condition for the number of games, now determined by the league with prices and team skill levels taken as parameters, and the first-order condition for prices, with number of games taken as a parameter, are fully differentiated with respect to skill. After rearranging terms,

(9.0)
$$\sum_{i=1}^{N} \sum_{\substack{j=1 \\ j \neq i}}^{N} \frac{\partial B_{ij}^*}{\partial S_i} \left[2P_i^* \frac{\partial Q_d^i}{\partial B_j} + P_i^* B_{ij}^* \frac{\partial^2 Q_d^{ij}}{\partial B_{ij}^2} \right]$$

$$= \sum_{i=1}^{N} \sum_{\substack{j=1 \\ j \neq i}}^{N} \left[2 \frac{\partial C}{\partial S_i} - P_i^* \frac{\partial Q_d^{ij}}{\partial S_i} \right]$$

(10.0)
$$\sum_{i=1}^{N} \sum_{\substack{j=1 \\ j \neq i}}^{N} \frac{\partial P_i^*}{\partial S_i} \left[2a_{ij} B_{ij}^* \frac{\partial Q_d^{ij}}{\partial P_i} + a_{ij} B_{ij}^* \frac{\partial^2 Q_d^{ij}}{\partial P_i^2} \right]$$

$$= - \sum_{i=1}^{N} \sum_{\substack{j=1 \\ j \neq i}}^{N} a_{ij} B_{ij}^* \frac{\partial Q_d^{ij}}{\partial S_i}.$$

Assume for simplicity that $\partial B_{ij}^*/\partial S_i$, $\partial P_i^*/\partial S_i$ are identical for all $i = 1, \cdots, N$. This allows us to factor $\partial B_{ij}^*/\partial S_i$ and $\partial P_i^*/\partial S_i$ from the left side of equations (9.0) and (10.0). Then equation (9.0) implies that $\partial B_{ij}^*/\partial S_i$, the change in the profit-maximizing number of games caused by a change in the skill level of team i, is sign indeterminate. Equation (3.2) indicates that the parenthetical term on the left-hand side of equation (9.0) is negative. The sign of $\partial B_{ij}^*/\partial S_i$ therefore depends on the terms of the right-hand side of equation (9.0)—that is, on the changes in marginal cost and revenue per game resulting from a skill change.

That the right-hand side of equation (10.0) is negative is shown by equation (1.3), and that the parenthetical term on the left-hand side is negative by equation (4.2) (and because the sum of negative numbers is itself negative). Hence equation (10.0) implies that $\partial P_i^*/\partial S_i > 0$—that is, the change in the profit-maximizing ticket price caused by a change in team skill is positive. Likewise, a decrement in skill implies a decrease in ticket price.

CHAPTER FOUR

Attendance and Price Setting

ROGER G. NOLL

THE FORMULATION of rational public policy toward professional sports requires some empirical knowledge of the industry's sources of demand and pricing practices. This knowledge is important in several ways. First, it provides some sense of the economic importance of various restrictive practices of teams and leagues. Second, it indicates the extent of viable economic demand for professional sports—that is, the number of teams that can profitably survive, and the cities that can support them. Third, it is pertinent to understanding the motivations of sports management: do team owners seek to win games regardless of the financial losses involved, or are they profit-oriented entrepreneurs differing little from other businessmen?

This chapter consists of a statistical investigation of the demand for sports contests. A section outlining the general approach is followed by an analysis of each of the four major team sports. As much as possible of the detailed explanation of methodology is relegated to footnotes, which can be ignored by the reader unfamiliar with statistical terminology without losing track of the argument.

Factors Influencing the Demand for Games

A list of factors that, a priori, ought to influence attendance at professional sports contests is not difficult to assemble. Fans presumably prefer good to poor games, skillful to unskillful players, and a winning to a losing home team. Most of the factors influencing attendance could be expected to interact with the population of the city in which the game is played: that is, variations in team quality, prices, and other demand-related factors should produce greater variation in attendance in larger cities. For example, Kareem Abdul-Jabbar should attract a larger crowd in New York or Los Angeles than in Phoenix or Portland. Consequently, in the following statistical analysis, most of the variables used to explain attendance are products of population and another variable, such as ticket prices or number of star players.[1] The only factors that were not multiplied by population are stadium capacity, which acts as a constraint on attendance, and population itself.[2]

Data for all sports were collected in essentially the same way, and sources and procedures are described in notes to the tables. Two variables need to be explained in some detail.

Average ticket prices were calculated from sales brochures supplied by all but a handful of teams; to derive the average stadium price, prices of individual seat locations were weighted by the fraction of seats at that price, the weights being calculated from diagrams of stadiums. The resulting variable is an average price per seat, not per ticket sold, since not all seat locations are likely to be sold with the same frequency unless the stadium is always sold out. To the extent that the average quality of seats differs among stadiums, the effect of the average ticket price on attendance will be more complex. A stadium with a relatively large number of good seats will have a higher average ticket price, all other things being equal,

1. Regressions were also run without multiplying the other independent variables by population. Both linear and logarithmic-linear equations were estimated. In all cases, the statistical quality of these results was much lower than for the regressions based upon normalized data: few regression coefficients were statistically significant and of the correct sign, and the equations had low correlation coefficients. The procedure of multiplying the independent variables by population rather than using attendance per unit of population was chosen because of the serious errors in variables that the latter would have created. Standard metropolitan statistical area (SMSA) population is not anything like an exact measure of the market for a team, though it is highly correlated with the size of the team's market. In addition, most regressions were performed on data for two seasons, and reliable annual series on SMSA population are not available.

2. The model proposed here is an aggregation of individual demand functions for the population of the metropolitan area in which a team is located. This raises the possibility that the model is significantly heteroskedastic, since the number of demand curves differs from city to city. Accordingly, all the regressions were also estimated after multiplying each observation of each variable by the inverse of the square root of the appropriate SMSA population, the normal procedure for dealing with heteroskedasticity of this type. This procedure did not improve the statistical significance of the regression coefficients—in many cases, indeed, it made them less significant—although it did have the expected result of increasing the correlation coefficients to near unity. Because this procedure did not improve the basic quality of the equations, while making them more difficult for the casual reader to interpret, it was abandoned. Only the ordinary least-squares results are reported here.

but the higher price will presumably not reduce attendance to the same extent as higher prices for seats of any given quality would.[3]

The number-of-stars variable was not calculated in a very scientific manner. All-star team rosters for the past few years were consulted, but in the end players were classified as stars according to the personal judgment of the author. The initial designations of stars were not altered on the basis of the results of the statistical analysis. The purpose of the star variable is to measure the drawing power possessed by some especially exciting players that is beyond their contribution to the playing successes of their teams. For example, Elgin Baylor and Willie Mays, though no longer the most effective players in their sports, were still attracting fans in the period covered by this study.

The remaining variables are more straightforward. To capture the effect of team quality, several measures were used: percentage of games won, number of games behind the league leader at various times during the season, and playing success in past seasons as indicated by winning percentages and championships won. These measures were always highly correlated, so that only one or two were needed to capture the full effect of team quality.[4] In all cases the one or two team-quality variables that explained the greatest amount of interteam differences in attendance were retained in the final results.[5]

Another factor that should affect attendance is the amount of entertainment competition the team faces. Two variables were used to measure this factor. First, the total number of other teams in major-league professional sports (baseball, football, basketball, and hockey, excluding soccer) located in the city indicated sports competition. Second, on the grounds that bigger cities have more entertainment options, the population of the metropolitan area was used as a rough index of nonsports competition.[6]

3. One consequence of this problem is that the regression results yield an underestimate of the elasticity of demand.

4. Adding more measures of quality did not increase the explanatory power of the equation, and, due to multicollinearity, destroyed the estimates of the standard deviations of the regression coefficients.

5. They had the highest t-statistics and contributed the most to the equation's coefficient of determination.

6. The population surrogate for nonsports entertainment might enter the individual demand functions in many ways. Three possibilities were considered: the inverse of population, the logarithm of population, and population itself. In the aggregate demand relation, when multiplied by population, these would become respectively a constant, the product of population and the logarithm of population,

The ways in which income might explain attendance are numerous, so that the results cannot properly be used to measure the effect of generally rising income on the demand for sports. Intercity differences in per capita income reflect, among other things, differences in industrial structure, region, and the educational attainment and age composition of the population.[7] Per capita income tends to be lower in a city that is in the South or that has an abnormally large fraction of residents who have not finished high school, who are very young or very old, or who work in blue-collar occupations. It tends to be higher in a city that is in the North or that has more workers in white-collar occupations, more of its population of prime working age, or more college graduates.

The stadium or arena in which a team plays can also affect total attendance. First, a newer facility may attract fans because of its greater comfort or because it affords a better view of the game; this factor was found to be important only in baseball. Second, the capacity of the stadium obviously puts an upper limit on attendance. In general, an attempt was made to avoid the use of this variable. If stadium capacity explains a substantial part of attendance that cannot be explained by other variables, then the proper conclusion is that the sport in question has excess demand at the going price. In nearly all cases, stadium capacity by itself could explain much of the intercity differences in attendance, but, in all sports except football, when it was included with the other variables in the same equation it added little or no explanatory power. In the long run, one would expect cities to build sports facilities and teams to set prices so that attendance and capacity would be highly correlated, because both are determined by the underlying demand for sports in the city.

---

and the square of population. Note that the aggregate equation would have no intercept unless the inverse of population appeared in the individual demand function. In all cases, the constant intercept was highly significant and of the correct sign (positive). When replaced by either of the other alternatives, the equation lost much explanatory power, and the replacement was itself usually not statistically significant, though usually having the proper sign (negative). When both an intercept and one of the other population variables were included, the latter was always highly insignificant. Since the intercept can be important for many reasons, including misspecification of the important independent variables or of the functional form, it cannot be concluded that nonsports competition is necessarily reflected in the estimated relation. Nevertheless, when all independent variables except population are set at mean values, the resulting equation predicts a declining ratio of attendance to population.

7. A fruitful line of future research would be to attempt to capture the effects of all these factors separately. At the time this research was carried out, data from the 1970 Census of Population, the best source for such information, were not yet completely available.

The racial composition of a city was included as a variable, since sports entrepreneurs have long regarded it as important in determining attendance. Industry sources believe that a smaller fraction of blacks are fans, and some have argued that whites attend games less frequently if more blacks turn out. For each sport, the percentage of blacks in the metropolitan area was used to measure this effect. Since this variable, like the others, was multiplied by total population, the actual numbers used represented the total black population in each area.

Weather conditions may play a role in determining attendance. Two factors are at work here: fans may stay home if the weather is bad; but fans living in cities with generally good weather attend less frequently since they have greater opportunities for more active outdoor recreational pursuits. In private conversation, Baseball Commissioner Bowie Kuhn has said that he believes the second factor at least offsets, and perhaps dominates, the first—that is, he expects attendance to be no worse, and perhaps better, in areas with bad weather. To measure this effect, the number of days of sunshine per year in the metropolitan area was used. Unfortunately, this variable, like any measure of climate, is strongly correlated with the region of the country, so the effect measured may reflect factors other than weather conditions.

Finally, an attempt was made to capture the effect on attendance of close competition for a playoff position. Several variables were tried, such as the average difference in winning percentages of first- and second-place teams, or the number of games behind of the second-place team. These were important in baseball and hockey, but not in football and basketball, where the end-of-season playoff and the small number of teams in each division probably reduce the importance of this variable. In football, a further mitigating factor is that, with only a fourteen-game season, races are *always* close, so the special effect of closeness cannot be measured.

For baseball and basketball, data on team characteristics were collected for two seasons,[8] but reliable data on income, population, and ticket prices were not available for both seasons.[9] Thus, in those sports, data on the

8. Football data were not aggregated over several years because of the special problems presented by the recent merger and by the fact that teams have played to nearly full capacity since 1969.

9. Population and income statistics for metropolitan areas in intercensal years are not particularly reliable, especially for measuring year-to-year changes. Ticket price information was provided by most teams only in the form of the current season's ticket brochure. Teams were generally unwilling to supply more accurate information on prices actually charged, or to supply brochures for past seasons. Some refused to send current ticket information until the request was masqueraded as an inquiry from a potential customer.

performance of a particular team for both seasons are related to the same data for the latter variables. (For example, 1970 population figures are used for both the 1970 and 1971 playing seasons.) Such a procedure leads to an underestimate of the importance of these variables; however, it avoids the noncausal correlation that arises simply because all economic variables tend to increase over time.

Baseball

Results of the analysis of baseball data for the 1970 and 1971 seasons are shown in Table 1. Each of twenty-three teams[10] accounts for two of the data observations for each variable.[11] Since the meaning of several of the variables is not obvious, the reader is encouraged to read the notes to the table. All variables with t-statistics exceeding unity are included in the table for the convenience of the reader; however, only coefficients with t-statistics exceeding 1.65 are statistically significant by conventional standards.[12] Since most of the variables are scaled by the SMSA population, the coefficients are somewhat difficult to interpret. Table 2 therefore breaks down the second set of results in Table 1 into three categories by metropolitan area population: 1.5 million (about the size of the smallest cities having baseball teams), 3.5 million (the baseball-wide average, and roughly the size of the sixth largest SMSA having a baseball team), and 12 million (representing New York).

Interpretation of the Results

Several interesting results are apparent in the two tables.

INCOME. Given the negative correlation between attendance and income, baseball appears to be a working-class sport. (Of course, the negative coefficient should not be interpreted to mean that poor people are the

10. The Dodgers, who did not respond to requests for ticket price information, are excluded.

11. Reliable annual figures were not available for income, population, and price, so the same value for each of them was used for both years.

12. That is, at the 95 percent confidence level for a one-tailed t-test; a 1.0 t-statistic indicates only about an 80 percent likelihood that the true sign of the coefficient is the same as the estimated sign. For a two-tailed test, which should be applied to the population and income variables, the 95 percent confidence value of the t-statistic is roughly 2.0. The variables that were included in the analysis but failed to have t-statistics greater than unity were team batting average, team earned run average, annual number of sunny days, and the league in which the team played.

Table 1. Regression Results for Baseball Season Attendance Correlated with Selected Variables, 1970 and 1971 Seasons[a]

Variable or summary statistic	Coefficient	
	Equation (1)	Equation (2)
Variable		
Constant	952.24	540.56
	(9.66)	(3.78)
Population[b]	63.91	984.02
	(2.98)	(3.81)
Per capita income[b] × population	...	−134.89
		(3.00)
Ticket price × population	...	−54.12
		(1.59)
Stadium age[c] × population	...	9.82
		(2.28)
Number of star players[d] × population	...	21.74
		(1.83)
Close pennant race[e] × population	...	37.02
		(1.54)
Sports competition[f] × population	...	−24.12
		(2.16)
Recent pennant win[g] × population	...	68.91
		(5.04)
Games behind[h] × population	...	−1.79
		(1.36)
Black population[b]	...	−475.74
		(1.83)
Summary statistic		
R^2	0.17	0.76
$\overline{R}^2$	0.15	0.69
Degrees of freedom	44	35

Sources: Attendance, *The World Almanac and Book of Facts, 1972 Edition* (Newspaper Enterprise Association, 1971), p. 909; population and income, U.S. Bureau of the Census, *Statistical Abstract of the United States, 1971* (1971), sec. 33; league standings, *World Almanac, 1972*, pp. 910, 913, and *1971*, pp. 872, 875; information on ticket prices, age of stadiums, and number of star players (see text), collected by author.

a. Data are for all twenty-four major-league baseball teams except the Dodgers, who failed to provide ticket price information. Attendance is measured in thousands of official paid admissions per season; the coefficients are thus the effect in thousands on regular-season attendance of an increase of one unit in the corresponding independent variable. The numbers in parentheses are *t*-statistics.

b. Population in 1970 (in millions) and per capita personal income in 1969 (in thousands of dollars) are for the relevant SMSAs.

c. This variable is eleven minus the age of the stadium, except it is zero for stadiums over ten years old. Information collected from teams and city officials.

d. This variable is one greater than the number of stars, except it is zero for teams with no stars. This procedure was chosen because in a regression in which the first star was one variable and the remaining stars were a second, the first coefficient was approximately twice as large as the second.

e. A divisional championship race was judged close if the second-place team averaged five games or less behind the leader between August 1 and the end of the season. The choice of five games was not critical; no divisional races would have switched categories had the choice been any number between 4.5 and 8.25.

f. The number of other professional teams in the four major team sports—baseball, basketball, football, and hockey—located in the city.

g. This variable is two if the team had won a pennant in the past four years, and one if it had won between five and nine years previously. The two periods are combined because when they are entered as separate dummy variables the coefficient of the first is almost exactly twice the second. The periods were chosen simply because the statistical significance of the dummy variable greatly exceeded the significance of several other alternatives, including years since the last pennant won.

h. Refers to the standings of teams relative to the divisional champions at the end of the season. Since a disproportionately large share of baseball attendance occurs in September, end-of-season standings produced the best results.

Table 2. Coefficients for Baseball Season Attendance, by Standard Metropolitan Statistical Area Population, 1970 and 1971 Seasons[a]

	SMSA population (millions)		
Variable	1.5	3.5	12.0
Constant	2,016.59	3,984.63	12,348.80
Per capita income	−202.34	−472.12	−1,619.35
Ticket price	−81.18	−189.42	−649.71
Stadium age	14.73	34.37	117.84
Number of star players	32.61	76.09	260.88
Close pennant race	55.53	129.57	444.24
Sports competition	−36.18	−84.42	−289.44
Recent pennant win	103.37	241.19	826.92
Games behind	−2.69	−6.27	−21.48
Percent black population	−713.61	−1,665.09	−5,708.88

Source: Derived by multiplying coefficients in equation (2) of Table 1 by SMSA populations of 1.5, 3.5, and 12.0 million.
a. See notes to Table 1 for dimensions of the variables.

most likely to attend baseball games; extrapolation of the differences in average income among cities to predictions about individuals at the extremes of the income distribution is not valid.) Two factors may account for the sign of the income variable. First, baseball tickets are relatively cheap, compared both to other sports and to other types of entertainment. Most baseball teams have some seats priced at or below $1.50; very few teams in other sports have any seats under $2.50. Second, persons in less physically exerting occupations may find the rather sedate pace of baseball less attractive. If so, cities having relatively more higher-paying, white-collars jobs—such as in finance or government—would have lower attendance figures. Both factors are suggestive of the source of the long-term relative decline in the popularity of baseball: rising income is associated with both a declining sensitivity to price differentials among entertainment options and a smaller relative number of persons in physically exerting occupations.

PLAYING SUCCESS. Winning a pennant apparently has a strong effect on attendance in the winning season and also in several succeeding years. In fact, attendance in the pennant-winning year will actually be less than in the next few years if the team, though not continuing to win pennants, can at least stay close behind the league leader. For example, suppose a team in a city of 3.5 million that won a pennant five years ago finishes twenty games behind in one year, wins a pennant in the second, and finishes ten games behind in the third (all three races being "not close"). From the first to the second year the predicted rise in attendance is 125,000; from the second to the third year attendance will rise another 180,000. This result is probably partly due to the effect of a pennant-winning season on season-ticket sales, the volume of which must obviously be based largely on past performance. If a pennant-winning team can sell 2,500 more season tickets the next year, it will attain the predicted 180,000 gain in total attendance even if it sells 20,000 fewer tickets to individual games. This suggests that aggregate league attendance will be substantially higher if several teams alternate in winning pennants than if one team tends to dominate, and provides a partial explanation for the wide divergence in attendance figures between the National and American Leagues.

The games-behind variable is not statistically significant by conventional standards; however, its correlations with such other factors as the number of recent pennant wins, the number of star players, and the closeness of a pennant race suggest that its significance may be greater than estimated. The value of its coefficient seems plausible: in a city with a metropolitan population of 3.5 million, finishing an additional ten games behind results in a drop in attendance of 63,000.

NUMBER OF STAR PLAYERS. Stars add substantially to the drawing power of baseball, even without considering their effects on the playing success of their teams.[13] In the average-sized baseball city of 3.5 million, the first star will add an estimated 150,000 fans to season attendance; at $3.00 per ticket, this amounts to over $450,000 in revenues. Adding the roughly 40 cents per fan in concession profits that, according to Bill Veeck,[14] the typical team earns and subtracting the visiting team's share of the gate and the stadium rental, net revenues generated by a star are more than $385,000. The second star, by similar calculation, is worth nearly $200,000.[15] These estimates are *not* based on a highly restrictive

13. Compare the "folk hero" effect hypothesized by Ralph Andreano in *No Joy in Mudville: The Dilemma of Major League Baseball* (Schenkman, 1965).

14. See Bill Veeck with Ed Linn, *Veeck—As in Wreck: The Autobiography of Bill Veeck* (Putnam, 1962), p. 121. His estimate is roughly consistent with the financial data presented in Chapter 1.

15. To these figures must be added the revenues the team obtains for every game and pennant won because of the star player's superior skills. If finishing one fewer game behind the league leader generates approximately 6,000 fans for the season, then each additional game that a star player causes to be won is worth at least $15,000 to his team (and the same amount in losses to the team he defeats). If a star causes his team to win ten additional games a year, he generates another $150,000 in revenues.

definition of a superstar. The number of players so classed was twenty-three for 1970 and twenty-four for 1971. Despite their high salaries, star players apparently generate much more revenue for their teams than they are paid.

SPORTS COMPETITION. For several reasons, the number of competing sports teams is a weak, though not readily improvable, measure of inter-sports competition. First, not all sports offer competition for fans to the same degree, since their seasons overlap to varying extents. Second, the effect of one team on the attendance of another probably depends upon the relative playing success of the teams. Third, the effect of the number of sports teams is not independent of the general interest in sports in a city, so that the estimated extent of intersports competition tends to be biased downward (that is, cities with more sports interest will tend to have both higher attendance per team and more teams, limited only by the institutional restrictions on multiteam cities in each sport). Despite these and other problems, the coefficient of the number of major-league teams is statistically significant by conventional standards. It suggests that attendance in the average baseball city (with 3.5 million metropolitan population and three other major-league teams in the four sports) is about 250,-000 lower—about 21 percent—because of intersport competition. This finding offers another partial explanation for the relative decline in the popularity of baseball. Of the sixteen original baseball franchises, twelve faced more competition from other professional sports teams in 1971 than they did in 1958 (the average increase in total sports competition being five-eighths of a competitor per team), and none faced less. The expansion teams in baseball face fewer competitors, but the overall average for baseball has risen because the other professional sports have added more teams than baseball has.

STADIUM AGE. New ball parks appear to be responsible for a significant increase in attendance. In a city of 3.5 million, a new stadium will cause attendance to increase by 378,000 in the first year. This prediction is borne out by the experience of the Philadelphia Phillies, whose attendance doubled when it switched fields in 1971. The variable used in the equation, which shows a steady, linear decline in the attendance generated by a new stadium, proved much more significant than alternatives, such as dummy variables for "very new" and "middle-aged" stadiums, indicating the validity of the belief that the novelty of a new stadium wears off slowly but steadily.

TICKET PRICES. The estimated coefficient of average ticket price indicates that the demand for baseball is inelastic at current prices—that is, that baseball teams could increase their revenues by raising prices. Nevertheless, the possibility that the demand is elastic cannot be rejected out of hand. In Table 2, the coefficient of price for an average team (in a city of 3.5 million, drawing 1,179,000 fans and charging an average of $3.04 per seat) would have to be 388 (instead of 189) in order for the estimated demand elasticity to be unity, and this figure is not significantly different from the estimated value. Furthermore, the coefficient of price—and hence the estimated elasticity—is biased downward because it does not correct for differences among stadiums in the quality of the average seat. Since larger parks tend to have a greater proportion of bad seats, their average price per seat would be lower if all seats of a given quality were the same price as in a smaller park; yet, all other things being equal, this difference in average price would not in reality affect total attendance. Finally, the *total* cost of attending a game—including parking, concessions, and so forth—is what is relevant to the sports fan. If the price of the ticket represents only half the cost of attending the game, the coefficient of price would have to be 194 (essentially the estimated value) in order for the estimated demand elasticity to be unity. Thus, the results do not warrant the conclusion that baseball prices are below the revenue-maximizing level.

If demand were inelastic, the belief that team owners do not maximize profits would gain important support. An owner wanting both to build a winning team and to provide a public service would not only overspend on player development but would also engage in cost-plus pricing; that is, ticket prices would be set just to cover the operating costs of the team and its player development system. If this "sportman" attitude were characteristic of owners, prices would be lower for a team with greater attendance, regardless of quality, and over the long run the profitability of all viable teams, regardless of attendance, would be about the same (except, of course, for teams with very low attendance figures that have difficulty covering costs).

Actual ticket prices do exhibit roughly this tendency, as shown in Table 3; however, the price differentials are not nearly large enough to offset cost differences. The average team in Group (I) receives roughly $1.7 million more in gate revenues than the average for all teams. Of that, $200,000 goes to higher stadium rents, which are usually based on revenues, and $450,000 to additional player development. On the other side of the ledger, a Group (I) team receives approximately $150,000 more in con-

Table 3. Final Standing and Average Ticket Price for Baseball Teams, by Season Attendance, 1970 and 1971 Seasons

Season attendance (millions)	Number of teams	Average final division standing	Average ticket price (dollars)[a]
(I) Over 1.4	8[b]	3.0	2.94[c]
			(0.28)
(II) 1.0 to 1.3	6	2.7	3.02
			(0.31)
(III) Under 1.0	9	4.7	3.15
			(0.44)
All teams	23	3.5	3.04
			(0.36)

Sources: Same as Table 1 for relevant variables.
a. Standard deviation in parentheses.
b. The Dodgers are excluded since they did not supply ticket price information.
c. $3.05 if "sportsman-owned" Cubs and Red Sox are excluded.

cession profits and $600,000 more in broadcasting revenues.[16] This leaves about $1.8 million in additional net revenues for each Group (I) team. The two remaining expenditure items that vary with attendance and team success are player salaries and stadium maintenance and operation. Since total expenditures per team on these items are less than $2.0 million, the difference between Group (I) and the baseball-wide average cannot account for all of Group (I)'s greater profits. Furthermore, nearly all the difference between the prices of Group (I) and the other groups is accounted for by the presence of the two "sportsman-owned" teams in Group (I), the Cubs and the Red Sox: with these two teams excluded, average ticket price is $3.05. But even without this alteration, the price differences among the groups are statistically insignificant, although Red Sox prices are significantly below the Group (I) average.

In short, the available data do not support the hypothesis that teams use an average-cost or cost-plus pricing policy, and hence that team owners are sportsmen rather than businessmen. Furthermore, the hypothesis that teams charge a revenue-maximizing price (indeed, a profit-maximizing price, since variable costs per fan are nearly zero) cannot be rejected, except in the case of the Red Sox.

POPULATION. A crucial factor in the success of a team is its hometown population. Table 1 permits an estimate of the attendance generated by

16. These data are derived from the profitability estimates in Chapter 1.

a team of a given quality in cities of different sizes. If all variables except population are assumed to take values equal to the average for all teams, then 1 million SMSA residents will produce about 237,000 fans.[17] In order to draw 1 million fans, a team with average characteristics (including average playing success) would have to be located in a metropolitan area with a population of about 1.9 million. But a team that finished thirty-five games (instead of the average eighteen) out of first place and had not won a pennant in the past ten years (and had otherwise average characteristics) would have to play in an SMSA with 2.9 million population in order to draw 1 million fans. Since all the metropolitan areas of this size or larger have higher than average per capita income, the use of actual income values in the equation produces the result that in only six SMSAs—New York, Los Angeles, Chicago, Detroit, Philadelphia, and Boston—will a persistent loser draw as many as 1 million fans annually.[18] At the other extreme, a team with average characteristics located in a metropolitan area of two million is expected to draw about 1.1 million fans if it wins a pennant, and in the following season, even if it finishes ten games behind, 1.2 million. By contrast, a team in New York that wins a pennant every ten years will average about 1.3 million fans in years when it is of average quality (eighteen games behind the leader), and will peak at over 2 million for a few years after winning a pennant, assuming that it remains a contender.

Tables 1 and 2 also imply a magnified effect of the other variables in the larger cities. For example, a New York team will gain over 500,000 fans with the acquisition of its first star. This accounts for 20 percent of the team's attendance even in its best years. In a city of 1.5 million, the first star adds about 65,000 fans, or about 6 percent of total attendance. Likewise, a team that improves its won-lost record by ten games increases attendance by 25,000 in the small city and 210,000 in New York.

For some extreme values of the independent variables, attendance can

17. This estimate exceeds the coefficient of the single-variable regression reported in equation (1) of Table 1 because of the effects of correlations between population and other variables that are picked up in the single-variable model. Note that these additional one million residents have the same proportion of blacks as the average for all teams, since the percentage of blacks in the population is one of the variables held constant.

18. In 1971, four teams finished thirty or more games out of first place. Only one, Philadelphia, drew more than 1 million fans. The Philadelphia SMSA contains nearly 5 million inhabitants and has a new stadium. All the other teams are located in areas under 3 million in population.

be negatively related to population. For example, a team that is persistently bad (never winning a pennant and finishing fifty games behind), that has no stars, that competes against six other major professional sports teams, and that plays in an old stadium will, according to the estimated equation, do better in smaller cities. Furthermore, when differentials in income and sports competition between large and small cities are taken into account, even a moderately bad team—always thirty to forty games behind—will do better in smaller cities. This prediction is consonant with the larger number of entertainment options, both sports (professional and collegiate) and nonsports, in a large city, which might well cause interest in a poor team to flag more quickly than it would in a smaller city. The experiences of the Chicago White Sox and the California Angels in the late 1960s bear this out, although the early years of the New York Mets provide a remarkable exception.

BLACK POPULATION. Table 1 shows that a larger black population in an area leads to lower attendance. The negative coefficient of black population has three possible interpretations. First, even when income differences are corrected for, blacks may just be less interested in attending baseball games. Second, as baseball spokesmen have argued,[19] especially strong white racism could be responsible, so that if one black attends a game, more than one white who would otherwise have attended will stay home. Third, cities with large black populations also tend to be the larger, older cities in which the baseball stadium has inadequate parking facilities and is located in an unattractive, perhaps even dangerous, slum: Yankee Stadium, Comiskey Park, and Cleveland Municipal Stadium come immediately to mind. In other words, the black-population variable may actually be a measure of stadium quality.

The magnitude of the coefficient of black population is too great for the first explanation to be the most important. According to the equation, increasing the black population of a metropolitan area by 1 million (holding the number of whites constant) causes attendance to decline by 168,000 annually.[20] The minimum possible effect of the hypothesis that blacks are *less* likely to attend games would be that more blacks would cause a very small *increase* in attendance, but not a decrease.

19. See Chapter 7.
20. This estimate takes account of the fact that total population would increase by 1 million, also. If 1 million blacks replace 1 million whites, attendance falls by 476,000. If the total population increases by 1 million (including 15 percent blacks), attendance goes up by 237,000. Thus, the effect of adding 1 million blacks is to cause attendance to change by 237,000 − (0.85) 476,000 = −168,000.

The second explanation requires the assumption that a fairly large proportion of fans in the larger cities are black. In a metropolitan area with a population of 5 million, 15 percent of which are black, and with all other characteristics at the average for baseball, total attendance is predicted to be 1.7 million. To allocate this figure by race, income effects must be taken into account. If racial differences in income are at the national average, per capita income for whites would be about $1,500 higher than for blacks. Applying this to the results of Table 1, the 1.7 million fans should include about 420,000 blacks, or 25 percent.[21] An increase in the black proportion of the population to 17 percent would cause attendance to fall by 48,000, including an increase of 56,000 blacks and a decrease of 104,000 whites, so that 29 percent of those attending would be black. In both cases, the fraction of blacks attending games would be much higher than that for the metropolitan population. While no data are available on the distribution of baseball fans by race, casual observation suggests that the fraction of blacks at baseball games is substantially below their proportion of the population. Therefore the "white racism" hypothesis alone cannot explain the magnitude of the negative correlation of black population and attendance.

Suppose, instead, that blacks are less interested in baseball than whites to the extent that the fraction of blacks in attendance is half their fraction in the SMSA population. Then the hypothetical team in an area of 5 million population, 15 percent of which are black, would have 128,000 blacks among its 1.7 million total attendance. If the number of blacks rose to 17 percent, black attendance would rise only 35 percent as much as in the preceding example, or by 17,000. White attendance would then have to fall by 65,000—that is, each black would displace nearly four whites—to make total attendance fall by 48,000. And as the fraction of blacks attending falls below half their proportion of the population, the ratio of the decline of white fans to the increase in blacks must grow. This suggests that the "lesser interest" and "white racism" hypotheses together can explain the results in Table 1 only if white racism is especially virulent.

If this extent of white racism is rejected as unlikely, a major source of the measured effect must be the correlation of black population with undesirable stadium location. (It would, of course, be preferable to measure the effect of stadium location directly through some sort of index of the

21. With the coefficient of black population zero and the constant in Table 1 divided proportionately among blacks and whites, black attendance (with $3,000 per capita income) becomes $81,000 + 450,000$ times black population (in millions).

relative squalidness of areas surrounding baseball parks.) The results do not establish a causal chain between urban blight and the racial composition of a city.[22] The connection is simply that ball parks located in undesirable neighborhoods tend to be old stadiums in very large cities in the North and Midwest, and these cities also tend to have atypically large black populations.

Implications for Expansion

The preceding statistical results have important implications for the number of teams that could feasibly be added to the major-league baseball roster. Within the industry, a common rule of thumb is that a team needs to attract about 850,000 fans to home games in order to break even.[23] Judging by the financial information presented in Chapter 1, a team should be able to earn a modest profit of $100,000–$200,000 if its home attendance is 1 million. Unless a philanthropic owner can be found, this level of profit is probably the minimum necessary for a team to remain in a city.

By this criterion, very few additional cities could support a team. New York City could probably support one more team with an attendance of 1.0 to 1.1 million in an average year. A few other cities without teams in 1973 could probably support one: the Washington, Toronto, and Newark areas all have populations sufficient to support a team, as does the new home of the former Washington Senators, Dallas–Fort Worth. A team of average quality should draw at least 1 million fans in these areas, assuming the availability of an adequate playing facility.

Many other cities that are often mentioned as possible expansion territories—such as Miami, New Orleans, Denver, Indianapolis, Memphis, Phoenix, and Buffalo—are not likely to be able to support a profit-seeking franchise. Three cities with teams in 1973 are also probably not viable franchise locations: Kansas City, Milwaukee, and San Diego. Atlanta and

22. Elsewhere I have argued at length against casual use of racial composition as an index of social problems. See Roger G. Noll, "Metropolitan Employment and Population Distribution and the Conditions of the Urban Poor," in John P. Crecine (ed.), *Financing the Metropolis: The Urban Affairs Annual Review*, Vol. 4 (Sage Publications, 1970), pp. 481–509 (Brookings Reprint 184).

23. Figure quoted to the author by both Baseball Commissioner Bowie Kuhn and Bill Veeck. This provides enough revenues to cover operating costs but no return to investment (and no interest payments should borrowed capital be used to pay for part of the purchase price of the franchise). Of course, this is only a rough estimate; the precise attendance required for break-even operations depends on ticket prices, broadcast income, and team costs.

Seattle, respectively a present and a former franchise site, are on the borderline of viability; both would normally be too small to support a team, but each has the advantage of access to a large regional broadcast audience, and Seattle is in addition close to another population center, Tacoma. Finally, one other area, San Francisco–Oakland, now has more franchises than it is likely to be able to support. Thus, the prospects for further expansion in the foreseeable future are not good. Judicious reshuffling of the existing franchises would probably locate teams in all of the areas that can support one.

The dim prospect for future expansion is a direct consequence of the gate-sharing arrangement used in baseball, whereby the home team keeps 80 (AL) to about 90 (NL) percent of the receipts. If revenues were split evenly, substantial expansion would be possible, even taking account of the smaller expected broadcasting revenues of teams in smaller cities. For example, a team in a city with 1.4 million metropolitan population would be expected to draw 900,000 fans at home if it finished twenty games behind the leader, a noncontending but respectable showing. The team would probably draw about 1.15 million on the road, about the average for all teams. With an 80–20 gate-sharing arrangement, the team would receive the revenues from 950,000 fans (720,000 at home and 230,000 on the road). If revenues were shared equally by home and visiting teams, the hypothetical team would receive the revenues from 1,025,000 fans. Under current rules, if the team drew 1 million fans at home (the minimum profit-making attendance), it would receive the revenues from 1,030,000 fans (800,000 at home, 230,000 on the road). If revenues were shared equally the team would need to draw only about 900,000 fans at home to maintain the same profits, thus reducing the minimum viable size for a franchise area from 1.9 million to 1.5 million population. If broadcast revenues were also proportionally lower, the minimum size would be close to 1.6 million. An even gate split would therefore make at least five, and perhaps seven, more teams financially viable, including only one (Milwaukee) of the four teams that, in 1973, appeared to have the worst prospects.

Basketball

Tables 4 and 5 report the results of an analysis of the factors affecting attendance at professional basketball games during the 1969–70 and

Table 4. Regression Results for Basketball per Game Attendance Correlated with Selected Variables, 1969–70 and 1970–71 Seasons[a]

	Coefficient	
Variable or summary statistic	Equation (1)	Equation (2)
Variable		
Constant	5,130	6,307
	(8.81)	(15.24)
Population[b]	545	−4,520
	(3.99)	(3.82)
Fraction of games won × population	...	2,740
		(3.23)
Black population[b]	...	−6,535
		(3.65)
Number of star players[c] × population	...	412
		(3.41)
Per capita income[b] × population	...	743
		(3.03)
Ticket price × population	...	−116
		(1.97)
NBA membership[d] × population	...	773
		(5.37)
Summary statistic		
R^2	0.242	0.861
$\overline{R}^2$	0.211	0.839
Degrees of freedom	50	44

Sources: Population, income, ticket prices, and stars, see Table 1; NBA attendance, 1969–70, box scores in *Sporting News*, relevant issues, and 1970–71, Harvey Pollack, *Philadelphia 76ers Press Guide* (Novelty Printing, 1970; processed); ABA attendance, tabulations supplied by the ABA, supplemented with site attendance data for 1969–70 from conversations with team officials; games won, *1970–71 Official American Basketball Association Guide* (Sporting News, 1970), *National Basketball Association Official Guide for 1970–71* (Sporting News, 1970), and box scores in *Sporting News*, relevant issues.

a. Attendance is measured by average attendance per game. The coefficients are the change in attendance per game from an increase of one unit in the corresponding independent variable. The numbers in parentheses are *t*-statistics.

b. Population in 1970 (in millions) and per capita personal income in 1969 (in thousands of dollars) are for the relevant SMSAs.

c. This variable is one greater than the number of stars, except it is zero for teams with no stars.

d. This variable is one for a team in the NBA, zero for a team in the ABA.

1970–71 seasons. Average attendance per game, rather than total season attendance, is used because of the variance among teams in the number of games played at home. The number of home games varies from thirty-two to forty-two, and some teams divide their home games among several cities.[24]

24. Like population, variation in number of games played raises the possibility of a heteroskedasticity problem; however, transforming the data for each team by the square root of the number of games played does not materially affect the significance of the coefficients in the regression.

Interpretation of the Results

While the results for basketball and baseball are broadly similar, some important differences do emerge. The most important is the weak relation between population and attendance in basketball.

POPULATION. When the other variables listed in Table 4 take average values, the second equation predicts attendance per game based only on the population of the metropolitan area. The resulting correlation between population and attendance is slightly positive in the National Basketball Association and slightly negative in the American Basketball Association. The probable source of this moderate correlation is the high correlation among the other variables in the table. If the true demand equation has a different functional form than that assumed in the statistical analysis, some of the true relationship between population and attendance is likely to be picked up in the other coefficients.

The single-variable analysis in equation (1) produces results that seem to be more reasonable, predicting that 1 million residents in a metropolitan area will add about 550 fans per game to attendance, on average, for both leagues. But several factors that are positively correlated with population—notably income, team quality, and league membership—also produce greater attendance, so that this result could be an overestimate.

For the NBA, at least, calculations similar to those performed for baseball can be made to estimate the minimum size of a metropolitan area that could support a franchise. To break even, a basketball team must average

Table 5. Coefficients for Basketball per Game Attendance, by Standard Metropolitan Statistical Area Population, 1969–70 and 1970–71 Seasons[a]

	SMSA population (*millions*)		
Variable	*1.5*	*3.5*	*12.0*
Constant	−473	−9,513	−47,933
Fraction of games won	4,110	9,590	32,880
Percent black population	−9,803	−22,873	−78,420
Number of star players	618	1,442	4,944
Per capita income	1,115	2,600	8,916
Ticket price	−174	−406	−1,392
NBA membership	1,160	2,706	9,276

Source: Derived by multiplying coefficients in equation (2) of Table 4 by SMSA populations of 1.5, 3.5, and 12.0 million.

a. See notes to Table 4 for dimensions of the variables.

either 8,000 fans per game and make the playoffs, or 9,000 fans per game without making the playoffs; this allows for no payments, not even interest, to investors, and neglects the effects of player depreciation on book losses and tax liabilities.[25] An NBA team of average quality in a city of 3.5 million with typical population and income characteristics would draw about 8,000 fans per game. Thus, a team of average quality would have to be located in a metropolitan area of nearly 3.5 million in order to break even, and then only if it made the playoffs.

As with baseball, this result depends upon the revenue-sharing practices within the sport. Basketball awards all gate receipts, less a 6 percent payment to cover league costs, to the home team. If revenues were split evenly, the high returns of teams in large cities and with winning records would make some teams drawing fewer than 8,000 fans per game financially viable. Unless more even gate-sharing arrangements are made, it appears that most professional basketball teams are located in cities too small to allow a team to show an operating profit.[26]

NUMBER OF STAR PLAYERS. In a metropolitan area of 2 million population—slightly below average for basketball—the first star player on a team's roster adds about 1,650 fans per game to attendance, not including his effect on the won-lost record.[27] For forty home games, this gives an increase in season attendance of 66,000. At a ticket price of $3, which is above average for the ABA but below average for the NBA, this represents nearly $200,000 in revenues. In addition, a star contributes to the winning percentage of his team. If he makes the difference between winning and losing in ten games during the season, he brings in another 690 fans per game, or 28,000 fans per season, thus generating an additional $84,000 in revenue. A small portion of this revenue must go to costs attributable to the additional fans, which, combined with rent, accounts for at most $1 of the $3 ticket price. But even so, the estimated total value of a star to the average team is at least $190,000 a year.

As in the case of baseball, the definition of a star was not very restrictive. The average number of stars per team was 1.1, with some teams having as many as three. Given their worth to their teams, it is not sur-

---

25. Based on financial data in Chapter 1.

26. Of course, tax advantages may still make most of these teams financially viable for their owners, even though they show operating losses. See Chapter 5.

27. As with baseball, when a regression was run with one variable for the first star and another variable for subsequent stars, the coefficient of the second was almost exactly half the coefficient of the first.

prising that, especially during the competition between the ABA and NBA, the annual salaries of many star players exceed $100,000. It is also not surprising that each year several rookie players receive very high salaries. If a star player can be expected to have a playing career of about ten years—three years more than the average for professional basketball —then three or four new stars begin their careers each year who, in a competitive environment, can command salaries of about $200,000 annually.

The very best players are, of course, worth much more than the average value of the twenty-five men identified as stars for the analysis reported in Table 4. For example, the Kentucky Colonels reported that the addition of Artis Gilmore to their roster has increased attendance by nearly 3,000 per game.[28] Buffalo reported a similar gain due to the acquisition of Elmore Smith.[29] Over a forty-game season, this will add approximately $250,000 (over arena costs) to the revenue of their teams. Furthermore, these players would be worth even more if they played in a large city. If, for example, Jim Chones develops into the superstar that the New York Nets expect him to be, he could be predicted to increase the Nets' attendance by over 190,000 because of his star status and by 130,000 if he increased the number of Nets victories by 10 percent. This would bring in additional net revenues of about $500,000 annually. Even if the Nets believed the chance was only fifty-fifty that Chones would become just an "average" star, he was still an even bet for the team at an annual salary of $250,000.

The preceding analysis indicates that basketball stars are probably not overpaid in relation to their value to a team, but it does not indicate whether they are overpaid in relation to their value to the sport at large. The contribution made to one team's victories naturally leads to an increase in another team's losses. If stars were equally distributed among teams, these effects would exactly offset each other, and the attendance gains of winners would balance the attendance losses of losers.[30] Consider-

28. *Washington Post*, Nov. 16, 1971.

29. Peter Carry, "Fortunes of a New Tough Cookie," *Sports Illustrated*, Vol. 35 (Nov. 22, 1971), p. 76. Contrary to published reports, the Buffalo gains are probably not entirely due to Smith, since the team also acquired other key players who improved its quality. Kentucky, however, had essentially the same team as the previous year, except for Gilmore.

30. Stars are not in fact evenly distributed. The average population of metropolitan areas having basketball teams is 2.87 million, while the average population of metropolitan areas weighted by the number of stars per team is 3.5 million. Thus,

ing the attendance gains attributable solely to "star quality," the presence
of the first star can be predicted to add, on the average, nearly 100,000
fans per season at home and some unknown number, probably close to
that amount, on the road. Subsequent stars add 50,000 to home attendance. Thus, the contribution to total league attendance of the average
star, one-quarter of whom are "second" stars, is somewhere between
85,000 and 180,000, accounting for a minimum increase in net revenues
(after game costs but neglecting his salary) of between $170,000 and
$360,000. In fact, since teams in large cities and with better records tend
to charge higher prices, the contribution of the average star is probably
greater than this. So, even when allowance is made for his effects on other
teams' attendance, the average star is probably not overpaid in relation to
his contribution to total league revenues.

TICKET PRICE. The statistical significance of the ticket price coefficient
in Table 4 is a pleasant surprise. The price data available from ticket brochures are notoriously unreliable, because basketball, more than any other
sport, engages in widespread ticket discounting. In 1970–71, one ABA
team actually realized less than $1 per fan in gate receipts, and several
other ABA teams realized under $2.[31] On the other hand, the richer NBA
teams engage in very little discounting. Thus, the ranking of all teams by
stated ticket price is essentially the same as the ranking by actual discounted price, and the coefficient in equation (2), while confirming the
negative relation between price and attendance, has little quantitative
significance unless the relationship between measured and actual ticket
prices is known.[32]

---

if a star increases the number of games won by his team, he will, on the average,
increase the attendance of his own team by more than he reduces attendance elsewhere. For example, if the average star increases his own team's won-lost record by
ten percentage points, he adds about 7,500 fans to the total season attendance of
the league.

31. See "Statement by Roger G. Noll and Benjamin A. Okner," in *Professional
Basketball,* Hearing before the Subcommittee on Antitrust and Monopoly of the
Senate Committee on the Judiciary, 92 Cong. 2 sess. (1972), Pt. 2, pp. 1042–56
(Brookings Reprint 258).

32. The data on average revenue per fan are not suited for use in the demand
equation for several reasons. First, local admissions taxes have been subtracted
from gross revenues. Tax rates differ among cities and must be counted in the price
paid by fans. Second, average revenue reflects the average price of seats actually
bought, not the average price of seats offered for sale. Since few teams are sold out
for most of their games, the distribution among price categories of tickets sold can
differ widely from the distribution of seats available. Third, average revenue may
be biased by overstatement of attendance, because teams may either overstate the

Table 6. Basketball Ticket Prices, by 1970–71 Season Attendance of Teams

Season attendance	Number of teams	Average ticket price (dollars)[a]
(I) Over 350,000	5	5.20
		(1.36)
(II) 300,000 to 350,000	5	3.80[b]
		(0.52)
(III) 200,000 to 300,000	6[c]	4.29
		(0.26)
(IV) Under 200,000	6[d]	3.87
		(0.90)
All teams	22	4.27

Sources: Same as Table 4 for relevant variables.
a. The numbers in parentheses are standard deviations.
b. $4.19 if Indiana and Kentucky are excluded.
c. Excludes San Diego.
d. Excludes Dallas and Virginia.

The tendency of the better teams to charge much higher prices is especially apparent. Table 6 groups according to 1970–71 season attendance the twenty-two teams for which price information was available.[33] The team with the greatest attendance—nearly 200,000 ahead of the next greatest—is the New York Knicks, who also charge the highest prices ($7.45 per seat, on average). Next most successful are the Lakers and the Bucks, who are the only other teams with average seat prices of $5.00 or more. A fourth member of Group (I) is the Chicago Bulls, who have a very low average price of $3.35; however, this figure is misleading because 40 percent of the seats at the Chicago arena have a poor or obscured view of the court. Two members of Group (II) are Indiana and Kentucky of the ABA, whose prices are the lowest in either league. But, again, this is misleading, since in both arenas nearly half of the seats are behind the backboard, the two highest fractions of such seats in professional basket-

---

number of fans in attendance or count last-minute give-aways, particularly to children's organizations. (One team reportedly once used the "first quarter" method of counting attendance: if the score at the end of the quarter was 34–27, attendance was reported as 3,427.) Fourth, when a game is sold out, ticket "scalping" usually occurs, so that some fans in attendance may have paid far more than the face value of the ticket. Thus, the actual price paid by fans for tickets could be significantly higher than average revenue to the team per person attending the game.

33. Data were not supplied by San Diego, then in the NBA, and Dallas and Virginia in the ABA.

ball.[34] Both Indiana and Kentucky are among the eight teams that tie for the highest prices in the ABA for good seats; however, all ABA teams charge less for good seats than the cheapest NBA team, Detroit, which also is the only team in the league that drew under 200,000 fans in 1969–70.

The data suggest that basketball teams charge profit-maximizing, rather than cost-plus, prices, though this conclusion must be somewhat tentative because so few basketball teams are securely profitable. However, even the pessimists agree that the four Group (I) teams are very profitable, and three of these charge amazingly high prices. The Knicks, in particular, must have amassed, over the years, the highest gross gate receipts of all professional sports teams, except the Mets and perhaps the Dodgers.

NBA MEMBERSHIP. The NBA dummy variable tests the value to ABA teams of merging with the NBA. It indicates that NBA membership is worth 1,500 fans per game in a city of 2 million population. How much of this is actually due to the membership status of a team and how much to differences between the leagues in team quality is impossible to estimate. Nevertheless, separate analyses of the two seasons combined in Table 6 shed some light on this issue. For 1969–70, the coefficient of NBA membership was 40 percent larger than that reported in Table 4 and had a t-statistic of 5.03, indicating that it was very important indeed in explaining attendance. In 1970–71, however, the coefficient was only about one-third the size of that in Table 4, with a t-statistic less than unity, indicating that NBA membership was not an important source of inter-team variation in attendance during that season.[35]

Since the ABA has been progressively more successful in signing the best players, it is reasonable to suppose that play within the league is getting better. If so, the single-season analyses suggest that the NBA membership variable is really a measure of quality, that quality differences between the leagues are disappearing, and that simply joining the NBA will not add materially to ABA attendance.

34. *Professional Basketball,* Hearing, p. 404.

35. The single-season regressions were, in general, quite similar otherwise. The star player variable in the 1969–70 regression and the team record variable in the 1970–71 regression were slightly less than conventionally acceptable. Despite the lack of significance of some variables, the correlation coefficient for the 1970–71 regression (corrected for degrees of freedom) was 0.870, and for the 1969–70 regression, 0.830.

If the values in Table 4 are accepted, the effect of NBA membership in a city of 1 million population is an estimated 773 fans per game. In the same equation, the effect of a winning team is 27 fans per game for each percentage point of games won. To calculate the total effect of merger requires combining the positive effect of NBA membership with the negative effect of losing more games. Assuming a realignment that called for each ABA team to play each NBA team twice (thirty-four interleague games), and assuming that the ABA teams won 30 percent of the interleague battles, the typical ABA team would win seven fewer games per season, meaning a decline of nine points in its percentage of games won. This, in turn, would lead to a drop in attendance of 247 fans per game. Thus, the net benefit for an ABA team of joining the NBA, under favorable assumptions about the significance of the league variable, is 526 fans per game, or 20,000 fans a year. Subtracting rents and admissions taxes, this is a net gain of $40,000 a year in revenues. The cost to ABA teams of joining the NBA is, by comparison, $125,000 annually for ten years.

After a few years the leagues would reach parity in playing strength; however, the net gain to an ABA team would still total less than $125,000 a year. Obviously, the ABA's desire for the merger must rest on more than its effect on attendance; it must lie instead in the possibility of lower costs and greater broadcasting revenues. At the time the merger was negotiated, the ABA did not have a national broadcasting contract for regular-season games, whereas the NBA did. The two leagues agreed to share in a combined broadcasting package when contracts effective at the time of merger expire.

PERCENTAGE OF GAMES WON. The quality of a team is extremely important in professional basketball. A comparison shows the relative importance of winning in baseball and basketball. A baseball team in a city of 2 million will increase its attendance by 0.4 percent of the average for the major leagues if it wins 1 percent more of its games. A basketball team in the same size city will, if it wins 1 percent more of its games, raise its attendance by 0.8 percent of the average for the sport. Thus, winning is roughly twice as important a factor in success at the gate in basketball as it is in baseball.

Whether this result is intrinsic to the sport is, of course, debatable. Possibly the fact that basketball teams vary in quality much more than baseball teams, at least in terms of their winning percentages, causes basketball fans to lose interest in poor teams more quickly. In other words, the positive correlation between attendance and quality can be offset if games are closer and more exciting, with the outcome more uncertain. Attempts to capture a "closeness of competition" measure for basketball comparable to the "close pennant race" variable for baseball were unsuccessful, but this may be due only to the fact that basketball divisional championship races are rarely close and, in addition, are relatively meaningless (in the years examined, both teams in a two-team race qualified for the playoffs). The winning percentages of teams also, of course, allow them to be ranked according to quality, and in the regression equation a decline in winning percentage is equivalent to a decline in the relative (as well as absolute) quality of a team. Whether fans of the best teams would be more or less willing to patronize them if relative quality rankings remained the same but the absolute quality differences between good and bad teams narrowed is an open question.

INCOME. The contrast between basketball and baseball is also particularly apparent in the relationship between income and attendance. In both cases income is about equally (and highly) significant in explaining attendance, and in both cases the relationship of the coefficient to average attendance is about the same—in a city of 2 million, a change of $1,000 in per capita income accounts for a change in attendance equal to about one-fourth the average attendance for the sport. But in basketball, the effect is positive, whereas in baseball it is negative; that is, baseball is more successful in cities with lower average income, while basketball is more successful in richer cities.

BLACK POPULATION. A very high, and very significant, negative correlation exists between the fraction of a metropolitan area that is black and attendance at basketball games. As with baseball, the size of the coefficient is too large to be reflecting simply a lower interest level among blacks, because, according to the equation, adding blacks to the population of a metropolitan area while keeping all other variables, including income and white population, constant leads to a lower predicted attendance. For the same reasons advanced in the discussion of baseball, part of the effect being measured here is probably the location of the arena. Cities with large black populations seem more likely to have arenas located in downtown neighborhoods that are less attractive to fans. At the same time, the data could reflect a combination of lower black interest combined with especially virulent white racism, for the same reasons advanced in the discussion of baseball.

Football

Of all professional sports, football is the one with the most obvious excess demand for its product. In 1970, roughly two-thirds of the National Football League teams were either completely sold out or within a few thousand fans per game of being so. This situation makes estimation of the demand for football very difficult, for no reliable measure of excess demand is available. Even the length of the waiting list for football tickets is not very useful, because the existence of a waiting list discourages some people from applying for tickets even though they would be willing to pay the price if tickets were available.

The results of the statistical analysis of the determinants of football regular-season attendance in 1970 are reported in Table 7. As is obvious, the capacity of the stadium explains nearly all the interteam difference in attendance. Since most stadiums, particularly the smaller ones, are sold out, the size of stadium capacity comes very close to predicting size of attendance. The only other factor that proved important is the record of the team in the previous year. And, since nearly all sales are for season tickets, it is only the previous year's record that can affect ticket sales. If a team's performance deteriorates during a given season, season-ticket holders cannot back out on their purchases; if a team improves, several games (with some empty seats) must pass before fans recognize the improvement and purchase the few remaining seats. Note that even though the past record is statistically significant, the magnitude of its effect is rather small. A team in a city of 2 million population that improves its record from 10 percent wins to 70 percent wins will attract only about 9,000 more fans a season. Even among the teams that are not always sold out, very few seats will become available if the team performs poorly.

The present excess demand for football is a recent phenomenon, which explains why adjustments to it—in terms of more games, higher prices, more team and leagues, larger stadiums—are still being made. As recently as 1968, only five teams were sold out, so that stadium capacity was not nearly so binding a constraint on total attendance. Table 8 shows the results of an analysis of 1968 attendance, using the same variables shown in Table 7; the difference in the results is, to say the least, striking. Several variables are statistically significant, and removing stadium capacity from

Table 7. Regression Results for Football Season Attendance Correlated with Selected Variables, 1970 Season[a]

Variable or summary statistic	Coefficient				
	Equation (1)	Equation (2)	Equation (3)	Equation (4)	Equation (5)
Variable					
Constant	62.2	68.4	61.5	63.6	338.7
	(1.82)	(2.14)	(1.87)	(1.93)	(10.09)
Population[b]	...	...	20.6	46.2	107.3
			(1.64)	(1.56)	(1.04)
Stadium capacity[c]	5.6	5.2	5.4	5.3	...
	(9.51)	(9.23)	(9.54)	(9.38)	
Previous record[d] × population	...	7.5	14.5	14.5	29.1
		(2.13)	(2.16)	(2.16)	(2.06)
Ticket price × population	...	...	...	−3.2	−7.6
				(0.96)	(1.01)
Percent sunshine[e] × population	...	...	−43.1	−48.5	...
			(1.88)	(2.05)	
Per capita income[b] × population	...	...	...	...	−13.4
					(0.84)
Summary statistic					
R^2	0.790	0.825	0.852	0.858	0.256
$\overline{R}^2$	0.782	0.810	0.823	0.823	0.114
Degrees of freedom	24	23	21	20	21

Sources: Population, income, and ticket prices, see Table 1; attendance, data supplied by the National Football League Players Association; stadium capacity, National Football League, *1970 Official Record Book* (NFL, 1970), pp. 353–78; previous record, ibid., p. 118; percent sunshine, *Statistical Abstract of the United States, 1970*, p. 186.

a. Regular-season attendance is measured in thousands of official paid admissions. The numbers in parentheses are *t*-statistics.

b. Population in 1970 (in millions) and per capita personal income in 1969 (in thousands of dollars) are for the relevant SMSAs.

c. Measured in thousands.

d. Fraction of games won in 1969.

e. Percent of sunny days during the season.

the analysis does not completely destroy its explanatory power. Unfortunately, the possible effect of ticket prices could not be estimated. 1968 prices could not be obtained, and the 1970 prices in Table 7 obviously reflect the substantial growth in the popularity of football (particularly among the old American Football League teams) in the intervening two years. Conclusions about the effects in 1968 of the other factors can, however, be drawn, since it is unlikely that in two years a massive shift could have occurred in the relative importance of the determinants of attendance.

Interpretation of the Results

Stadium capacity explains nearly half the interteam variance in attendance in 1968, although it is much less important than in 1970. In principle, stadium capacity is a constraint on attendance, not a factor in an individual's decision to attend, and should adjust, more or less, to the demand for games. It is apparent from equations (3) and (4) in Table 8 that stadium capacity is correlated with several of the other variables: the

Table 8. Regression Results for Football Season Attendance Correlated with Selected Variables, 1968 Season[a]

Variable or summary statistic	Coefficient				
	Equation (1)	Equation (2)	Equation (3)	Equation (4)	Equation (5)
Variable					
Constant	308.6	6.37	...	275.10	...
	(11.06)	(0.09)		(7.74)	
Population[b]	10.4	...	166.61	161.96	8.06
	(1.59)		(2.51)	(1.79)	(1.73)
Stadium capacity[c]	...	5.84	4.93	...	5.51
		(4.71)	(10.82)		(16.19)
Previous record[d] × population	...	...	70.42	102.54	...
			(3.22)	(3.66)	
Percent sunshine[e] × population	...	...	−104.14	−86.33	...
			(2.18)	(1.39)	
Per capita income[b] × population	...	...	−32.38	−39.14	...
			(2.24)	(2.06)	
NFL membership[f] × population	...	...	16.85	28.92	...
			(2.35)	(3.09)	
Summary statistic					
R^2	0.096	0.480	0.710	0.503	0.538
$\bar{R}^2$	0.059	0.458	0.638	0.378	0.519
Degrees of freedom	24	24	20	20	24

Sources: Population, income, and percent sunshine, *Statistical Abstract of the United States, 1970*, sec. 33 and Table 281; attendance, *World Almanac, 1970*, p. 851; stadium capacity and previous record, see Table 7.

a. Regular-season attendance is measured in thousands of official paid admissions. The numbers in parentheses are *t*-statistics.

b. Population in 1968 (in millions) and per capita personal income (in thousands of dollars) are for the relevant SMSAs.

c. Measured in thousands.

d. Fraction of games won in 1967.

e. Percent of sunny days during the season.

f. One if in NFL, zero otherwise.

old NFL teams and the teams with better records tend to play in larger stadiums. But these correlations only emphasize the adjustment of capacity to demand, since the old NFL teams and the teams with better records would tend to have greater demand for games. Equation (4) can thus be used to analyze further the demand for football games. It assumes (implicitly) that stadium capacity will adjust to demand, and hence it can predict long-run attendance when capacity is not a constraining factor. The simplified version of equation (4), in which coefficients of the explanatory variables are calculated for metropolitan areas of various sizes, is shown in Table 9.

POPULATION. As with the other sports, in football success at the gate is dependent on population, although the relationship is not as strong as in baseball. An additional 1 million in population will attract about 25,000 football fans per season, or about 7 percent of average attendance in the sport.[36]

INCOME. Football attendance, like baseball, is negatively associated with income; however, in this case the reliability of the result may be suspect. The negative coefficient reflects mainly the relatively high football attendance in the South, an area that has a lower average income. But since southern cities also have lower ticket prices, the income variable is probably picking up some of the effects of price.

WEATHER. Football is the only sport in which weather seems to be a significant factor in attendance: the fewer the number of sunny days, the greater the popularity of football.[37] Whereas the income variable picks up the popularity of football in the South, the sunny-days variable reflects its popularity in the Great Lakes area.

PREVIOUS RECORD. The past record of a team also is an important factor in attendance, especially in the large cities, although it is not as important as in basketball.[38] In a city of 1 million, a team that can improve its record by 25 percentage points will draw 26,000 more fans during the season (an 8 percent increase over average attendance). In a city of 3

36. In baseball, 1 million metropolitan residents add attendance equal to 20 percent of average annual attendance.

37. Baseball Commissioner Bowie Kuhn, in an interview with the author, hypothesized the importance of this variable for baseball; however, it is apparently important only in football. His reasoning was that areas with good weather have more recreational alternatives to professional sports contests.

38. In a city of 2 million, a gain of 1 percent in the won-lost record is worth about 0.6 percent in average season attendance, a ratio that is comparable to baseball's.

Table 9. Coefficients for Football Season Attendance, by Standard Metropolitan Statistical Area Population, 1968 Season[a]

Variable	SMSA population (millions)		
	1.5	3.5	12.0
Constant	517.9	841.9	2,218.6
NFL membership	43.4	101.2	347.0
Per capita income	−58.7	−137.0	−469.7
Previous record	153.8	358.9	1,230.8
Percent sunshine	−129.5	−302.2	−1,036.0

Source: Derived by multiplying coefficients in equation (4) of Table 8 by SMSA populations of 1.5, 3.5, and 12.0 million.

a. See notes to Table 8 for dimensions of the variables.

million, a similar improvement will add over 77,000 fans (a 23 percent gain). Because of the relatively even split of gate receipts, the entire league benefits if the big cities have good teams; the persistent strength of the New York, Chicago, Los Angeles, and Detroit teams indicates that this is generally the case, although Philadelphia is a clear exception.

LEAGUE MEMBERSHIP. Table 8 shows that, by the time the AFL and NFL had completed their merger, the difference in the drawing power of the leagues was significant but not great. Except for Oakland, New York, and Boston, the AFL teams were in smaller cities. AFL membership cost teams such as Kansas City and San Diego about 35,000 fans a year, and Oakland and Boston about 90,000.

UNIMPORTANT VARIABLES. Other variables that did not prove to explain attendance deserve mention. One is the number of stars on the team. Several methods of creating a star-player variable were tried—separating backs from linemen, offense from defense, and so forth—but nothing proved significant. A second insignificant variable is the number of competing professional sports teams, and a third is the percentage of the SMSA population that is black.

Implications for Expansion

The prospects for further expansion would appear to be particularly bright. Apparently a team can average as little as 35,000 fans a game and still turn a profit,[39] which is outside the range of prediction of the equation.

39. Based on the financial data in Chapter 1 (see especially Table 7).

Virtually any metropolitan area with about 1 million population probably could support a football team, making football viable in Indianapolis, Seattle, Phoenix, Anaheim, Tampa–St. Petersburg, Newark, San Jose, and Portland. Furthermore, additional teams could probably succeed in New York, Chicago, Los Angeles, Philadelphia, Detroit, and possibly Boston and Washington. Memphis and San Antonio fall somewhat short of the population standard; but because they are in the South and have relatively low average income, the equation in Table 8 predicts that they, too, could support a football team. This situation is a consequence of the gate-sharing arrangements in football, since such wholesale expansion would be financed to some degree by games in larger cities that attract more fans.

Hockey

The problems that arise in analyzing the determinants of hockey attendance are similar to those for football. Many hockey teams are sold out for every game; this is especially true for several old teams in the National Hockey League (NHL), which have been sold out for every game for several years. An additional complication is that a new league, the World Hockey Association (WHA), began operation in 1972–73. Attendance in the new league is unlikely to have found its long-run level in one year, and attendance in the NHL may have been temporarily destabilized by its emergence. Nevertheless, attempts to estimate hockey attendance in 1972–73 were surprisingly successful, as shown in Table 10.

Interpretation of the Results

The attendance data used to produce the estimates in Table 10 were the per game averages (for all teams in both leagues), as reported in the press, for roughly the first two-thirds of the 1972–73 season. Unfortunately, attendance figures reported in newspapers may be inaccurate; some teams may overstate attendance for public relations reasons, and some may include in the count those who received free tickets. Since the weaker franchises are most likely to misreport paid attendance, the possible distortion in the reported figures probably does not much affect the relative rankings of the teams by average attendance; instead, it just creates an underestimate of the interteam attendance differences.

Table 10. Regression Results for Hockey per Game Attendance Correlated with Selected Variables, 1972–73 Season[a]

Variable or summary statistic	Coefficient			
	Equation (1)	Equation (2)	Equation (3)	Equation (4)
Variable				
Constant	−3,132	−3,173	7,186	6,924
	(1.56)	(1.34)	(5.17)	(4.92)
Arena capacity	1	1	...	...
	(6.68)	(4.70)		
Fraction of games won[b] × population[c]	...	659	3,444	2,844
		(0.53)	(2.27)	(1.76)
Canadian team[d] × population	...	451	...	1,213
		(0.54)		(1.05)
NHL membership[e] × population	959	808	1,305	1,379
	(4.96)	(2.49)	(3.11)	(3.25)
Temperature[f] × population	−25	−23	−29	−31
	(5.29)	(2.12)	(1.89)	(2.00)
Sports competition × population	...	−40	−354	−268
		(0.25)	(1.72)	(1.22)
Close playoff[g] × population	...	−131	731	749
		(0.37)	(1.75)	(1.80)
Summary statistic				
R^2	0.808	0.821	0.604	0.624
$\bar{R}^2$	0.776	0.750	0.497	0.499
Degrees of freedom	23	19	21	20

Sources: Population, see Table 1; attendance and games won, *Sporting News*, relevant issues; arena capacity and temperature, *The World Almanac, 1972 Edition*.

a. Based on games played up to February 15, 1973. Since there were small differences among the teams in the number of home games played up to that time, average attendance per game was used as the dependent variable. One possible source of error, particularly in the measurement of the effect of NHL membership, was that attendance in the WHA was apparently growing during the season, so that the average attendance for the full year would be greater.

b. Calculated excluding ties. Again, combination of league data causes a problem, since the WHA plays overtime periods to break ties and the NHL does not, resulting in substantially fewer ties in the WHA. The decision to count only games ending in a victory for either side is based on the assumption that if the NHL had the same rule, each team would win about the same fraction of games in overtime as it wins during regulation play.

c. Population in 1970 (in millions) for the relevant SMSAs.

d. Variable is one if the team's home city is in Canada, zero otherwise.

e. Variable is one for NHL teams and zero for WHA teams.

f. Mean temperature during the month of December.

g. Variable is one for all teams within five points of fourth place in each division (as of February 15, 1973). (In hockey, league standings are determined by points instead of percentage of games won; a team receives two points for a victory and one point for a tie.) Third-place teams that led the fourth-place team by five points or less were considered to be in a close race for the playoff, and by this criterion roughly half the teams in hockey were judged to be in a close race. As with baseball, the choice of five points was not critical—any number between three and eight would have produced essentially the same results.

As Table 10 shows, the capacity of a team's arena is a very important factor in determining attendance. But, unlike football, the presence of the capacity variable does not destroy the explanatory value of all the other variables. Hockey in 1972–73 was similar to football in 1968 in that stadium capacity was the most important factor in an explanation of attendance, but an analysis that excludes it still produces a reasonably good explanation of much of the interteam attendance differences.

Equation (4) in Table 10 seems to offer the most useful results for the purposes of this analysis.[40] Table 11 shows the relationships between attendance and the variables in equation (4), calculated for three different assumptions about the metropolitan population of a team's home city. These two tables suggest several interesting conclusions about hockey attendance.

PLAYING SUCCESS. As in other sports, playing success and close competition are important in hockey. A team in an average-sized metropolitan area of 3.5 million can increase its attendance by nearly 1,000 fans per game if it wins 10 percent more games. With overall hockey attendance averaging about 10,000 per game, this increase represents 10 percent of average attendance, and so is roughly comparable to the importance of winning in baseball.

The nature of the hockey data makes estimation of the importance of close competition especially difficult. The spread in won-lost records is greater in the NHL than the WHA, but any attempt to measure this effect would be unsuccessful because it cannot be separated from the other effects of league membership. Past information for the NHL is not very useful, since the league had only six teams and one division during the years when competition within it was less imbalanced.

Three measures of competition that did not correspond closely to league membership were developed, and two produced similar results. The best results, reported in Tables 10 and 11, were obtained by making a variable of whether or not a team was a close contender for a spot in the league playoffs. Teams assured of making the playoffs and teams hopelessly be-

40. While two of the variables exhibit less statistical significance than would normally be required in such an analysis, there are good reasons to accept their importance. First, their influence seems relatively stable in several different statistical analyses, and their coefficients have reasonable values. Second, as in the other sports, the factors influencing attendance are highly interrelated, which causes an underestimate of the statistical significance of all variables. For instance, Canadian hockey teams win more games, have less competition from other sports teams, and are more likely to qualify for a playoff, thus making these variables highly correlated.

Table 11. Coefficients for Hockey per Game Attendance, by Standard Metropolitan Statistical Area Population, 1972–73 Season[a]

Variable	SMSA population (millions)		
	1.5	3.5	12.0
Constant	6,924	6,924	6,924
Fraction of games won	4,266	9,954	24,128
Canadian team	1,820	4,246	14,556
NHL membership	2,069	4,827	16,548
Temperature	−47	−109	−372
Sports competition	−402	−938	−3,216
Close playoff	1,123	2,622	8,988

Source: Derived by multiplying coefficients in equation (4) of Table 10 by SMSA populations of 1.5, 3.5, and 12.0 million.

a. See notes to Table 10 for dimensions of variables.

hind in the standings were thus differentiated from those still battling for third and fourth places in their divisions. Similar results, though with less statistical significance, were obtained from a variable that for each team was set equal to the number of teams in its division that were playoff contenders (that is, teams whose standing had not yet assured them of either making or not making the playoffs). Finally, attempts to measure the effect of a close race for first place in a division met with no success. Neither a division of a league nor a team contending for first place receives a measurable boost in attendance from a close race.

These results illustrate the effect of organizing a league so that the champion is determined by a playoff that includes a large proportion of the teams in the league. The best teams have higher attendance because of their above-average winning percentages, but the average teams also receive a boost in attendance because they usually are still in close competition for a playoff spot. In the NHL, the best teams win about 75 percent of their games (excluding ties). Having a winning percentage this much above average is worth about 2,500 fans per game in a city of average population. But even an average record, if the team is in a close race for the last playoff spot, is worth 2,600 fans per game in the same size city.

Unfortunately, it is only in hockey that the relation of attendance to a close playoff race can be measured, for it would be especially interesting to see if the same results held for all sports.[41] The only counterpart is the

41. The other two sports with extensive playoffs offer too little variation in the closeness of competition to make estimation of its effect feasible. In football, few teams are eliminated from playoff competition during the first two-thirds of the

close-pennant-race variable in baseball, which also proved to be important in explaining attendance. But there, since only one team in a division qualifies for the playoff, only the best teams benefit from uncertainty over playoff qualification. In hockey, and presumably also in football and basketball, if the latter could balance competition and the former could fill its excess demand, it is the average teams that benefit from a close playoff race.

HOCKEY AS A REGIONAL SPORT. The belief that hockey's appeal is regional received some verification in the analysis reported here. Two measures of regional interest were used: whether a team's home city was in Canada, and the average December temperature in a team's home city. Both appear to be important. In a Canadian city of 3.5 million, attendance will average, all other things being equal, over 4,000 fans per game higher than in the United States.[42] A city of similar size with a mean December temperature of 20 degrees will draw about 2,000 more fans per game than one with a mean temperature of 40 degrees.[43] The long hockey tradition in eastern Canada is obviously reflected in attendance figures for that area, and the spread of hockey's popularity has been more rapid and complete in regions where winter weather permits amateur hockey to be played more extensively.

SPORTS COMPETITION. The number of competing major-league teams in all sports also appears to affect hockey attendance. A team in an average-sized city that competes with one team in each of the other three professional sports will average about 2,800 fewer fans per game. This relation probably does not measure simply the direct competitive effect of other teams. Instead, it is a measure of the general availability of enter-

---

season; and, in any event, with excess demand for the sport creating a situation in which nearly all seats are sold on a season-ticket basis, the ability of attendance to respond to the closeness of a race is minimal. In basketball, competition has been too unbalanced to create uncertainty over the playoff positions. In 1972–73, the NBA attempted to change this by making a team's overall record, not just its position in the division, a qualifying factor for the playoffs, but even this failed to create any uncertainty over as much as one playoff spot by the time the season was a month old.

42. Since no Canadian cities are anywhere near as large as the five largest American cities, the values implied by the coefficient of the Canadian variable should not be taken too seriously when population becomes very large. The estimate that attendance per game in New York would be more than 14,000 higher if Gotham were moved 300 miles north is far outside the reliable range of prediction of the equation.

43. The mean December temperature averaged 30 degrees for all teams, with a standard deviation of 12.5 degrees.

tainment options and perhaps also an index of the diversity of sports interests in the city.

One other competitive factor was formulated as a variable that took the value of one if a team was located in a city with a team of the other league, and zero if it was not. This variable always had a positive sign—that is, more hockey competition was associated with greater attendance; it was less significant statistically, however, than the variables reported in equation (4) in Table 10.[44] Of course, it is unlikely that the direct effect of more hockey competition is to increase per game attendance. To the extent that this variable measures something of importance, it is testimony to the wisdom of the WHA in choosing to compete with the NHL in those cities where the demand for hockey was already greater than average (given population and the other factors that conventionally affect demand).

LEAGUE MEMBERSHIP. NHL teams have much greater attendance than WHA teams, but much of the attendance differential can be explained by factors other than league membership. According to Table 11, a city with the average (for hockey) population of 3.5 million will produce nearly 5,000 fans per game more for an NHL team than for a WHA team. This variable thus measures the difference in the overall attractiveness of the two leagues, reflecting partly differences in playing quality and partly the difficulties a new league has in marketing its product. The actual difference between the two leagues in average attendance per game is much greater than this figure, being in fact more than 9,000.[45] Nearly half the difference between the leagues can be explained by the size of the cities in which the teams play, the number of competing teams, and the fact that the WHA has placed a lower proportion of its best teams in its biggest cities.[46] In the two cities—Los Angeles and Boston—where both leagues have fielded teams of similar quality, attendance has differed by much less than the 9,000 per game average.[47]

44. Its t-statistic ranged between 0.26 and 0.68.

45. During the first two-thirds of the 1972–73 season, attendance averaged over 14,000 per game in the NHL and about 4,700 in the WHA.

46. The top two teams in each NHL division in 1972–73 were Montreal, New York, Chicago, and Philadelphia, and in the WHA they were New England, Cleveland, Winnipeg, and Houston.

47. In Boston the difference has been about 7,500 per game, but the WHA Whalers have had to play over half their games in the tiny Boston Arena. In Los Angeles, the difference has been about 5,500. This is less than equation (4) predicts in a metropolitan area of that size, but in 1972–73 the WHA Sharks had a better record than the NHL Kings.

A further attempt to measure a difference between the NHL divisions proved unsuccessful. Instead of using a single variable for league status, two were used, one for each division. Each took the value of zero for all WHA teams and for NHL teams in the other division of the league. The coefficients of both were essentially identical. This indicates that the attendance differential between the two divisions is explained by other factors, notably the quality of the teams.

POPULATION. The relationship between population and attendance, while complicated, appears to bear out the general tendency of larger cities to draw larger crowds. For an NHL team of average quality located in the United States and in contention for the playoffs, each 1 million in metropolitan area population adds 2,010 to attendance per game. In Canada, population has a more positive effect on attendance. In the WHA, it has less effect than in the NHL.[48]

As in baseball, a very poor team will actually do better in a smaller city. A WHA team that wins one-third of its games, is not a contender for the playoffs, and is located in the United States will draw 590 fewer fans per game for each additional 1 million people in its home city. In the NHL, a U.S. team must lose 94 percent of its games (excluding ties) before attendance begins to decline with larger population.

In order to estimate the minimum viable population for an NHL franchise, assumptions must be made about the team's playoff chances and the country in which it is located. If a team is in a close race for a playoff spot half the time, and over the long run wins as often as it loses, then the relationship between attendance and population for a U.S. team is 1,640 additional fans per game for each 1 million population. An American city of 900,000 population should draw about 8,400 fans per game, which is roughly the attendance required for break-even operations. In Canada, a similar team would draw an additional 1,200 fans for each 1 million population, so that the break-even population in Canada is about 520,000.[49]

According to these calculations, the WHA suffers from a problem similar to that of the ABA. Several of its franchise sites will not be viable even if the WHA becomes as attractive to fans as the NHL. Quebec City and

48. Equation (3) in Table 10, which excludes the national location of a team, perhaps offers a more plausible relationship between population and attendance. It predicts that for *all* teams in contention for the playoffs the increase in attendance produced by an additional 1 million in population is essentially the same—2,080 per game in the NHL—as the estimate for U.S. teams derived from equation (4).

49. The same calculation based on equation (3) in Table 10 results in a minimum population in either country of something over 700,000.

Edmonton are well below even the low Canadian standard for minimum viable population, and Ottawa and Winnipeg are doubtful. Of the WHA teams in the United States, only Houston appears to be of doubtful viability as a site for a hockey franchise (and that only because of its high mean December temperature). This means that nearly half the WHA teams are located in cities that may not be able to support a franchise, even if the WHA attains parity with the NHL.

In the NHL, Atlanta is the only questionable franchise location, because of its weather. Several cities now without a franchise, including Baltimore, Cincinnati, Columbus, Indianapolis, Milwaukee, and Newark, should prove able to support one, with Seattle in the borderline category. The two most recent additions to the NHL, Washington, D.C., and Kansas City, should also prove to be viable franchise sites.

The preceding analysis suggests that further increases in the number of hockey teams are probable. The WHA is likely to succeed, for most of its teams are located in areas that can support a team, and there are several viable alternative locations for the weaker WHA teams if the present sites should prove to be unsuccessful. The NHL is also likely to be able to add several additional franchises.

UNIMPORTANT VARIABLES. Three other factors that proved important in other sports were omitted from the hockey analysis.

First, per capita income was included in several analyses, but it proved to be statistically insignificant in all instances. Second, no attempt was made to construct a hockey counterpart to the superstar index developed in the other sports. Hockey fans are attracted to players for many reasons, one of which is their combativeness on the ice. Since expertise in fighting does not normally confer star status, there is no way to determine which players attract fans on this count without having a detailed knowledge of the game—which I do not have. In addition, at the time this analysis was undertaken, the WHA teams had not been playing long enough for a formal all-star roster to have been compiled.

Finally, information on ticket prices could be obtained for only a handful of NHL teams, so prices could not enter into the statistical analysis. Among those teams that did supply information, there was a slight, but statistically insignificant, positive correlation between prices and attendance, indicating that if any relation exists, it is that the more popular teams charge higher prices.

Some additional information on ticket prices was submitted as evidence in antitrust suits arising from the emergence of the WHA. In 1969–70, the second season after the NHL formed its Western Division of expansion teams, average ticket prices were $4.44 in the Eastern Division but only $3.96 in the Western Division. In the same year, attendance in the Eastern Division was over 50 percent higher than in the Western Division.[50] This conforms to the general pattern in sports, and adds more support to the view that sports enterprises are profit oriented, engaging in monopolistic, rather than cost-plus, pricing practices by charging higher prices in areas with greater demand.

Conclusions

The preceding analysis enables us to draw several conclusions about the role of attendance in the operations of sports teams.

1. In all sports there is a tendency for a team of any given quality to have greater attendance if it is located in a big city. Some qualifications to this conclusion must be made for basketball and hockey, which are more regional in appeal and in which conditions created by the rapid increase in the number of teams may still be clouding the true relationship between attendance and population. Nevertheless, in all sports, most of the teams in the half-dozen or so largest metropolitan areas are among the most successful, and few teams in these areas draw badly even when their record is poor. This suggests that the protection against competition each league gives to its teams prevents an economically viable increase in the number of teams in the largest cities. The only way demand for sports in large cities can be satisfied is by the formation of new leagues, but this can occur only when new teams are economically justified in several cities. Thus, the exclusive territorial rights of big-city teams act as an important restriction to competition that benefits teams at the expense of sports fans and players.

2. The pricing policies of teams do not appear to be motivated by any goal other than profits. Prices tend to be positively correlated with attendance, which indicates that team owners respond to higher demand by raising prices. If owners sought only to cover costs while maximizing the strength of the team, a positive correlation between attendance and prices would occur only to the extent justified by costs. But, as shown in Chapter 1, the best teams generally have the highest profits, indicating that owners

50. *Philadelphia World Hockey Club, Inc.* v. *Philadelphia Hockey Club, Inc.,* U.S.D.C. Eastern Pa., C.A. 72-1661 (1972), Exhibit 59.

raise prices above the level necessary to produce a team of high quality. In fact, the cost data indicate that a strictly cost-plus pricing policy, which would leave all profitable teams with about the same amount of total profit, would require a negative correlation between prices and attendance, at least among those teams operating in the black. Two teams appear actually to follow such a policy—Thomas A. Yawkey's Boston Red Sox and Philip K. Wrigley's Chicago Cubs, both of which have above-average attendance and charge the lowest prices in their leagues for teams of above-average quality.

3. In football and baseball, several cities that could support franchises do not have teams. The close control leagues exercise over the number of franchises awarded is thus denying baseball fans in cities such as Washington, Toronto, and Newark, and football and hockey fans in as many as a dozen cities, teams that would probably be economically viable. Furthermore, if baseball and hockey revenue-sharing arrangements awarded more of the gate to the visiting team, some franchises now in financial difficulty would become viable, and several other cities would become profitable sites for a franchise.

In basketball, the formation of a new league appears to have exhausted the number of cities that could support a team, although additional teams may be feasible in a few of the largest cities. In the absence of a merger between the ABA and the NBA, the ABA could be expected to attempt to compete for fans in cities such as New York, Los Angeles, and Chicago (assuming that the potential market for basketball in these cities is as great as the statistical analysis indicates) by expanding or by moving existing weak franchises. In hockey, the emergence of the WHA has served the same function that the ABA has in basketball, by establishing teams in several viable franchise sites that had been passed over by the NHL. No conclusions about the future of hockey leagues can be made until the following questions are answered: Will the WHA teams, with perhaps a few exceptions, survive and become profitable? And will the largely regional appeal of hockey grow into national popularity so that cities in the South and West become viable franchise sites? If the answer to these questions is yes, as early returns indicate, the competition between the two leagues will cause expansion to continue until essentially all of the viable franchise sites have teams, as appears to have happened in basketball.

4. In all sports, a winning team draws more fans than a losing one; and, at least in basketball and baseball, star players add significantly to

attendance. Furthermore, the importance of having a good team increases with the size of the city, so that owners of teams in larger cities have a greater financial incentive to produce a winner. Since teams in the same city will compete to some extent for the same fans, successful competition against a team in the same city produces greater rewards than against a team in another city. As a result, placing more teams in big cities will not eliminate the greater incentive for big-city teams to win. It will, however, affect the incentive of the entire league. While it would increase the total profits of a league to have one strong team in a big city, it would not pay to make all teams in the same big city strong, since the additional attendance a second strong team would capture would be largely at the expense of the first and would not, therefore, add to the total revenues of the league.

5. Despite their high salaries, star players in basketball and baseball are probably paid substantially less than they contribute to the revenues of their teams. In both sports, the player's star status generates revenues more than equal to his salary, even excluding the economic consequences of his effect on the won-lost record of his team and the additional attendance he generates at away games. These results support the view that the restrictions on competition among teams for players reduce the salaries of the best players, for in a competitive environment each team would be willing to bid for a player up to the point where his salary equaled his contribution to the revenues of the team.

Star players also draw many more fans in large cities than in small ones, so that big-city teams have more incentive to recruit and develop stars. The disparity in the value of stars is sufficiently great that a "second" star in a large city draws more fans than the "first" star in a small city. In a competitive environment, this would drive the salaries of stars up to an even higher level than they are at now, since there would be more big-city teams that would engage in competitive bidding for stars. For the same reason that increasing the number of big-city teams will not eliminate their incentive to win, the addition of stars to big-city teams will not reduce demand for them there.

6. In baseball and hockey, sufficient variance in the closeness of championship races was present to provide a rough estimate of the importance of uncertainty of outcome for attendance. The results indicate that a league benefits from lessening the quality differences among teams. While no proof is available that the other sports are similarly affected by closeness of competition, it is reasonable to suppose that they are. The playoff in football and basketball probably guarantees sufficient uncertainty about

the identity of the ultimate champion to diminish the effect of a runaway regular-season race. Nevertheless, leagues in all sports probably have not taken full advantage of the stimulating effect on attendance of closer competition. The leagues in which competition has been closest are the NFL and the National League in baseball, but it is not clear that this is the result of conscious actions of the owners.

For football, the shortness of the playing season and the frequency of injuries to key players may make the sport intrinsically more subject to uncertainty of outcome. In addition, the findings that stars are not a significant factor in explaining football attendance and that playing success, while statistically significant, does not account for a large fraction of attendance indicate that football owners have relatively little incentive to concentrate strength in big-city teams. Thus, the comparatively close competition in football is probably a consequence of the environment in which the sport operates, rather than of its institutional arrangements.

In baseball, the circumstances in which the National League operates do not appear to provide an explanation for its high degree of competitiveness. A baseball team owner has a strong incentive to improve the quality of his team beyond the point that maximizes league profits. The long playing careers of star players would seem to make the dominance of the sport by a single team relatively easy, as the history of the American League would suggest. And the long playing season makes it highly likely that a team of superior quality will win.[51] Why, despite all of these circumstances, the National League has remained remarkably competitive (while still keeping its big-city teams a little stronger, on the average) remains an intriguing but unanswered question.

51. Hockey has many of the same characteristics as baseball, and has also gone through long periods in which one or two teams were dominant.

CHAPTER FIVE

Taxation and Sports Enterprises

BENJAMIN A. OKNER

TO MOST PEOPLE "sports" simply means athletic contests. But professional sports is also a business that can generate substantial income for team owners and investors. Various provisions of the tax laws and regulations are advantageous to owners because they tend to make the true rate of return on investments substantially higher than it appears to be in accounting records. Team owners, of course, like other astute businessmen, attempt to minimize their tax liability by taking advantage of as many tax provisions as they can; indeed, they would (and should) be criticized by their stockholders or fellow investors if they did not. This chapter does not pass judgment on the morality of such actions. Instead, it is confined to an examination of the effects of some federal income tax provisions on the profitability of sports enterprises and an assessment of their implications for the sports industry.

The tax provisions examined include the basic tax statute and Internal Revenue Service (IRS) rulings and regulations that clarify and elaborate upon sections of the Internal Revenue Code (IRC). The Code itself does not treat professional sports enterprises specifically; it was written for, and applies to, all individuals and businesses. Like any other business, a team sums gross revenues, subtracts the ordinary and necessary costs of doing business, and pays income tax computed on the difference (taxable income) if it is positive. If taxable income is negative—that is, if costs exceed revenues—no income tax is paid.

This seemingly straightforward definition of net taxable income encompasses a multitude of thorny issues in the definition of both revenues and costs, most of which are the province of accountants. Economists generally agree that gross economic income should be defined as comprehensively

159

as possible and should include all revenues, from whatever source they are derived.[1] This implies, for instance, that the full amount realized from the sale of capital assets should be subject to tax along with all other income, and, on the cost side, that the value of the economic resources expended in producing this income should be offset against gross receipts. In many instances, the true economic cost may differ greatly from the cost calculated by the generally accepted accounting principles permitted by the Internal Revenue Code. Thus, firms in the extractive industries can take advantage of special tax provisions for depletion costs and intangible drilling expenses, while in residential real estate it is possible to use accelerated methods of calculating depreciation costs. Such costs are very different from the amounts that would be computed as the true economic costs of production in these industries. These differences are recognized by accountants and taken into account when certifying financial statements prepared for stockholders of publicly held corporations or for submission to government regulatory agencies. Thus, while accelerated depreciation or intangible drilling expenses would be shown as deductible expenses on a firm's tax return, they would be handled differently on a certified public statement.

This chapter examines most of the accounting practices that reduce (or defer) the tax liabilities of individuals or businesses to less than the figure that true economic cost and income would produce. The provisions that are most important to professional sports—the method of calculating the annualized cost of player contracts and the capital gains treatment of the disposition of assets—apply to other industries as well. Taxing profits from the sale of capital assets more lightly than other forms of income is, of course, a widespread practice in all sectors of the economy.

The amount of player contract cost that is properly charged as an expense against the current year's income is especially difficult for accountants to determine. Over the years, the Internal Revenue Service has issued different rulings on how to handle player acquisition costs, and, in fact, before 1967 the costs of acquiring baseball player contracts were fully deductible in the year of acquisition.[2] In 1967, the Internal Revenue Service reversed its earlier position and now requires that contract costs

1. The Sixteenth Amendment to the U.S. Constitution, which authorizes the individual income tax, states that "the Congress shall have power to . . . collect taxes on incomes, from whatever source derived. . . ." Similar language is found in sec. 61 of the IRC.

2. U.S. Internal Revenue Service, *Internal Revenue Bulletin: Cumulative Bulletin 1954-2* (1955), Revenue Ruling 54-441, p. 101.

be capitalized and written off over the asset's useful life. However, determining the useful life of a player is difficult, so the number of years over which the contract cost should be written off remains questionable. Another difficulty in determining the true financial status of teams is that very few American professional sports teams—14 of 96 in 1973—are publicly held corporations. The other clubs are not required to have certified financial statements prepared; so most financial data presented here are not audited and there is little reason to believe that the clubs are not writing off their player contract costs as rapidly as allowed by Internal Revenue rulings.

To the extent that the rate at which the cost of a player contract is written off diverges from the "true" rate at which its value declines, the use of depreciation in sports is similar to the use of accelerated depreciation on residential real estate,[3] which can often make profitable ventures appear quite unprofitable. A similar result may often obtain in sports. The difference is only that the use of tax provisions is not as highly publicized in sports as in other industries, and that fewer people are probably benefited.

Sports as a Business

In many respects, professional sports clubs are similar to other enterprises engaged in selling a service to the public. The club sells a service consisting of a sporting event produced jointly with another team. The production elements include players, trainers, coaches, and managers; playing equipment; a facility to house the contest and spectators; the entrepreneurial skill to organize and finance the enterprise; and some mechanism for arranging the contests (the only element unique to sports).

Team Assets

Aside from a small amount of equipment (and a stadium for teams that own their facilities), one of a club's two major assets is its right to the services of players. The club's contracts with its players derive their value from the restrictions on competition for players imposed by league

3. Before enactment of the Tax Reform Act of 1969, accelerated depreciation was generally available for all real estate. Since then, depreciation on new, nonresidential real property has been limited to the amount calculated using the 150 percent declining-balance method.

rules. The value of a contract is determined by the extent to which the club's exclusive right to bargain with the player keeps his salary below what the club would have to pay in a competitive environment. In practice, as noted below, the accounting values of the contracts are assigned arbitrarily. The other major asset owned by a sports club is its "franchise." Franchises give clubs certain privileges, including the right to be the sole provider of league contests within a specific geographic area.[4] Consequently, the market power generated by the team franchise is of considerable economic value.

Some idea of the magnitudes of team assets in basketball can be obtained from Table 1. It is evident that the allocation of a team's assets varies widely both among teams in the same league and between the two leagues. Player contracts represent a larger proportion of assets for National Basketball Association (NBA) teams than they do for American Basketball Association (ABA) clubs. This is because the NBA clubs have generally been in existence longer than the average ABA club, so the player cost represents purchases of contracts over a longer period of time. The newest NBA teams have the greatest percentage of total cost allocated to player contracts, since these clubs, created by league expansion in 1970, purchased players from the existing teams.

Sports Profits and Franchise Prices

The limited financial data available to the public do not indicate that professional sports teams show large accounting profits. For 1970, it was estimated that seven of the twelve American League baseball teams suffered losses.[5] In basketball, all of the ABA teams and twelve of the fifteen NBA teams for which information is available showed accounting losses for the 1970–71 season.[6] Substantially the same picture emerges from another survey,[7] which estimated that only twelve of the twenty-four

---

4. For example, no new football team can locate within seventy-five miles of an existing franchise without the latter's permission. When the New York Jets entered the National Football League in 1966, the Giants were granted compensation totaling several million dollars for invasion of their territorial rights.

5. "Who Says Baseball Is like Ballet?" *Forbes*, Vol. 108 (April 1, 1971), p. 30.

6. "Statement by Roger G. Noll and Benjamin A. Okner," in *Professional Basketball*, Hearing before the Subcommittee on Antitrust and Monopoly of the Senate Committee on the Judiciary, 92 Cong. 2 sess. (1972), Pt. 2, p. 992 (Brookings Reprint 258).

7. "Pro Sports: A Business Boom in Trouble," *U.S. News & World Report*, Vol. 71 (July 5, 1971), p. 58.

Table 1. Franchise and Player Contract Costs of Basketball Teams Operating in 1971

Team[a]	Cost of team (thousands of dollars)			Player contracts as percentage of total costs
	Franchise	Player contracts	Total	
American Basketball Association				
A1	250	0	250	0
A2	100	885	985	89.8
A3	n.a.	n.a.	n.a.	n.a.
A4	15	280	295	94.9
A5	200	1,350	1,550	87.1
A6	172	280	452	61.9
A7	20	0	20	0
A8	n.a.	n.a.	606	n.a.
A9	425	373	800	46.6
A10	255	0	255	0
A11	6	100	106	94.3
All ABA teams	1,443	3,270	5,319	69.4
National Basketball Association				
N1	250	250	500	50.0
N2	1,100	4,500	5,600	80.4
N3	1,035	4,140	5,175	80.0
N4	400	3,200	3,600	88.9
N5	400	3,037	3,437	88.4
N6	50	1,200	1,250	96.0
N7	416	600	1,016	59.1
N8	200	478	678	70.5
N9	465	3,170	3,635	87.2
N10	101	1,056	1,157	91.3
N11	100	0	100	0
N12	180	1,727	1,907	90.6
N13	331	3,166	3,496	90.5
N14	25	0	25	0
N15	50	2,990	3,040	98.4
N16	0	23	23	100.0
N17	150	1,284	1,434	89.5
All NBA teams	5,253	30,821	36,073	85.4

Source: "Statement by Roger G. Noll and Benjamin A. Okner," in *Professional Basketball*, Hearing before the Subcommittee on Antitrust and Monopoly of the Senate Committee on the Judiciary, 92 Cong. 2 sess. (1972), Pt. 2, p. 1000 (revised, with supplementary information) (Brookings Reprint 258). Figures are rounded.

n.a. Not available.

a. Teams are not identified in the material published by the Subcommittee; the notation used here is the same as that in the Subcommittee report.

major-league baseball teams and nine of the twenty-eight basketball teams made a profit or broke even in the 1970 season. Hockey and football appear to be more profitable: eleven of the fourteen major-league hockey teams and all twenty-six football teams probably either made money or broke even.[8]

Sports ventures are obviously risky undertakings. Some teams in all sports do well financially, but many teams, according to their financial statements, either just break even or lose money. Consequently, it seems difficult to understand why a rational investor would buy such an enterprise at any price. Moreover, current owners might be expected to be anxious to sell their clubs—or even give them away—in order to cut their losses on a bad investment.

Yet, in the face of large book losses, expansion clubs and new leagues are being formed, and the values of established clubs (as measured by sales prices) are generally rising. In basketball, for example, where information is available about five transfers of ownership from 1965 to 1971,[9] the total difference between the sales prices and original costs of the five teams was $7.9 million. The increases in value per team ranged from about $300,000 to $3.8 million, yet not one of these teams showed an accounting profit during the period between sales. The values of baseball franchises have also increased greatly. *Forbes* estimated that the aggregate increase in franchise value since acquisition was between $74 and $122 million for American League baseball teams and between $46 and $160 million for National League teams.[10] These data indicate an average increase in franchise value of $6 to $10 million per club in the American League and $4 to $13 million per club in the National League.[11]

The apparent contradiction between profitless operations and rising franchise prices can be explained, in part, by the accounting practices that arise from the tax provisions available to sports enterprises. Even more of the contradiction is explained if the additional tax advantages that accrue to wealthy individuals and profitable corporations through team ownership are taken into account. These advantages stem from the fact that the amount of income that can be sheltered from tax by writing

8. Ibid.
9. Noll-Okner testimony, pp. 998–99.
10. "Who Says Baseball Is like Ballet?" p. 30.
11. A notable exception to the general pattern of increasing franchise prices was seen in the 1973 sale of the New York Yankees for $10 million, which was $3.2 million less than the team cost the Columbia Broadcasting System, its former owner (*New York Times*, Jan. 4, 1973).

off the value of player contracts usually exceeds the operating profits that can be earned by the team even if it is exceptionally well managed. Consequently, the true profitability of a franchise can be much greater than the published, "bookkeeping" amount. In some cases, however, the actual losses of teams are large. For some owners, a team may provide nonpecuniary benefits that offset low profits or even actual losses. Nevertheless, the apparent irrationality of even the *worst* sports investment is largely explained by the effects of full utilization of the available tax benefits.

Tax Treatment of Player Contracts

Sports clubs appear to be unique in their accounting treatment of employee contracts: no other industry treats employment contracts as capital assets of the enterprise.[12] Since the team's contracts with its players usually comprise a substantial part of its total assets, the manner in which these contracts are acquired and treated for tax purposes has an important effect on its financial position and tax liability. Because the method of valuing a player contract depends on how it is acquired, the cases of newly purchased teams, expansion clubs, and established teams are examined separately.

Purchasing an Established Team

If an existing team is sold to new owners, the valuation of contracts will be based on the actual price paid for the club. Suppose a group of businessmen pays $2 million for a basketball team. For this amount, the new owners acquire (1) the team's franchise; (2) the player contracts owned by the team; and (3) a few other assets, such as equipment and office furniture. In establishing an accounting system, the new owners must allocate the $2 million among these three asset groups.

A club normally allocates as large a share as possible to the player contracts, because they may be depreciated[13] over their estimated useful

12. Of course, businesses may capitalize and write off for tax purposes many other intangible assets, such as contracts involving leasehold improvements, customer lists, covenants not to compete, and other types of contracts that create an intangible asset with a determinable useful life.

13. Actually, contracts are intangible assets and are therefore amortized rather than depreciated; but the depreciation terminology is used here because it is more familiar.

life in computing taxable income.[14] Hence, the greater the proportion allocated to contracts, the smaller the club's taxable profits. The percentage of the total cost allocated to player contracts, as well as the useful life over which their cost may be depreciated, are subject to review by the Internal Revenue Service, but the probability of a resulting adjustment appears to be low. For example, the relatively complete financial information available for basketball teams for the period 1967–71 (a total of ninety-seven team years) reveals only one Internal Revenue Service audit. In that case, the allocation of initial cost to player contracts was lowered from 90 percent to 50 percent.[15] Another instance of IRS examination resulting in a change in allocation involves the Atlanta Braves. When the team moved to Atlanta in 1966, they allocated about $5.5 million, or 99 percent of the total cost, to player contracts. However, the team's 1970 financial report stated that after IRS examination, a tentative agreement had been reached to increase the amount initially allocated to the franchise by $450,000. This would reduce the proportion of cost initially allocated to player contracts from 99 percent to about 90 percent.[16]

If the team's profit, after the deduction of player contract depreciation, is negative, it will pay no income tax. If it is organized as a corporation, the loss may be carried forward for up to five years to offset any taxable income earned in that period. If the team is a small business corporation (under Subchapter S of the IRC) or a partnership, the current year's loss, subject to certain limitations, will be distributed among the owners and can be used by each to offset other taxable income on individual income tax returns.[17]

To illustrate these possibilities, assume that the new owners of the

14. Specific rulings to this effect actually exist only for baseball and football, but the same procedures are followed in the other sports. See U.S. Internal Revenue Service, *Internal Revenue Bulletin: Cumulative Bulletin 1967-2* (1968), Revenue Ruling 67-380, p. 291, and *Internal Revenue Cumulative Bulletin 1971-1* (1971), Revenue Ruling 71-137, p. 104.

15. Noll-Okner testimony, p. 1000.

16. Atlanta Braves, Inc., "1970 Annual Report," note 2 to "Consolidated Financial Statements, October 31, 1970."

17. This assumes that the investment of the owners is large enough to enable them to take the net loss on their individual income tax returns. In a partnership, a partner's distributive share of partnership loss for any year is limited to the adjusted basis of his interest in the partnership at the end of the partnership year (IRC, sec. 704(b)). A shareholder's portion of the net operating loss of a Subchapter-S corporation for any taxable year is limited to the sum of the shareholder's equity in the corporation and the indebtedness of the corporation to the shareholder (IRC, sec. 1374(c)(2)).

hypothetical team allocate $1.5 million of the $2 million price to player contracts and depreciate them over a five-year period. Since straight-line depreciation must be used for intangible assets, the annual depreciation expense will be $300,000. If the net income of the team before depreciation is $100,000, the depreciation deduction will result in a $200,000 net loss. This loss is distributed among the owners (assuming the club is a partnership or Subchapter-S corporation) and is reported separately by them for individual income tax purposes. If the owners' taxable incomes from other sources are high enough to place them in the 70 percent marginal tax bracket, every dollar of this loss will reduce their personal tax liability by 70 cents.[18] Under these circumstances, the $200,000 net loss reduces the taxes for which they otherwise would be liable by $140,000. Thus, the owners will realize $100,000 in cash-flow profits and $140,000 in personal tax relief, for a total cash-flow return from the team of $240,000—the team, meanwhile, reporting a $200,000 bookkeeping loss. This situation is shown in Table 2. Even with a book loss of $800,000, which implies an actual loss of $500,000 in the team's cash flow, an owner's after-tax position is $60,000 better than a nonowner's. In fact, the book loss of the team in this example would have to be almost $1 million before the owner experienced an actual deterioration in his personal after-tax cash position. Any actual investment situation would, of course, be much more complex than these hypothetical cases, but the fundamental point of the example—that bookkeeping and cash-flow results are not necessarily the same—holds.

The example also serves to illustrate the difference between "economic cost" and "accounting cost." When a business acquires a depreciable asset, its value is normally the amount paid for it, which, in turn, represents the cost of the economic resources that were used up in producing it. This economic value depreciates (is used up) during the asset's useful life, so the loss in value is properly deducted from gross receipts to determine the net income from production.

When an established team is purchased, as in the example, the amount allocated to the player contracts does not represent the true economic cost of the asset's "development or construction," but is instead simply an arbitrary proportion of the owners' total investment. In contrast to the practice in other industries, the amount deducted each year as deprecia-

18. This assumes that they are subject to the maximum marginal tax rate under the federal individual income tax. Since the marginal rates start at 14 percent, a dollar of loss might theoretically reduce personal tax liability by only 14 cents.

Table 2. Before-Tax and After-Tax Financial Status of a Hypothetical Sports Team Owner and Nonowner

Thousands of dollars

Item	Nonowner	Team owner, assuming	
		$200,000 book loss	$800,000 book loss
Taxable cash income other than from team	1,000	1,000	1,000
Less team book loss[a]	...	−200	−800
Taxable income	1,000	800	200
Actual cash flow from team	...	100	−500
Total before-tax cash income	1,000	1,100	500
Less individual income tax[b]	−671	−531	−111
After-tax cash income	329	569	389
Effect of team ownership on after-tax cash position	...	240	60

Source: Calculated from provisions of the 1972 Internal Revenue Code. Figures are rounded.

a. After deduction of $300,000 depreciation on player contracts.

b. Based on rates in the 70 percent bracket for married couples filing joint returns, and assuming that "other" taxable cash income does not include any net long-term capital gain or other items subject to preferential tax treatment. It is also assumed that the 50 percent maximum tax on earned income is not applicable.

tion is related neither to what the team might actually have to spend to replace the players nor to their economic value to the team's success during their useful life. Thus, in the example above, the new owners might well have allocated only $500,000 of the total cost to player contracts (perhaps as a compromise with the IRS). Still assuming a five-year useful life, the annual depreciation would then be reduced from $300,000 to $100,000, which would lead to a break-even position rather than a $200,000 loss after depreciation. Yet this would still not affect the club's *actual* financial performance. It would, however, affect the owners, who would suffer a $140,000 loss in their after-tax cash position.

Purchasing Player Contracts from Other Teams

When the contract of a player is purchased from another team, the tax treatment is essentially the same as when an entire team is bought. The amount paid for the contract is taken as its initial book value, and this is then depreciated over the expected duration of the player's career. The only difference from the purchase of an entire team is that no arbitrary allocation of costs between player contracts and the franchise is involved.

Although established teams frequently buy and sell player contracts, the practice is most apparent when a new team is created through expansion, since the expansion team must acquire its roster of players by purchasing contracts from the established teams in the league. The expansion team receives authorization to operate in a designated place, and in return it pays a fee to the league. A small part of this sum is shared by league members as payment for the franchise and is not depreciable. The remainder is distributed as payment for player contracts, and is treated as a depreciable asset,[19] so that most of the cost of an expansion team can be written off as depreciation expense during the first few years of its operation.[20]

One of the recent NBA expansion teams, for example, paid about $3.0 million for its franchise. It allocated $2.5 million, or about 83 percent of the total, to its player contracts and wrote off this amount over eighteen months. Thus, nearly two-thirds of the cost was depreciated during the team's first year of operation. In summary form, the accounting statement for the first year was as follows:

Item	Amount (thousands of dollars)
Revenue	
Gate receipts	958
Sales of players	260
Total	1,218
Costs	
Other than player depreciation	1,245
Player depreciation	1,575
Total	2,820
Book loss	− 1,602

According to the books, the team lost $1.6 million during its first year of operation. But, in terms of cash-flow income, the situation is not quite so bleak. In addition to the $1.6 million depreciation cost, there was $0.3 million in deferred salaries and other noncash expenses for the year. By taking advantage of these deferred expenses and the player depreciation, the team turned the $1.6 million loss into a $0.3 million cash-flow

19. *Internal Revenue Cumulative Bulletin 1971-1,* Revenue Ruling 71-123, pp. 227–28. This ruling was made for football, but it would undoubtedly apply to other sports.

20. Since the established teams can protect their better players from purchase by an expansion team, the quality of players on new teams is initially well below the league average. Because of this, the useful life of the players is short, and the team is justified in depreciating their costs over a short period of time.

profit. And if the tax benefit to the owners from the $1.6 million book loss is calculated at a modest 50 percent tax rate, the $1.6 million loss is converted into a $1.1 million profit![21]

Acquiring Player Contracts through Negotiation with New Players

Except in the case of recent expansion teams, most player contracts were not acquired through purchase of a franchise or even through trades or sales of players. Rather, they were acquired after negotiations between a team and a potential player. A new player may be acquired by a professional team in one of two ways: first, especially in baseball and hockey, he may be signed to play in the minor leagues until the major-league club feels he is sufficiently proficient to play in the big leagues; second, he may be signed to begin playing immediately for the major-league team.

The size of the bonuses that new players may receive when they are signed by a team has caused considerable public confusion. It is true that many basketball players have received $1 million or more in their initial contracts, and, with the formation of the World Hockey Association in 1972, multimillion dollar contracts also began to appear in hockey.[22] But the highly publicized $1 million contract is usually more precisely a "$1 million package," which may include such perquisites as an interest-free loan, a new automobile every year or two, and a cash bonus. In most cases, the player's salary for the duration of a multiyear contract represents a large proportion of the value of the package. Cash bonuses are usually very small.[23]

For tax purposes, a team is expected to capitalize signing bonuses and write them off during the useful life of the players' contracts. Although it

21. Noll-Okner testimony, p. 1036. While these are actual figures for an existing NBA team, the team may be required to change its allocation and/or write-off period upon examination by the IRS.

22. The record shows that large financial inducements for players prevail only as long as leagues compete for their services. For instance, the heyday of large football payments ended when the two leagues merged in 1966 and adopted a common player draft. Similarly, large rookie bonuses all but disappeared in baseball when the free-agent draft was instituted. The maximum bonus in baseball is now probably in the $10,000 to $14,000 range.

23. For example, of the fourteen top ABA rookies signed in 1971, only ten received a bonus. The payments ranged between $7,500 and $55,000 and averaged about $31,000. Besides the signing bonus, the average package involved a three- to five-year contract (although one player signed for a ten-year period) at an average annual salary of $77,000 and other allowances valued at $18,000. Six of the fourteen also had contract provisions for deferred compensation averaging $343,000 annually for periods after expiration of their initial contracts.

is hard to know exactly what teams actually do, some bonuses probably are treated as a current expense rather than being capitalized and depreciated. For example, in 1969 the former Los Angeles Stars basketball team expensed $125,000 in player signing and acquisition costs.[24] The Baltimore Orioles' financial statement for 1970 showed a deduction of $1.3 million for team replacement expenses. The statement also contains the following explanatory note:

The Internal Revenue Service requires the cost of purchased player contracts together with payments of certain types of bonuses to be capitalized and amortized over the estimated number of years that the individual player can reasonably be expected to play. The Company, however, has always charged these type expenditures to operations as they were incurred and is continuing to do so.[25]

Undoubtedly, the rare very large cash bonus is capitalized, but small ones may not be.[26] The paucity of publicly available financial information makes it impossible, however, to assess the extent of this practice.

If a team does expense bonus payments, its net income and tax liability for the year will not normally be appreciably affected. For example, approximately 1,100 new players were signed each year in professional baseball from 1965 to 1968.[27] The average bonus was about $4,400, and among drafted players it was about $7,500. The standard baseball contract is for one year, and most first contracts are not renewed. Since the average bonus amount is quite small and would be written off over a short period, whether it is expensed or capitalized has little effect on annual expenses as long as the team's experience in writing and renewing new contracts does not vary much over a period of years.

The principal effect of capitalizing the bonus is on the book values of player contracts, for without capitalization they will always be zero.[28] This,

24. Material submitted by James J. Kirst, former owner of the Los Angeles Stars, in *Professional Basketball,* Hearing, Pt. 2, p. 597.

25. Baltimore Baseball Club, Inc., and Subsidiary, "Report to Stockholders, October 31, 1970."

26. One team official said in a personal interview that his practice was to expense bonuses of $20,000 or less and capitalize those over $20,000.

27. All data cited here are from testimony presented in *Curtis C. Flood* v. *Bowie K. Kuhn et al.,* 316 F. Supp. 271 (S.D.N.Y. 1970).

28. For example, from 1958 to 1969, average total bonus payments per major-league baseball team were about $280,000 annually. Assuming a steady flow of expenditures and a four-year depreciation period, the amount written off in any one year would be $280,000—$70,000 for the current year and $70,000 from each of the three preceding years. So the effect on net income and tax liability is the same whether the bonus payments are depreciated or expensed, although with capitalization the book value of all player contracts will be $420,000 in any year.

in turn, affects a team's income and tax liability only if the player's contract is sold. If the bonus has been treated as an expense, the income from sale of the contract will be taxed mainly at capital gains rates rather than at the higher rates applying to ordinary income.[29] If the bonus has been capitalized, income from the sale, up to the amount of depreciation claimed on the contract, is subject to "depreciation recapture"—that is, it is taxed as ordinary income. Only the amount by which the price of the contract exceeds the depreciation taken on it is taxed at capital gains rates. Thus, to the extent that bonuses are expensed and player contracts are sold, teams may avoid or defer tax payments.

The avoidance of depreciation recapture can be very important when leagues expand. In 1968–69, each baseball league expanded from ten to twelve teams. Each of the two new American League clubs paid $5.25 million to the established teams for the right to draft thirty players, while the two new National League teams paid $6 million each for thirty players (plus an additional $4 million each for the franchise). This yields an average payment of $175,000 per player in the American League and $200,000 per player in the National League. Although documentation is impossible, it is likely that the selling teams paid only capital gains tax on much of the $30.5 million total. The 1968 income statement of the Atlanta Braves shows net extraordinary income of $1.4 million resulting from the sale of players in the expansion ($2.0 million less tax of $0.6 million). Similarly, the Baltimore Orioles reported net extraordinary income of $0.7 million ($1.0 million less tax of $0.3 million). The 30 percent tax rate reported on these transactions was the maximum alternative capital gains rate for corporations in prior years, and the team's published financial statements do not indicate that there was any depreciation recapture in connection with the sales.[30]

29. Part of the income may be subject to ordinary tax rates on the grounds that the signing expense reduced income subject to ordinary rates in prior years. See U.S. Internal Revenue Service, *Internal Revenue Bulletin: Cumulative Bulletin 1968-1* (1968), Revenue Ruling 68-104, p. 361, for an application of the tax benefit rule relating to the treatment, at the time of sale, of assets that resulted in a reduction of ordinary tax in prior years. This treatment is similar to the recapture of excess depreciation discussed below except that there is, of course, no depreciation to recapture if the asset was expensed.

30. The Braves' financial statement, however, notes that their treatment of the sale was questioned by IRS examiners and that they may be liable for additional tax on the transaction. Before 1967, it was common practice for clubs to treat as expense the amounts paid for player contracts, but this practice was supposed to end with the issuance of Revenue Ruling 67-380. When the expansion took place

Acquiring Player Contracts through Trades

When player Jones on Team A is traded for Smith on Team B, Jones's contract and depreciation costs stay with Team A and are applied to Smith, who was acquired in place of Jones. Smith's cost and depreciation stay with Team B and are applied to Jones, who was acquired by Team B in the trade.[31]

The tax situation is more complicated when a player is traded for another team's draft choice rather than an active player. For example, assume that player Jones's adjusted value on Team A's books is $25,000 (derived by subtracting past depreciation of $400,000 from a $425,000 initial cost of his contract). Even if Jones is traded for one or more of Team B's draft choices rather than a player, the transaction would probably still be considered a tax-free exchange of like property. Since a draft choice has no tax cost, Team A will wind up with an asset with a $25,000 *book* value (the draft choice), and Team B will wind up with Jones's contract with a basis of zero. The owners of Team B would find this transaction especially attractive if they were planning to sell the club or to improve their cash flow by selling player contracts. After the transaction, Jones's contract would have a book value of zero, so the proceeds from its sale by Team B would be subject only to capital gains tax.

Tax Treatment of Asset Sales

When all or part of the assets of a team are sold, taxes must be paid on any profits realized. As in any other business, the total gain on a sale is computed as the difference between the sales price and the cost or adjusted basis of the assets sold.[32] Part of the total gain may then be subject to capital gains tax rates and the remainder taxed as ordinary income.

---

in 1968–69, the IRS had just issued Ruling 68-104, which created uncertainty about the extent of ordinary tax treatment required on the sale of player contracts during expansion. Presumably, there will be stricter adherence to the rulings (and a greater degree of ordinary tax treatment) for such transactions in the future.

31. This would be considered a tax-free exchange of like property under IRC, sec. 1031. Sometimes cash is also involved in the trade, in which case the amount of cash represents the maximum capital gain on the transaction.

32. The adjusted basis is generally equal to original cost less any depreciation previously charged against the asset.

Excess Depreciation Recapture

The "depreciation recapture" provision of section 1245 of the Internal Revenue Code requires a taxpayer to report as ordinary income (and pay tax at ordinary rates on) any excess depreciation claimed on an asset in previous years. For a sports enterprise, this means that a player contract that has been depreciated is subject to recapture if the sales price exceeds the depreciated book value (adjusted basis) of the contract at the time of sale.

When an entire team is sold, the tax treatment is the same as if all the team's assets were sold separately. A portion of the proceeds is allocated to each asset, including the player contracts, and contracts that would be subject to depreciation recapture if sold separately are also subject to recapture when the entire team is sold. In allocating the proceeds among the various team assets, the sellers will try to assign as little as possible to the player contracts, so as to minimize the amount of depreciation recapture subject to ordinary tax. (This, of course, is just the reverse of what happens at the time of purchase.) Again, while it is difficult to know, in the absence of their financial records, what clubs actually do, there does not seem to be any impediment to allocating the sales proceeds in the way most favorable to the club—even if it differs from the allocation at the time of purchase—if the club can justify such a procedure to the Internal Revenue Service.

Table 3 illustrates how depreciation recapture works. The excess depreciation is determined by comparing the actual decrease in the asset's value (as measured by the difference between cost and sales price) with the claimed decrease (as measured by the depreciation charged against the asset). In Case A, the actual decrease in the asset's value is $7,000 ($10,000 cost less $3,000 sales price), while the claimed decrease (depreciation) is $8,000. Since the depreciation exceeds the actual decline in value by $1,000, this amount would be taxed as ordinary income.

Like other taxpayers, team owners prefer paying the lower capital gains tax rate on their incomes. For clubs organized as corporations, capital gains are taxed at a maximum rate of 33.75 percent (this includes the effect of the 10 percent minimum tax) rather than the 48 percent rate levied on ordinary net income. If a team is operated as a partnership, each partner includes in his individual tax return his pro rata share of capital gains income along with any other income from capital assets. He is allowed to exclude from taxable income one-half of his net long-term

Table 3. Depreciation Recapture on the Sale of a Depreciable Asset
Dollars

Item	Case A	Case B
Cost of asset	10,000	10,000
Less depreciation written off over period owned	8,000	8,000
Adjusted basis at time of sale	2,000	2,000
Sales price	3,000	12,000
Less adjusted basis	2,000	2,000
Total gain on sale	1,000	10,000
Part of gain taxed as ordinary income[a]	1,000	8,000
Part of gain taxed as capital gain	0	2,000

Source: Derived from provisions of 1973 Internal Revenue Code.

a. Gain from the sale of depreciable personal property must be reported as ordinary income unless the depreciation on the property is less than the gain. In that case, gain to the extent of the depreciation is taxed as ordinary income and the remainder is taxed as a capital gain.

capital gain, and generally the maximum tax he would pay on the remainder is 36.5 percent (if he is in the 70 percent tax bracket and also has enough preference income to be subject to the 10 percent minimum tax enacted in 1969).[33] The procedure for taxing capital gains of small business corporations is very complex, so it is difficult to state simply what the combined corporate and personal tax rate on capital gains is.

To summarize, the income tax liability on the net long-term capital gain realized by a team as a result of selling its assets depends on how the team is organized. The tax may vary between 33.75 percent for corporations to 36.5 percent for taxpayers in a partnership.[34] Ordinarily, capital gains income will be subject to maximum effective tax rates of 30 to 35 percent. Any ordinary income resulting from recapture of excess depreciation would be taxed at 48 percent for corporations and at regular individual income tax rates for partners or shareholders in Subchapter-S corporations.

Asset Exchanges

There appears to be another way in which to "sell" a sports club and completely avoid any tax on the transaction, as illustrated by the three-

33. The alternative tax on the first $50,000 of net long-term capital gain is 25 percent. It rises to the higher level only on net gains in excess of $50,000.

34. These are the maximum rates. If the capital gain is $50,000 or less, it would be subject to only one-half the maximum tax rate of the individual stockholders, up to a maximum of 25 percent; this could be as low as 7 percent (one-half of 14 percent, the lowest individual income tax rate).

way transaction involving Carroll Rosenbloom, former owner of the Baltimore Colts; the estate of the late Daniel Reeves, owner of a majority interest in the Los Angeles Rams at the time of his death; and Robert Irsay, the current owner of the Colts.[35] Rosenbloom wanted to sell the Colts and acquire another football team. After the death of Reeves, the Reeves estate and the other Rams stockholders were willing to sell their stock for approximately $19 million.[36] Irsay was willing to buy the Colts from Rosenbloom for $19 million, but Rosenbloom was reluctant to sell because he would have to pay $4 to $6 million in capital gains tax.[37] So instead of buying the Colts, Irsay purchased the Rams for $19 million, and then he and Rosenbloom swapped the Los Angeles and Baltimore assets. If the trade qualifies as a tax-free exchange of like assets,[38] Rosenbloom will avoid the $4 to $6 million capital gains tax on the "sale," and the Reeves estate will pay little or no tax because of the increased basis of its Rams stock.[39]

Evaluation of Sports Investments

Every financial investment—including those in sports enterprises—is based on an evaluation of whether (on the basis of the best available estimates about unknown future events) it is likely to be recovered with a sufficiently attractive rate of return. The true rate of return cannot be known until the investment is terminated; hence, calculations of the

35. These transactions occurred during the spring of 1972 and are described in Research Institute of America, *Tax Coordinator,* Vol. 3, §I-2814 (Oct. 11, 1973). So far, the IRS has not reacted adversely to the transaction, and, if the facts reported are accurate, it would seem to be allowable under sec. 1031 of the Internal Revenue Code.

36. In this instance, the sale would presumably have been tax free to the estate because of the increased basis allowed for the valuation of estate assets at time of death (IRC, sec. 2032).

37. Rosenbloom's initial purchase price for the Colts reported in the *Tax Coordinator* was $1.2 million, and it was estimated there that the capital gains tax on the sale would have been $6.23 million. Another report on the transaction estimated a tax liability of $4.4 million ("Nay on the Neighs, Yea on the Baas," *Sports Illustrated,* Vol. 37 [Aug. 14, 1972], pp. 67–69).

38. See IRC, sec. 1031.

39. The presentation here is considerably simplified in order to concentrate on the salient economic aspects of the transactions. Thus, there was probably a liquidation of the old Rams corporation when Irsay bought it in order to get a higher basis for the assets. In addition, there may be some capital gains realization if there are any cash payments involved in the transaction.

prospective rate of return can be considered only estimates. Thus, an investor will often require a rate of return on an investment that includes a substantial risk premium or a payoff period for recovering the investment that is substantially shorter than would be necessary for investments involving less risk. For instance, if risk-free United States Treasury securities yielding a 6 percent return are readily available, an investor might require a yield of 8 or 10 percent to make a risky investment equally attractive to him.

All the useful procedures for evaluating investments take into account the time value of money, the annual flow of expected receipts and disbursements, and the period over which the funds are to be invested. Two factors are especially important in evaluating a prospective investment in a sports club: the effects on net income from the investment of depreciation and of income taxes. (Of course, these two items are interrelated, since the treatment of depreciation affects net income as computed for tax purposes.)

The central task of depreciation accounting is the allocation of the cost (less salvage value, if any) of assets among the years of their useful service. Thus, the conventional treatment of depreciation disregards such matters as prospective increases (or decreases) in the market value or the value to the owner of assets, although these may be important considerations in making an investment decision. Since depreciation accounting is concerned solely with the amortization of the initial asset cost, the book depreciation expense is, in effect, capital recovery computed without any return on the initial investment. The profit after depreciation shown in the accounting records is, therefore, only an estimate of the return on an investment and often bears little relationship to the actual rate of return realized.

In evaluating a prospective financial investment, book depreciation is of value primarily in determining the expected flow of net receipts or disbursements. In calculating future flows, income taxes must also be considered. Income tax payments made by a profitable enterprise will reduce cash flow, so they should be treated in the same way as any other disbursement. Similarly, to the extent that there are losses that offset income that otherwise would be subject to tax, the tax value of losses should be treated in the same way as receipts.

As noted above, it is never possible to calculate the true rate of return until an investment is sold or otherwise disposed of. Even after termination, when all the financial data are assembled, computing the rate of return can be a complex operation. Receipts and disbursements will have fluctuated from year to year; some players on the team at the outset will have been sold, retired, or traded during the period of ownership; other income of the owners may have fluctuated, with the result that the marginal tax rates used in determining the tax effects of club profits and losses will have been different in various years.

While these and many other factors make computation of the actual rate of return difficult, it is possible if all the pertinent financial information is available. Unfortunately, this information is not available for sports enterprises. Nevertheless, the following calculations, based on the hypothetical example of a club purchased for $2 million, will serve to illustrate the possible effects of various tax provisions on the profitability of investment in a sports enterprise.

Several simplifying assumptions underlie these calculations: (1) the club is held for five years and then sold by the owners; (2) the owners are individuals or partners (or constitute a corporation that has elected to be taxed as a partnership); (3) the investment made by the owners is in the form of equity rather than debt; (4) the roster of players at the time of purchase remains unchanged; (5) the annual cash receipts and expenditures are constant, with annual operating profits of $100,000; and (6) the club's only assets are its player contracts and the franchise. Table 4 shows how, under these assumptions, the possible rates of return to the owners are affected by the percentage of initial cost allocated to player contracts, the length of time over which they are depreciated, the marginal individual income tax rates of the owners, the price for which the club is sold, and the allocation of the sales proceeds between the franchise and contracts. Different sales prices and allocations will, of course, result in different amounts of total realized gain, depreciation recapture taxed at ordinary tax rates, and profit subject to capital gains rates.

Since the number of possible combinations of all these variables is very large, only a few are presented in the table. The rates of return shown represent the interest yield on a $2 million investment, which pays the investor various amounts of income during a five-year period plus repayment of the principal at the end of the period. The calculations indicate that the combined effects of the various assumptions cause the rate of return to vary widely. All other things remaining constant, the rate of return is higher: (1) the larger the proportion of initial cost allocated to the player contracts; (2) the shorter the period of time over which the player contracts are depreciated; and (3) the higher the sales price of the club.

Table 4. Rates of Return to Team Owners on a \$2 Million Investment under Alternative Tax and Sales Assumptions

Item	Case A	Case B	Case C	Case D
	Club sold for \$2 million			
Percentage of purchase price allocated to player contracts	50	50	50	50
Number of years for contract depreciation	5	5	3	3
Owners' marginal tax bracket (percent)	50	70	50	70
Rate of return on initial investment (percent)				
50 percent of sales proceeds allocated to player contracts	2.8	1.7	2.9	1.9
25 percent of sales proceeds allocated to player contracts	4.0	3.6	4.3	3.9
	Club sold for \$4 million			
Percentage of purchase price allocated to player contracts	75	75	75	75
Number of years for contract depreciation	5	5	3	3
Owners' marginal tax bracket (percent)	50	70	50	70
Rate of return on initial investment (percent)				
75 percent of sales proceeds allocated to player contracts	15.6	13.9	16.6	15.3
50 percent of sales proceeds allocated to player contracts	16.1	14.7	17.2	16.2

Source: Derived by author.

The rate of return depends especially on the price at which the assets are sold and the percentage of the proceeds allocated to the player contracts.[40] In all instances in which the sellers used the same allocation of sales proceeds as was used at the time of purchase, the rate of return on investment declines as the owners' marginal tax bracket rises (for example, compare Cases A and B or Cases C and D in the 50 percent allocation row). This somewhat surprising outcome is the result of the large amount of gain taxed as ordinary income, due to excess depreciation recapture. When a larger proportion of the sales proceeds is allocated to the franchise, the rate of return on investment rises as the owners' marginal tax bracket

40. The allocation of sales proceeds to player contracts and the franchise need not be the same as the allocation at the time of purchase. In the example shown in Table 4, for instance, the sellers might argue that the players' talents had been depleted during the five-year period and that the new owners were buying mainly the franchise rather than the "worn-out" roster of players.

increases, because there is substantially less depreciation recapture taxed at ordinary rates.

The relative importance of the write-off period and sales allocation can be seen by comparing Cases A and C or Cases B and D. With a 50 percent tax bracket (A and C), shortening the depreciation period from five to three years raises the rate of return from 2.8 percent to 2.9 percent. For the same cases, allocating 25 percent rather than 50 percent of the sales proceeds to the player contracts and using the shorter write-off period raises the rate of return to 4.3 percent.

The most unrealistic assumption made in these examples is that the club has the same roster of players at the end of the five-year period as when it was purchased. In practice, at least some of the original players would have retired or been released by the time of sale. Such personnel changes were not taken into account, since they would involve capital gains and losses that would greatly complicate the computations. Their effects, however, would generally be to increase the rates of return in a manner similar to that shown for the more favorable allocations of sales proceeds, since little depreciation would be taken on the contracts of new players, and hence there would be less recapture at the time of sale.

These examples, of course, are hypothetical and are not meant to describe any particular club in the four major professional sports. Furthermore, as in every industry, some sports enterprises yield low returns, some high returns. What the examples do indicate is that it is often misleading to judge the profitability of a sports enterprise on the basis of its unaudited accounting records or tax statements. In Table 4, Cases A and B would have shown accounting losses in all five years, and those cases do in fact have the lowest rates of return. But C and D—the most profitable investments—also would have had substantial book losses during the first three years, and relatively modest bookkeeping profits in the last two years. Since a dollar today is worth more than a dollar to be received next year (and considerably more than a dollar to be received four or five years from now), the more quickly an investment is recouped, the more profitable it will be (all other things being equal).

The Effects of Special Tax Provisions

The immediate effect on a team of the special tax provisions is to increase its after-tax profitability: an owner who takes advantage of these tax provisions can turn a seemingly profitless venture into a very attractive investment. For all sports, the maximum possible gain from these tax provisions, arrived at using accepted accounting procedures, is much larger than the operating profit of an average team. This fact helps to explain why investors continue to sink several million dollars in professional sports clubs that persistently operate in the red.

Since astute businessmen can be expected to invest their money in enterprises that yield a satisfactory after-tax rate of return, the material presented in this chapter is not very surprising. Nor is the federal tax revenue forgone because of these tax provisions very large[41] compared to the implicit costs of numerous other tax shelters available to wealthy individuals. In fact, the primary purpose of this chapter lies not in estimating the revenue loss from the tax provisions that apply to sports clubs, but rather in examining how these provisions affect the operations and ownership structure of teams.

Any factor, including favorable tax provisions, that increases the profitability of sports enterprises relative to investments elsewhere in the economy will tend to have two effects. First, the price of franchises will increase, since prospective owners will bid up the price of assets that are expected to yield higher returns. Second, the number of economically viable franchises will grow, resulting in an expansion of old leagues or, if the rate of expansion does not match the growth in the demand for fran-

41. The annual total is perhaps a few million dollars. It is difficult to estimate because the necessary financial data for individual teams are not available. One large source of income subject to special tax treatment is the compensation for players purchased from existing team rosters during league expansions. Payments to the existing teams in the most recent expansions in the four major sports are estimated to have totaled $76.5 million and involved the purchase of 280 player contracts. Assuming that the sales of baseball and hockey contracts involved no depreciation recapture and that, on the average, basketball and football contracts were subject to a recapture of $25,000 each, $73.5 million of the total were taxed at capital gains rates and $3.0 million in depreciation recapture were taxed at ordinary income tax rates. The difference in tax payments between the 30 percent capital gains rates and the 48 percent ordinary income rates is $13.2 million, which, when spread over the period during which the payments are to be made, amounts to $2.6 million a year of revenue loss.

The other tax provisions are too complex, and the necessary financial data too scarce, to permit a calculation of their effects on the tax liabilities of individual teams. All that is known is that a few sports franchises are sold each year for several million dollars apiece, and that a large part of the sales price is allocated to player contracts and depreciated. A single transaction of the magnitude of the 1973 Yankees sale, for example, is likely to provide between $500,000 and $1 million a year in tax reduction (or, at least, deferral) for the new owners.

chises, the emergence of new leagues. The number and prices of franchises will then increase until the profitability of an investment in sports is again roughly comparable to the profitability of an investment in other industries.

Sports leagues carefully control the number of member teams. Consequently, the principal effect of an increased profit potential in sports has been a rise in franchise prices. By limiting the number of teams, owners increase the value of their own investments and ensure maximal prices for the occasional expansion franchises they grant. The only check on this practice is the possibility of the formation of new leagues, which tends to bid up player salaries and adversely affect the value of both established and expansion franchises in the old league. Because new leagues are costly, risky ventures, the threat that they might emerge somewhat retards, but does not prevent, the general upward drift of franchise prices in the established leagues.

The most important tax provision affecting sports clubs—that which allows most of the club's cost to be allocated to player contracts and depreciated—is a relatively recent phenomenon, becoming widely used only in the late 1960s. The resulting rise in franchise prices has had a profound effect on the operation and ownership of teams. Because the potential tax benefits from owning a team generally exceed the team's operating profit, only individuals and corporations having substantial income from other sources can take full advantage of the tax provisions available to a sports enterprise; thus, only wealthy persons and large corporations can afford to pay the high prices that franchises now command. Conversely, an individual who must rely on the return from a sports franchise as his primary source of income and whose main interest is the club's operating profit can no longer afford to buy a team. The days of such owners as Bill Veeck, George Halas, and Calvin Griffith are over; such men simply cannot compete with rich businessmen like Ewing Kauffman and Robert Short, or large, profitable corporations, like CBS or Anheuser-Busch, in bidding for franchises that become available.

The change in the nature of ownership has had several effects on sports operations. First, the new owners have numerous other business interests and have less time to devote to their teams. They enter the sports business with little expertise in running a team, and because of their other commitments are slow in gaining it through experience. Second, the principal source of the owner's profit derives from the tax provisions available to him, not from the operation of the team. Thus, he is more likely to regard the team as a hobby rather than a business. One manifestation of this attitude is the tendency of an inexperienced owner to take full command of team operations, and undermine the quality of the team through a series of bad drafts, trades, purchases, and sales of players. Third, the owner derives full benefit from team ownership only for as long as the tax advantages persist, that is, until his players are fully depreciated, usually in five to seven years. Then he will sell the team to another wealthy individual or corporation that can also take advantage of the same tax provisions. This gives the owner a very short perspective on team operations. His decisions will tend to be based more on the effect they will have on the price the team can command in a few years than on the long-term viability of the franchise. Since the next buyer is not likely to be sophisticated in sports operations, the current owner has an incentive to engage in practices that sacrifice the future performance of the team to its present status, such as trading draft choices and young, developing players for aging veterans. Furthermore, since the highest bidder for a franchise is primarily interested only in the short-term attendance potential of the franchise, he may very likely wish to change the location of the team, for an area that has not had a major-league team in a particular sport is likely to find a new team something of a novelty and to provide it with more fan support for a few years than the team's old hometown would.

In sum, then, special tax provisions, and their effect on franchise prices and team owners, are factors that tend to introduce considerable instability into sports operations. It is inaccurate and unfair to attribute all instability in professional sports to tax considerations; there are many legal and institutional arrangements that also have significant effects on professional sports operations. However, there seems to be little doubt that tax considerations play a prominent part.

CHAPTER SIX

Labor Relations in Sports

JAMES G. SCOVILLE

THE GROWING MILITANCY of player associations, underscored by the first league-wide strikes in history, has made labor relations in sports a matter of considerable public concern. This chapter develops some hypotheses about the labor markets in professional sports, explores the particular industrial relations arrangements of the sports industry, and investigates the public and private policy issues involved.

Labor Markets in Sports

The market process by which wages are determined is unusually complex in professional sports, especially since the service being bought and sold is more than just skill. Although the typical player contract asserts only that the club is buying and the player is selling "skilled services as a ——— player," the player actually agrees to perform certain specific functions (for example, to permit his picture to be taken for publicity), to carry out a range of vaguely defined duties (maintain a first-class physical condition, evidence proper personal conduct, display good sportsmanship), and to refrain from a number of activities (playing more or less of the sport than the club desires, playing in another sport, whether for pleasure or pay, and, in some sports, owning part of his club). The service traded thus includes a more significant restriction of personal freedom than is usual in employment relationships.

The Demand for Players

The theoretical conception of the demand side of the labor market for a particular sport assumes a fixed number of employers, each limited in his hiring decisions by rules covering the maximum number of players he may employ. The worth of a player to an employer depends on a variety of factors, some related to performance productivity, some to revenue productivity, and others reflecting interactions between individual performance, team performance, and the gate.[1] Since the equilibrium state for a league involves a stable number of employers, total demand for labor in each league remains constant for long periods of time, which serves to reduce upward pressures on salary levels. Additional anticompetitive devices (particularly the reserve clause) ensure that wage competition is minimal within the league.

This description is, of course, oversimplified. Owing to differences in wealth among owners, the number of players controlled varies widely from club to club. This is especially true in baseball, with its well-developed farm system: in 1956 the average American League team controlled 289 players, with a range from 206 (White Sox and Senators) to 425 (Yankees); for the National League the average was 391, ranging from 279 (Cubs) to 549 (Dodgers).[2] Nevertheless, the number of major-league players active at any time depends solely on the number of clubs.

The Supply of Players

The supply of labor is composed of individual players selling their personal skills and characteristics to specified buyers. A striking feature of the labor pool is the persistence of a distinct regional pattern of recruitment. Baseball, for instance, is said to be a small-town sport, although this may simply reflect "the disproportionately large share [of players] contributed by the states of the South and Southwest."[3] Otherwise, baseball recruitment patterns parallel the distribution of population. In football, although the greatest number of college and professional players come from the major cities and from western Pennsylvania, the per capita pattern is different. The Ohio–Pennsylvania mining area produces an unusually large number of players, with the other areas of highest per capita output scattered in a band running northwest from Texas to the

1. For a trenchant and humorous summary, see Walter C. Neale, "The Peculiar Economics of Professional Sports," *Quarterly Journal of Economics,* Vol. 78 (February 1964), pp. 1–14.

2. *Organized Professional Team Sports,* Hearings before the Antitrust Subcommittee of the House Committee on the Judiciary, 85 Cong. 1 sess. (1957), Pt. 2, pp. 1901–03.

3. Ralph Andreano, *No Joy in Mudville: The Dilemma of Major League Baseball* (Schenkman, 1965), p. 136.

Rocky Mountains. Notably, big cities are not very productive in relation to their size.[4] Basketball, on the other hand, appears to draw heavily on the black population of inner cities.

The labor pool can be usefully divided into three broad classes, which differ not only in level of athletic proficiency but also in supply elasticity.

STARS. A common belief among fans, players, owners, and sportswriters is that the supply of competent players in any sport is quite small. It is true that the number of exceptional players is small indeed, especially since stardom is measured in relation to the skills of other players and depends on the number of "famous" names that the public can keep in its collective mind.[5]

JOURNEYMEN. These players are the regulars of the game, whose performances are at or above their league average, whose careers span several years if they can avoid serious injury, but who never achieve all-star status. They occupy from one-third to two-thirds of the positions on a team's roster, depending on the quality of the team.

HELPERS. These players are the semiskilled or apprentice workers of sports. They occupy several positions on even a good team, but in the absence of injuries to a regular they see little playing action. The supply of helpers must be virtually unlimited. In every sport, but especially in hockey and baseball, hundreds of these players populate the rosters of minor-league and semiprofessional teams.[6]

The Player's Reservation Price

The minimum salary, or reservation price, that a player of any quality will accept is determined primarily by two factors.

4. John F. Rooney, Jr., "Up from the Mines and Out from the Prairies: Some Geographical Implications of Football in the United States," *Geographical Review,* Vol. 59 (October 1969), pp. 471–92.

5. The method of identifying stars used in Chapter 4, which is based primarily on all-star rosters, yields an estimate of the number of stars that averages slightly more than one per team.

6. Some idea of the pyramidical structure of the pool of potential professional players was given by Lawrence Fleischer of the National Basketball Association Players Association (in a private conversation, April 21, 1971), who estimated that 60,000 high school students play varsity basketball. Most are weeded out at the next stage: college varsity rosters number about 13,000 players, of whom perhaps 3,000 graduate each year. Of these, about 40 enter one of the two major professional leagues. Another indication of the excess labor supply in basketball is the growth of the Italian Professional Basketball League, many of whose best players come from the United States.

The first is earning potential in other occupations. For a star, outside earning ability is determined less by actual skills than by his fame, which in turn depends upon his athletic accomplishments and the number of years he has been a star. His most lucrative alternative is likely to be in some other form of entertainment (the "Jim Brown Phenomenon"), advertising, or politics (the "Vinegar Bend Mizell Effect"), where his athletic fame, rather than any particular occupational skills, will pay dividends. For journeymen and helpers, too, outside earning capacity is related to athletic fame, but probably the extent to which their sports abilities carry over into other employment is also important.[7] Certainly the publicity value of an athlete to an employer, and perhaps the self-confidence that comes with success in sports at a high level of proficiency, are the chief qualifications of athletes for the sales-oriented jobs they often occupy, such as the current favorite, dealing in tax-exempt bonds.

The second factor in determining a player's reservation price is the nonpecuniary or psychic income (or loss) he receives from being a professional athlete. In comparing an athletic career with another occupation, a player will consider more than incomes in the two occupations; he will also make allowances for his devotion to sports. Obviously, many athletes find sports careers very attractive and are willing to make a financial sacrifice to pursue them.[8] Others find athletics less attractive.[9] These attitudes cause the athlete to make a compensating adjustment in his outside earning potential when calculating his reservation price for a sports career.

For stars, earning capacity in and out of sports is large, but, at least during most of their careers, it is likely to be much higher in sports—too high to be much affected by adjustments for nonpecuniary factors. Consequently, the supply of stars is likely to be inelastic, that is, not closely related to wages in either sports or other occupations. For journeymen, outside income potential is relatively more important, and their supply is

7. The extent of the relationship between athletic ability and other marketable skills is debatable. Nevertheless, deans and admissions directors of medical and dental schools believe that undergraduate athletes, particularly football players, are good candidates for success in these occupations because their athletic background is evidence of an ability and pleasure in "working with their hands."

8. Most books written by athletes, even some written by the more iconoclastic players, express this point of view. See, for example, Jim Bouton's *Ball Four: My Life and Hard Times Throwing the Knuckleball in the Big Leagues* (World, 1970), and Bernie Parrish's *They Call It a Game* (Dial, 1971).

9. See, for example, Dave Meggyesy's *Out of Their League* (Ramparts Press, 1971).

probably more closely related to their earnings. For helpers, outside income prospects are probably good compared to jobs in sports, particularly to jobs outside of the major leagues. Small changes in wages in either sports or alternative occupations are thus likely to have a significant effect on the number of helpers willing to accept sports employment. Nonpecuniary income is also probably an important factor in the helper's decision to participate in the industry.

If the player market were competitive, the salaries of journeymen and helpers would equal the reservation price of the last player in each category to enter the sport. They would also equal the value to a team of the last player in each category added to its roster.[10] The salaries of stars, since their supply is inelastic, would probably exceed each star's reservation price but would still equal the value of the last star added to a roster. In all cases, all players except the last journeyman and helper entering the sport would receive more than their reservation price.[11]

The Salary Determination Process

Salaries in professional sports are not, in fact, determined in a competitive market. The process is complicated by the institutional arrangements imposed by leagues to restrict competition for players. The effect of these restrictions is to give the team an opportunity to force the salary of each player closer to his reservation price. The extent to which a team can succeed in this attempt depends upon the bargaining positions of the players and teams and differs significantly among the three classes of players.

A simple model of salary determination at the team level can be developed that incorporates the most important of the institutional and market phenomena described above. The club's objective is to maximize profits, π, given by

$$(1) \qquad \pi = R(s,j,h) - w_s(s)s - w_j(j)j - w_h(h)h,$$

where $R(s,j,h)$ expresses revenue as a function of the number of stars (s), journeymen (j), and helpers (h) employed. The club intends to maximize

10. In a completely competitive player market teams would have differing numbers of players. Teams in cities with greater drawing potential would hire more players, so that the value of the last player hired would be the same everywhere.

11. This argument depends on the assumption that players fall into three homogeneous classes. If, as in Chapter 2, playing skill is allowed to be different for all players, the market equilibrium is more complicated to describe, but the conclusion is essentially the same.

the difference between gross revenue and the three categories of wage cost, w, subject to the condition that the number of players $(s + j + h)$ equal the roster limit, k.[12] The following three equations (in addition to the constraint, not shown) must be satisfied if profits are to be maximized, with each equation representing the salaries of a class of players:

(2a) $w_s(s) = R'(s) - sw'_s(s) - \lambda$

(2b) $w_j(j) = R'(j) - jw'_j(j) - \lambda$

(2c) $w_h(h) = R'(h) - hw'_h(h) - \lambda,$

where λ is the value to the team (the "shadow price") of violating, if it could, the roster limit, k. If roster limits are an effective constraint on total employment by the club, λ must be positive.

Thus, the equations show that *all* players are "exploited" in the sense that their wages are below the marginal revenue product of players in each class by a minimum of λ. In addition, as the second term on the right-hand side of equations (2a), (2b), and (2c) shows, each group of players is exploited according to its supply elasticity to the team. These elasticities depend both on supply elasticities of each class of players for the entire sport and on the extent to which a team has a monopsony bargaining position over its own players. Team supply elasticities are likely to differ significantly among the classes of players, in part because the sport-wide elasticities differ and in part because the team's monopsony power differs among the classes.

At one end of the scale are the stars. Usually one and never more than a few stars are on the roster of any single team, so that a star bargains with only one team, and the typical team bargains with very few stars. The club has slightly more flexibility, for it may purchase the contract of another star from another team, but this is a very imperfect check on the star's bargaining position. First, if another star is receiving a salary significantly below his value to his team, the team is likely to charge a high price for his contract. Second, the adverse publicity surrounding the outright sale of a superior player to another team may cause his cost to the selling team to exceed the contribution he makes to team revenues. For the "superstar"—the Bobby Hull who may make or break a fledgling league —the market may degenerate to a pure case of bilateral monopoly. The

---

12. Strictly speaking, $(s + j + h)$ must be less than or equal to k. For simplicity, and since clubs never stay below the roster limit for appreciable periods of time, the above formulation may be regarded as acceptable.

market for the more numerous "ordinary" star players involves a monopsonistic club and a few players who are near monopolists.

The team can usually be expected to have the upper hand in bargaining, partly because of the background of many new players. The team negotiator generally has more education, sophistication, and business experience than the player, and knows how much players of a given quality normally earn. The player often is inexperienced in business affairs, comes from lower-income sections of the country, has little sense of his true value to a team, and may be influenced by family and peers to overvalue the psychic rewards of sports. Only as a star's career draws to a close, when he has had several years of negotiating experience and his athletic fame begins to generate real outside earning potential, is his bargaining ability likely to approach that of the owners. During his early playing years, it is the team that derives major benefit from the bilateral bargaining situation.

At the other end of the scale in the player market are the helpers. The player reservation system gives teams monopsony rights to a large pool of these players. In football and basketball, the pool consists mainly of the first-year players recently drafted; a player who does not make the twelve-man roster in basketball or the forty-man roster in football must be released. Nevertheless, each summer a football or basketball try-out camp has several times as many helpers trying to make the team as there are helper positions available on the roster. In baseball and hockey, the pool includes an enormous number of minor-league players who are bound to player contracts containing a reserve clause.

Assuming that helpers are available in perfectly elastic supply, the value of $w_h'(h)$ in equation (2c) is zero at all levels of helper employment, so that helper salaries must be equal to their marginal revenue product (minus λ) and identical with their reservation price.

Of course, all helpers do not have the same reservation price. The player reservation system allows a team to discriminate fully among helpers not only according to their sophistication about the economics of sports, but also according to the psychic satisfaction they derive from playing. In fact, a belief has developed in professional sports that a player whose abilities are questionable but whose attitude is especially good is of enormous value to a team. (In baseball, such a player is often referred to as a "holler guy.") Whatever the truth of this, the nature of the player market tends to foster a greater emotional attachment to the sport in helpers. Since numerous helpers are available, teams will hire those with the lowest reservation prices—that is, those with the greatest emotional attachment to the game. The bilateral negotiation system will depress to some degree even the salaries of stars who are "devoted" players, but for stars the effect is not as great because of the limited number of high quality players available to any team. For helpers, there is no countervailing influence to the tendency of a player's salary to be reduced to his reservation price.

In theory, the full power of monopsony comes to bear on the salaries of journeymen. The wage of a journeyman is depressed by the positive supply elasticity of this class of players. Thus, their salaries are placed at a level below the λ-adjusted marginal revenue but above the reservation price of all but the last journeyman employed. In reality, the salary outcome for journeymen is modified by the fact that these players possess moderate amounts of individual bargaining power. A team normally has rights to several journeymen, but not enough to fill all of the important positions on its roster. Thus, it often has to negotiate with a journeyman in a modified bilateral monopoly situation: although the player may be one of several journeymen on a team, he may also be the team's only competent left-handed reliever, free safety, defensive forward, or goalkeeper.

Still, a journeyman will be less likely to capture the full value of his contribution to his team than a star. In addition to all the factors relating to experience and sophistication that undermine the bargaining position of most athletes, the journeyman faces a much greater threat from player trades and sales than the star. He does not have the degree of support from his hometown fans that a star enjoys, so his transfer to another team would generate less protest. Furthermore, because his numbers are greater, some team is sure to have more than one journeyman with his particular set of skills and is, therefore, likely to be interested in a deal. Since transfer to a new team is costly to a player, and since the possibility of obtaining a similar player from another team makes a journeyman's security more precarious, the player reservation system weakens the position of the journeyman more than it weakens that of the star.

The Impact of Unionization

Although the player reservation system weakens the bargaining position of all players in markets dominated by monopsony power, the formation of player associations raises the reservation price of whole classes of players, thereby limiting the amount by which clubs can reduce salaries. To be effective, a union must obtain the voluntary support of most workers or control access to the labor market. Only then can it gain market power over the sale of labor services and, like a monopolist, force wages above the level that would otherwise prevail.

Most major-league athletes are journeymen, and most of the remainder are helpers; relatively few are stars. Thus, the success of a player association depends primarily on its attractiveness to journeymen, secondarily on its appeal to helpers, and only from a public relations or "solidarity" viewpoint on its appeal to stars. Control of the most interchangeable and replaceable players is essential. It is not surprising that the areas in which player associations have been most active are those that affect journeymen and helpers, such as minimum salary levels and fringe benefits. Raising minimum salaries directly benefits helpers by limiting the extent to which a team can force a player's salary down to his reservation price. It also benefits journeymen, for the maintenance of a salary structure that provides incentives for improved performance requires a significant differential between the journeyman and the helper.[13] But it provides little benefit to the star, whose earnings are so far above the other two classes that he is not much affected by changes at the other end of the salary schedule. Other activities of the player associations, however—negotiations to provide safer playing conditions, to improve scheduling, to give players the right to be represented by counsel during contract negotiations, and to weaken the player reservation system—strengthen the bargaining position of all players, including stars.

The Financial Outcome

The overall earnings in the sports labor market, summarized in Figures 1 and 2, give an indication of the factors influencing player salaries.[14] Figure 1 presents age-income profiles for three education levels. The average income of active male athletes is higher than for all males in the labor force and peaks at least a decade earlier than theirs.

13. As shown in Chapter 7, the salary structure in baseball resembles a well-designed job evaluation scheme, in that there is a high correlation between measures of output and income.

14. These figures show the income of all persons reporting themselves as athletes in the 1960 Census (U.S. Bureau of the Census, *U.S. Census of Population, 1960, Detailed Characteristics: United States Summary,* Final Report PC(1)-1D [1963], p. 528). The fact that the number of athletes fell from over 11,000 in 1950 to around 4,000 in 1960 casts doubt on the purity of these figures. The decline in minor-league baseball is not sufficient to account for a drop of this magnitude.

Figure 1. Age-Income Profiles for Male Athletes and Male Experienced Civilian Labor Force, by Educational Level, 1959

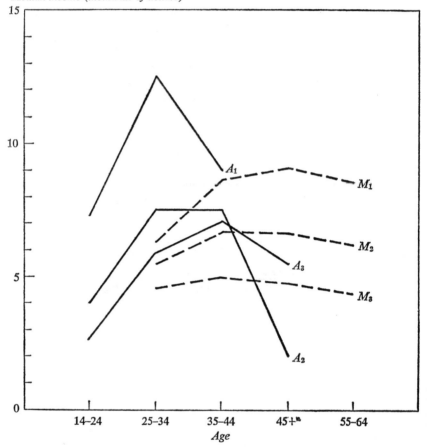

Median income (thousands of dollars)

A_1 = athletes finishing college M_1 = males finishing college
A_2 = athletes not finishing college M_2 = males not finishing college
A_3 = athletes not attending college M_3 = males not attending college

Sources: Total labor force, from or estimated from U.S. Bureau of the Census, *U.S. Census of Population, 1960, Occupation by Earnings and Education,* Final Report PC(2)-7B (1963), Table 1; athletes, estimated from the same census, *Characteristics of Professional Workers,* Final Report PC(2)-7E (1964), Table 7.
a. Includes all athletes 45 and older and persons 45 to 54 only in the male labor force.

The distributions of income for athletes and for all males are shown in Figure 2. The most notable difference between the two distributions is at middle income levels. The center of the income distribution is dramatically

Figure 2. Distribution of Income of Male Athletes and Male Experienced Civilian Labor Force, by Income Classes, 1949 and 1959[a]

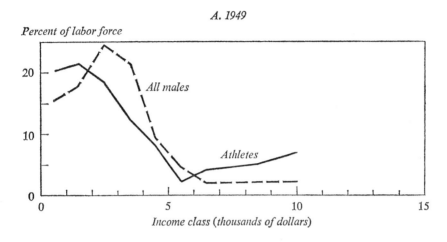

A. 1949

Percent of labor force

Income class (thousands of dollars)

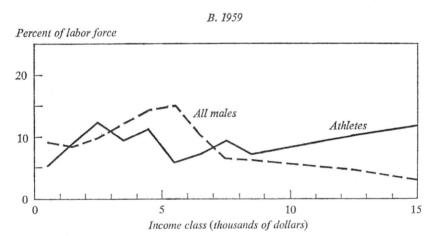

B. 1959

Percent of labor force

Income class (thousands of dollars)

Sources: U.S. Bureau of the Census, *U.S. Census of Population, 1950*, Vol. 4, Special Reports, Pt. 1, *Occupational Characteristics* (1956), Table 19, p. 183; Bureau of the Census, *U.S. Census of Population, 1960*, Subject Reports, *Occupational Characteristics*, Final Report PC(2)-7A (1963), Table 25, p. 296.

a. Data are plotted at the midpoint of the income class. Percentages for athletes are based on all male athletes in the experienced labor force with income, and for total males, on the total male experienced labor force with income.

underrepresented among athletes, which is consistent with the above statements about the position of journeymen and helpers in salary bargaining. In 1949, athletes were considerably more concentrated at both the bottom and top income levels. By 1959, the lower ranges of the two distributions were much alike, while the upper end showed relatively many more athletes. The reduction in the relative number of athletes at the bottom end is partly due to cutbacks in minor-league baseball, which was the major employer of helpers at notoriously low pay. The increased divergence between athletes and other males at upper income levels may simply reflect the general prosperity of sports.

A striking feature of the sports industry is the disparity of average compensation among clubs in the same sport. Table 1 shows a set of salary estimates for the National Football League in the 1970 season. The average salary in the best-paying club was almost double that in the worst-paying club. Similarly wide distributions were revealed during the 1957 House hearings on baseball,[15] and continue to prevail: in 1967, the range of mean salaries by club was from $12,007 to $29,470.[16] In the National Basketball Association, team average salaries ranged from $30,000 to $83,000 in 1970–71.[17]

The following regression, fitted to the data of Table 1, shows that the most important determinants of this phenomenon in football are the age and playing success of the team.

Variable	Coefficient (dollars)	t-value
Intercept	+ 21,339	10.5**
Fraction of games won, 1967–69[18]	+ 10,686	5.0**
Dummy: 1 if in "second expansion," around 1965	− 3,128	2.4*
Dummy: 1 if in "first expansion," around 1960	− 2,146	2.4*
Dummy: 1 if for Green Bay	+ 3,417	1.6

$R^2 = 0.724$**

** = significant at 1 percent level; * = significant at 5 percent level

By far the most important factor in the regression is the percentage of games won. The two dummy variables for expansion rounds show that

15. *Organized Professional Team Sports*, Pt. 2, p. 2056.
16. Personal communication from Marvin J. Miller, May 25, 1971.
17. "Statement by Roger G. Noll and Benjamin A. Okner," in *Professional Basketball*, Hearing before the Subcommittee on Antitrust and Monopoly of the Senate Committee on the Judiciary, 92 Cong. 1 sess. (1971), Pt. 1, Table 5, p. 406 (Brookings Reprint 258).
18. Calculated omitting ties. For Cincinnati, applies to 1968 and 1969 only.

Table 1. **Average Salaries of National Football League Players, by Team, 1970 Season**

Team	Number of players reporting	Average salary (dollars)
Baltimore	25	31,300
Green Bay	23	30,900
Minnesota	19	30,800
Cleveland	14	30,000
Los Angeles	28	29,600
New York Jets	26	28,900
Kansas City	18	28,300
New York Giants	36	27,800
St. Louis	16	27,800
Oakland	41	27,500
Washington	38	26,600
Detroit	16	26,100
San Francisco	37	24,900
Miami	19	24,200
Philadelphia	32	24,000
Dallas	15	24,000
San Diego	40	23,500
Boston	18	23,500
Chicago	25	23,300
Houston	25	23,100
Pittsburgh	29	23,000
Denver	40	22,700
New Orleans	24	21,700
Buffalo	32	21,000
Atlanta	16	19,800
Cincinnati	25	18,600

Source: *Philadelphia Inquirer*, July 24, 1971.

significantly lower salaries are paid by the newer franchises.[19] By multiplying all coefficients by forty (the roster limit), the equation can be converted into an equation for the team's wage bill, thus permitting a rough estimate of the cost in player salaries of improving the relative quality of a team (its won-lost record). For example, raising the fraction of games won by 0.2 (about three games per year) would raise the team wage bill by $85,000. If a single player accounts for the improvement, this figure

19. Several other variables were tried but rejected for the final equation. Size of metropolitan area (which accounts for the Green Bay dummy variable), presence of another football franchise in the metropolitan area, and league affiliation were not significant. The latter (positive NFL correlation) did enter the equation at an early stage but was subsequently replaced by the more meaningful expansion dummies.

can be interpreted as being the amount by which his salary would exceed the average salary for the team, giving him a total salary of about $110,000. This seems reasonably near newspaper estimates of offers to the best quarterbacks, and so provides a crude verification of the meaningfulness of the equation.

Are Players Exploited?

The proposition that in sports the buyer of labor is able to exert market power over the seller is difficult to test because relevant data are hard to come by. Such figures as are available, summarized below, appear only sporadically and are of less than perfect quality. They indicate that reservation rules in sports have succeeded in keeping player salaries lower than they would otherwise be, but that the degree of exploitation is, if anything, declining.

That restraints on competition in player markets usually succeed in holding down salaries is most evident from the pattern of wage increases during periods of interleague competition for players. Data for four struggling NBA teams (Fort Wayne, Boston, Rochester, and St. Louis), during a period (1952–53 season to 1956–57 season) when there was no competition among teams for players, show that average player salaries rose by 33 percent.[20] In contrast, the median salary in the NBA rose about 60 percent between 1967 and 1971 (a period of interleague competition for players), as shown in Table 2.

The emergence of the World Hockey Association (WHA) in 1972 had a similar effect on salaries in hockey. In its first year of operation, the WHA competed vigorously for National Hockey League (NHL) players, and succeeded in signing seventy-nine NHL players, sixty-six of whom had played as regulars in the NHL during the 1971–72 season. The average salary in the WHA for the sixty-six former NHL regulars was over $53,000.[21] Although data are not available on what these players had earned in the NHL during the previous season, it is apparent that their salaries increased by 50 to 100 percent. The average salary of NHL players during 1971–72 was $24,000,[22] and in 1972–73 it rose to $40,000.[23] The

20. *Organized Professional Team Sports,* Hearings, Pt. 3, pp. 2928, 2932.
21. All 1972–73 WHA data are from the league file of contracts of all WHA players as of October 1, 1972.
22. *Philadelphia World Hockey Club, Inc.* v. *Philadelphia Hockey Club, Inc.,* U.S.D.C. Eastern Pa., C.A. 72-1661, Opinion (Nov. 8, 1972), p. 14.
23. *Washington Post,* March 1, 1973.

Table 2. Player Salaries, National Basketball Association, 1967–70 Seasons[a]

Thousands of dollars

Salary	Number of players			
	1967–68	1968–69	1969–70	1970–71
Under 10	6	...	...	...
10 to 15	26	17	2	...
15 to 20	21	24	15	20
20 to 30	25	25	32	44
30 to 40	21	30	20	40
40 to 50	21	30	16	32
50 to 60	10	7	7	17
60 to 70	10	7	5	10
70 to 80	10	7	6	8
80 to 90	4	3	1	2
90 to 100	4	3	1	5
Over 100	4	6	12	18
Median	$25,000	$30,000	$35,000	$40,000

Source: NBA Basketball Players Association.
a. Data are for players on the rosters at the end of each season.

salary history of three former Boston Bruins indicates the effects of inter-league competition:[24]

		Salary (*dollars*)	
		1972–73	
Player	1971–72	WHA	NHL offer (*rejected*)
John McKenzie	48,000	100,000	100,000
Derek Sanderson	50,000	300,000	80,000
Gerry Cheevers	47,500	200,000	70,000

The effect of the emergence of the WHA was not confined to former NHL players. WHA players who had not played in the NHL in 1971–72 received an average salary in 1972–73 of nearly $22,000—almost equal to the average NHL salary in the previous year, and double the average

24. Figures do not include performance bonuses. McKenzie data from *Philadelphia World Hockey Club;* Sanderson and Cheevers data from *Boston Professional Hockey Association* v. *Derek Sanderson* (D.C. Mass. 1972), C.A. 72-2490c.

minor-league salary in 1971–72.[25] For example, Nick Polano moved from the minor-league Providence team to the Philadelphia Blazers of the WHA, with whom he signed a three-year contract calling for salaries of $24,000, $27,000, and $28,500, and a $5,000 bonus for signing.[26] The most spectacular deal was the offer made to Bobby Hull, the former Chicago Black Hawks star. In addition to a ten-year contract calling for annual salaries ranging from $187,500 to $250,000, each of the twelve WHA teams also paid Hull $62,500 just for agreeing to enter the league.[27]

Prosperity does not seem to be the dominant factor in generating salary increases of such magnitude. An examination of the effects of the AFL-NFL merger showed that salaries for promising new players have fallen by one-third to one-half since the common draft began, despite the fact that football is probably the most prosperous sport and has continued to prosper in the years after the merger. Curiously, the effect seems to have taken several years to appear in any dramatic fashion.[28] At the other extreme, basketball salaries have skyrocketed because of competition, even though basketball is the least prosperous of the four major sports.

The available data do not indicate that the financial health of the professional athlete was failing, even before the revival of some militancy among the player associations and the periods of interleague competition in football and basketball. For example, although the mean salary of baseball players increased by only 9.6 percent between 1952 and 1956,[29] while the nation's median family income rose 23.1 percent, this discrepancy can be explained by the fact that these were years of stagnant or falling attendance in baseball. In contrast, during the same years average salaries in the increasingly popular NFL went up by 24 percent, slightly above the national rate.

25. *Philadelphia World Hockey Club,* p. 14.

26. Ibid., Exhibit 103.

27. According to press reports and the judge's decision in the ensuing court case, Hull's signing bonus was $1 million, but the records submitted in evidence in the lawsuit document payments of "only" $750,000. In addition, Hull's ten-year contract has a no-cut clause for only the first five years. After that, if he fails to make the team, he is guaranteed a management job with his WHA team (Winnipeg) at $100,000 annually, considerably less than what he would earn if he were an active player. Since Hull will be over forty years old when the contract expires, it seems unlikely that he will realize the full potential gain from the contract.

28. Morton Sharnik, "The Buckeyes Don't Have It," *Sports Illustrated,* Vol. 35 (July 5, 1971), p. 31.

29. *Organized Professional Team Sports,* Hearings, Pt. 2, pp. 1414, 2056.

Some aggregate figures for the 1950s further support the contention that exploitation of players did not increase during the decade. These data include sports other than those under discussion here, and have other drawbacks as well, but yield a definite general impression. Between 1950 and 1960, personal consumption expenditures on spectator sports rose 31 percent; baseball attendance rose about 15 percent; and NFL attendance rose 59 percent.[30] However, the median income of male athletes climbed 131 percent, compared with 77 percent for the rest of the male labor force.[31] These comparisons cannot be considered conclusive, as they ignore broadcast fees and some other less important sources of club revenue, but they suggest the general picture.[32] The Census figures, in fact, probably understate the increase in salaries: as seasons have been lengthened, the outside income component has probably fallen relative to the total, so that sports income probably rose faster than total income.

The effect of the recent increased activity of player associations is difficult to detect in aggregative data, but the evidence is strong that the salary structure has been significantly altered by the unions. In all sports, the minimum salary has risen; in basketball, it has tripled in the past ten years. The change in basketball salary ranges is further evidence of the strength of the player association. According to the hypotheses formulated above about the supply elasticities of stars, journeymen, and helpers, vigorous competition for players during the ABA-NBA "war" should have caused the salary structure to widen. Instead, as a result of the success of the union in raising the minimum salary, the ratio of interquartile range to median salary fell from 1.25 to 0.75 over the four-year period.[33]

30. U.S. Bureau of the Census, *Statistical Abstract of the United States, 1970* (1970), pp. 204, 205.

31. U.S. Bureau of the Census, *U.S. Census of Population, 1950,* Vol. 4, Special Reports, Pt. 1, *Occupational Characteristics* (1956), Table 22, and *U.S. Census of Population, 1960,* Subject Reports, *Occupational Characteristics,* Final Report PC(2)-7A (1963), Table 25.

32. Except for the fragmentary information given in Chapter 8, broadcast revenue figures on a time series basis are unavailable; they are not included even in the U.S. Census of Business reports for selected service establishments. However, a rough measure of income can be obtained by adding the personal consumption expenditures per team and the broadcast revenues given in Chapter 8: this gives an increase in total revenue of 20 percent in baseball and 30 percent in the NFL from 1950 to 1960. For the more interesting decade of the sixties, no data on the income of athletes are available at this writing.

33. Derived from Table 2. The interquartile range is the difference in salaries between the twenty-fifth and seventy-fifth percentile.

The Industrial Relations System in Sports

The concept of an industrial relations system embraces the interactions of three actors (managers, workers, and government) against the background of market, technological, and power constraints. The outputs of the industrial relations system take the form of a "web of rules." These rules fall into three general categories: (1) substantive rules (how much shall be paid to the man who does a specific job?); (2) rules about the application of substantive rules (what are the procedures and routes of appeal in a case of termination for cause?); and (3) rules about the making of rules (how, when, and by whom are the rules governing the employment relationship to be enunciated or changed?).[34] Public attention has tended to focus on changes (sometimes spectacular) in various substantive rules in professional sports, and to overlook the possibility that, more than the substantive rules, the rules about the making and application of rules have been at the root of increased player organization militancy.

In any industry, the nature of the product market and of the technology employed tends to produce organizational structures, interests, and behavior patterns for the "actors" that reflect the peculiarities of that industry. The following sketch of the organization and activities of the actors in the sports industry provides abundant illustrations of this proposition.

Management

The management component of an industrial relations system consists of owners and "operating" managers. In sports, owners typically play a larger role in the direct management and supervision of their enterprise, particularly in hiring and compensation decisions, than is common in other industries (although this may change, particularly if corporations based outside sports continue to buy clubs). This means that the lowest level of management in sports (managers, coaches) also has a different role than in industry (foremen, supervisors). The latter employees usually have greater job security than the workers they direct, and frequently have the

34. For a concise development of these concepts, see John T. Dunlop, *Industrial Relations Systems* (Holt, Rinehart, and Winston, 1959), Chaps. 1–4.

power to hire and fire. The less secure and powerful position of the operating managers in sports undoubtedly contributes to many of the personal animosities that make the sports pages.

In addition to the club owners, the league, which is a cartel in sports, has important functions. Traditionally it has exercised unilateral control over almost all conditions of work except the individual's salary, which was subject to bargaining between the player and the club. The league is in a curious position from an industrial relations viewpoint. Not only has it exercised control over the internal labor market of the sport (through reserve clauses, draft rules, and so forth), over major aspects of compensation (such as the granting or refusal of pension systems), over the product market (through determining the location and price of franchises, granting broadcast rights, and so forth), but it even legislates the "technology" of the industry.[35] The player associations have had, and probably will continue to have, their greatest success in curtailing this element of management.

At the club level, the most important of the customary managerial prerogatives generates many problems in labor relations. In all industries, management traditionally has the right and the power (and perhaps, from the consumer's point of view, the duty) to evaluate the quality of output and judge the competence of employees. As employers, sports clubs must also have this right. Yet objective evaluation of competence in sports is exceptionally difficult, and, moreover, depends on a host of factors other than individual performance. (Scientific evidence on this point can be collected in any taproom in the nation in the wake of trading activity.) The lack of absolute standards of competence gives management a powerful weapon against labor organizations.

Moreover, this management power is not tempered by a well-functioning labor market, which would provide an effective recourse for an underpaid or wrongfully discharged player. The options now available to him—internal grievance procedures, proceedings in court or with the National Labor Relations Board (NLRB), or playing out his option—while better

---

35. This power can have important effects on the sport. For at least a decade, for instance, there has been public debate on changing the "equilibrium technology" of baseball, which dates from the last century, in order to speed up the game in line with the faster modern pace. Other examples of differentiated technology are the AFL two-point conversion after a touchdown, and the ABA three-point basket and multicolored ball. The three-point basket may actually have affected hiring decisions or may simply have been a tacit admission that in the early years of the ABA the dunking-style superstar was going to the NBA anyhow.

than nothing, still leave him in a position of weakness. Under present arrangements the issues of the reserve clause and recourse from managerial judgments of competence are so intimately linked that player interests cannot be adequately protected. Alternative contractual arrangements might reasonably be developed that would preserve some protection of team interests while making punitive actions by management at least more costly.

In addition to its other advantages, sports management enjoys a virtual monopoly of prestige in contrast to player associations. The sports pages give the impression, for example, that the NBA-ABA struggle is a silly feud, the sooner ended by merger the better,[36] and the objections from the NBA Basketball Players Association are brushed off as "obstructionist."

Player Associations

Each of the four major team sports has a player association that includes most of its major-league players. These organizations, along with the baseball umpires' association, comprise the trade union sector of the sports world.[37] For several reasons, one would expect unions of professional athletes to be potentially strong. The labor force they represent is fairly homogeneous with respect to social background and occupational status. Since stars have usually been willing to stand by their associates who have less bargaining power, race has been the only important divisive factor. Finally, because the industry is a cartel, entry into which is almost totally blocked, and because its product has only very imperfect substitutes, an organization that can shut it down has great potential power and the possibility of capturing large monopoly profits. Nevertheless, strikes

36. A moderate statement of this position is given by Peter Carry, "Meanwhile, Back at the Merge," *Sports Illustrated,* Vol. 34 (May 24, 1971), p. 68: "While the Stars and Colonels bulled at each other for six games . . . the owners of the two leagues got together and—in a rare moment of sanity—agreed to merge."

37. Although none is a member of the AFL-CIO, these associations are, in fact, labor organizations as defined in the Labor Management Relations Act of 1947, sec. 2(5) (61 Stat. 138): "The term 'labor organization' means any organization of any kind, or any agency or employee representation committee or plan, in which employees participate and which exists for the purpose, in whole or in part, of dealing with employers concerning grievances, labor disputes, wages, rates of pay, hours of employment, or conditions of work." For refusal of an exemption under sec. 14(c)1 of the act, as amended, see the Dec. 15, 1969, decision of the NLRB in Case 1-RC-10414, *American League of Professional Baseball Clubs and Association of National Baseball League Umpires, Petitioner,* 180 NLRB 190–94.

have in fact occurred only infrequently in sports. Through 1973, entire leagues have been shut down just twice—the football strike of August 1970 and the baseball strike of April 1972—and only the latter action caused any games to be canceled.

The football dispute had two phases: a management lockout from July 13 to July 29, 1970, followed by a strike lasting until August 3. The major issues were pay for preseason training and games, and the amount and financing of owners' contribution to pension funds. Agreement was reached on a four-year, $19.1 million package for pensions, disability, and other (including maternity) benefits. This represented an increase of $11 million over benefit levels of 1969. A prominent feature of this episode was the players' solidarity: only 21 of 1,300 veteran players reported to camps during the strike.[38]

The baseball strike lasted from April 1 to April 13, 1972. Again, the amount and financing of pensions and medical benefits were the primary concerns. As these issues neared resolution, a new problem appeared: whether games that had been canceled because of the strike should affect player compensation. Because players are paid a yearly salary, rather than on a per game basis, they maintained that canceled games were irrelevant. On April 10, however, the owners proposed that salaries be reduced in proportion to the duration of the strike and that all canceled games be made up in double-headers or on open dates. This plan would have caused an actual reduction of wages per game. Fortunately for the players, the owners were split, along league lines, on this issue. The final agreement added contributions by the owners of $490,000 to medical insurance and $500,000 to pension funds, and provided that none of the eighty-six canceled games be made up.[39] Finally, the strong desire of some owners (as expressed by Robert Short)[40] to break the players' union seems to have been thwarted.

In both strikes, two characteristics are apparent. First, the issues involved, particularly the level and funding of fringe benefits, were rather ordinary and predictable, and thus do not confirm fears that union activity will produce radical changes in the nature of sports. Second, the processes, results, and rhetoric associated with these examples of collective bargaining are, if a certain amateurism due to inexperience is discounted, remarkably similar to those prevailing in other industries. Clubs and players, in

38. *Monthly Labor Review,* Vol. 93 (October 1970), p. 56.
39. *Monthly Labor Review,* Vol. 95 (June 1972), p. 62.
40. *New York Times,* April 2, 1972.

fact, appear to function in a manner much more like than unlike that of their industrial counterparts, employers and workers.[41]

It was not always thus. Although player associations are almost as old as professional sports,[42] they have rarely had a powerful effect on labor relations. They appear to have been especially dormant during the 1950s, to judge from the testimony of players and player representatives at congressional hearings since 1957. A revival occurred in the mid-1960s, when new executive directors appeared almost simultaneously in the baseball, basketball, and hockey player associations. The NBA Basketball Players Association, for example, was a weak group when Lawrence Fleischer took charge. It did not have a regular dues structure, and its player representatives did not reflect the composition of the clubs. (In particular, all the representatives were white, while the league was close to being two-thirds or more black.) Copying the old trade union practice of putting locals into trusteeship, Fleisher appointed new club representatives. At the end of two years, he asserts, the organization had established itself as the most militant and united of the player associations.[43] Its success in staging annual ABA-NBA all-star games against the wishes of the owners is evidence of its unity and power.

Achieving recognition as bargaining agents and entering into formal collective agreements has not always been easy. At one point in 1946, the American Baseball Guild, led by Robert Murphy,[44] claimed to have majority membership on six teams. It extracted some concessions from the owners but was never recognized by them.[45] On the petition of the Guild,

41. Both players and management often contend that industrial relations in sports are not similar to other industries. With few exceptions, the participants from the industry at the Brookings conference on sports took this position, stressing numerous attitudinal differences between, on the one hand, players and owners and, on the other hand, labor and management in other industries.

42. Baseball began as a nomadic enterprise with little management activity; so it is not surprising that player associations are roughly coeval with the National League itself. In 1890, in fact, players established their own competitive league, although they were forced to disband after one year. A resurgence of player organization in the Baseball Players Fraternity caused considerable turmoil in the mid-teens of this century.

43. Conversation with Fleisher, April 21, 1971.

44. "Murphy money," the weekly expense allowance paid in spring training, commemorates him.

45. Television spots during the 1971 World Series commemorated the twenty-fifth anniversary of the pension fund; similar spots explained fringe benefits for players during the 1972 Series. In both cases, the foresight and liberality of the owners were praised but the Guild's role was never mentioned.

the Pennsylvania Labor Relations Board ordered a certification election in Pittsburgh; the Guild lost, 15–3, and promptly vanished.

More recently, the associations have been more successful: clauses in standard contracts for baseball, basketball, and hockey players have been altered by collective agreement. Although collective bargaining cannot negotiate individual salaries, it can effect changes in the salary determination process that improve the player's bargaining position. Player associations have accomplished this by obtaining such concessions as imposing and continually raising the minimum salary in a league, thus exerting upward pressure on the whole salary structure; permitting a player to be accompanied by a lawyer when negotiating his contract (a major achievement in baseball); and capturing more liberal severance pay arrangements. Perhaps the most important gains of this kind are the arrangements in hockey and baseball for the arbitration of salary disputes.

In hockey, disputes are to be settled by a permanent, impartial umpire, who can compare the aggrieved player's pay and performance with those of other players in the league, but who is expressly forbidden to take into account the financial position of the club involved—an important provision if wealth is unevenly distributed within a league.[46] In baseball, professional arbitrators can be called in at the request of a player with two years' major-league service to decide between the last offer of the club and the player's demand, but they are not allowed to name figures other than these.[47] While arbitration is an important gain for players, it will not raise salaries to competitive levels. Since arbitration decisions are based upon the existing salary structure in a league, their main effect will be to raise the unusually low pay of some players. The case of John McKenzie, whose salary was arbitrated during the 1971–72 season, provides evidence that arbitration does not produce competitive results. The arbitrator settled on the $48,000 salary McKenzie received that season, which was less than half that offered by both the WHA and NHL teams that desired his services the next year.[48]

There is still plenty of scope for further growth in the power of associations and the variety of issues they may deal with. A conspicuous ex-

46. Complete details of the hockey arrangement can be found in the records of any of the lawsuits involving players who joined the WHA for the 1972–73 season.

47. *Washington Post*, March 1, 1973. This provision reflects the greater emphasis in the baseball association on journeymen rather than helpers, since the latter rarely remain in the majors for more than two years.

48. *Philadelphia World Hockey Club,* Exhibit 72.

ample of an issue associations might well contest is the unilateral authority of management to make hiring and firing decisions. As the following two cases show, the modern equivalent of baseball's traditional blacklists is the "judgment of competence."

The 1968 labor dispute in the NFL appears to have resulted in punitive action against the player representatives. Gwilym S. Brown writes that, although representatives are chosen partly for their playing excellence, "a player rep's chance of being traded, waived or cut is about three times as high as that of a player who minds his own business. . . . In addition, reps have been demoted to the taxi squad, benched, and pressured."[49] Illegal reprisals for union activity are clearly the issue here, but management's extensive rights to judge competence makes the case hard to prove.

A somewhat different issue is raised by the case of two American League umpires who claimed that they had been discharged for organizing a union. The league argued explicitly that the men, who had twenty years' experience between them, had been released for incompetence, and the League President Joseph Cronin claimed that he was unaware of their role in the Association of Major League Umpires. The NLRB examiner rejected the arguments of the umpires on the ground that they had not *proved* that organizing activity was the cause of their dismissal.[50] This burden of proof is a legal standard applied to other industries, which may, however, be hard to apply to sports, where the excuses available for discharge are almost innumerable. If current contracting arrangements are retained, the thorniest industrial relations problem will be the development of substantive and procedural standards of due process in questions of professional competence.

In the performing arts, the closest parallel to sports, nonrenewal of contract counts as a grievance and can (under some union contracts) be arbitrated. The consensus of opinion in this field appears to be that an arbitrator should infringe on management's right to dismiss only if it can be proved that nonrenewal was based on considerations other than artistic competence (racial discrimination, for example). In practice, most performers seem to prefer to leave quietly, salvaging what is left of their careers, rather than to create a furor producing questionable personal

49. "Owners Can Be Tackled, Too," *Sports Illustrated,* Vol. 3 (March 22, 1971), p. 19.

50. Bureau of National Affairs, *Daily Labor Report,* Issue 226 (Nov. 20, 1970), pp. A-13.

returns.[51] There would surely be more cases in sports, as there would be more causes of grievance (player trades and sales in addition to releases and demotions). But many problems would arise. If, for instance, a player were reinstated, how long would an owner have to wait before releasing him again? The Alex Johnson case illustrates how difficult these matters can be. Johnson was suspended by the California Angels for lackadaisical play and otherwise improper behavior brought on by mental illness. Johnson fought the suspension, and won his case on the ground that mental and physical ailments are equally valid reasons for being placed on the full-pay disabled list. But the arbitrator's decision is of little practical help to his future in baseball.[52]

The right of teams and leagues to fine a player for unsatisfactory performance or violation of conduct rules also raises difficult problems of protecting the rights of players. In 1972, the NFL Players Association won a legal action against the NFL for automatic fines imposed on any player engaging in a fight during a football game, but this did not destroy the ability of management to mete out penalties to individuals on a selective basis. The case of Jim Snowden, occurring soon after the NFL players won their case, illustrates the point. Snowden, a member of the Washington Redskins, was injured and unable to play in the 1973 Super Bowl. Nevertheless, Coach George Allen fined him $1,000 for missing a team curfew a few nights before the game. As with judgments of competence, the likely, though imperfect, solution to arbitrary and capricious fines is probably arbitration. Since fines are very common and generally involve not more than a few hundred dollars, each sport might reduce the costs of the arbitration process by retaining a permanent umpire for these cases.

Many other practices are likely targets of action by the player associations. The following list summarizes the areas that have been explored during past negotiations, and includes several not discussed above:

1. infractions for which penalties may be imposed (such as elimination of fines for "indifferent play" in the NHL)
2. methods of imposition and amounts of fines and suspensions

51. Michael H. Moskow, in *Labor Relations in the Performing Arts: An Introductory Survey* (Associated Councils of the Arts, 1969), cites only four cases in symphony orchestras of nonrenewal taken to arbitration.
52. See the *New York Times,* Sept. 29, 1971. The Johnson case ended happily, as he subsequently found employment with the Cleveland Indians and the Texas Rangers.

3. rules on termination payments
4. rules on transfers, payments of moving costs, and so forth
5. pension, health insurance, and other benefits
6. subsistence, food, and lodging allowances and standards of accommodation
7. scheduling of games
8. frequency of play
9. length of the season
10. changes in working conditions (for example, introduction of artificial turf in football)
11. distribution of championship playoff, all-star games, and other proceeds
12. grievance procedures in connection with any of the above.

Other labor relations problems could be added to the associations' agenda for action. The nature of the industry has led to adoption of a bargaining unit that was appropriate for the issues to be collectively negotiated. Because of the importance of rules governing movements from team to team, the fact that the usual industrial concept of seniority has no applicability to these enterprises, and the need for a common portable pension scheme, bargaining currently takes place at the industry (or cartel) level. But "local" bargaining also has a potentially important role. Many issues arise at the team level, and formal machinery does not now generally exist for dealing with them (except, to some extent, in baseball). In particular, many of the racial discontents seem to be problems associated with the managing and coaching staff. Other issues could include profit sharing, the quality of clubhouse facilities, and team travel arrangements. The player associations must develop the capabilities of their "locals" if the issues of concern to the players of an individual club are to be resolved.

In light of the preceding discussion, what is to be made of the popular journalistic claim that "unions will wreck sports"? A sophisticated variant of this position was given by Robert Creamer:

Whenever owners and players bicker, the fans are the ones who get it in the neck. When a strike is on they are threatened with no pro football. When it is settled they pay the added cost. . . . What the owners and players were fighting about [in the 1970 NFL strike], then, was the money in the wallets and checking accounts of people whose only connection with the game is emotional. If someday the fans were to become disenchanted, if in an involuntary display of unity they all suddenly decided to go on strike themselves and neither buy tickets nor watch pro football on television, where would that leave the owners and the players?

It can't happen, of course. At least, not all at once.[53]

Is this just the age-old argument against unions that management in almost all industries has voiced? If not, what do the fans fear? Of course, they dislike being inconvenienced, but strikes or threats thereof at "inconvenient" times (*not,* for example, during preseason training, such as the "holdout" or the 1970 football strike) are the most powerful weapons the players can have. This problem is probably foremost in the public mind, but in comparison to the inconveniences caused by other labor disputes in the United States, this is trivial indeed.

Perhaps fans are unhappy about the rising number of legal squabbles in sports. But the purpose of bargaining and legal conflict, however unpleasant, is to allow the participants to resolve problems and live together more harmoniously. The squabbles are symptomatic of more basic conflicts, not the cause. The public may also be concerned that union activity will reduce the quality of play. It is possible that drastic changes in personnel might become more difficult to make, either through limitations on management's right to fire or through restricting trades. Still, direct implications for the overall level of play are difficult to identify. Finally, fans may fear that union activity will raise wages and benefits, which, in turn, will cause ticket prices to go up. The importance of the television sector of the market makes this a point of questionable significance, particularly in view of evidence that a number of football franchises currently face excess demand for tickets. Moreover, to the extent that gains in compensation come out of monopoly profits, the effect of higher player salaries on prices is likely to be minimal.

Government

The most important governmental influences on labor relations in sports have been in the form of application of the Labor Management Relations Act and the procedures of the National Labor Relations Board to the industry. Several practices that are or have been common in professional sports are explicitly contrary either to the LMRA or to rulings of the NLRB. In the past, for example, owners financed player associations, which is a violation of the LMRA.

53. "Scorecard," *Sports Illustrated,* Vol. 33 (Aug. 10, 1970), p. 6.

More difficult to establish, but also illegal, are refusals to bargain in good faith over "wages, hours, and other terms and conditions of employment." All of the major-league player associations have attempted to submit the player reservation system to collective bargaining, but apparently only in basketball have the owners been willing to bargain at all on this issue.[54] The transcript of the Curt Flood case challenging baseball's reserve clause is replete with claims by player representatives that the owners have refused to bargain at all on the reserve system.[55] The joint study provided for by the 1973 contract between major-league baseball and the player associations could represent a break in this logjam.

A similar refusal to bargain appears to have arisen in hockey. After reviewing the history of bargaining in the sport, Judge A. Leon Higginbotham, Jr., who issued the preliminary injunction that enabled Bobby Hull and John McKenzie to play in the WHA, concluded: "There is no indication that for any of the benefits offered the players that the owners would have been willing to modify the reserve clause in lieu of the other benefits given. Thus in that context there does not appear to have been any 'collective bargaining' on the reserve clause except as to arbitration of salary."[56]

Management has also violated established rules in labor relations by treating agreements in a rather cavalier fashion. After an agreement between the NFL Players Association and the owners was reached in the summer of 1970, the players complained to the NLRB that the owners were making unilateral changes on matters previously agreed to collectively but, several months later, still not written into a formal document. An NLRB examiner had to order the clubs to put the agreement on paper or have a hearing before the Board.[57] Similarly, the National Hockey League was slow in ratifying an agreement that its negotiating committee reached with the NHL Players Association. In November 1972, Judge Higginbotham noted that "there is no evidence that the so-called arbitration agreement of March 29, 1972 . . . has ever been formally approved or

54. The incentive for agreement on this issue was greatly increased by the surprising difficulty the ABA and NBA encountered in obtaining approval of a merger.

55. *Curtis C. Flood* v. *Bowie K. Kuhn et al.,* 316 F. Supp. 271 (S.D.N.Y. 1970). Jim Bouton reported having suggested at a bargaining session that the reserve clause expire on the player's sixty-fifth birthday. The owners turned down the proposal (pp. 1893–94 of the trial transcript). Perhaps they feared that Satchel Paige would make another comeback!

56. *Philadelphia World Hockey Club,* p. 47.

57. *New York Times,* May 27, 1971.

adopted by the Board of Governors of the National Hockey League, as required by NHL By-Laws 2.2(a)."[58]

Existing antitrust laws and labor relations practices interact to raise another interesting issue of public policy. In each sport, the standard player contract is incorporated in the collective bargaining agreement between the player association and the owners. The Clayton Act (sections 6 and 20) exempts labor organizations from antitrust liability, at least to some degree, and owners have claimed that this exemption prevents antitrust actions against the reserve clause.[59] Although the legal precedent is by no means clear, the most common view is that the exemption applies if the "union acts in its self-interest and does not combine with non-labor groups."[60] This view was enunciated more clearly in *Allen Bradley* when the Supreme Court held that "Congress never intended that unions could, consistently with the Sherman Act, aid nonlabor groups to create business monopolies and to control the marketing of goods and services."[61] In a similar vein, *United Mine Workers* v. *Pennington* held that a collective agreement creating wage cost barriers to entry was not exempt from antitrust proceedings.[62] In another case, restrictions on marketing hours arising from a union contract were held to be covered by the antitrust exemption.[63] The Supreme Court was willing to apply the exemption in this instance because it determined that the collective bargaining agreement was primarily in the interests of the union, only secondarily affecting competition in the product market. According to the Court, "the crucial determinant is not the form of the agreement—e.g., prices or wages—but its relative impact on the product market and the interests of union members."[64] Judge Higginbotham, after reviewing these and other cases, ruled that the Clayton Act exemption did not apply to the reserve clause in hockey. Presumably his ruling would have equal validity for the other sports. His decision was based upon the following conclusions:

First, those cases [where the exemption was applied] all involved situations

58. *Philadelphia World Hockey Club*, p. 58.

59. The case is most completely made in Michael S. Jacobs and Ralph K. Winter, Jr., "Antitrust Principles and Collective Bargaining by Athletes: Of Superstars in Peonage," *Yale Law Journal*, Vol. 81 (November 1971), p. 28.

60. *United States* v. *Hutcheson*, 312 U.S. 219 (1941) at 232.

61. *Allen Bradley Co.* v. *Local Union No. 3, International Brotherhood of Electrical Workers*, 325 U.S. 797 (1945) at 808.

62. *United Mine Workers* v. *Pennington*, 85 Sup. Ct. 1585 (1965).

63. *Local Union No. 189, Amalgamated Meat Cutters & Butcher Workmen of North America, AFL-CIO* v. *Jewel Tea Co.*, 381 U.S. 676 (1965) at 684.

64. Ibid. at 690.

where the union had been sued for its active, conspiratorial role in restraining competition of a product market, and the union, not the employer, sought to invoke the labor exemptions. . . .

Second, the cases cited above pertained to issues which furthered the interests of the union members and on which there had been extensive collective bargaining. . . .

Finally, even if, *arguendo,* there had been substantial arm's-length collective bargaining by the National Hockey League and the Players' Association to revise the perpetual option provision of the reserve clause . . . those negotiations would not shield the National Hockey League from liability in a suit by outside competitors who sought access to players under the control of the National Hockey League.[65]

Of course, Judge Higginbotham's preliminary injunction in a district court does not necessarily make long-standing precedent. Nevertheless, the current state of judicial opinion appears to be that the player reservation system does not qualify for the labor exemption from antitrust; or at least that emergent leagues and players wishing to join them may seek to use antitrust as a means to open up interleague competition in the player markets. This gives player associations less reason to fear that by negotiating changes in the reservation system they are precluding other means of changing or abolishing the system. Whether the players can achieve their goals through bargaining is as yet an unanswered question; perhaps recent court decisions will induce the owners to bargain seriously on the reserve systems. If the parties cannot resolve the issue themselves, outside agents (Congress or the courts) will have to do it for them.

Public and Private Policy Issues in Industrial Relations

This chapter has touched on a wide range of problems and inequities in the labor relations aspect of sports. They are summarized here in order to explore how policy toward them should be formulated. In this connection, the following questions must be answered: How should these issues be resolved? What role should or need the government play? Which problems are most likely to reach equitable and workable solutions through collective bargaining or other private mechanisms? Should policy be formulated and administered publicly or privately?

The Reserve Clause

The central problem of sports labor relations is management power and prerogatives, and the most important current issue is the player reservation

65. *Philadelphia World Hockey Club,* pp. 77–78.

system. Success in the use of antitrust laws to attack the reserve clause has been mixed, with attacks most likely to succeed when a new, competing league tries to lure players from the old league. Antitrust may in theory be an effective weapon, but the expense and protractedness of cases makes its practicability limited.[66] Collective bargaining seems more promising, but here the players must overcome the objections of owners who have thus far been extremely reluctant to allow the issue to be subject to negotiation.

The 1973 baseball agreement will undoubtedly cause the issue to be brought to a head. It calls for a three-year study by players and owners of realistic mechanisms for revising the player reservation system. The study is to serve as the basis for negotiating changes when the basic agreement is renegotiated in 1976. Marvin Miller, the executive director of the Major League Baseball Players Association, a man with a lifetime of experience as a labor negotiator, is a tough and able union leader who is strongly committed to significantly weakening, if not eliminating, the reserve clause. Unless the owners depart from their historical reluctance to weaken the reservation system in any fashion, the 1976 negotiations are likely to be tumultuous, perhaps culminating in a strike or lockout of long duration. Unless the reserve system is dismantled by the courts, these negotiations will probably be the definitive test of whether player associations have the strength to force significant changes in the institutional structure of the sports labor market.

If the baseball players should fail, or if they should succeed only at the cost of a long-term strike, public intervention could emerge as the least of the evils necessary to resolve the issue. The other professional sports are likely to draw their cues for future actions in this area from the outcome of the baseball negotiations. Failure by the baseball players would likely destroy the player association; other player unions would not risk a similar fate, but would instead turn to government. A costly strike in baseball, whatever the outcome, might make both sides in other sports more willing to defer the matter to government decision, either by requesting specific legislation defining the legitimate bounds of anticompetitive restrictions in the player market, or by supporting the proposal to establish a regulatory commission for professional sports.

A possible advantage of government intervention on this issue, aside from avoiding a period of strife, is that such action is more likely to respond to the interests of the unrepresented participants in the player

66. See Chapter 11 for a full discussion.

market. The player associations represent only the established players, those on the roster of a major-league team. In baseball and hockey, enormous numbers of minor-league players are not represented, nor, in all sports, is the amateur about to embark on a professional career. This is hardly unusual: industrial unions typically have no concern with potential employees of the establishments they cover. Nevertheless, because the composition of the nonmajor-league pool of players is so fluid, so that they are not likely to be effectively organized, and because management's prerogatives and practices are at least as harsh in the minors as they ever were in the majors, government intervention might be desirable as a means of extending to minor leagues some of the protections and benefits achieved by collective bargaining in the major leagues.

The major disadvantage of government control, except for the normal problems of bureaucratic behavior,[67] is that it may be insufficiently responsive to differences among sports. The needs of hockey and baseball, for example, which do not benefit from as extensive a player preparation system in colleges and high schools, are likely to be quite different from the needs of basketball and football, where there is no investment in minor-league training that clubs protect through restrictions on competition for players.

Player Compensation

Although individual player salaries are unlikely ever to be determined through collective bargaining, other matters are ripe for continued negotiation, whatever the eventual status of the reserve clause. Players will continue to want pension rights, living allowances for away games, and other fringe benefits to be kept in line with inflation and take-home pay, and this is most easily and effectively accomplished through collective bargaining.

The other major collective bargaining issue relating to player compensation is the procedure for arbitration of salary disputes. Unlike the fringe benefit issue, this seems likely to wither away should the player reservation system be eliminated or significantly weakened. If teams compete for players, the highest salary offered is presumed to be a fair estimate of the player's worth. The need for arbitration arises only if interteam competition for players is restricted. Nevertheless, until such competition is al-

67. See Chapter 12.

lowed, players in the sports without salary arbitration arrangements (football and basketball) are likely to demand and eventually receive it.

Other Issues

The power of teams to control the behavior of players and to fine, suspend, or fire them on the basis of a unilateral determination of the extent to which they conform to this code is also likely to be a continuing matter for collective bargaining. Because professional sports does require that employees maintain their bodies in acceptable physical condition, owners are always going to insist on having some control over players in this area. While such control may be necessary to the success of the industry, it also creates opportunities for abuse, and hence will continue to evoke a collective bargaining response. For the same reasons, working conditions, such as field composition and clubhouse accommodations, are likely to continue to be a management prerogative, but one subject to increasing scrutiny by player unions.

Another unresolved issue is the status of personnel other than players in the collective bargaining system. In baseball, almost all coaches, managers, and trainers are members of the player association, but they are not covered by the players' basic agreement with the leagues. Since their numbers are relatively small compared to the number of players, these groups are unlikely ever to be well represented within the player association; and, in any event, their interests often do not coincide with those of the players. Even more removed are the referees, umpires, and other officials, who are employed by the leagues rather than the teams and who are not in a position to be closely associated with players. All of these groups are likely to be effectively represented only by their own unions; and since wages, working conditions, rules of conduct, and fringe benefits are as important to them as to anyone else, such unions seem likely to be established along the pattern of that of the baseball umpires.

Finally, what should be the role of the players in choosing the commissioner of their sport? Some player associations have complained that they have no role in the selection of a commissioner, but others have argued that they want no such role, preferring to see the commissioner clearly identified as the spokesman for the owners. The situation is complicated by the fact that the commissioner is currently the final interpreter of league rules. In baseball, for example, any penalty levied by the commissioner for actions that would undermine the integrity of baseball or weaken the public's confidence in the honesty of the sport cannot be appealed. The history of sports—notably the Black Sox scandal in baseball—indicates that it is probably necessary for someone to have such sweeping power. But, while it makes sense to have a spokesman for the owners (the commissioner) who can deal directly with a spokesman for the players (the executive director of the Players Association), the players allow enormous power to a representative of the owners by not participating in the selection of a commissioner. There seem to be two alternatives: either the players will gain some power over the commissioner's office, or the development of a comprehensive arbitration system for fines and penalties will effectively redefine his role.

Conclusions

Unions of professional athletes are really in their formative stages. They have become active and powerful only since the mid-1960s, and are still learning the extent of their strength and of the issues they might attack. It is reasonable to expect that they will become more important in the future and will succeed in reducing the degree to which industrial relations and salary determination are dominated by the owners.

The major factor working to inhibit the unions is the strength of the owners' position. Although unions have overcome antiunion employers in other industries, the problem is probably more difficult in sports than elsewhere. The owners enjoy much prestige, and usually receive favorable treatment from the press (which in turn depends primarily upon the owners for access to news). The position of the owners is further strengthened by the fact that most have diverse business interests and derive much of their financial benefit from sports from the tax advantages of ownership.[68] These tax advantages would persist even if a long strike ensued, and, since the entire profit, if any, of many teams derives from the tax advantages,[69] they could avoid operating losses by simply refusing to stage games. Nevertheless, in both instances in which player strikes did occur, the owners did not choose to try to break the union. It is, therefore, likely that these associations are permanent features of the sporting scene.

This conclusion may not please the public; yet, aside from the space it steals from real sporting news on the sports pages of American news-

68. See Chapter 5.
69. See the profit figures in Chapter 1.

papers, this development has little consequence for the fan. The small size of the industry and the absence of important linkages with other parts of the economy mean that labor strife in sports has minimal impact. And, since teams normally operate in a monopoly market when selling their services, the financial consequences of collective bargaining are likely to be confined to the distribution of monopoly profits between owners and players and not passed on as increases in the ticket prices paid by fans.

CHAPTER SEVEN

Discrimination: The Case of Baseball

GERALD W. SCULLY

---

*All his past fame was forgotten—he was now a hopeless
  "shine"—
They called him "Strike-out Casey" from the mayor down
  the line;
And as he came to bat each day his bosom heaved a sigh,
While a look of hopeless fury shone in Casey's eye.*[1]

MAJOR-LEAGUE BASEBALL is America's oldest and most venerable
professional sport, billed from the beginning as the national pastime. It
has cultivated an ethos of "fair play" in an effort to protect its privilege
of self-regulation and to secure immunity from the standards by which
others are judged. The motives of men in baseball are rarely questioned,
and their actions tend to be rationalized as being in the interest of the
"integrity of the game."

Major-league baseball is more than a business and a sport. It has long
been regarded as a symbol of the American meritocracy. Ethnic minorities
have sought through sports, which requires only particular athletic skills,
what they could not attain elsewhere because of educational and language
difficulties. On the field, it was and is asserted, all men compete equally.
For Germans, Irish, Italians, and, now, Negroes, baseball has been the
symbolic exit from the ghetto.

1. From a poem by James Wilson, quoted in Hy Turkin and S. C. Thompson,
The Official Encyclopedia of Baseball (5th ed. rev., A. S. Barnes, 1970), p. 642. The
term "shine," of course, is colloquial, ethnic in origin, and pejorative in tone.

Despite the image of sports as a symbol of opportunity, those seeking to better their circumstances through baseball and other sports may incur great disappointment.

At the most, sports has led a few thousand Negroes into a better life while substituting a meaningless dream for hundreds of thousands of other Negroes. . . . For every Willie Mays or Bob Hayes there are countless Negroes who obviously had abundant will and determination to succeed, but who dedicated their childhoods and their energies to baseball gloves and shoulder pads. If there were other ways out and up, they were blinded to them by the success of a few sports celebrities. . . . This has been the major effect of sports on the Negro, and it overrides all others.[2]

It is a commonly held belief that baseball, unlike the greater society at large, has afforded Negroes equal status and equal opportunity. Nevertheless, "Negro athletes do not agree. . . . [They] say they are underpaid [and] shunted into certain stereotyped positions."[3] Surely, evidence cannot be found to sustain such a charge against major-league baseball! After all, the Negroes who have made it in the sport are successful by any standard. Nearly 25 percent of all major-league players are black, and many earn $100,000 or more annually. Yet, there is in fact evidence of racial discrimination in baseball: Negro ballplayers face markedly stiffer entrance requirements and earn significantly less for equivalent performance than whites do. This chapter explores the history and present status of these findings.

The Roots of Discrimination

The signing of Jackie Robinson, on October 23, 1945, to play with the Dodger organization at Montreal was widely touted as the beginning of a new phase in race relations in the United States. But the monumental efforts required of the civil rights movement during the fifties and sixties belie the wider importance of the Robinson event, although the signing was certainly an important breakthrough for both baseball and society as a whole. In any event, the signing of Robinson at least made public declarations of racist attitudes in baseball unfashionable. Personalities in baseball, both black and white, became silent on the race issue. It is significant that not one word concerning race discrimination was uttered

2. Jack Olsen, "The Cruel Deception," *Sports Illustrated,* Vol. 29 (July 1, 1968), p. 16.
3. Ibid., p. 15.

either in testimony before the Celler committee in 1951[4] or in the Senate hearings conducted by Senator Estes Kefauver in 1958.[5] This silence created the illusion that baseball had adjusted to the presence of blacks in its ranks. Even Jackie Robinson, who was later to speak of the opprobrium that had been heaped on him,[6] was silent on the problem of the Negro ballplayer in his testimony before the Senate.[7] Thus, the period from 1947 until about 1970, when some black athletes began to speak critically about their position in professional sports, was characterized by a sense of euphoria about the state of race relations in sports. The large number of Negro major leaguers and the high salaries of the black superstars have contributed to the illusion that racial inequalities do not exist in baseball. This section establishes that with the signing of Robinson discrimination was not eliminated, but simply became more subtle in form.

Discrimination during the Early Period, 1845–98

Baseball originated in the urban areas of the North before the Civil War. The first professional baseball team, the Knickerbocker Club of New York City, was founded in September 1845. The institution of baseball quickly came to be regarded as a perfect manifestation of American democratic principles. Though dating from the First World War, the remarks of John K. Tener, president of the National League and former governor of Pennsylvania, accurately reflect the feelings of men in baseball throughout its history: "I tell you that baseball is the very watchword of democracy. There is no other sport or business or anything under heaven which exerts the leveling influence that baseball does. Neither the public school nor the church can approach it. Baseball is unique. England is a democratic country, but it lacks the finishing touch of baseball."[8] Indeed, in many respects, baseball was ahead of its time in measuring men by ability and not by

4. *Study of Monopoly Power,* Pt. 6, *Organized Baseball,* Hearings before the Subcommittee on Study of Monopoly Power of the House Committee on the Judiciary, 82 Cong. 1 sess. (1952).

5. *Organized Professional Team Sports,* Hearings before the Subcommittee on Antitrust and Monopoly of the Senate Committee on the Judiciary, 85 Cong. 2 sess. (1958).

6. Carl T. Rowan with Jackie Robinson, *Wait Till Next Year: The Life Story of Jackie Robinson* (Random House, 1960).

7. "Statement of Jackie Robinson, Formerly with the Brooklyn Dodgers," in *Organized Professional Team Sports,* Senate Hearings, pp. 294–302.

8. Harold Seymour, *Baseball: The Early Years* (New York: Oxford University Press, 1960), p. 83.

ethnic origin. Throughout the post–Civil War period, minority groups, especially those of Irish and German descent, represented the majority of professional ballplayers.[9]

The opportunities available for Negroes were always limited. As early as 1867, Negro players and clubs were formally banned from playing with white teams. The National Association of Baseball Players (NABBP), at its national convention in Philadelphia in 1867, approved the proposal of its nominating committee to exclude Negroes from baseball. It was accurately reported that the purpose of the ban was "to keep out of the Convention the discussion of any subject having political bearing. . . ."[10] This motivation is borne out by the official records of the convention.[11]

The NABBP ban was effective for a while. Although the National Association of Professional Baseball Players (NAPBBP), formed in 1871 to replace the NABBP, did not incorporate a formal ban on Negro players, they were effectively excluded for a time by a "gentleman's agreement." But the ban against Negroes was never totally effective after the establishment of the NAPBBP. John W. (Bud) Fowler, who was the first paid Negro ballplayer, was on a white team in New Castle, Pennsylvania, in 1872.[12] It is also believed that there were "one or two other Negro players on white teams during the late 1870s and early 1880s."[13]

Opportunities for blacks in the early period reached their height in 1884–88; some have judged that this was a period when baseball was actually integrated.[14] But even in the peak year of 1887, the number of Negro players on white teams or in white leagues was minuscule. The period was initiated by the signing of Moses Fleetwood Walker with Toledo in 1883. The following year, Toledo entered the old American Association, making Walker the first Negro major leaguer. Later in the 1884 season his younger brother Weldy W. Walker played in six games when Toledo was shorthanded, thus becoming the second Negro major leaguer. At the end of the 1884 season, Fleet Walker was released by

9. Seymour (ibid., p. 334) notes that "so many Irish were in the game that some thought they had a special talent for ball playing. Fans liked to argue the relative merits of players of Irish as against those of German extraction."

10. *Beadle's Dime Base-Ball Player* (New York: Beadle and Co., 1868), p. 55.

11. Seymour, *Baseball,* p. 42.

12. A. S. ("Doc") Young, *Negro Firsts in Sports* (Johnson, 1963), p. 16.

13. Robert Peterson, *Only the Ball Was White* (Prentice-Hall, 1970), p. 21. This is a good account of the history of the Negro leagues.

14. Young, *Negro Firsts,* p. 56.

Toledo after several disabling accidents, and Negroes were not to play in the majors again until 1947. In 1885, only Fleet Walker and Bud Fowler were in the organized white leagues.[15] In 1886, with the addition of George W. Stovey and Frank Grant, four Negroes played on white minor-league teams.[16] By 1887, the number of Negro players had grown to about eight.[17] More importantly, in the same year the League of Colored Base Ball Clubs obtained recognition as a legitimate minor league; however, it collapsed almost immediately owing to the precarious financial position of its teams.

Despite these gains, there was every indication that the integration of Negroes into organized baseball would be only temporary. The fielding of Fleet Walker by Toledo caused several players and teams to declare that they would refuse to play if Walker were in the lineup. For example, in 1887, Adrian ("Cap") Anson refused to allow the Chicago White Stockings to play in an exhibition game against Newark until Stovey and Walker were removed. In the same year, the entire St. Louis Browns team, except Charlie Comiskey and Ed Knouff, signed a letter protesting a scheduled exhibition game with the Cuban Giants, the first Negro professional team.[18] Syracuse and Buffalo also had protests from their white players because of the signing of Robert Higgins and Frank Grant.[19] Douglas Crothers and Henry Simon, two white players at Syracuse, refused to have their picture taken with Higgins in an incident that was obviously racial in origin.[20]

To counteract the growing prejudice against Negroes, blacks and whites inside baseball adopted the ploy of advertising Negroes as Cubans or Spaniards. In 1886, when Frank Grant moved from Meriden, Connecticut, of the Eastern League, to Buffalo, of the International Association, the Buffalo *Express* reported that Grant was a Spaniard.[21] The first Negro professional team called itself the Cuban Giants and spoke in faked Spanish on the field.[22] Of the same genre was the attempt of John J. McGraw

15. Peterson, *Only the Ball Was White,* p. 24.

16. Ibid., p. 25.

17. Ibid., p. 26. Lee Allen, *100 Years of Baseball: The Intimate and Dramatic Story of Modern Baseball from the Game's Beginnings up to the Present Day* (Bartholomew House, 1950), p. 282, claims that there were about twenty Negro players on white teams in 1887, but this estimate seems high.

18. *Sporting Life,* Vol. 9 (Sept. 21, 1887), p. 3.

19. Ibid.

20. *Sporting Life,* Vol. 9 (June 11, 1887), p. 1.

21. *Express* (Buffalo), July 13, 1886.

22. Interview with Sol White, reported in Alvin F. Harlow, "Unrecognized Stars," *Esquire,* Vol. 10 (September 1938), p. 75.

in 1901 to field the great Negro second baseman Charles Grant by advertising Grant as an Indian named Charlie Tokohoma.[23]

By 1887, player pressure was building to formally exclude Negroes from
the minor leagues. At the meeting in Buffalo of the International League
clubs on July 14, 1887, "several representatives declared that many of the
best players in the League were anxious to leave on account of the colored
element, and the board finally directed Secretary White to approve of no
more contracts with colored men."[24] The International League "liberal-
ized" its racial ban the following year in a meeting in Toronto: it agreed
to a policy of one Negro per team.

In 1888, John Montgomery Ward attempted to sign George Stovey,
who had won thirty-five games for Newark during the previous season,
for his New York Giants. Cap Anson, who emerged as a powerful figure
in baseball during this period as the head of the Chicago White Stockings,
succeeded in blocking the deal.[25] After the 1888 season, a few Negro
players continued in organized baseball, but clearly the death knell had
been sounded for the participation of Negroes in white baseball. The last
Negro team to play white teams was the Acme Colored Giants, who
played in the Iron and Oil League until mid-July 1898.[26]

From 1898 to 1946, Negroes were barred from organized baseball by
an unwritten rule. They continued to play the game, but were confined to
their own leagues. On a few occasions, teams attempted to add colored
players to their rosters, but failed. The extent of racial discrimination is
indicated by the attempt of Walter McCredie, the manager of Portland
in the Pacific Coast League, to add Lang Akena, a player of Chinese-
Hawaiian origin, to his roster. Akena was released because of "strenuous
objections from prospective team mates."[27]

Racial Attitudes, 1933–45

With few exceptions, little of importance concerning the Negro in organized baseball appears to have occurred from 1898 until the 1930s. In
the thirties, agitation began for the admission of Negroes into baseball's
ranks. Influential sportswriters, such as Heywood Broun, Jimmy Powers,
and Shirley Povich, spoke out against the ban. Their main theme was that

23. Lee Allen, *The American League Story* (Hill and Wang, 1962), pp. 20–22.
24. *Sporting Life,* Vol. 9 (July 20, 1887), p. 1.
25. Young, *Negro Firsts,* p. 56, and Allen, *100 Years,* pp. 282–83.
26. Peterson, *Only the Ball Was White,* pp. 50–51.
27. *Chicago Daily Defender,* Jan. 16, 1916.

a great wealth of Negro playing talent was going untapped. They argued that the skill of such outstanding athletes as Leroy (Satchel) Paige, James ("Cool Papa") Bell, Walter (Buck) Leonard, Slim Jones, and Josh Gibson would benefit baseball as much as it would the "Negro cause." Baseball's spokesmen were divided on how to respond to the pressure, and many of the statements of the baseball leadership on this issue during the thirties and forties were self-contradictory or conflicted with one another.

One defense was to deny that a ban against Negroes existed. In 1933, the president of the National League, John A. Heydler, stated: "I do not recall one instance where baseball has allowed either race, creed or color to enter into the question of the selection of its players."[28] In response to a charge by Leo Durocher that the commissioner of baseball was blocking the signing of Negroes, Judge Kenesaw Mountain Landis replied: "Negroes are not barred from organized baseball by the commissioner and never have been during the 21 years I have served as commissioner."[29]

In 1942, the *Pittsburgh Courier* contacted twenty-six owners and managers concerning the color ban, six of whom replied. Two said nothing. Three agreed with Landis, but had no suggestions on how to introduce Negroes into the structure of baseball. Clark Griffith of the Washington Senators offered this solution: "My idea is that the Negro leagues should be developed to the place where they will also assume a commanding place in the baseball world . . . Someday the top teams could play our top clubs for the world championship and thus have a chance to really prove their calibre."[30]

Shortly thereafter, baseball's unofficial voice, *Sporting News,* finally spoke out on the color ban:

There is no law against Negroes playing with white teams, nor whites with colored clubs, but neither has invited the other for the obvious reason they prefer to draw their talent from their own ranks and because the leaders of both groups know their crowd psychology and do not care to run the risk of damaging their own game. Other sports had their Joe Louis, Jesse Owens, Fritz Pollard, and like notables, respected and honored by all races, but they competed under different circumstances from those dominating in baseball.[31]

The editorial went on to make three further points: (1) fan-player and interplayer relationships would probably take on racial overtones, which

28. *Pittsburgh Courier,* Feb. 25, 1933.
29. Ibid., July 25, 1942.
30. Ibid.
31. *Sporting News,* Vol. 113 (Aug. 6, 1942), p. 4.

would be damaging to the game; (2) Negro players were doing well in the Negro leagues, and competition by the white teams for Negro players would decimate the Negro leagues financially; and (3) Negro agitators pressing for integration of organized baseball had the interests of neither the sport nor their race at heart.

In the early 1940s, several attempts were made to arrange tryouts for Negro players. In the spring of 1943, tryouts were promised by two Pacific Coast League executives, Clarence Rowland, president of the Los Angeles Angels, and Vince DeVencenzi, owner of the Oakland club, but in both cases, the offers were withdrawn.[32] In the same year, Bill Veeck announced plans to purchase the Philadelphia Phillies and resuscitate the team with Negro players for the 1944 season. According to Veeck, although an agreement had been reached and financing arranged, Landis blocked the deal.[33] Finally, in 1945, Negro players were given tryouts by the Dodgers, the Red Sox, and the Braves. None resulted in signings, although one of the players who tried out for the Red Sox was Jackie Robinson, who later charged that the Red Sox had not been serious.[34]

Baseball's Adjustment to Integration, 1946

Robinson and baseball were not to be denied. Within six months, Branch Rickey announced that Jackie Robinson had been signed to play in the Dodger organization at Montreal. Baseball's official response to the agitation for racial integration and to the signing of Robinson was to create a steering committee "to consider and test all matters of major league interest."[35] Uppermost in the minds of the owners were the Mexican league, the growing attacks on the reserve clause, attempts at the unionization of players, and the player demands for a pension fund. But also to be considered was how baseball should respond to the pressure for racial integration. The report of the committee was the last official racist statement from organized baseball. Considering that Robinson was already playing for Montreal, the tone of the report is surprising. A few passages will indicate the depth of the anti-integration sentiment within the baseball hierarchy. Among the arguments made were the following:

32. *Pittsburgh Courier,* May 15, 1943.
33. Bill Veeck with Ed Linn, *Veeck—As in Wreck: The Autobiography of Bill Veeck* (Putnam, 1962), pp. 171–72.
34. Rowan, *Wait Till Next Year,* pp. 99–100 .
35. *Organized Baseball,* House Hearings, p. 474.

(1) *Integrationists are no good*

Certain groups in this country, including political and social-minded drum-beaters, are conducting pressure campaigns in an attempt to force major league clubs to sign Negro players. Members of these groups are not primarily interested in professional baseball. They are not campaigning to provide better opportunity for thousands of Negro boys who want to play baseball. They are not even particularly interested in improving the lot of Negro players who are already employed. They know little about baseball—and nothing about the business end of its operation. They single out professional baseball for attack because it offers a good publicity medium.

(2) *Black fans will ruin the game*

The employment of a Negro on one AAA League club in 1946 resulted in a tremendous increase in Negro attendance at all games in which the player appeared. The percentage of Negro attendance at some games at Newark and Baltimore was in excess of 50 percent. The situation might be presented, if Negroes participate in major-league games, in which the preponderance of Negro attendance in parks such as the Yankee Stadium, the Polo Grounds, and Comiskey Park could conceivably threaten the value of the major league franchises owned by these clubs.

(3) *Negroes cannot play baseball as well as whites*

Comparatively few good young Negro players are being developed. This is the reason that there are not more players who meet major-league standards in the big Negro leagues. Sam Lacey, sports editor of the Afro-American newspapers, says, "I am reluctant to say that we haven't a single man in the ranks of colored baseball who could step into the major-league uniform and disport himself after the fashion of a big leaguer . . . There are those among our league players who might possibly excel in the matter of hitting or fielding or base running. But for the most part, the fellows who could hold their own in more than one of these phases of the game are few and far between—perhaps nil." Mr. Lacey's opinions are shared by almost everyone, Negro or white, competent to appraise the qualifications of Negro players.

(4) *Separate but equal status benefits blacks*

[The] Negro leagues cannot exist without good players. If they cannot field good teams, they will not continue to attract the fans who click the turnstiles. Continued prosperity depends upon improving standards of play. If the major leagues and the big minors of professional baseball raid these leagues and take their best players—the Negro leagues will eventually fold up—the investments of their club owners will be wiped out—and a lot of professional Negro players will lose their jobs.

(5) *Segregation is good business*

The Negro leagues rent their parks in many cities from clubs in organized baseball. Many major and minor league clubs derive substantial revenue from these rentals. (The Yankee organization, for instance, nets nearly $100,000 a year from rentals and concessions in connection with Negro league games at the Yankee Stadium in New York—and in Newark, Kansas City, and Norfolk.)[36]

Fear of economic loss weighed heavily on the minds of the club owners. It was believed that the introduction of black players would, by raising Negro attendance, drive away white fans. Another concern was the loss of frequently lucrative stadium rentals to teams in the Negro leagues. The solicitude expressed for the financial status of the Negro leagues was gratuitous, and the charge that few black players were of major-league caliber, spurious.

While baseball management was less than enthusiastic about the prospect of Negroes playing in the majors, some of the players felt strongly enough actually to attempt to block Robinson's appearance. Rickey was alleged to have asked each player, when he signed, if he had any objections to the transfer of Robinson from Montreal.[37] During spring training in 1947, there was a near mutiny of the Dodgers players,[38] but Rickey was able to quell the player revolt before it became effectively organized. Early in the season, the Phillies, Cubs, Cardinals, and possibly the Pirates threatened strikes. Some Phillies players showered Robinson with such scurrilous abuse that National League President Ford Frick and Commissioner Albert ("Happy") Chandler had to warn them against further racial baiting.[39] The threatened Cardinals player strike was the most serious, although baseball has never officially acknowledged that such a strike had been planned. Ford Frick prevented the disaster by threatening to suspend all strikers.

Racial Attitudes Today

The existence and depth of racial prejudice in baseball can be documented only before 1947. Since then, sports commentators, owners, managers, and both black and white players appear for the most part to have

36. "Report of Major League Steering Committee for Submission to the National and American Leagues at Their Meetings in Chicago," in *Organized Baseball*, House Hearings, pp. 483–84.

37. Arthur W. Mann, *Branch Rickey: American in Action* (Houghton Mifflin, 1957), pp. 256–57.

38. Rowan, *Wait Till Next Year*, pp. 175–76.

39. *Sporting News*, Vol. 123 (May 21, 1947), p. 4; Rowan, *Wait Till Next Year*, p. 183.

entered into a conspiracy of silence concerning racial tension and discrimination in the sport.

Prejudice among Fans

Baseball management was concerned that attendance would decline with the introduction of Negro players. In 1946, attendance was 18.5 million for both leagues; in 1970, it was 28.7 million. Measured in terms of average attendance per team, however, this growth was insignificant.[40] Although the popularity of baseball may not have actually declined, this does not necessarily mean that the introduction of Negro players into the game did not adversely affect attendance. Fans are attracted to ball parks by the quality of team performance, among other things, and may or may not consider the race of the players in their decision to attend. It is difficult to separate variations in attendance that are due to team performance from those that are due to the presence of Negro players if the team is used as the unit of measurement.

The following test, which uses the player as the unit of measurement, attempts to determine if racial prejudice is a characteristic of the American baseball fan. The only position in which players are rotated on a regular basis is pitcher. Moreover, starting pitchers are announced in the press before the game. The variation in pitchers and the advance knowledge of who will start offers the discriminatory fan the opportunity of deciding whether to attend on the basis of the race of the pitcher.

The average home attendance of fifty-seven National League starting pitchers was calculated for the entire 1967 season.[41] It was hypothesized that the average home attendance would vary by the pitcher's team and by the mix of games pitched (that is, the percent of games pitched after July 1 and the percent of night games, double-headers, and weekend

40. In 1946, there were sixteen teams, with an average attendance of 1.2 million per team. In 1970, there were twenty-four teams, also with an average of 1.2 million. Barry R. Chiswick has pointed out that constant average attendance per team implies a decline in attendance per game, since the number of games per year increased. This is not surprising, given the growth of competing sports (football, golf, basketball), the development and decreasing cost of television, and the rise in the opportunity cost of time (attending a game requires more time than observing it at home, and the value of time increases as earning capacity rises). However, the impact of television may be somewhat softened by the fact that baseball is probably the game that is least adaptable to television coverage because of the size of the viewing area required for full appreciation of the play.

41. Source: *New York Times,* issues during the 1967 baseball season.

games). Finally, a binary variable for race was included to determine if average home attendance with black pitchers differed significantly from that with white pitchers. The following linear multiple regression equation was obtained (the numbers in parentheses are t-statistics):

$$\bar{A}_i = 24{,}574 + 4{,}473 \text{ SF} - 7{,}804 \text{ CHI} - 10{,}776 \text{ CIN}$$
$$\phantom{\bar{A}_i = 24{,}574 +} (2.68) \qquad (4.01) \qquad (4.80)$$

$$- 10{,}876 \text{ PHIL} - 12{,}559 \text{ PITT} - 12{,}030 \text{ ATL}$$
$$ (6.71) \qquad (7.40) \qquad (6.92)$$

$$- 6{,}235 \text{ LA} - 2{,}274 \text{ HOU} - 5{,}484 \text{ NY}$$
$$ (3.86) \qquad (1.33) \qquad (3.21)$$

$$+ 272 \text{ JULY} - 1{,}046 \text{ NIGHT} + 4{,}158 \text{ DH} + 253 \text{ WEEKEND}$$
$$ (0.18) \qquad (0.36) \qquad (1.40) \qquad (0.09)$$

$$- 1{,}969 \text{ NEGRO}$$
$$ (1.78)$$

$$R^2 = 0.86; \text{ degrees of freedom} = 42.$$

The constant intercept is the average attendance per game of the first-place St. Louis Cardinals. The coefficients of the nine dummy variables assigned to the other teams are the divergence in average attendance per game from the St. Louis attendance. Clearly, intercity variation is the most important variable in explaining differences in average home attendance of starting pitchers. Except for the San Francisco Giants, whose average home attendance was significantly higher than that of St. Louis, lower ranked teams lagged behind first-place St. Louis in attendance by as few as 2,274 to as many as 12,559 fans per home game. It is interesting to note that winning affects attendance less for the newer teams: Houston and New York finished at the bottom but ranked third and fourth in average home attendance. The variables designed to capture differences in the mix of games pitched were generally not statistically significant at an acceptable level,[42] undoubtedly because there is little systematic variation in the pitching schedule rather than because the variables have little effect on attendance variation.

The most important feature of the regression results is the sign of the race variable, which suggests that an average of 1,969 fewer fans attend

42. The coefficient of the double-header variable is significant at the 90 percent level.

games pitched by blacks than those pitched by whites.[43] The variable does not measure racial differences in pitching performance, since black pitchers have significantly better pitching records than whites.[44] For example, in the 1967 season, black pitchers won an average of 2.7 more games than white pitchers. Thus, it appears that fans do alter their attendance on the basis of the race of the pitchers.

Discrimination in Hiring Players

That racial entry barriers continue to exist in baseball today is a view that is not widely shared. In 1972, blacks occupied every position except that of manager, and very often their presence was disproportionately large. If a comparison is drawn between the proportion of blacks in baseball and in the population at large, a convincing case can be made that baseball is free of racial bias in its hiring and promotion practices. By 1957–58, the percentage of blacks in baseball was about the same as in the U.S. population, but before 1953 (and for some teams even today), "tokenism" would accurately describe the racial hiring practices of most baseball teams.

The period 1947–53 was one of slow expansion in the number of black players fielded. The National League averaged three additional black players every two years, and the American League about one every two years. After 1953, black players were added more rapidly. From 1953 to 1960, the percentage of black players rose by 2.2 points per year in the National League and by 0.6 points per year in the American League. The slow response of the American League in hiring Negroes created an ever-widening interleague differential, but in 1960, the American League began to accelerate its hiring of blacks, while the increase in Negro players in the National League slowed. From 1960 to 1971, the American League added blacks at a rate that increased their share of the total available positions by 1.4 percentage points annually, in comparison to 0.6 points in the National League. In 1964, the interleague differential nearly vanished, but accelerated hiring of blacks in the National League thereafter kept it ahead of the American League in the number of black players.

Substantial differences exist in the number of black ballplayers per team. Pittsburgh, with the most black players, averaged about 35 percent black from 1960 to 1971 (see Table 1), and in 1967, over half of the

43. On a one-tail test, the coefficient is significant at the 5 percent level.
44. See Tables 6 and 9.

Table 1. Percentage of Black Players on Major-League Baseball Teams, 1960–71

Team	Average, 1960–71	1971	1970	1969	1968	1967	1966	1965	1964	1963	1962	1961	1960
National League													
Atlanta[a]	27	40	40	32	28	28	24	32	16	24	20	16	24
Chicago	19	12	20	20	24	24	28	16	20	16	20	16	16
Cincinnati	25	32	28	36	28	32	24	24	16	20	20	20	20
Houston[b]	24	36	36	32	28	28	32	16	12	12	12	..	..
Los Angeles	22	24	24	16	20	12	32	24	20	24	20	24	20
New York[b]	18	16	16	20	16	12	16	24	16	20	20	..	..
Philadelphia	26	20	24	28	24	28	20	32	20	20	24	32	28
Pittsburgh	35	48	44	36	44	56	44	32	28	32	28	16	16
San Francisco	28	24	20	28	32	32	32	32	32	28	28	20	28
St. Louis	28	32	44	36	36	40	24	24	16	24	20	16	24
Montreal[c]	20	8	20	32	..	..	..	..	..	..	..	..	..
San Diego[c]	24	16	24	32	..	..	..	..	..	..	..	..	..
Average	25	26	28	29	28	29	28	26	20	22	21	20	22

American League

Baltimore	17	36	36	36	24	12	12	8	12	8	8	4	12
Boston	14	12	12	12	24	24	24	12	12	8	8	8	4
California[b]	17	24	20	20	16	16	20	24	16	16	8	8	…
Chicago	18	28	20	24	16	20	20	20	20	12	12	20	8
Cleveland	21	20	16	24	40	32	20	16	16	28	12	20	12
Detroit	18	16	20	28	16	20	24	20	20	16	20	16	4
Minnesota[d]	22	24	32	24	24	32	24	24	20	16	16	12	16
New York	17	20	20	28	20	20	20	16	16	12	12	12	8
Oakland[e]	21	24	28	24	12	24	24	16	24	24	20	8	…
Washington[b]	17	28	24	16	24	16	16	12	16	16	8	16	…
Kansas City[c]	24	16	28	28	…	…	…	…	…	…	…	…	…
Milwaukee[e,f]	19	20	12	24	…	…	…	…	…	…	…	…	…
Average	18	22	22	24	22	22	20	17	17	16	12	12	9

Source: Calculated on the basis of data on black major leaguers available in *Ebony*, June issues, 1960–71. Figures are rounded.

a. Franchise located in Milwaukee until 1966.
b. Expansion team in the American League in 1961 and the National League in 1962.
c. Expansion team in 1969.
d. Franchise located in Washington, D.C., until 1961.
e. Franchise located in Kansas City until 1968.
f. Milwaukee franchise formerly located in Seattle.

Pittsburgh team was black. On September 1, 1971, the Pirates fielded an all-black team in a game against the Phillies.[45] Second-ranked San Francisco and third-ranked St. Louis fall considerably short of Pittsburgh in percentage of blacks. Los Angeles, which pioneered the use of black players, has recently ranked toward the bottom of the league in percent black. In the American League, the average spread between the first- and second-ranked teams is substantially less than in the National League. Cleveland, the first American League team to integrate in 1947, has remained among the leaders in hiring blacks: in 1968, 40 percent of the team was black. Only one other American League team could approach such a record for any year. Even so, only two National League teams (except the new franchise at Montreal)—Chicago and New York—have averaged fewer blacks than Cleveland over the entire period. The least integrated teams in the American League are Boston, which was the last team to integrate when it hired Elijah ("Pumpsie") Green in 1959, California, and Baltimore (which, however, has recently increased its number of blacks).

Interteam differences in the percent of black players, like the interleague differential, have remained fairly constant. The trend in intraleague inequality can be determined from the coefficients of variation presented in Table 2. In the American League, the coefficients of variation show no definite trend, with the values fluctuating around an average of 30.3 percent. In the National League, there is evidence of growing inequality among the teams.[46]

The Economics of Hiring Black Players

Increased hiring of black players, particularly in the National League from 1953 to 1960, may be explained in part by changes in the cost differential in acquiring blacks and whites of comparable talent. Pascal and Rapping concluded that other clubs followed Brooklyn's lead for solid

45. *Sports Illustrated,* Vol. 35 (Sept. 13, 1971), p. 14.
46. Anthony H. Pascal and Leonard A. Rapping, "The Economics of Racial Discrimination in Organized Baseball," in Anthony H. Pascal (ed.), *Racial Discrimination in Economic Life* (Heath, 1972), pp. 146–47, suggest that competitive pressures within the league would bring about an equalization of the proportion of black players among the teams. That is, in view of the superior playing ability of the black players, no team that wanted to win could afford to have its percentage of black players fall too far below that of its competitors. The data in Table 2 do not support this hypothesis.

Table 2. Intraleague Variations in the Percentage of Black Major-League Baseball Players, 1962–71

	Coefficients of variation	
Year	National League[a]	American League[b]
1962	21.7	38.7
1963	25.8	37.5
1964	31.1	22.1
1965	24.6	31.5
1966	28.6	19.6
1967	43.8	30.5
1968	28.6	38.5
1969	26.1	28.4
1970	35.6	32.0
1971	39.5	24.4
Average, 1962–71	30.5	30.3

Source: Calculated from Table 1.
a. Excludes Montreal and San Diego.
b. Excludes Kansas City and Milwaukee.

economic reasons: the period of unlimited free-agent bonus competition raised the relative price of white ballplayers and compelled teams to substitute lower-cost black players of comparable quality.[47] The increase in black players did coincide with an increase in bonus payments, which were becoming more and more of a drain on team resources (see Table 3). The bonus costs to teams in the major leagues from 1958 to 1969 were $63.2 million. In 1961, the year of the first American League expansion and a peak year in bonus payments, major-league teams spent about $8.5 million acquiring potential talent, with an average of about $470,000 per team. Since average team salaries per player were about $17,350 in 1961,[48] bonus costs actually exceeded player salaries for the twenty-five-man roster.

The data further show that a greater proportion of white ballplayers (over one-third) received bonus payments in excess of $20,000 in the

47. Ibid., pp. 134–35.
48. Calculated on the basis of: (1) average player salaries for 1956, estimated at $13,800 from data available in *Organized Professional Team Sports*, Senate Hearings, pp. 794–99; and (2) player salaries for 1965, averaged at $19,500 (from Arthur D. Little, Inc., "Economic Analyses of Certain Aspects of Organized Baseball" [n.d.; processed], p. 3).

Table 3. Bonus Payments to Players Signing Their First Major-League Baseball Contracts, 1958–69

Year	Number of players	Total bonus payments[a] (thousands of dollars)	Average bonus payments per team[b] (thousands of dollars)	Average bonus per player signed (dollars)	Percent of players drafted[c]	Average bonus of drafted players (dollars)	Average bonus of nondrafted players (dollars)
1958	1,473	6,456	404	4,383	...	...	...
1959	1,144	4,880	305	4,266	...	...	...
1960	1,277	5,352	335	4,191	...	...	...
1961	1,486	8,460	470	5,693	...	...	...
1962	1,113	3,863	193	3,471	...	...	...
1963	1,083	3,479	174	3,212	...	...	...
1964	1,117	5,134	257	4,596	...	...	...
1965	1,084	4,610	231	4,253	38.8	8,059	1,837
1966	1,149	4,985	249	4,339	48.8	7,756	1,077
1967	1,173	5,216	261	4,447	57.8	6,786	1,243
1968	1,109	5,249	262	4,733	58.5	7,249	1,182
1969	1,340	5,549	231	4,141	54.7	6,605	1,166
Total	14,498	63,233	...	...	...	...	...
Average	1,208	5,269	281	4,361	51.7	7,291	1,301

Source: *Curtis C. Flood v. Bowie K. Kuhn et al.*, 316 F. Supp. 271 (S.D.N.Y. 1970), trial transcript.

a. Does not include salaries or college scholarship commitments.

b. From 1958 to 1960, there were sixteen teams; in 1961, eighteen teams; from 1962 to 1968, twenty teams; and in 1969, twenty-four teams.

c. The free-agent draft was introduced in 1965.

period 1959–61 than in 1958 or earlier;[49] yet there were only three black players receiving such bonuses in the period. It seems reasonable to infer that the unlimited free-agent bonus competition, which began in 1947 as a response to rising postwar attendance and the maldistribution of talented ballplayers and as a by-product of Branch Rickey's development of the farm system,[50] pressured teams to search for a supply of talented but less expensive players. A pool of qualified blacks willing to join teams for smaller, or no, bonus payments provided the answer.

In 1961, the leagues attempted to restrain bonus competition by requiring the clubs "to keep bonus rookies on the major league roster for two years before playing them."[51] This action, coupled with other measures, reduced bonus payments significantly in 1962 and 1963;[52] simultaneously, the percentage of black players in the National League leveled off. In fact, between 1962 and 1964, the number of black players in the National League declined. By checking bonus competition, baseball had altered the relative prices of black and white players and thus reduced the economic incentive of teams to hire blacks. The adoption of the free-agent draft in 1965 seemed to have no appreciable effect on average bonus costs per team or the average bonus payment per player. While average payments have never returned to the 1961 high, they rose steadily through 1968. Negro players were still relatively more attractive financially to the teams, which probably contributed to the renewed increase in their employment.

Racial Performance Differentials and Equality of Opportunity

Comparison of the percentage of blacks in baseball with their proportion in the population may give a misleading picture of the racial situation in the major leagues. Rosenblatt suggests that numbers do not necessarily imply equality of opportunity.[53] Superior performance appears to be a requirement for the entry and retention of blacks in the game. Rosenblatt uses lifetime batting average as a measure of ability for nonpitchers,[54] and

49. Pascal and Rapping, "Economics of Racial Discrimination," p. 136.

50. Ralph Andreano, *No Joy in Mudville: The Dilemma of Major League Baseball* (Schenkman, 1965), p. 120.

51. Ibid., p. 121.

52. See Table 3.

53. Aaron Rosenblatt, "Negroes in Baseball: The Failure of Success," *Transaction*, Vol. 4 (September 1967), pp. 51–53.

54. Batting average is, of course, only one component of performance. Performance measures are discussed below.

shows that during the period 1953–65 a racial differential of about twenty points existed.[55] In 1965, 36 percent of the black players hit 0.270 or better and well over 50 percent hit 0.250 or above. Although the black superstar may not be affected, "more places are available in the majors for the substar white player than for the comparably able Negro."[56] Moreover, there is no evidence that the differential is narrowing. On the contrary, the average rate of change in the batting average differential from 1957 (the year when the percentage of blacks in baseball approximated that in society) to 1965 was +0.8 percentage points per year. If anything, the performance criterion for blacks is becoming stiffer.

Two rationalizations, other than discriminatory hiring and promotion practices, for the racial performance differential have been advanced: (1) the existence of racial differences (in the means or in the variances) in the distribution of baseball playing talent; (2) the existence of "endemic societal wage discrimination in most callings and lesser discrimination in baseball [that] may result in a systematic difference in the ability distributions of black and white baseball players through the process of occupational choice."[57]

The belief that blacks are genetically endowed with more athletic skills than whites is widespread and not without some basis in fact. It is known, for example, that Negro and Caucasian skeletons have somewhat different properties. At birth, holding prenatal environment constant, Negroes and whites differ in body weight.[58] Furthermore, Negro motor skill development proceeds more quickly during the early period of childhood.[59] But, for the genetic argument to be given serious consideration requires more than isolated and tenuously connected associations. It requires that particular baseball skills be isolated, that the differences in the amount of these skills within any group be shown to be due to genetic factors, and that the amount of these particular skills be demonstrated to vary by race. Until such an investigation is undertaken, arguments based on genetic differences must be viewed as speculative.

The second hypothesis is based on the argument that if there is discrimination in nonbaseball occupations, the incomes of blacks will be higher in the sport than outside. However, if the initial distribution of

55. Pascal and Rapping found this still to be true in 1967.
56. Rosenblatt, "Negroes in Baseball," p. 52.
57. Pascal and Rapping, "Economics of Racial Discrimination," p. 141.
58. Arthur R. Jensen, "How Much Can We Boost IQ and Scholastic Achievement?" *Harvard Educational Review,* Vol. 39 (Winter 1969), p. 87.
59. Ibid., pp. 86–87.

playing skills is racially invariant, there is no reason to expect that the black players attracted to the sport for economic reasons will have *higher* average ability.

Pascal and Rapping[60] argue that, while baseball would attract a higher percentage of above-average blacks, mediocre black players would also be attracted by the wage differential, so that the net effect on racial ability distributions would be unclear. The existence of racial income differentials does not ensure a uniform impact on supply. The supply of players of both races at any given ability level is determined by the elasticity *at that level*. In any range of ability, the supply of black players will be more elastic than that of whites, so that the fraction of players who are black should exceed the fraction of blacks in the total population. However, the income differential between sports and other occupations widens at higher ability levels, until it is finally so large as to make the "stars" of both races perfectly inelastic with respect to salary. If ability distributions are assumed to be invariant by race, the proportion of "stars" that are of a particular race should equal the proportion of that race in the total population.

Racial Entry Barriers by Position

It is possible that racial differences in ability (as measured by lifetime batting averages) could be accounted for by other factors, such as the racial distribution of players by position. For example, since outfielders have higher mean batting averages than infielders, a higher proportion of black outfielders could be the source of the performance differential. Table 4 shows that, in 1969, blacks occupied 24.1 percent of all of the available playing positions, but that their representation by position was not uniform. Specifically, relatively more blacks were in the outfield (49.6 percent) and relatively fewer in pitching (11.0 percent). Moreover, if Latin American blacks are removed from the sample, the proportion of North American blacks in the outfield becomes nearly three times (40.0 percent) that of their representation in all positions (15.8 percent). Furthermore, North American blacks are found in significantly smaller numbers in both infield (10.0 percent) and pitching (8.1 percent) positions. The absence of blacks from coaching and managerial positions is well known: in 1969, only 4.2 percent of the coaches and none of the managers were black.

The distribution of black players by position is relatively stable, as

60. "Economics of Racial Discrimination," pp. 141–42.

Table 4. Percent of Available Positions[a] Filled by Blacks, and by Blacks Born in North America, Major-League Baseball, 1969

Position	Filled by blacks	Filled by blacks born in North America
All playing positions	24.1	15.8
Outfielder	49.6	40.0
Infielder	23.1	10.0
Pitcher	11.0	8.1
Nonplaying positions	3.4	3.4
Coach	4.2	4.2
Manager	0	0

Sources: *Ebony*, Vol. 24 (June 1969), pp. 138ff.; *New York Times*, April 6, 1969; *Sporting News*, Vol. 167 (April 26, 1969).
a. Available positions obtained from the 1969 opening day rosters.

shown in Table 5. In 1960, the ratio of black infielders to black pitchers was about 2.6. In the period 1967–70, this ratio varied from about 2.4 to 2.7, but in 1971 it fell to 2.2. The real gain for black players was in the outfield. Where there were 5.6 times as many black outfielders as pitchers

Table 5. Percent of Available Playing Positions[a] Filled by Blacks in Major-League Baseball, 1960–71

Year	Position		
	Outfield	Infield	Pitcher
1960	33.3	16.0	6.0
1961	34.0	16.5	5.0
1962	37.0	15.0	8.5
1963	44.0	16.0	9.5
1964	47.0	15.0	7.5
1965	50.0	16.3	9.0
1966	58.0	22.0	9.5
1967	57.0	25.0	10.0
1968	60.0	22.5	9.5
1969	56.7	26.7	11.3
1970	59.2	24.6	9.2
1971	61.7	20.0	9.2

Source: *Ebony*, June issues, 1960–71.
a. Available playing positions per team were assumed to be five positions for outfield, ten for infield, and ten for pitchers, to form a twenty-five-man roster. This division is quite close to the actual average divisions by positions in recent years.

in 1960, by 1971 there were over 6.7 times as many. Since 1960, of a net increase in black players of eighty-four, forty-eight were outfielders. During the same period, blacks increased their share of the available outfield positions at the average annual rate of 2.4 percentage points. Meanwhile, blacks, mostly Latin American blacks, increased their share of the infield positions at the average annual rate of only 0.34 percentage points. Most of the increase in black infielders occurred after 1965. In 1969, a peak year, twenty-seven blacks (seven of them Latin American) held one of the approximately two hundred forty pitching slots. From 1960 to 1971, the average annual increase in the share of pitching slots going to blacks was 0.26 percentage points.

The performance differential apparent in the aggregate also persists at a more disaggregated level. Furthermore, the magnitude of the performance differential is related systematically to the proportion of black ballplayers. From a sample of 453 veteran ballplayers, Pascal and Rapping have calculated racial performance differentials by position. For nonpitchers they followed Rosenblatt and used cumulative lifetime batting averages. For pitchers, they measured performance by the number of games won in the 1967 season. Their calculated performance differentials are shown in Table 6. All differences in the means are significant at the 5 percent level, except for the second baseman and shortstop category. The existence of performance differentials that favor blacks is consistent with the view that baseball has racial entry barriers. Moreover, these barriers are higher for certain positions than for others. Generally, where

Table 6. Performance Differentials by Race and Position, Major-League Baseball, as of 1967

Position	Percent black	Performance differential[a]	Black-white performance ratio
Outfielder	56.6	0.120	1.047
Catcher	8.6	0.320	1.141
First and third base	33.3	0.190	1.075
Second base and shortstop	29.5	0.010	1.004
Pitcher	10.9	2.7	1.360

Source: Anthony H. Pascal and Leonard A. Rapping, "The Economics of Racial Discrimination in Organized Baseball," in Anthony H. Pascal (ed.), *Racial Discrimination in Economic Life* (Heath, 1972), pp. 138–39.

a. Except for pitchers, where the measure is games won during the 1967 season, the performance measure is the arithmetic averages of individual lifetime major-league batting averages through 1967.

there is less exclusion of blacks, the performance differential is narrower than in the high exclusion positions of catcher and pitcher.[61]

Another possible explanation for the racial difference in the distribution of positions may lie in the different early environment of black and white players. Opportunities for supervised amateur and semiprofessional baseball are probably more available to young whites than to young blacks. In the South, school and societal segregation may have caused young black players to play on poorer fields without instruction. And in northern cities, opportunities for recreation off of the streets are limited. Under those circumstances, defensive skills would probably become relatively less developed among blacks than among more intensively supervised whites. Hitting ability probably develops more fully without supervision and independently of the quality of the playing field. Consequently, the poorer environment in which blacks learned the game may be responsible for their superior hitting records.

While this explanation accounts for the relatively high proportion of Negroes in the outfield, it is inconsistent with their superior pitching and fielding performance. Negro players are among the top ten lifetime fielding leaders in nearly every playing category,[62] and as pitchers they win more often than whites. While early environment may well have been unfavorable to the development of black catchers, pitchers, and infielders, racial entry barriers appear to be the primary cause for the lower representation of Negroes in these positions. Perhaps the intensive coaching, in both the minor and major leagues, that white coaches would be required to devote to black infielders and pitchers leads to racial bias in the selection of players by position. Perhaps, since team leadership cannot easily be exercised except in the infield, it is an unwillingness to assign leadership responsibilities to blacks.

Or, perhaps it is because the real drama of baseball takes place in the infield. It is true that outfielders more frequently are the superstars, but they are not the featured actors in the game. To the stadium fan, his proximity to the outfielder is inversely related to the price of his seat; the inexpensive seats are closer to the outfield than to home plate. The television fan sees the outfielder only when he bats and fields, except momentarily during a break in the action or at the end of the inning as he trots off the field. If the pitching is at all effective, this exposure is only a frac-

61. Although it may not be strictly proper to compare the performance differentials for positions that required a different measure of performance.
62. *The Baseball Encyclopedia* (Macmillan, 1969), p. 71.

Table 7. Skin Color and Position Assignment of Black Baseball Players, 1969

Skin color	Percentage of nonoutfielders
Very light	80.0[a]
Light brown	67.9[a]
Medium brown	56.8
Dark brown	53.5
Very dark	25.0[a]
All black players	54.8

Source: Calculated from the sample of 159 black ballplayers in *Ebony*, Vol. 24 (June 1969), pp. 138–46.
a. Significant at the 1 percent level.

tion of the viewing time devoted to the battery (the catcher and pitcher). The greater frequency of fielding plays in the infield and the occasional conference of infielders at the pitcher's mound means that the exposure of infielders is between that of the battery and the outfielders. Skin color and un-Caucasian-like facial features, rather than race per se, may thus be the prime factor in blacks being all but excluded from battery positions and having lower representation in the infield than in the outfield.

The possibility that skin color was associated with the distribution of blacks by position was tested, using the pictures of all black major leaguers published annually by *Ebony* magazine (see Table 7). The 159 players were identified only by code, and grouped by skin color using five color classifications that largely followed those of G. Franklin Edwards.[63] It was hypothesized that the proportion of nonoutfielders in each skin color category would be the same as their proportion among all black ball-players. This hypothesis had to be rejected in three cases: very light and light brown players had significantly higher representation in the infield, catching, and pitching positions than predicted, while very dark brown players had significantly lower representation.

Major-league baseball has no black managers and only a few black coaches. In part, this may reflect the relatively small supply of former black players with the necessary skills and experience for these jobs. But the exclusion of blacks from coaching and managerial positions can also be related to certain characteristics of managers—their regional origin and former playing position. From 1947 to 1967, there were one hundred

63. *The Negro Professional Class* (Free Press, 1959). Edwards found that black lawyers, physicians, and teachers had significantly lighter skin than blacks as a group.

Table 8. Characteristics of Major-League Baseball Managers, 1947–67

Characteristic	Percent of total
Background	
Former player	93.5
Outfield	17.6
Infield	67.6
First base	12.1
Catcher	19.4
Other	36.1
Pitcher	8.3
Nonplayer	6.5
Region of birth	
Non-South	66.7
Northeast	22.2
Midwest	32.4
West	12.0
South	33.3

Source: Calculated from data in *The Baseball Encyclopedia* (Macmillan, 1969), pp. 356–453, 501–1688, 2206–37. Figures are rounded.

eight individuals who managed major-league teams (some, of course, managing more than one team). The regional origin of managers (see Table 8) conforms closely to the regional origin of ballplayers. About two-thirds of the managers came from nonsouthern states, while 74 percent of the 9,659 known U.S.-born players and managers in the major leagues from 1871 to 1968 were born outside of the South.[64] On the other hand, about 63 percent of the North American blacks in the 1969 sample used in Table 7 were southern born.[65] Even more striking is the fact that 67.6 percent of all managers were former infielders,[66] but only 26.3 percent of the available infield slots were filled by North American blacks in 1969.

Most managers have had some previous coaching experience. The majority of a team's coaching staff devotes itself to the infielders, catchers, and pitchers, so it is reasonable that coaches are selected predominantly from these positions. Of the four black coaches in 1969, all had been infielders. That former infielders, rather than pitchers, tend to become man-

64. *The Baseball Encyclopedia*, p. 30.
65. Calculated from the sample of 159 black ballplayers in *Ebony*, Vol. 24 (June 1969), and data on place of birth from *The Official Encyclopedia of Baseball*.
66. Infielders constitute about 40 percent of a team roster.

agers probably stems from the fact that infielders have leadership responsibilities. (Most team captains are infielders.) Pitchers, on the other hand, play, at most, 20 percent of the time and are segregated from the rest of the team during the game. Furthermore, they are relatively passive in team decision making on the field, as are outfielders.

The exclusion of blacks from managerial and coaching positions thus appears to be intimately linked to the underrepresentation of blacks in the infield. This underrepresentation certainly is not connected with poorer performance on their part; their performance is, in fact, superior to that of whites. The evidence points to the conclusion that racial prejudice is responsible for this pattern.

The Theory of Discrimination in Major-League Baseball

Prejudice against black players has three possible sources: the fan, the team owner, and white players. Prejudicial acts have economic consequences only when the discriminatory activity can be translated into an objective (money) or subjective (dissatisfaction or disutility) result.[67] If the fielding of blacks comparable in quality to whites results in a torrent of racial epithets from the grandstand but gate receipts remain unchanged, then fan prejudice has no economic consequence.[68] If owners and players are prejudiced against blacks but require no additional compensation for associating with them or impose no restrictions on their employment, then economic discrimination is not present.

Most prejudicial acts, however, do have economic consequences. Prejudice against blacks can be expressed in the baseball labor market in two ways: by excluding Negroes whose ability is equal to that of existing white players, or by paying Negroes a salary less than that paid white players of equal ability. For example, social custom may be the criterion for allocating the number and type of positions open to blacks in baseball. Before 1947, social custom dictated that blacks be totally excluded from organized baseball, no matter what their ability and no matter what their supply price relative to white players. From 1947 to 1953, the social custom of "tokenism" appears to have fixed the number of positions open

67. Gary S. Becker, *The Economics of Discrimination* (University of Chicago Press, 1957), pp. 6–7.
68. Although it would, of course, be discriminatory from a sociological perspective.

to Negroes at 5 percent or less of the total. It is possible that social custom continues to allocate the number or type of positions available to black ballplayers.

The alternative to exclusion is to compensate those who are prejudiced for tolerating the presence of blacks. For example, if the owner dislikes association with black players, a wage differential against blacks, which would compensate his disdain, would permit the employment of Negro players.

The Player's Contribution to Team Revenues

Fan discrimination can affect the net revenues generated by black ball-players.[69] Fans purchase tickets because they derive satisfaction from watching the game.[70] Their satisfaction, and hence the number of tickets sold, is assumed to be determined by the ability of the ballplayers. But if baseball viewers, a majority of whom are white, are prejudiced, black players will tend to lower gate receipts. This lowers the contribution to team revenues of blacks relative to whites of equal skill, and hence reduces the demand for black players relative to white players.

In the absence of fan discrimination, only a player's ability determines his contribution to the revenues of the team. If ability does not differ systematically between black and white players, only discrimination can cause differences in the revenues produced by players of different races. If fans discriminate, ticket sales fall as the number of black players increases, with playing skills held constant. Thus, where there is fan discrimination, contributions to team revenues can be made racially equal only by systematically requiring higher performance levels for black players.[71]

The effect of owner discrimination is conceptually the same as that of fan discrimination, since it determines the value to the owner of employing players of each race, irrespective of the effect of the player on revenues. Again, the demand for players is affected.

Player discrimination, while having no effect on the revenues produced

69. Wage discrimination in other occupations will also cause a constant wage differential (due to racial differences in the reservation prices) between black and white ballplayers, irrespective of ability differentials. See Pascal and Rapping, "Economics of Racial Discrimination," pp. 141–43.

70. It is assumed that television and radio revenues are proportional to gate attendance, so that the present discussion can be confined to gate receipts.

71. See the Appendix for a more detailed treatment of this argument.

by a player, alters the minimum wage at which players are willing to play (the supply price). If fan and owner discrimination are held constant, a wage differential emerges from changes in the supply of white ballplayers due to discrimination: white ballplayers who dislike playing with blacks will demand higher salaries if more blacks are added to the team; conversely, black ballplayers who like playing with other blacks will play for lower salaries if a team has more blacks.

Differences in Bargaining Positions

A ballplayer's salary is affected by his relative bargaining power. Even in the absence of any market discrimination, black-white salary differentials could emerge if black players generally had less bargaining strength than white players and if this difference varied systematically among performance levels. One possible explanation for this is that owners are prejudiced against black ballplayers and so, other things being equal, will develop a stronger bargaining posture against blacks than against whites. Another possible explanation is that blacks might be less skilled in bargaining.[72]

Summary

In the presence of market discrimination, several factors would contribute to a racial salary differential. Fan and owner discrimination both lower the owner's valuation of blacks. Salaries offered blacks then reflect the lower gate receipts from fans or the dissatisfaction owners incur from associating with black players. Player discrimination may also lower black salaries by altering supply prices.[73] Finally, educational and economic discrimination outside of sports may weaken the bargaining power of blacks relative to whites.

72. Previous exclusion from opportunities to bargain or lower educational attainment might cause group differences in bargaining strength. On the latter point, Pascal and Rapping, "Economics of Racial Discrimination" (pp. 122–23), studied the educational characteristics of 784 major-league players for the 1968 season and found that North American black players had completed about twelve median school years, in comparison to about thirteen years for whites. See also Chapter 6.

73. If blacks and whites are equally prejudiced against blacks, or if whites gain as much satisfaction from playing with blacks as other blacks do, no salary differential would be caused by the supply side. Overall player salaries would be higher in the first situation than in the second.

Salary Differences by Race

Black athletes believe that they must possess greater skills than whites to obtain positions on major-league rosters and that they are underpaid.[74] How can this be when, according to one estimate, of the ten major-league baseball players earning $100,000 or more in 1970, no less than seven were blacks?[75] Furthermore, position by position, blacks earn more, on the average, than whites. (Since, on the average, they outperform whites, this is not so startling.) But higher average salaries for blacks do not insure that baseball is free of salary discrimination. When the relationship between performance and salary is examined, there is evidence of pervasive racial discrimination. For instance, in 1971 Carl Yastrzemski earned $35,000 more than Hank Aaron and Willie Mays, although Yastrzemski had been playing fewer years and had not come close to matching Aaron's and Mays's performances.[76]

The Relationship between Performance and Salary

The belief that performance determines player salaries is almost universal in baseball circles. Players share the view that they "have generally been paid in accordance with their value to the clubs."[77] The players' position is well summarized in the 1958 salary report commissioned by the player representatives. While conceding that "a base hit cannot be translated into a precise dollar value," they argue that "the nature of baseball does provide statistics which afford some measure of evaluation. Batting averages and pitching records provide considerable weight in finding a player's true value."[78] However, the existence from year to year of a number of contract holdouts is a small indication of the differences between owners and players in their expectations of future player performance. Few would agree with Fred Hutchinson, who said, when he was a player

74. Harry Edwards, *The Revolt of the Black Athlete* (Free Press, 1970), p. 22.
75. *Ebony,* Vol. 25 (June 1970), pp. 128–30.
76. *Ebony,* Vol. 26 (June 1971), p. 94.
77. "Statement of Frederick Hutchinson, Pitcher, Detroit Tigers," in *Organized Baseball,* House Hearings, p. 840.
78. "Salary Report for Major League Baseball Players," Prepared Pursuant to Resolution of Player Representatives, printed in *Organized Professional Team Sports,* Senate Hearings, p. 806.

representative, that the differences between players and owners seldom represented more than a few hundred dollars.[79] Nor is there much support for Bill Veeck's claim that contract negotiations were easily completed and holdouts were solely for publicity, that in the end players knew that "Ole Will would give them a fair shake."[80] A "fair shake" seems to mean a salary commensurate with the player's ability, as measured by his past performance. The area of dispute is in what constitutes a meaningful measure of player performance.

Measuring Player Ability

Lifetime batting average, batting average in the previous season, runs batted in, home runs, times at bat, hits, and runs scored are some of the numerous statistics that are used to measure a hitter's ability. For pitchers, recognition is commonly based on won-lost record, games won, earned run average, and strikeouts per season. Although these performance measures are largely accepted by fans, owners, and players, it is true that "most of baseball's statistics are arbitrary and do not always reflect the player or team's total ability."[81] This is because they measure only one aspect of a player's ability and because they are not wholly independent of factors beyond the player's control. Lifetime batting average, for instance, the most commonly accepted yardstick of hitting performance, suffers from some conceptual weaknesses. First, it is biased against those who draw more walks, are hit by pitched balls more frequently, and sacrifice, even though these factors all contribute to the offensive strength of a team. More importantly, extra-base hits are not recognized in the statistic, so that there is a bias against the long-ball hitter, who may strike out more frequently and have fewer hits but whose hits have greater scoring power. Finally, the lifetime batting average is biased if the level of a player's ability changes over the course of his career. It may, specifically, underestimate ability during the early period of the player's career and overestimate ability during the closing phase, when he has already "peaked."

Pitching measures also suffer from conceptual weakness. A won-lost record for a pitcher is not independent of the entire team's performance. Winning against an upper division team requires greater ability than defeating a lower division team. The earned run average, which Branch

79. *Organized Baseball,* House Hearings, p. 849.
80. Veeck, *Veeck—As in Wreck,* p. 133.
81. Andreano, *No Joy in Mudville,* p. 29.

Rickey believed was a good measure of pitching ability and Donald Barker found to be the strongest measure of pitching effectiveness, shows surprisingly little variation between great and not-so-great pitchers.[82]

More sophisticated measures of performance have been suggested. Rickey proposed, apparently with some seriousness, "a complicated but not very useful index"[83] that would "gauge and analyze performance on a team basis," but would have "certain elements in it [to] provide a yardstick for measuring individual talent."[84] This index expanded the concept of batting average to incorporate the ability to get on base and produce extra-base power. Earnshaw Cook[85] developed an average scoring index that takes into account almost all of the available statistics in baseball. None of these composite indexes, whatever their merit, has captured much attention. And, in any case, they do not appear to be used in salary negotiations.

Most measures of performance are not, in fact, independent, as Barker's sophisticated statistical analysis clearly reveals.[86] Since any a priori justification for selecting one performance measure over another is lacking, the measures discussed below were chosen on empirical grounds. Recognizing that most fans have their own ideas as to which measures are preferred, some measures that were rejected will be discussed, as well as some other factors related to salary that were considered and rejected.

A useful point to begin is the formulation of salary equations by Pascal and Rapping. For hitters, they used lifetime batting average, home runs, times at bat last season, age, and education. The performance measures for pitchers were games won per full season played, innings pitched per full major-league season, total major-league games won, total major-league innings pitched, total seasons pitched, and difference between performance last year and lifetime performance. In one form or another, these variables explained a considerable portion of the differences in players' salaries.[87]

To improve upon these results, the inquiry was extended here in two

82. Branch Rickey in *Life,* Vol. 37 (Aug. 2, 1954), p. 84; Donald G. Barker, "The Factor Structure of Major League Baseball Records," *Research Quarterly,* Vol. 35 (March 1964), pp. 75–79.

83. Andreano, *No Joy in Mudville,* p. 30.

84. *Life* (Aug. 2, 1954), p. 79.

85. Earnshaw Cook with Wendell R. Garner, *Percentage Baseball* (Williams and Wilkins, 1964).

86. Barker, "The Factor Structure."

87. See Pascal and Rapping, "Economics of Racial Discrimination," Table 4-3.

directions. First, other performance measures were tried: for nonpitchers, total bases, runs produced, extra-base power, on-base percentage, base stealing, and fielding measures, adjusted for position; for pitchers, pitching percentage, earned run average, hits divided by total batters faced, and games completed divided by games started. Second, certain factors not explicitly related to past performance were also considered. Since salary negotiations are based on expected performance, there is a certain risk associated with the prediction. Past deviations from average performance seemed to be an appropriate way of measuring risk. Minimum performance requirements are likely to differ by position, and attempts were made to take such differences into account.[88] Finally, no matter how well qualified the players, "there are clubs in the major leagues who cannot . . . pay as much money as some other clubs."[89] The average team salaries for 1952–56, which were made available to the Senate in 1958,[90] reveal widespread differences. Some of the variance, of course, is due to differences in the quality of teams. But part of the difference in average team salaries may be due to intercity differences in attendance.

All these factors were taken into account in the course of the statistical investigations reported below. The fact that one performance measure or another or one plausible effect or another does not appear in the following analysis does not mean that the measure or effect was not associated with salary variations. On the contrary, many of the effects described above were frequently correlated with other performance measures as well, so that their unique effects could not be isolated. For example, last year's batting average and its percentage deviation from the player's lifetime batting average were significantly related to hitters' salaries, but were highly correlated with lifetime batting average.

The Determinants of Player Salaries

Three factors apparently play an essential role in salary determination: hitting or pitching performance as measured by the lifetime slugging aver-

88. For example, outfielders are expected to bat better than infielders, and infielders are expected to field better than outfielders. Also, among infielders, first basemen and, to a somewhat lesser degree, third basemen and catchers are thought to hit better than other infielders. Such differences were taken into account by estimating separate relationships for outfielders and infielders and utilizing dummy variables for the various infield positions.

89. "Statement of Branch Rickey, Jr.," in *Organized Baseball,* House Hearings, p. 1025.

90. *Organized Professional Team Sports,* Senate Hearings, pp. 795–98.

age (equals total bases divided by times at bat) for outfielders, the life-time batting average for infielders, and the lifetime power pitching for pitchers; years in the majors or years as a regular; and superstar versus nonsuperstar status.[91]

A desirable feature of the performance measures used in this study is that they are easily perceived as independent measures of the individual's past contribution to the team—his productivity. For both conceptual and empirical reasons, lifetime batting average was used as the productivity measure for infielders and the lifetime slugging average for outfielders. In the game plan of baseball, outfielders traditionally have been assigned the role of hitting the long ball. Thus, extra base hitting would appear more important in the determination of the outfielder's salary, and less important for the infielder. This conceptual difference is verified in the statistical analysis.

Power pitching, or the ratio of strikeouts to walks, seems conceptually superior to most other pitching statistics because it does not depend systematically on the performance of the team. The pitcher contributes to victory by minimizing the number of walks and maximizing the number of strikeouts. A second variable that was significantly related to pitchers' salaries was the lifetime average percentage of innings pitched out of total innings per season. That is, the number of innings pitched was divided by the total number of possible innings (nine times games per season times years in majors).[92] This variable might be interpreted as a measure of work effort. Alternatively, it may be another dimension of pitching quality: better pitchers work more frequently.

The second factor affecting player salaries is years spent in the majors (M) or as a regular (R). For a hitter, R differs from M by the length of time it takes a player to become one of the first eight men on the team roster. For a pitcher this is defined as playing one hundred or more innings or having ten or more decisions (a win, loss, or save).[93] The length of time it takes to become a regular differs from position to position. There-fore, both variables were tried in the salary regressions and the best result selected. It is not entirely clear what these variables measure. First, M

91. Since salary is determined on the basis of past performance, all of the values of the independent variables were calculated on the basis of the player's statistics in the previous season. That is, since player salaries here are for the 1968 and 1969 seasons, all the independent variables were for the 1967 and 1968 seasons.
92. Extra-inning ball games should be randomly distributed among pitchers.
93. These are the definitions used in *The Baseball Encyclopedia*, pp. 78–79.

or R could measure a pure seniority effect; that is, salary may have to rise with age, independent of ability, to preserve team morale.[94] While such an interpretation cannot be rejected out of hand, competitive sports generally do not put such a premium on age. A more plausible interpretation is that the variables measure the separate contribution of experience to playing ability.[95] Alternatively, M or R may indicate the phase in his career that a player has reached, and hence may adjust the mean performance measures for the trend, or even the growth, of the player's bargaining skills.

Finally, something other than performance and experience determines the recognition afforded some ballplayers. Superstars all measure high in performance criteria and most have been in the majors for a relatively long time, yet these factors do not adequately explain their high salaries. Attempts to obtain independent measures of the superstar phenomenon failed.[96] The phenomenon was in the end accounted for by recognizing the nonlinearity that the high marginal value products of superstars would introduce into the salary relationships. Players like Willie Mays, Carl Yastrzemski, and Jim Bunning draw fans. Undoubtedly, their superior playing ability, their productivity to the team, and the years they have spent in the game contribute to this facility. But, conceptually, it is useful, to the extent possible, to separate the influence of contributions to team revenues from the player's athletic performance. This was accomplished by estimating the salary relationships in semilogarithmic form.[97]

There were two primary sources for the data used in the salary equations. All the values of the independent variables were obtained or calculated from or based on information in *The Baseball Encyclopedia*. The salary data were made available to the author by Pascal and Rapping, and hence are from the same salary sample used in their study.[98] The salary

94. Pascal and Rapping note the possibility of a seniority effect and cite team morale as a possible justification ("Economics of Racial Discrimination," p. 128).

95. This is Pascal and Rapping's interpretation of their age variable (ibid.). Age would appear to be a less satisfactory measure than years in the majors or years as a regular, since entry and promotion (from the minors) age are not uniform among major-league players.

96. One measure that is conceptually appealing—the number of times the player appeared on the all-star roster—while very successful in that it was highly correlated with salary, created unacceptable collinearity problems.

97. Normally, one would expect diminishing returns to salary with respect to performance. But if superstars attract fans for reasons other than their productivity to the team, the second derivative may well be positive over the observable range.

98. Pascal and Rapping also verified the salary data with Marvin Miller, head of the Major League Baseball Players Association. Their data were obtained from re-

sample is not fully representative of all major-league players, for players with high salaries are overrepresented. The mean salary of all players in the sample was $48,100, compared to the reported average salary of $42,200 for 209 veterans on major-league teams in 1970.[99] Of the 148 observations, 87 are for 1968 salaries and the remainder for 1969. Forty-one players appear in both the 1968 and 1969 data, and 107 players are represented in the total sample. The salary range is from $10,000 to $125,000, with 34 instances below $25,000. Thus, about 25 percent of the sample is at the lower end of the salary scale. Enough observations over the whole salary range are present to make inferences about general salary conditions feasible.

Players were separated into outfielders, infielders, and pitchers, and salary equations were estimated for each group.[100] Table 9 gives the means and standard deviations for all divisions of the sample used in the salary equations. The substantial difference in the mean salary of outfielders is immediately noticeable. While this could be due to the characteristics of the sample, it is more likely that outfielders on the average *are* paid more. Of the ten players earning more than $100,000 in 1970, seven were outfielders.[101] Since long-ball hitting is a characteristic of outfielders, a premium must be paid for those willing and able to "swing for the fences." Looking at the means and standard deviations, the distribution of salaries in each subsample seems reasonably uniform.[102]

---

ported salaries in twenty local newspapers and *Sporting News.* Use of the same salary sample permits the reader to compare the results obtained by Pascal and Rapping with those reported here, with the knowledge that the divergent results were not caused by differences in the samples. It had been hoped that actual salary data could be obtained from the teams, but they were reluctant to cooperate. According to Pascal and Rapping, there is "reason to believe that the data are fairly accurate and, equally important, there is no a priori reason to think that reporting errors, if any, are systematically related to any of the variables used in our analyses" ("Economics of Racial Discrimination," p. 127).

99. Testimony of John Clark, Jr., in *Curtis C. Flood* v. *Bowie K. Kuhn et al.,* 316 F. Supp. 271 (S.D.N.Y. 1970), p. 1660 of the trial transcript.

100. Where players did not clearly occupy one position, the total number of games in the position was used to make the assignment.

101. *Ebony,* Vol. 25 (June 1970), pp. 128–30.

102. On the average, outfielders outslug and outhit infielders and are more consistent in both categories. Both the mean lifetime slugging and batting averages of outfielders are higher than those of infielders, and the variances are less. The average period of time spent in the majors is about the same for both positions, although outfielders appear to gain regular status somewhat more quickly. This difference may be due to the fact that the ratio of playing positions to players on the roster is higher in the outfield than in the infield. Seldom more than five outfielders appear on the

Table 9. Means and Standard Deviations for Salary Regressions for Baseball Major Leaguers, by Position and Race, Late 1960s[a]

Position and race	Salary (dollars)	Slugging average $\overline{SA}$	Batting average $\overline{BA}$	Years in majors $\overline{M}$	Years as a regular $\overline{R}$	Percent innings pitched $\overline{IP}$	Power pitching index[b] $\overline{PP}$
Outfielder	61,791	0.449	0.278	8.2	6.4	...	...
	(33,204)	(0.072)	(0.031)	(4.1)	(4.2)		
White	56,900	0.433	0.272	7.7	6.0	...	...
	(31,111)	(0.062)	(0.027)	(3.8)	(3.2)		
Black	66,043	0.463	0.283	8.7	6.8	...	...
	(35,047)	(0.077)	(0.033)	(4.4)	(5.0)		
Infielder	44,470	0.411	0.257	7.8	5.4	...	...
	(22,523)	(0.086)	(0.030)	(3.6)	(3.7)		
White	40,757	0.393	0.250	7.7	4.8	...	...
	(20,770)	(0.079)	(0.027)	(3.5)	(3.4)		
Black	53,133	0.455	0.275	7.9	6.8	...	...
	(24,758)	(0.089)	(0.029)	(4.0)	(3.9)		
Pitcher	43,354	...	...	5.8	4.7	14.2	2.28
	(26,884			(3.3)	(3.1)	(2.8)	(0.53)
White	38,432	...	...	5.4	4.4	13.9	2.25
	(19,852)			(3.4)	(3.3)	(2.7)	(0.47)
Black	59,910	...	...	7.5	5.9	15.2	2.38
	(39,838)			(2.4)	(2.2)	(3.0)	(0.73)

Sources: Salaries, *Sporting News*, various issues, and twenty local newspapers; other values, *The Baseball Encyclopedia* (Macmillan, 1969).

a. Based on 87 observations for 1968 salaries and 61 observations for 1969, 41 of which appear in both years. The total sample comprises 107 players. The numbers in parentheses are standard deviations.

b. Ratio of strikeouts to base-on-balls.

The statistical analysis of the determinants of salary for the three positions is presented in Table 10. The results indicate that a substantial proportion of the variance in individual player salaries is explained by the models. The statistical results are interpreted more easily if the coefficients are converted to the elasticities at the mean values of the independent variables (the average elasticities).

For every 1 percent increase in their lifetime slugging average, outfielders, on the average, increase their salaries by 2.3 percent, other factors

team roster for the three outfield positions, but about ten infielders compete for the five infield positions. Pitchers, on the other hand, appear to have a considerably shorter half-life than nonpitchers, with at least two fewer years in the majors than other players. Possibly because of the higher rate of depreciation of pitching talent, the gestation period before attaining regular status is shortened to an average of only one season.

Table 10. Salary Regressions for Baseball Major Leaguers, by Position, Late 1960s[a]

Position	Constant	Productivity	Experience	Hitter without power dummy	Percent innings pitched	R^2 and degrees of freedom
Outfielder	7.9909	0.0052 $\overline{SA}$ (5.25)	0.0625 R (3.82)	0.4996 $D_{\overline{BA}}$ (4.25)	...	0.8015 39
Infielder	6.9953	0.0113 $\overline{BA}$ (7.36)	0.0835 M (6.55)	...	...	0.7908 47
Pitcher	8.2883	0.3358 $\overline{PP}$ (3.87)	0.0891 M (7.15)	...	0.0670 $\overline{IP}$ (3.96)	0.7408 44

Source: Table 9.

a. See Table 9 for definition of symbols. The regressions are semilogarithmic, with the dependent variable being the log (base e) of the players' salaries. The numbers in parentheses are *t*-values. All are significant at the 1 percent level or above. Slugging and batting averages were multiplied by 1,000.

being constant. Infielders experience a 2.9 percent increase in salary for every 1 percent increase in their lifetime batting averages. The salary of outfielders will rise about 4 percent for every 10 percent increase in the number of years they spend as regulars. This suggests that outfielder salaries rise on the average about 6 percent per year, holding the influence of their lifetime slugging averages constant. Infielder salaries will rise about 8 percent per year. Finally, one further difference between the statistical results for the outfielders and the infielders is worth noting. Although there was a close association between the lifetime slugging and batting averages of outfielders, adjustment for below-average sluggers who had above-average lifetime batting averages was required. In other words, some outfielders hit well but without power. This was accounted for simply by introducing a variable ($D_{\overline{BA}}$) that took the value of one for those outfielders with below-average lifetime slugging averages and above-average lifetime batting averages. Similar adjustments for infielders who were below-average hitters but above-average sluggers, despite the presence of first basemen in the infielder sample, proved unnecessary.

Pitchers earned about 3.4 percent more in salary for every 0.1 percentage point increase in their strikeout-to-walk ratio. The average value of the power pitching variable $\overline{PP}$ was 2.28, and its highest value in the sample was Juan Marichal's 3.64. Close behind Marichal was Dick Hughes of St. Louis. The lowest $\overline{PP}$ value was 1.37, attained by a pitcher who would undoubtedly prefer anonymity. Pitchers were also rewarded substantially for percentage point increases in their share of the pitching—about 4.1 percent for pitching about one full game above the average. The average pitcher worked about 14 percent of the innings (207 innings or 23 game equivalents). Highly paid pitchers like Jim Bunning and Juan Marichal pitched over 18 percent of the scheduled innings of play, but some less highly paid pitchers like Jerry Koosman, Dick Hughes, and Tom Seaver pitched about as much.[103] Finally, pitchers' salaries rise more rapidly with seniority than the salaries of infielders and outfielders. The average pitcher's salary rises 8.9 percent for each year he remains in the majors. In part, this may be a reflection of the shorter major-league careers of pitchers.

Evidence of Salary Discrimination

With a satisfactory salary model at hand we can proceed to investigate whether there is any evidence of racial salary discrimination in the major leagues. The simplest way to approach this question is to separate the players by race and reestimate the salary equations. Inferences about the direction and magnitude of the discrimination can be made through comparison of the coefficients and intercepts.

A comparison of the means supports the view that "the highest paid, and best, professional athletes in baseball . . . are Negroes."[104] On the average, blacks earn more in each position than whites (see Table 9). The differential is as large as about $21,500 for pitchers and as little as about $9,000 for outfielders. Again, the sample characteristics are within tolerable limits, although the sample included only eleven black pitchers (a reflection of the scarcity of black pitchers in the majors).

All the means of the independent variables favor blacks. That is, blacks have higher average performance measures and more years in the majors or as regulars. In the outfield, there is an 0.030 spread in the lifetime slugging average $\overline{SA}$ and an 0.011 difference in the lifetime batting average $\overline{BA}$, both of which favor blacks. The corresponding racial difference for infielders, which again favors blacks, is 0.062 points in $\overline{SA}$ and 0.025 in $\overline{BA}$. These differences confirm the proposition that where there are

103. Eight percent of the innings pitched (about 100 innings) per season was defined as the minimum amount for a regular starter or reliever in *The Baseball Encyclopedia*, p. 79. This reduced Pascal and Rapping's sample of pitchers from fifty-five to forty-eight.

104. Young, *Negro Firsts*, pp. 116–17.

relatively fewer blacks, the performance differential is widest. The average number of years it takes to achieve regular status is somewhat less for whites. There is a gap of 1.7 years between years in the majors M and years as a regular R for white outfielders, and 1.9 years for blacks. Black pitchers, also, appear to wait longer. On the other hand, black infielders become regulars much more quickly than whites.

The actual salary regressions by position and race appear in Table 11. The statistical analysis of outfielder and infielder salaries reveals: (1) a constant salary differential favoring blacks (that is, if all the variables are set at zero, blacks earn more than whites); (2) that whites appear to earn more than blacks for every increase in their hitting performance; and (3) that blacks earn larger increments in salary over their playing careers than white players do. Of principal interest is whether, for any given position, the coefficients of a particular variable differ for blacks

Table 11. Salary Regressions for Baseball Major Leaguers, by Position and Race, Late 1960s[a]

Position and race	Constant	Productivity	Experience	Hitter without power dummy	Percent innings pitched	R^2 and degrees of freedom
Outfielder						
White	7.1982	$0.0077 \, \overline{SA}$	$0.0312 \, R$	$0.4451 D_{\overline{BA}}$	...	0.7567
		$(3.52)^b$	(0.74)	$(2.13)^c$		16
Black	7.9349	$0.0051 \, \overline{SA}$	$0.0622 \, R$	$0.5870 \, D_{\overline{BA}}$	...	0.8589
		$(4.34)^b$	$(3.71)^b$	$(4.00)^b$		19
Infielder						
White	6.6399	$0.0134 \, \overline{BA}$	$0.0612 \, M$	...	...	0.7870
		$(5.71)^b$	$(3.32)^b$			32
Black	6.9707	$0.0107 \, \overline{BA}$	$0.1049 \, M$	...	...	0.7962
		$(3.88)^b$	$(5.21)^b$			12
Pitcher						
White	8.6280	$0.3254 \, \overline{PP}$	$0.0782 \, M$	...	$0.0483 \, \overline{IP}$	0.6757
		$(3.24)^b$	$(5.98)^b$		$(2.74)^b$	33
Black	7.1025	$0.2675 \, \overline{PP}$	$0.1525 \, M$	...	$0.1251 \, \overline{IP}$	0.9245
		(1.72)	$(4.72)^b$		$(3.17)^b$	7

Source: Table 9.

a. See Table 9 for definition of symbols. The regressions are semilogarithmic, with the dependent variable being the log (base e) of the players' salaries. The numbers in parentheses are t-values. Slugging and batting averages were multiplied by 1,000.

b. Significant at the 1 percent level or above.

c. Significant at the 5 percent level or above.

and whites. A crude test of this can be made by estimating the pair of equations for each position as a single equation, in which each of the variables is multiplied by two dummy variables, one for whites and one for blacks (D_W and D_B). For example, the single equation for outfielders would then include among its variables both $\overline{SA} \cdot D_W$ and $\overline{SA} \cdot D_B$. The difference between these coefficients could then be tested for statistical significance. The t-statistics for the coefficient differences in each equation are as follows:

Position	Variable	t-statistic
Outfielder	$\overline{SA}$	1.04
	R	0.61
	$D_{\overline{BA}}$	0.59
Infielder	$\overline{BA}$	0.75
	M	1.63
Pitcher	$\overline{PP}$	0.32
	M	2.18
	$\overline{IP}$	1.71

Since only the last two differentials in black-white performance levels are statistically significant at the 95 percent level, it is not possible to confirm the hypothesis that the coefficients for blacks exceed those for whites. That the general pattern of differences in coefficients is so consistent (only the power-pitching variable not following the pattern) seems far more important. The nature of the salary discrimination process can be seen more clearly by expressing these results graphically. Figure 1 shows the relation between salary and performance for outfielders and infielders, setting the effect of R or M equal to the mean of the entire sample. It can be seen that among experienced ballplayers, blacks, on the average, earn less than whites of equal ability, except at performance levels below those required for retention in the majors. That is, among experienced outfielders, if blacks and whites have lifetime slugging averages below 0.355, then blacks will tend to earn more than whites, other things being equal. Among experienced infielders, blacks will tend to earn more than whites at lifetime batting averages below 0.249.

Pay differentials between whites and blacks of equal ability persist throughout the observed performance levels of experienced players. To earn $30,000, black outfielders must outperform whites by about 0.020 in slugging average. Alternatively, if both a black and a white have slugging averages of 0.450, the estimated salary of a white outfielder is

Figure 1. Salary and Performance Levels for Baseball Players, by Race, Late 1960s[a]

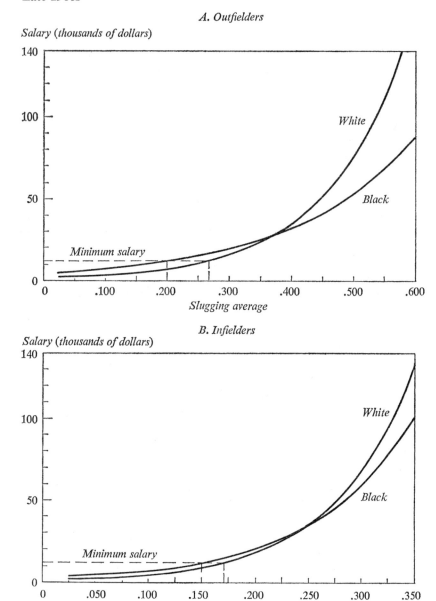

A. Outfielders

Salary *(thousands of dollars)*

White

Black

Minimum salary

Slugging average

B. Infielders

Salary *(thousands of dollars)*

White

Black

Minimum salary

Batting average

Source: Table 11.
a. The effect of experience as a regular or in the major leagues is set equal to the mean of the entire sample.

nearly $11,000 more than the black. Among infielders, the estimated salary discrimination is less severe. For experienced infielders with eight years in the majors, blacks actually earn more than whites until the batting average reaches 0.249; but among superior experienced infielders, whites earn more than blacks for equivalent performance. At a batting average of 0.280, for example, the expected earnings of white infielders are about $4,000 more per season than those of blacks.

The estimated white-black salary differential widens with improved performance, as shown in Figure 1 and, most clearly, Figure 2. The relative salary (the ratio of the predicted white to the predicted black salary) is plotted on the vertical axis against performance. At 1.0, white and black salaries are equal. For the most part, equality of earnings occurs below minimum major-league performance levels for experienced ballplayers. At the average level of outfielder performance ($\overline{SA} = 0.450$), whites earn about 25 percent more than blacks, and among the best outfielders, whites earn substantially more than blacks. The racial salary gap, while present, is not as severe among outstanding infielders.

As the statistical results in Table 11 indicate, M and R significantly affect the racial salary differential in baseball. Blacks earn more for each year they stay in baseball than whites do. Black outfielders average about a 6.2 percent annual increase in salary, holding $\overline{SA}$ constant, while whites average a 3.1 percent increase. Among infielders the respective annual figures are 10.5 and 6.1 percent. Clearly, in the course of time black-white player salaries can be expected to converge. Two questions arise. First, what is the reason for the higher coefficients for R and M among black players? Second, how long must the black player of any given ability wait before his earnings approach those of whites of equivalent ability?

There are several possible interpretations for the observed racial differences in R and M. These variables measure in part an experience effect, but they may also measure other dimensions of player performance, for which blacks would then be earning more than whites. Another possibility is that the variables capture evidence of a retention barrier: that is, not only do blacks have to outperform whites to get into baseball, but they must consistently outperform them in order to stay in baseball. Over time, they will be rewarded, albeit differentially, for their superior performance. If this interpretation is correct, there should be some evidence of a widening in the racial performance differential as the length of time in the majors is increased. The evidence presented in Table 12 is consistent with this

Figure 2. Racial Inequality in Baseball Salaries, by Performance Level, Late 1960s

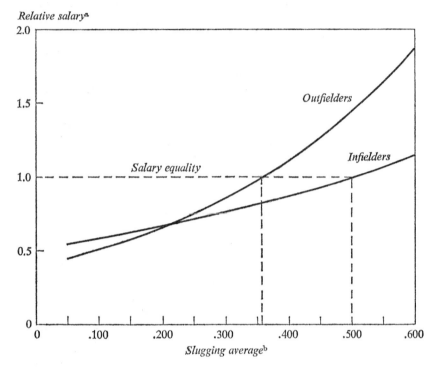

Relative salary[a]

Slugging average[b]

Source: Table 11.
a. Ratio of predicted white to predicted black salaries.
b. Batting average = 0.5 of slugging average.

interpretation for outfielders, but not for infielders.[105] Average performance improves with an increase in years in the majors. This observation reflects the attrition of the poorer players. Among outfielders, the difference in performance is widest among players with eleven or more years of experience. Among infielders, the pattern is not clear; in part, this may be caused by the greater heterogeneity of positions. Also consistent with the evidence is that the entry barriers in baseball were stiffer in the past than they are now. Another interpretation that cannot be rejected out of hand is that the less attractive occupational opportunities outside baseball for black star players causes them to stay in baseball longer than whites of equal ability.

105. The calculations in Table 12 were made on the basis of the entire roster of major-league players for the 1968 season.

Table 12. Performance Differentials and Career Length for Baseball Players, by Race, 1968 Season

	Outfielders			Infielders		
Years in majors	Mean $\overline{BA}$,[a] blacks	Mean $\overline{BA}$,[a] whites	Perfor-mance differential	Mean $\overline{BA}$,[a] blacks	Mean $\overline{BA}$,[a] whites	Perfor-mance differential
2–3	0.213	0.230	− 0.017	0.248	0.221	0.027[b]
4–5	0.245	0.246	− 0.001	0.245	0.233	0.012[b]
6–7	0.261	0.251	0.010	0.269	0.238	0.031[c]
8–10	0.285	0.263	0.022[b]	0.260	0.247	0.013
11 or more	0.299	0.270	0.029[c]	0.274	0.261	0.013

Source: Same as Table 9.
a. $\overline{BA}$ = lifetime batting average.
b. Significant at the 5 percent level or above.
c. Significant at the 1 percent level or above.

Whatever the cause of the racial differentials in the coefficients relating R and M to salary, Figure 3 verifies that taking those factors into account does not vitiate the findings regarding salary discrimination. Relative salaries were computed for outfielders and infielders, allowing for the effect of R or M, on the basis of high, average, and low values of $\overline{SA}$ and $\overline{BA}$. The results are clear: blacks must spend an exceptionally long period in the majors before they can expect equal pay for equal performance. If a black outfielder is an average player ($\overline{SA} = 0.450$), he can expect to earn the same as a white after fourteen years as a regular—considerably longer than the normal career of an exceptional, much less an average, baseball player. The exceptional black outfielder ($\overline{SA} = 0.525$) will never earn as much as the exceptional white outfielder, but below-average black outfielders ($\overline{SA} = 0.375$) will earn the same salary as below-average whites in about eight years; however, it is unlikely that below-average outfielders would stay in the majors for that long a period.

The salary prospect for black infielders is somewhat brighter. After about eight years in the majors, the average black infielder ($\overline{BA} = 0.260$) can anticipate salary equality with the average white. Superior black infielders ($\overline{BA} = 0.300$) need wait only eleven years, while below-average blacks ($\overline{BA} = 0.220$) will catch up to whites in only six years! Therefore, among both outfielders and infielders, an exceptionally long period is required for racial convergence in salary, and the longest wait is for the better players, who are the most likely to remain in baseball for a long period.

Figure 3. Racial Inequality in Baseball Salaries, by Career Length and Performance Level, 1968–69

A. Outfielders[a]

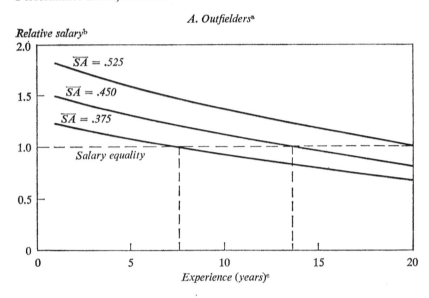

Relative salary[b]

$\overline{SA} = .525$

$\overline{SA} = .450$

$\overline{SA} = .375$

Salary equality

Experience (years)[c]

B. Infielders[d]

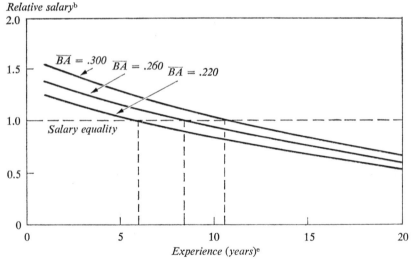

Relative salary[b]

$\overline{BA} = .300$ $\overline{BA} = .260$ $\overline{BA} = .220$

Salary equality

Experience (years)[e]

Source: Same as Table 9.
a. $\overline{SA}$ = slugging average.
b. Ratio of predicted white to predicted black salaries.
c. Years as a regular.
d. $\overline{BA}$ = batting average.
e. Years in the majors.

The statistical results for the black pitcher equations are not strong enough to draw firm conclusions about salary discrimination. In part, this result is predictable, since an effective exclusionary policy eliminates much of the incentive and opportunity for wage discrimination. The results for pitchers cannot be compared on a racial basis, since the productivity variable for black pitchers is not significant.

So, it would seem that the growing suspicion among black professional athletes that they are underpaid at any given performance level has some substance to it for baseball. Racial wage discrimination can be demonstrated, however, only through serious economic and statistical investigation. The more common measures of wage differentials, such as differences in the means, cannot be used because of the wide racial differences in performance (productivity).[106] That blacks consistently outperform whites is not fully reflected in salaries. Accordingly, and remembering all the caveats concerning investigations of this sort, it is concluded that racial wage discrimination is a feature of the baseball labor market.

Implications for Public Policy

Acts are said to be racially discriminatory in the labor market when they lead to the systematic exclusion of qualified individuals or to unequal compensation for equivalent performance. The present investigation into discrimination supports the view that labor practices in major-league baseball currently are racially discriminatory. A summary of the major findings follows.

• Although baseball has been the "national" pastime, blacks in its ranks have consistently been discriminated against. Fans, players, and owners have demonstrated prejudice, the existence and impact of which can be statistically verified.

• There is a historical and fairly constant interleague difference in the percentage of Negro ballplayers. Furthermore, the inequality in the distribution of black players among teams is growing.

• In every position, black players outperform whites, with the performance differentials widest in the positions where blacks are most excluded. That is, entry barriers are highest for black catchers and pitchers

106. Pascal and Rapping's study of discrimination in baseball suffers from this drawback. They used a race dummy to test for discrimination. Since the technique adjusts for differences in the means between the two races, it was inevitable that they would obtain the wrong sign for the race dummy variable.

and lowest for the outfield positions. Furthermore, the concentration of Negro players in the outfield has increased. Blacks are excluded from managerial and coaching positions; but, given the regional and positional origin of managers and coaches, it is likely that the lower concentration of blacks in the infield helps explain the lack of Negroes in managerial positions.

• Black ballplayers earn more on the average than white ballplayers. Since racial performance differentials exist, differences in average salary are not a proper measure of discrimination. Salary models for outfielders, infielders, and pitchers were estimated. Equations estimated for each racial group revealed evidence of salary discrimination against black outfielders and infielders, but not pitchers.

Theoretical elements of the racial wage differential in baseball were also identified. These consist of racial differences in the intercepts, due to a constant wage differential, and differences in the slopes of the salary functions. The reserve clause may be an important factor in the racial pattern of compensation in baseball; its elimination could remove differences in salaries due to racial differences either in the reservation prices of the ballplayers or in bargaining strength. The removal of both of these elements in the racial wage differential would be insured by interclub competition: players would be paid according to their marginal value products if buyers had to compete for their services.

The removal of the reserve clause would not guarantee racial wage equality. If market discrimination is a feature of the baseball labor market, racial wage differentials will persist. Racial differences in the marginal value products would sustain the racial wage differential in the absence of the reserve clause. Furthermore, market induced wage differentials are difficult to eradicate. The cost of a vigorously enforced equal pay provision is frequently a reduction in the percentage of Negro employment. To the extent that market discrimination is the exclusive source of wage discrimination in the baseball labor market, the relative economic position of black ballplayers would not be improved with the removal of the reserve clause.[107] The empirical results, while confirming the existence of wage discrimination, offer no clue as to what proportion of the wage differential is due to market discrimination and what proportion is due to the reserve clause.

---

107. At a minimum, it is likely that racial differences in reservation prices would have an effect on racial salary differences.

What are the implications of these findings for public policy? "No deployment of facts, no analysis of them, however correct, can ever yield an imperative for action until those facts have been compared with some kind of standard or norm of desirability."[108] A consensus does seem to have been reached in this country that earnings and the criterion for employment and promotion must be invariant with respect to race. Accordingly, racial equality of earnings and opportunity is the standard to which baseball must be made to conform. How might this be accomplished?

The elimination of the reserve clause might reduce the racial wage differential. Predictably, both Negro and white ballplayers would gain *absolutely* through the removal of the reserve clause. *Relatively,* blacks might gain and whites lose. Traditionally, attacks on the reserve clause have come through antitrust suits, such as the recent Curt Flood case. Another approach would be to declare major-league baseball in violation of Title VII of the Civil Rights Act of 1964. The section of that act relevant to the question at hand is as follows:

Sec. 703. (a) It shall be an unlawful employment practice for an employer—

(1) to fail or refuse to hire or to discharge any individual, or otherwise to discriminate against any individual with respect to his compensation, terms, conditions, or privileges of employment, because of such individual's race, color, religion, sex, or national origin; or

(2) to limit, segregate, or classify his employees in any way which would deprive or tend to deprive any individual of employment opportunities or otherwise adversely affect his status as an employee, because of such individual's race, color, religion, sex, or national origin.[109]

The equal employment opportunity title applies to all employers who employ twenty-five or more persons for at least twenty weeks. The definition of an employer is very broad under the act, so that major-league baseball would appear to be subject to it, while still exempt from the antitrust laws.

One of the difficulties in seeking relief from discrimination under Title VII, in addition to the cumbersome and time-consuming procedure required, is the necessity of demonstrating equal qualification. Most occupations require a certain level of educational attainment or specialized train-

108. M. A. Adelman, "The Measurement of Industrial Concentration," *Review of Economics and Statistics,* Vol. 33 (November 1951), p. 295, reprinted in Richard B. Heflebower and George W. Stocking (eds.), *Readings in Industrial Organization and Public Policy* (Richard D. Irwin, 1958), p. 44.

109. 78 Stat. 255.

ing. The courts have had difficulty evolving standards for determining whether discrimination or educational and training deficiencies are responsible for the racial employment and wage pattern in a given occupation. Hence, decisions under Title VII have had an ad hoc quality about them. In baseball, employment and salary depend almost solely on the ability to play the game; and baseball performance *can* be measured. The courts' attention could be directed to the existence of performance differentials favoring Negro ballplayers and the racial inequality of earnings. The courts' historical disdain for moderately sophisticated economic and statistical argumentation is a problem, though not necessarily an insurmountable one. The vulnerability of economic and statistical argument to counterargument places the courts in the position of having to adjudicate on the basis of evidence that they have little competence to evaluate. Hence, the outcome more often depends on the whim of the court than on the soundness of the economic and statistical argument.

Do these findings have any broader significance than their implications for organized baseball? The possibility immediately comes to mind that other professional sports may suffer from racial entry barriers and salary differentials. Furthermore, football and basketball have somewhat different contractual arrangements governing their labor markets, so that comparison with findings in baseball would shed some light on the relative degree of "exploitation" under the reserve clause. But the implications of these findings hopefully are even wider. The fact that discrimination in such an exposed business as major-league baseball has not been well understood points to the subtlety that racial discrimination can have in the American economy, and the extent to which the American people have not been willing to face it.

APPENDIX: A Model of Discrimination in Baseball

Gate receipts, G, are determined by the number of tickets, T, sold times a constant (average price), $\bar{p}$.

$$(1) \qquad\qquad\qquad G = \bar{p}T.$$

The number of tickets sold depends on the ability of the players, A, and on the number of black ballplayers, B. If the fan is white (black), his demand for tickets will rise with an increase in A, independent of the players' race, and fall (rise) with an increase in B.

$$(2) \qquad\qquad\qquad T = T(A, B).$$

The number of black ballplayers fielded will depend positively on the ability of black ballplayers, A_b, and negatively on the ability of whites, A_w.

$$(3) \qquad\qquad B = B(A_b, A_w),$$

where $\partial B/\partial A_w < 0$ and $\partial B/\partial A_b > 0$.

Substituting (3) into (2) and (2) into (1), the gate receipts equation can be rewritten as

$$(4) \qquad\qquad G = \bar{p}\{T[A, B(A_b, A_w)]\}.$$

Now the expression for a player's marginal value product, M_i, can be obtained by differentiating (4) with respect to A_i, where i represents the individual player.

$$(5) \qquad\qquad \frac{dG}{dA_i} = M_i = \bar{p}\left[\frac{\partial T}{\partial A_i} + \frac{\partial T}{\partial B}\frac{\partial B}{\partial A_i}\right], \ i = w, b,$$

where w, b represent individual white, black players.

The baseball player's salary, S_i, depends on his marginal value product, his supply price, and his bargaining power, λ.

$$(6) \qquad\qquad S_i = S_i\{M_i[A_i, B(A_i)], B[A_i], \lambda_i\}, \ i = w, b.$$

Differentiating S_i with respect to A_i, the impact of discrimination on the slopes of the salary functions of white and black ballplayers can be determined:

$$(7) \qquad \frac{dS_i}{dA_i} = \frac{\partial S_i}{\partial M_i}\frac{\partial M_i}{\partial A_i} + \frac{\partial S_i}{\partial M_i}\frac{\partial M_i}{\partial B}\frac{\partial B}{\partial A_i} + \frac{\partial S_i}{\partial B}\frac{\partial B}{\partial A_i} + \frac{\partial S_i}{\partial \lambda_i}\frac{d\lambda_i}{dA_i}.$$

In the presence of market discrimination, all the terms in equation (7) except the first may contribute to a racial salary differential. Setting i equal to w and b in equation (7), and subtracting each term in the black salary equation from its correspondent in the white salary equation, permits determination of the direction of the salary differential and the conditions under which it will exist.

The first terms in the equation, of course, are the marginal value products of the players in the absence of discrimination and bargaining. They are equal in the white and black salary equations. The second term represents the combined impact of fan and owner discrimination on the marginal value product schedules:

$$\frac{\partial S_w}{\partial M_w}\frac{\partial M_w}{\partial B}\frac{\partial B}{\partial A_w} - \frac{\partial S_b}{\partial M_b}\frac{\partial M_b}{\partial B}\frac{\partial B}{\partial A_b} > 0.$$

Since $(\partial S_i/\partial M_i)(\partial M_i/\partial B) < 0$, the signs are determined by $\partial B/\partial A_i$. It has already been noted that $\partial B/\partial A_w < 0$, while $\partial B/\partial A_b > 0$.

This result is shown graphically in Figure 4. In the absence of discrimination, $M_w = M_b = M$, and equal ability, at say A, will yield racial equality in salary, S^c. (Note that under competitive conditions, $\lambda_i = 1$.) Fan and/or owner discrimination alters the marginal value product schedules of white and black players by raising M to, say, M_w, and lowering M to M_b, respectively. With $\lambda_i = 1$, the effect of the differences in M_i are

Figure 4. Effect of Racial Discrimination on Salaries of White and Black Baseball Players

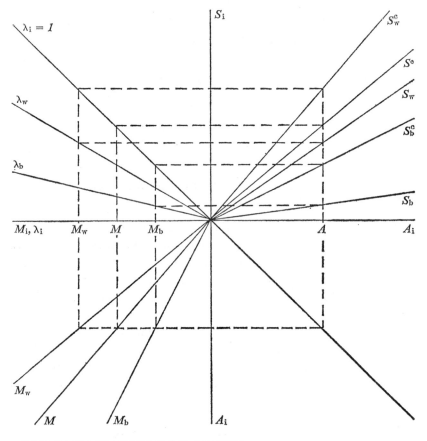

Source: Equation (7), where the symbols are explained.

corresponding differences in salary. M_w yields S_w^c, and M_b yields S_b^c. The slope of S_b^c is less than that of S_w^c.

The third term in equation (7) represents the effect of player discrimination.[110] If white players incur disutility from playing with blacks and blacks obtain utility, then

$$\frac{\partial S_w}{\partial B} \frac{\partial B}{\partial A_w} - \frac{\partial S_b}{\partial B} \frac{\partial B}{\partial A_b} > 0.$$

The effect of bargaining under the reserve clause may be an exacerbation of the racial wage differential. All the bargaining repercussions of discrimination can be seen in Figure 4. Essentially, whatever its source, discrimination would alter the player shares racially. It would be expected that $\lambda_b < \lambda_w$, given the expected direction of discrimination. In the diagram, with racial equality in ability, say at A, the white player's marginal value product is M_w and his share at $\lambda_w < 1$ yields a salary of S_w. On the other hand, at A, the black player produces M_b and with a smaller share, $\lambda_b < \lambda_w$, earns S_b. The salary differential under bargaining is greater than that under perfect competition. Alternatively, the slope of the black player's salary function, dS_b/dA_i, may be less under the reserve clause relative to dS_w/dA_i than it would be under perfect competition.

110. To simplify, the effect of player discrimination has not been plotted in Figure 4. Conceptually, it is the same as the effect of owner/fan discrimination. That is, in the presence of player discrimination the slope of S_w^c would be greater and that of S_b^c less than it appears in the diagram.

CHAPTER EIGHT

Sports Broadcasting

IRA HOROWITZ

WITH THE SPREAD of television to 96 percent of U.S. households, televised sports have assumed an important role in American life. Correspondingly, radio and television broadcasts of professional sports have become a central part of the corporate planning of major-league clubs, broadcasters, and the major national and regional firms in some industries. Sports broadcasts have thus given rise to a series of interesting economic issues and to important questions of government regulation, some of which are examined in this chapter. In particular, it is argued that regular-season broadcasts of professional sports have anticompetitive effects on three groups: clubs and leagues, broadcasters, and sponsors. The anticompetitive nature of sports broadcasting is of unusual interest because the government is at least partially culpable. The Congress has explicitly sanctioned the current institutional arrangements by exempting from the antitrust laws the pooled sale of broadcast rights by a professional league. Furthermore, since the networks are agents for federally licensed broadcasters, government regulatory policy has created a market in which a few oligopolistic agents trade with legalized cartels. Sports broadcasting policies are directly detrimental to the interests of the broadcast audience in that they tend to restrict viewing choice, and potentially detrimental insofar as consumers ultimately must bear advertising costs and will suffer the consequences of reduced competition in the marketplace. Yet, because of the high prices paid for broadcast rights and commercial time, and the clubs' desire to protect a lucrative revenue source, the public interest is increasingly ignored. In particular, broadcasting policies affect the public in the following ways.

• Franchise location decisions are influenced by potential broadcast revenues, to the detriment of areas with a small broadcast audience.

• Owners, leagues, and sponsors consider a broadcast to be an entertainment and commercial vehicle, rather than simply the factual reporting of an event. This leads to an avoidance of critical and controversial commentary and thus constitutes a kind of censorship of broadcasts by sports management.

• The present institutions restrict the public's viewing choice by limiting the number of dates on which games are telecast and the number of simultaneous telecasts in a given location.

• The framework of sports broadcasting increases prices all along the line, including prices paid by sponsors and, to the extent that sponsors do not completely absorb higher advertising costs, by consumers.

Institutional Framework

Authorization to broadcast a game[1] is granted by a professional club, subject to league regulations (where "league" refers to one of the two major leagues in basketball and hockey, and to the single major organizations in football and baseball). The procedures for selling these rights are affected by the sports antitrust broadcasting act,[2] an act "to amend the antitrust laws to authorize leagues of professional football, baseball, basketball, and hockey teams to enter into certain television contracts, and for other purposes."

Although the details of broadcasting arrangements differ among sports and over time, all follow the same general pattern. Each club has the right to determine whether its home games will be broadcast and to prevent broadcasts of any other games in its "home territory."[3] All clubs, however, have given up some part of these rights through various kinds of mutual

1. All-star, playoff, and championship games in each sport are also broadcast, but these specialty broadcasts are outside the scope of our main concern, the anticompetitive effects of regular-season broadcasts.

2. P.L. 87-331, approved Sept. 30, 1961 (75 Stat. 732).

3. Home territory has generally been defined as an area within a specified number of miles of the home city or stadium. Currently, home territory in baseball is the area within a radius of 50 miles of the home park. In football, the home territory is the area within 75 miles of the home stadium, and this definition has been interpreted to mean that a club may prevent any station whose signal carries into its home territory from telecasting its home games. On this basis, the St. Louis Cardinals prevented a station in Paducah, Kentucky, 135 miles from Busch Stadium, from telecasting Cardinal home games. (The broadcasts were eventually permitted when an antitrust suit was threatened.) In 1970, a Mason City, Iowa, station, more than 75 miles from Minneapolis, reduced its power while televising an important Vikings game so that its signal could not be received in Minneapolis.

agreements.[4] First, reciprocal agreements permit a club to broadcast its away games. Second, clubs may combine to sell broadcast rights to some games to a national network. The only control over these games retained by the club is its right to prevent its own city from being included in a national broadcast of its home games. Third, in two-team cities, a club has no control over the broadcasts of the other team in its home territory.[5]

Territorial restrictions, or blackout provisions, have two purposes. The more obvious one is to shield gate receipts from broadcast competition. Clubs are understandably anxious to avoid broadcasts of their own home games, and also fear the competition of telecasts of other teams' games. Broadcast restrictions seek to eliminate this potential competition by permitting each club to regulate competition to its own telecasts. The less obvious purpose of the restriction is to grant each club a monopoly on (or a duopolist's share in) broadcasts within its home territory. By eliminating competition to local broadcasts, each club increases the value of its home territory rights at the sacrifice of the possible sale of its rights in another team's territory.

Local Broadcasts

The "local rights" of a team include all broadcasting possibilities not subsumed under the national contract or proscribed by league rules. This includes the right of a team to form its own network for broadcasting games not included in the national contract in areas not within the home territory of another team.

Clubs have essentially three options in the sale of local rights. The most common practice is to sell rights to a station or network, which then "packages" the games—that is, hires the announcers and provides the technical crews and equipment—and sells commercial time to sponsors.

---

4. Sometimes under pressure, as, for example, in 1952, when the Browns and the White Sox resisted a reciprocal agreement in the American League (AL) to broadcast away games. Their capitulation was undoubtedly assisted by such league actions as a scheduling "quirk" that left the Browns without any lucrative weekend and night games in New York (*New York Times,* various issues, December 1952). (The *New York Times* and *Broadcasting* are the sources of much of the historical information in this chapter, but, for brevity, specific references are often omitted.)

5. The National Football League (NFL) is an exception. It tries to avoid direct conflicts between Jets or Giants away telecasts and the other's home games, and prohibits road telecasts of Raiders or 49ers games that conflict with the other's home games unless prior consent has been obtained from the home team.

In 1970, twenty-two of the twenty-six NFL clubs and eight of the twenty-four major-league baseball clubs followed this practice exclusively. A less common, but increasingly important, practice is for a club to package its own games, deal directly with sponsors, and then purchase station time. No NFL club retains its radio rights, but several baseball clubs package all broadcasts and others package either their radio or TV broadcasts. The third alternative is for a club to sell the rights directly to a sponsor. Three NFL clubs follow this procedure for radio rights, and seven baseball clubs sell either radio or TV rights to sponsors. The sponsor resells a portion of the rights to sellers of noncompeting products. Broadcast time is then purchased from individual stations.

All baseball and football clubs have regional networks that are generally, but not necessarily, located in an area contiguous to the club's home territory. If a club or a station owns the rights to broadcast games, it sometimes sells them, perhaps on a per game basis, to other stations, which in turn sell commercial time to local sponsors. In other cases, especially where a sponsor holds the rights, station time is bought on behalf of network-wide sponsors. Organizations such as the Hughes Sports Network (formerly Sports Network Incorporated) and the Television Sports Network specialize in setting up regional alignments composed primarily of independent stations.

National Rights

There have been three major variants in the sale of national rights, differing according to whether one, some, or all teams participate. In each case, the rights are sold to a network, which packages the games. The New York Yankees and the Cleveland Browns have each been the sole club in a national network. Groups of two or more clubs have also negotiated the sale of a national package, with the network paying each club either a flat fee (not necessarily the same for all clubs) or on the basis of the number of home game telecasts.

The culmination of the multiclub arrangement, the league-wide package, followed the passage of the sports broadcasting act. As soon as the individual clubs in each sport had fulfilled previous commitments, they pooled their national rights. When competing leagues have merged, they have also pooled their national rights, as in the case of the merger of the American Football League (AFL) and the NFL. National contracts have three important features. First, except for regular-season football telecasts, they do not prohibit the sale of local rights. Second, while the leagues or sponsors could in theory package the games, the networks have in fact done it. Third, since 1967, when the National Hockey League (NHL) and the Columbia Broadcasting System (CBS) entered into a three-year contract, revenues from national rights have always been divided equally among league members.

The History of Sports Broadcasting

Sports broadcasting became an important source of income for teams after the Second World War. The prospect of significant broadcast revenues, and the threat that broadcasts would adversely affect attendance, led to the adoption of rules in each sport that restricted interteam competition for the sale of broadcast rights. These rules subsequently became the focus of antitrust suits brought by the federal government and by private parties who believed they had been injured by the restrictive practices. When the courts ruled that antitrust statutes had been violated, professional sports turned to Congress for legislation that would exempt them from these laws. In 1961, Congress obliged.

An examination of the history of the clash between sports and the antitrust laws over broadcasting policy, in the decade preceding the 1961 legislation, reveals the arguments that were persuasive to the courts and the Congress about the extent to which anticompetitive practices in sports are "reasonable." Also, by indicating the issues that were not explicitly dealt with in the period, it explains why conflicts over public policy still surround broadcasting practices in sports today.

Baseball

In 1946, when the major leagues adopted a rule prohibiting a club from broadcasting a game in another club's home territory or from another stadium without the home club's consent, antitrust issues were first raised. As a result of a Department of Justice investigation into possible restraints of trade and a series of conferences between the clubs and the department, the rule was modified for the 1950 season to permit blackouts only in minor-league territories where a game was being played at home, or where the home club was telecasting a road game in its home territory. A renewed threat of Department of Justice action, which may well have been welcomed by major-league owners seeking to increase their broadcast revenues by encroaching on minor-league territories, led to the suspension of all broadcast restrictions as of the 1952 season.

Nonetheless, in February 1952, all but three clubs (the Dodgers, White Sox, and Reds), together with Baseball Commissioner Ford Frick and the league presidents, William Harridge and Warren C. Giles, were sued for $12 million by the Liberty Broadcasting System, which charged a "continuing conspiracy to monopolize and restrain competition" in broadcasting major-league games.[6] Liberty, which had "re-created"[7] American League (AL) games in 1950–51 and National League (NL) games in 1948–51, had grown to 435 stations. It already had a three-year contract with the White Sox and agreements with the Dodgers, Reds, and Boston Braves. But six teams asserted that they would not permit re-creations of their games under any circumstances. On April 14, 1952, Chicago Federal Court Judge John P. Barnes ruled that the clubs had a right to control and profit from broadcasts of their own games. As a result, Liberty, which contended it earned a $4 million profit from the broadcasts, was forced to suspend operations on May 15, 1952.[8] A $2.1 million suit by Liberty against the NFL in 1954 charging a system to "restrain trade unlawfully in broadcasting and to maintain a monopoly of the broadcasting" in home territory[9] was also unsuccessful.

In 1954, the Federal Communications Commission denied a petition to prevent the Trinity Broadcasting Corporation in Texas from re-creating major-league games. On February 28, 1955, however, the New York State Supreme Court ruled that unauthorized re-creations were illegal because authorized baseball broadcasts do not constitute news in the public domain. Following these decisions and the 1953 *Toolson* decision reaffirming baseball's special status under the antitrust laws,[10] each major league and the National Association (the organization of minor leagues) separately adopted a rule stating that a club does not have the right to authorize a broadcast within the home territory of another club. These rules do not, however, prevent a club in one major league from broadcasting in the home territory of a club in any other league.

6. *New York Times,* Feb. 22, 1952.

7. In a re-created broadcast, an announcer in the studio has access only to inning-by-inning summaries of the game provided by a news service. Normally the announcer exercises considerable dramatic license in filling in the details of play.

8. When Liberty appealed this decision, the clubs, allegedly to avoid the expense of a trial, offered, and, on January 26, 1955, Liberty accepted, a $200,000 settlement.

9. *New York Times,* Sept. 28, 1954.

10. *Toolson* v. *New York Yankees,* 346 U.S. 356 (1953).

Football

Broadcasting practices in professional football first captured public attention on October 9, 1951, when the Department of Justice filed a civil suit against the NFL.[11] Judge Allan K. Grim's decision of November 12, 1953, upheld the legality of an NFL bylaw preventing the telecasting of an outside game in a third team's home territory when that team had a home game. Judge Grim agreed that the effect of the rule was to allocate marketing territories for the purpose of restricting competition. While this is generally held to be illegal under the Sherman Act, the court found that such a restraint was reasonable because of the adverse effects that competitive outside telecasts would be likely to have on the home club's attendance.[12] In view of the mutual interdependence of the clubs, the court held that, by protecting the home attendance of the weaker teams, the restriction would help to preserve the league. This in turn would permit competition in the sale of TV rights in situations unaffected by the restriction.

The court did find illegal two other restrictions on broadcasts: the prohibition against telecasts by another team when the home club was also telecasting an away game in its home territory; and all restrictions on outside radio broadcasts. The court held that the primary reason for these restrictions was to enable each club to sell a home territory broadcast monopoly. The court stated that the first restriction clearly had no effect on home attendance, while the effect of the second had to be minimal, since NFL clubs did not fear the competition of home game radio broadcasts in their own home territories.

National Broadcasts

As NFL Commissioner Alvin (Pete) Rozelle later pointed out, Judge Grim's ruling had nothing whatsoever to do with a situation where all the clubs in a league collectively bargain as a cartel in negotiations for broadcast rights.[13] The National Broadcasting Company (NBC) and the National Basketball Association (NBA) signed the first league-wide pack-

---

11. *United States* v. *National Football League*, 116 F. Supp. 319 (E.D. Pa. 1953).

12. The evidence of adverse effects, which is not compelling, is discussed below.

13. *Telecasting of Professional Sports Contests,* Hearing before the Antitrust Subcommittee of the House Committee on the Judiciary, 87 Cong. 1 sess. (1961), p. 6.

age agreement in 1954. And, indeed, just six days after this ruling, Louis F. Carroll, acting on behalf of Commissioner Frick, submitted a plan to the Department of Justice for the baseball "Game of the Week" for the 1954 season. Under this plan, the commissioner would negotiate with telecasters for the sale of the broadcast rights of each club for a designated period. The proposal included a condition that a specified number of clubs would have to agree to participate. This proviso was defended on two grounds: first, a network "Game of the Week" was said to be of general interest and salable to a sponsor only if most clubs participated; second, multiclub participation would ease scheduling problems and guard against postponements. The plan also contained blackout provisions, on the grounds that they would protect attendance in the minor leagues. The welfare of the minor leagues was also argued to be better served if the commissioner's office handled the negotiations, since he could arrange compensation for the anticipated decline in minor-league attendance. The Justice Department advised Carroll that it would not approve the proposal, and by 1956 CBS had negotiated a network package involving less than half the clubs.

Broadcast competition in baseball reached its zenith in 1958. First, CBS began baseball telecasts on Sunday, the minor leagues' best drawing day. The commissioner's office again asked the Department of Justice to approve a home territory blackout rule, but the department refused, noting that the purpose of the rule was not to preserve the major leagues (the justification for Judge Grim's 1953 decision countenancing blackouts) but to protect other leagues from competition. Second, several National League teams decided to capitalize on the desertion of New York by the Giants and Dodgers. The Phillies televised seventy-seven games in New York City, and the Cardinals and Pirates televised twenty-two Giant and Dodger games in New York via a Jersey City station. These were in direct competition with Yankee home games, and with many of the road games the Yankees televised. One immediate result was a doubling of the Phillies broadcast revenues, putting them ahead of all teams but the Yankees.[14] But the fading loyalty of the Dodger and Giant fans, and perhaps the possibility of Yankee retaliation (the Philadelphia *Evening Bulletin* alleged that the Yankees had threatened to televise into Philadelphia),[15] caused the dropping of the Phillies, Cardinals, and Pirates

14. *Television Age,* Vol. 4 (March 25, 1957) and Vol. 5 (March 24, 1958).
15. *New York Times,* Dec. 6, 1958.

telecasts after one season. Phillies President Bob Carpenter stated that "the baseball television market is overcrowded." In 1959, Phillies' rights fees fell by half, and were surpassed by all teams except Washington.

In 1960, the newly formed AFL concluded an agreement with the American Broadcasting Company (ABC) for the league's pooled TV rights, and a similar agreement was reached between the NFL and CBS on April 24, 1961. Following the latter agreement, a petition seeking an interpretation of the 1953 decision was brought in Judge Grim's court.[16] The court held that by pooling TV rights, the member clubs eliminated competition among themselves in the sale of these rights. The court also held that by granting to CBS the right to determine which games would be telecast and where, the agreement violated the 1953 judgment enjoining the league from entering into any agreement that could tend to restrict broadcast areas. The court therefore held the CBS-NFL contract to be in violation of its 1953 judgment.

When Judge Grim's 1961 ruling was made, the leagues and the networks petitioned Congress for permission to pool. The interests of the minor leagues and the viewer, as well as the preservation of sporting competition, were discussed in the 1961 House hearing. Prospective profits received occasional mention, but only as a means of preserving the leagues and equalizing playing strengths—in the public interest—rather than of enriching club owners and networks. The result of the hearings was Public Law 87-331, approved September 30, 1961.

The new law amended the antitrust laws so that they "shall not apply to any joint agreement by or among persons engaging in or conducting the organized professional team sports of football, baseball, basketball, or hockey, by which any league of clubs . . . sells or otherwise transfers . . . rights of such league's member clubs in the sponsored telecasting of the games. . . ."[17] Excluded from this exemption was any joint agreement resulting in a blackout area beyond a club's home territory, and any joint agreement that would, in effect, result in professional telecasts competing with college football games. Since 1961, professional clubs have been permitted to negotiate as a cartel for the sale of national broadcast rights. The clubs in all four sports have taken advantage of this option; indeed, they employ it exclusively. Collective bargaining has, as one might expect, gone hand in hand with increasingly large national broadcast revenues.

16. *United States* v. *National Football League,* 196 F. Supp. 445 (E.D. Pa. 1961).
17. 75 Stat. 732.

The Effects of Broadcasts on Attendance

While restrictions on competition for broadcast rights undoubtedly raise team profits, the principal reason they have been given legal sanction is the fear that unlimited broadcasting would seriously undermine attendance, and thereby threaten the viability of all but the most successful teams. Or, in Frick's words: "Baseball faces the dilemma of being compelled to use a byproduct of its business (the broadcasting and telecasting rights) in a manner tending to destroy its main product (gate receipts)."[18] This argument has considerable merit when applied to minor-league baseball. Between 1949 and 1957, attendance in the minor leagues dropped from almost 42 million to about 15.5 million, a decline largely attributable to the introduction of nationwide major-league telecasts.[19] But this is hardly valid evidence that broadcasts could seriously erode attendance at major-league games. In fact, broadcasting could contribute to attendance by generating greater fan interest. As AFL Commissioner Joe Foss testified, ". . . it is important from the standpoint of each individual club that a broad exposure to the public on television be obtained . . . for prestige purposes in the home city, which clearly is reflected in home attendance . . ."[20] Further, Joe Reichler, representing the baseball commissioner, has stated: "Television tends to create fans, especially among women. Television night games have hurt the box office a little, because of traffic and the late hour, but more fans are created than stay away."[21]

To test the effects of TV on attendance, the Yankees announced in 1953 that five night home games would not be telecast. The Yankees were concerned about a drop in night game attendance from an average of over 50,000 in 1951 to 33,400 in 1952. After the first blacked-out game against a leading attraction, the Tigers, the New York Times wrote: "The contest, which was not televised, was watched by a somewhat disappoint-

18. *Organized Professional Team Sports,* Hearings before the Subcommittee on Antitrust and Monopoly of the Senate Committee on the Judiciary, 85 Cong. 2 sess. (1958), p. 203.

19. Ibid., p. 687. When the first national telecast of a World Series game took place in 1952, an article in the *New York Times* (Dec. 9, 1952) correctly predicted that this would lead to the demise of the minor leagues.

20. *Telecasting of Professional Sports Contests,* House Hearing, p. 51.

21. *Broadcasting,* Vol. 78 (Feb. 9, 1970), p. 27.

ing crowd of 24,990."[22] After a four-game average of 37,000, the fifth game to be blacked out was, in fact, televised.

A statistical analysis of the relationship between the number of telecasts and baseball attendance confirms the absence of any deleterious effects of television on the gate. In 1970, a typical year with respect to home, away, and total telecasts, there was a slight positive relationship between home attendance and the number of games televised by each of the twenty-three U.S. clubs. This positive relationship reflects the fact that the clubs in the more populous areas televise more games and draw larger crowds. Taking the effect of population into account causes the slight correlation between telecasts and attendance to disappear.

The baseball evidence has been held to be irrelevant for other sports. Most football and basketball fans, it is argued, watch the man with the ball, not the development of a play, and it is easier to follow the ball on TV. Furthermore, a football stadium at 10 degrees above zero, or the trip to a downtown basketball arena on a cold winter's night, can be most uncomfortable.

The classic example of the devastating effect of TV on football attendance is the case of the Los Angeles Rams. Commissioner Bert Bell testified[23] that in 1949 the Rams drew 205,000 fans. With the sponsor guaranteeing to make good any loss in gate receipts, the Rams televised their 1950 home games, and attendance dropped to 110,000. The Rams case is particularly interesting because it was a vital consideration in Judge Grim's 1953 decision. A check of the actual attendance records reveals that the Rams' situation was both misstated and misleading. The Rams, who won their conference championship in 1949, 1950, and 1951, drew crowds in those years of 308,722, 158,460, and 309,372, respectively, according to the *New York Times'* published accounts. In 1951, the Rams played seven home games, as opposed to six in 1949 and 1950. In 1949, 86,000 fans turned out to see the Chicago Bears, and 75,000 fans appeared at the Chicago Cardinals game at which the Rams were attempting to clinch their first championship. In 1950 the Rams' first game drew 18,000 and the *Times* reported that a pregame rain held down the crowd. Another 1950 crowd of 16,441 turned out to see the Baltimore Colts—a team that had lost eighteen straight games, going back more than a year. The Rams

---

22. May 20, 1953.

23. *Organized Professional Team Sports,* Hearings before the Subcommittee on Antitrust and Monopoly of the Senate Committee on the Judiciary, 86 Cong. 1 sess. (1959), p. 49.

played Green Bay at home in all three years and drew crowds of 37,000, 39,000 (televised), and 24,000, respectively.

Indeed, in 1950 attendance in the NFL in general was down. Speaking in New York about this decline, Earl ("Curly") Lambeau, coach of the Chicago Cardinals, commented: "I cannot understand the small turnouts. Some blame it on television, but though I am against television, I do not think that is the reason. I feel the owners missed the boat because of their policy on publicity . . . As regards television, continued small attendance may compel us to seek revenue from that medium, which will result in even smaller turnouts. Our stadiums may have to be turned into studios."[24]

In fact, after the Colts' 23–17 overtime victory against the Giants for the 1958 NFL championship, professional football was firmly established, in part because of TV. Cleveland Browns owner Arthur Modell commented that "without television, I'd be out of business. It has literally made the game by giving it exposure."[25] On November 22, 1970, the New York Jets (2–7), playing without Joe Namath against the Boston Patriots (1–8), drew 62,000 fans, although the first- and second-place teams in the Jets' division of the AFC, Baltimore and Miami, were on TV. Similarly, 62,000 Jets fans turned out the following weekend against the Vikings, although NBC carried one game and the Giants, battling for first, were televised on CBS. The next weekend, in a 34-degree temperature with a 23-miles-per-hour wind, and with two games televised, both the Giants *and* Jets drew 63,000 fans. Assuredly, nearly all of those attending had season tickets, but the TV football schedules were published well in advance of the season's start. Additionally, NBA attendance increased by an average of 30 percent a year from 1965, when the NBA returned to network TV, to 1970. On balance, then, it is by no means obvious that, over an extended period of time, telecasts—even of home games on a selective basis—have hurt, or would hurt, gate receipts.

The Importance of Broadcast Rights

Broadcast rights have been a steadily growing and increasingly important revenue source in sports. The figures in Tables 1 and 2 reveal the extent of this growth in baseball and football.[26] For baseball clubs, average

24. *New York Times,* Nov. 14, 1950.
25. *Wall Street Journal,* April 22, 1966.
26. The primary sources of broadcast rights data—the clubs and broadcasters—are reluctant to make this information public. Most of the data available are esti-

Table 1. Revenue from Baseball Broadcast Rights, Selected Years, 1933–71

Dollar amounts in thousands

Year	Number of teams	Revenue			
		Local[a]	National[b]	Total[c]	Per team[d]
1933	16	$ 18	...	n.a.	$ 1
1939	16	885	...	n.a.	55
1943	16	725	...	n.a.	45
1946	16	838	...	n.a.	52
1950	16	3,365	...	n.a.	210
1952	16	4,165[e]	n.a.	$ 5,400	260
1953	16	4,741[e]	n.a.	5,952	296
1954	16	5,556[e]	n.a.	6,741	347
1955	16	6,123[e]	n.a.	7,308	383
1956	16	7,206[e]	n.a.	8,366	450
1957	16	5,290	$1,750	10,290	440
1958	16	5,950	2,475	11,475	527
1959	16	6,315	3,225	12,790	596
1960	16	9,355	3,174	15,779	783
1961	18	10,780	2,666	16,696	747
1962	20	12,775	2,000	18,525	739
1963	20	13,000	2,225	18,775	761
1964	20	14,325	1,700	19,775	801
1965	20	15,970	5,950	25,670	1,096
1966	20	17,335	5,700	26,785	1,152
1967	20	17,125	5,700	28,925	1,141
1968	20	18,340	6,000	31,740	1,217
1969	24	21,690	8,800	37,190	1,270
1970	24	21,850	9,600	38,150	1,310
1971	24	22,451	9,600	40,751	1,335

Sources: 1933–50, *Study of Monopoly Power*, Pt. 6, *Organized Baseball*, Hearings before the Subcommittee on Study of Monopoly Power of the House Committee on the Judiciary, 82 Cong. 1 sess. (1952), pp. 968–70; 1952–56 local revenue, *Organized Professional Team Sports*, Hearings before the Antitrust Subcommittee of the House Committee on the Judiciary, 85 Cong. 1 sess. (1957), Pt. 1, pp. 354–59, and Pt. 2, pp. 2046–52; other data compiled from *Broadcasting*, *Television Age*, and *Sponsor* estimates and from published reports in the *New York Times*.

n.a. Not available.

a. Includes all broadcasts not covered by the national package or prevented by league rules.

b. Excludes World Series and all-star games.

c. Includes World Series and all-star games. Comparable data not available before 1952.

d. Local and national, excluding specials.

e. Includes national, which is not available separately.

mates by the broadcasting trade press, which quite naturally focus on baseball and football because these sports are of greatest significance to broadcasters. Because the estimates are of uneven quality, analysis of individual teams is not very reliable, but the broad picture that emerges from the aggregated data is undoubtedly roughly accurate.

Table 2. Revenue from Football Broadcast Rights, 1952–71

Dollar amounts in thousands

	National Football League			American Football League			Both leagues	
Year	Number of teams	Total revenue[a]	Revenue per team	Number of teams	Total revenue[a]	Revenue per team	Regular-season, national	Total revenue[b]
1952	11	$ 769	$ 70	...	...	...	...	...
1953	12	1,239	103	...	...	...	...	...
1954	12	1,764	147	...	...	...	...	...
1955	12	1,364	114	...	...	...	...	...
1956	12	1,720	143	...	...	...	...	...
1957	12	1,958	163	...	...	...	...	...
1958	12	2,296	191	...	...	...	...	...
1959	12	2,634	220	...	...	...	...	...
1960	13	3,100	238	8	$1,616	$202	...	$ 4,916
1961	14	3,510	251	8	1,805	226	...	6,005
1962	14	5,213	372	8	2,070	259	$ 6,530	7,973
1963	14	5,360	383	8	2,112	264	6,610	8,598
1964	14	14,848	1,061	8	2,787	348	16,700	19,730
1965	14	15,270	1,091	8	7,470	934	21,400	26,500
1966	15	20,072	1,338	9	8,108	901	26,550	32,385
1967	16	21,515	1,345	9	8,223	914	27,700	36,638
1968	16	21,621	1,351	10	8,823	882	28,200	36,944
1969	16	21,415	1,338	10	8,948	895	28,200	36,863
1970[c]	26	45,600	1,754	...	...	...	43,500	49,100
1971[c]	26	45,640	1,755	...	...	...	43,500	49,140

Sources: 1952–56, *Organized Professional Team Sports*, House Hearings, Pt. 3, pp. 2562–65; 1960–71, compiled from *Broadcasting* estimates and published reports in the *New York Times*; 1957–59, extrapolated from these figures.

a. Regular-season national and local broadcasts include AFL playoffs (1960–64) and NFL playoffs (1970–71).
b. Includes playoffs and the Super Bowl (beginning in 1967). Comparable data not available before 1960.
c. Figures are for all professional football teams, after the merger of the two leagues in 1970.

net revenues from regular-season broadcasts increased more than fivefold during the years 1952–71; average football revenues increased twenty-five fold. Because of expansion, the growth in total revenues has been even greater, eightfold and sixtyfold, respectively.

Clubs also benefit from the league's sale of playoff and all-star game rights. A portion of these revenues goes to the individual clubs, with the remainder going to the leagues and players. The players' share sometimes is included in a fixed payment to the participants, sometimes negotiated as a pension fund contribution.[27] The payments to the players are important to the clubs, for they represent a significant component of player compensation—and one whose source is the networks. If these payments are included in the total, revenues from the sale of baseball rights more than doubled during the past decade, while football revenues increased eightfold.

A similar pattern emerges from the scanty data that are available for basketball and hockey. In 1952, the NBA teams received around $130,000 for broadcasting rights. In the 1970–71 season, the national contract with ABC netted $5.5 million (no comprehensive data are available on local rights). In hockey, the four U.S. teams in the NHL received $132,000 in 1952.[28] This fell to $86,000 in 1956, but in 1967 the NHL signed a three-year contract with CBS that paid each U.S. team $100,000 a year the first two years and $150,000 the third. In addition, most teams received at least $200,000 in local rights revenues. In 1970, CBS renewed its contract with the NHL, even though hockey received the lowest Nielsen ratings of any sport.

As broadcast revenues have grown, teams in all sports, and especially in baseball and football, have become heavily dependent on broadcasting. Because broadcast rights have become an important source of revenues, they must play an important role in the financial planning of a franchise.

27. In baseball, for example, the 1957–61 agreement between the players and the clubs gave the players' pension fund $1.95 million of the annual $3.25 million paid by NBC for the World Series and all-star games. Between 1962 and 1966, the players' share was $2.75 million of the $3.75 million payment. The 1967 contract boosted the players' share to $4.1 million of the $6.1 million payment, and by 1970, $5.5 million of NBC's $6.7 million payment was going to the pension fund. In football, the $95,000 that Dumont paid for the 1951–56 NFL championships was placed in the players' pool. By 1964 the NFL players' pension fund was getting half of the $1.8 million that CBS paid for the championship.

28. *Organized Professional Team Sports,* Hearings before the Antitrust Subcommittee of the House Committee on the Judiciary, 85 Cong. 1 sess. (1957), Pt. 3, pp. 3131–35.

In baseball, broadcasting accounted for 0.3 percent of total revenues in 1933. This grew to 6.7 percent in 1943 and 16.8 percent in 1956. By the late 1960s, broadcasting accounted for between 25 and 29 percent of total revenues. Similarly, in football, broadcasting revenues grew from 9.2 percent of the clubs' income in 1952 to over 40 percent in the late 1960s.[29]

The trend has been similar, but less dramatic, in basketball and hockey. Broadcasting accounted for 8 percent of total basketball revenues in 1952; the 1970–71 national contract alone accounted for 15 percent of revenues. In hockey, broadcasting revenues were about 7 percent of the total in 1952; by 1967 they were between 15 and 20 percent.[30]

The importance of broadcasting in sports is perhaps most apparent when broadcast revenues are compared with total team profits. For most teams, game broadcasts generate no direct costs, for the teams do not package the broadcast or sell the advertising. Consequently, the contribution of broadcasting to profits is essentially equal to total broadcast revenues. In baseball, only one team would have shown a book profit in either 1952 or 1970, the first and last years for which relatively complete data are available, if broadcast revenues had been zero, and only four clubs would have been profitable without broadcasting in 1965.[31] The situation is essentially the same in football, where only the Giants and Redskins would have been profitable in 1952 without broadcast revenues. Although comprehensive data on football profits in recent years are not available, estimates indicate that only a handful of the most successful teams might be profitable without broadcasting.[32] In basketball, many teams are unprofitable even with broadcasting revenues, but this by no means diminishes the importance of such income. Only in hockey would it appear that most teams could operate profitably without broadcasting.[33]

29. Ibid., Pt. 2, pp. 2046, 2048, and Pt. 3, p. 2562; *Study of Monopoly Power, Pt. 6, Organized Baseball,* Hearings before the Subcommittee on Study of Monopoly Power of the House Committee on the Judiciary, 82 Cong. 1 sess. (1952), pp. 968–69; *Forbes,* Vol. 107 (April 1, 1971), p. 24.

30. Total revenue data for hockey for 1967 are not available; however, in that year the Boston Bruins had about $2.3 million in total revenues, and probably were more successful than most of the ten U.S. teams then playing. If total revenues average about $2 million per team, then the average broadcast revenues from national and local rights of between $300,000 and $400,000 were 15 to 20 percent of the total. Other data are from *Organized Professional Team Sports,* House Hearings (1957), pp. 2930–34-d, 3131–35.

31. *Organized Professional Team Sports,* House Hearings (1957), p. 354; *Forbes,* Vol. 107 (April 1, 1971), p. 30; *Wall Street Journal,* April 22, 1966.

32. See Chapter 1.

33. It is conceivable that this somewhat overstates the importance of broad-

The relative importance of local versus national rights varies enormously among sports, although in all cases national rights are growing in importance. The great contrast between baseball and football in this respect is also shown in Tables 1 and 2. Network rights rose from 25 percent of baseball's regular-season broadcast fees in 1960 to 30 percent in 1971. In football, the networks accounted for 90 percent of all regular-season fees in 1962, and 95 percent in 1971.

Differences in broadcast revenues among teams in a league are closely related to the relative importance of national rights, because the clubs divide national fees equally. Football has always exhibited less interclub disparity in broadcast revenues than baseball. In 1970, all twenty-six professional football clubs received between $1.7 and $1.9 million, whereas in baseball in 1971, the extremes were $2.2 million (the Dodgers) and $850,000 (the Pirates), including the $400,000 in network payments received by each team.

The hockey and basketball data, though sparse, reflect a spread in payments similar to baseball's. In 1967, total broadcast revenues in hockey ranged from $500,000 in Los Angeles to $190,000 in Pittsburgh. In basketball, each of the seventeen NBA clubs received $325,000 for network rights alone for the 1971–72 season, while the American Basketball Association (ABA) had no national contract. Most of the NBA teams received additional revenues for local broadcasts, while a few ABA teams received nothing here as well.

In 1952, the pattern of dispersion in broadcast revenues was similar to the situation twenty years later. Football revenues in 1952 ranged from $15,000 (Chicago Cardinals) to $158,000 (New York Giants), with the nine other clubs receiving between $24,000 and $100,000. In the same year baseball broadcast revenues varied between $9,000 (St. Louis Browns) and $580,000 (Brooklyn Dodgers). Two other clubs were above $400,000, and seven were under $180,000. In hockey, one team, the New York Rangers, received $93,000, which was two-thirds of the total broadcast revenues of the four U.S. hockey teams. Finally, in basketball, 1952

---

casting. First, broadcasts may detract from attendance at games and hence reduce revenues from ticket sales and concessions. But broadcasting generates interest in sports as well as competition for attendance. Second, since broadcasting contributes more to revenues than it detracts, it serves to increase the value of players and thereby raises their salaries. While these factors may be important, their net effect is probably quite small compared to total revenues, so that total broadcast revenues can be assumed to be reasonably close to the contribution of broadcasting to profits.

broadcast revenues varied from nothing in Boston to $62,000 in New York.[34]

The relatively equal revenues from broadcasting persisted in football even during the era of four competing national telecasts. In 1960, broadcast revenues in the NFL varied from $105,000 (Green Bay Packers) to $340,000 (New York Giants), but the other clubs were all clustered between $180,000 and $300,000. In the AFL, all teams received between $215,000 (Houston Oilers) and $194,000 (Oakland Raiders).[35] In contrast, revenues from broadcasting in baseball during the same year varied enormously. Local revenues ranged from $200,000 (Washington Senators) to $1 million (Los Angeles Dodgers), a spread that was actually even greater since only about half the clubs shared in the national broadcasting packages.

The importance of rights fees to a club's financial situation is not entirely reflected in the magnitude of the annual payments. Because the sale of rights generally involves a long-term contract, broadcasting provides a guaranteed revenue base that is independent of team performance and the vagaries of fan allegiance. This is particularly true of the national contract. The AFL's dependence on the sale of a long-term broadcast contract is unique. When the AFL began operations in 1960, it already possessed a five-year, $11 million contract with ABC that guaranteed each of its eight clubs $185,000 per year.[36] In 1964, at the height of the competition between the leagues for players, NBC obtained the AFL rights, agreeing to pay each team $900,000 a year for five years. The league probably could not have survived without the financial support and interest-generating exposure provided by the TV coverage.[37] The Oakland, Denver, and Los Angeles franchises, for example, together had a total 1960 attendance of 271,000, which was surpassed by eight NFL clubs. Dallas and Houston led the AFL with attendances of 171,500 and 140,127. Only the newly created Dallas Cowboys in the NFL fell below 140,000, and only St. Louis and the Redskins were below 170,000.[38] Yet,

34. *Organized Professional Team Sports,* House Hearings (1957), Pt. 1, pp. 354, 359, and Pt. 3, pp. 2562, 2930–35, 3131–35.
   35. *Broadcasting,* Vol. 61 (Aug. 28, 1961), p. 40.
   36. Ibid., p. 42.
   37. As Leonard Shecter has written: "What the AFL needed was enough money to go out and do battle for future stars with the NFL. To that end NBC decided to give—subsidize might be a better word—each club to the tune of a million a year for the next five years" (*The Jocks* [Bobbs-Merrill, 1969], p. 70).
   38. *Broadcasting,* Vol. 61 (Aug. 28, 1961), p. 40.

in 1961 the broadcast revenues of each AFL club approximated those of powerful Baltimore, which featured Johnny Unitas, then football's premier quarterback. As AFL Commissioner Foss commented in 1961: "Pro football survived without television, but the sport's period of expansion, solvency and growth is directly equated to its entrance into the field of television."[39]

Local Broadcast Rights

Local broadcast rights are a potentially valuable resource. Even without league restrictions, a club either has a monopoly on "broadcasts of the home team," or shares it with one other club.

No matter how the rights are acquired, the price ultimately depends upon sponsor interest and the club's bargaining position. The minimum price that a profit-conscious club might accept could be negative, as when a newly established club would be willing to sponsor itself in order to get audience exposure. The minimum would normally be higher for home games than for road games, since the former would be more likely to detract from attendance. The maximum price that sponsors (and hence broadcasters) are willing to pay depends on the size, composition, and loyalty of the average audience that the broadcasts are expected to draw, the extent of sponsor interest in reaching this audience, the number of broadcasts, and, if some games are not broadcast, the selection of games. Negotiations determine where between these limits the actual price will be, as well as the number and selection of games.

Since the final contract depends upon the bargaining skills of both parties, any statistical analysis attempting to "explain" rights fees in terms of the variables that affect the limits is unlikely to be very successful. Nonetheless, an effort to obtain some rough results is worth making. If local broadcast revenues are important to a club, as they are in baseball, and if the clubs are operating as profit-oriented business organizations, then the organization will take into account these factors in making business decisions, such as where to locate a franchise. Furthermore, determination of the factors that affect local revenues will help reveal sponsor motivations. If sponsors perceive sports broadcasts as giving them a unique competitive advantage, the special treatment accorded professional sports in

39. Quoted in *Broadcasting,* Vol. 53 (July 24, 1961), p. 61.

marketing broadcast rights can have undesirable effects on competition in the "sponsoring" industries.

Seven principal factors might plausibly influence local broadcast rights: (1) the size of the potential audience; (2) fan interest; (3) past performance and future prospects; (4) the number of competitive broadcasts; (5) the number of games broadcast; (6) the duration of the broadcast contract; and (7) bargaining skill. These factors occasionally overlap, and attempts to isolate and quantify their effects only served to emphasize the great complexity of the problem. In fact, the only quantitative variable that statistical analysis clearly singles out as important is the size of the potential audience, and even here the strength of the relationship is not especially great.

The effect of potential audience size is reflected in the correlations given in Table 3 between local rights fees in baseball and the standard metropolitan statistical area (SMSA) population of each club's home city. The correlations are based on observations for the fifteen clubs operating in both 1961 and 1971, but analogous results are obtained with all teams included. Correlations of like magnitude are found for the NFL teams before the development of a league contract.

These correlations are relatively small for three reasons. First, the local SMSA population is not an accurate measure of the potential audience within a home city's broadcast range, since broadcast signals normally can be received over a wider geographical area than the SMSA, and since some clubs have extensive networks that expand the potential audience well beyond that reached by the hometown station. Second, the geographical areas of some broadcast networks receive competitive sports broadcasts that reduce the size of the audience. Third, although a full schedule of radio broadcasts is the norm, the number of baseball telecasts differs widely among teams.

Attempts to consider systematically some of these variables, as well as others that might influence revenues, met with little success. When, for example, both the previous year's attendance, as a surrogate variable for fan interest, and current SMSA population are included in a statistical analysis of broadcast revenues,[40] the estimates for 1962 through 1967

40. For each year, a separate cross-section linear regression was performed. Since teams in larger cities generally have greater attendance, these equations have a serious multicollinearity problem. One difficulty of a statistical analysis based on annual data is that most clubs are bound by multiyear contracts. Even if an unanticipated improvement in a team's performance, heightened fan interest, or an

Table 3. Correlation Coefficients for Local Broadcast Revenues of
Selected Baseball Teams, by Team Characteristics, 1962–71[a]

Year	Attendance $(t-1)$	Won-lost percentage $(t-1)$	First-place difference $(t-1)$[b]	Hometown population (t)[c]
		Characteristic		
1962	0.5319	0.4055	−0.3188	0.6561
1963	0.5985	0.4280	−0.4845	0.7295
1964	0.5434	0.5919	−0.4714	0.7255
1965	0.4433	0.3364	−0.1888	0.6958
1966	0.2677	−0.0185	−0.0229	0.6526
1967	0.2251	0.1201	−0.0839	0.5818
1968	−0.1903	−0.3760	0.2842	0.8327
1969	−0.0031	−0.3825	0.3525	0.7832
1970	−0.0160	−0.3565	0.2626	0.7843
1971	−0.1878	−0.2743	0.3588	0.7131

Sources: Population, U.S. Bureau of the Census, *Statistical Abstract of the United States,* relevant annual issues (1962–64 by extrapolation); other data, *The World Almanac and Book of Facts* (Newspaper Enterprise Association), relevant annual editions. *t* signifies current year.

a. Includes the fifteen major-league teams operating in both 1961 and 1971.

b. Difference in won-lost percentage from first-place team.

c. Population of the standard metropolitan statistical area of each team's home city. (The Los Angeles and Anaheim SMSAs are combined.)

are extremely plausible: with varying degrees of statistical significance, teams located in more populous areas and drawing larger crowds at the box office tended to be paid more for broadcast rights. But after 1967, the effect of attendance essentially disappears, and the correlations become slightly negative (though statistically insignificant). Other, more direct measures of the attractiveness of a team, such as performance on the field, also proved to have no measurable effect on rights fees.[41]

extension of a club's network boosted fees, a statistical analysis of annual data might not reveal it. An analysis over several time periods also holds little promise of capturing more than the population effect because of the poor quality of the data on rights revenues and the details of broadcasting arrangements. For example, many teams no longer have records of how their rights were packaged in the past, or how many stations broadcast their games.

41. Team performance in the previous season was measured by won-lost percentage and the difference in that percentage between the team and the pennant winner. Neither had a consistent, systematic effect on rights fees, and indeed, for the fifteen-team sample, there was a negative relation between previous performance and broadcast revenues from 1968 to 1971. Only from 1962 to 1965 did previous performance have a statistically significant, positive correlation with broadcast revenues.

Two other interesting "nonresults" emerged from the statistical analysis of rights fees. First, the number of telecasts—home, away, or total—did not appear to have an important effect on rights fees. Second, the presence of a second local team in a broadcast market did not influence broadcast revenues.

In addition to population and, to some degree, fan interest, another factor that offers a partial explanation of broadcast revenues is the extent to which the club owner is profit oriented. In order to measure the effects of profit orientation, two additional variables were defined. The first assigned a value of one to those clubs in the sample that knowledgeable baseball sources considered to be most profit oriented—the Dodgers, Yankees, Twins, Giants, and Reds—and zero otherwise. The second assigned a value of one to the clubs in the sample judged to be owned by "sportsmen" (that is, the least profit-oriented executives)—the Cubs, Pirates, and Red Sox—and zero otherwise.

The results of a statistical analysis using the sportsman variable and SMSA population to explain broadcast revenues are reported in Table 4. The other profit-orientation variable and attendance were excluded because in an analysis that included all four variables, these proved statistically insignificant.[42] The three clubs with the least profit orientation are estimated to have averaged between $156,000 and $337,000 less in fees than did the other clubs, taking account of differences in population.

The pattern of the other clubs' broadcast revenues, although not as extreme, has equally evident explanations. For example, the broadcast revenues of Baltimore and St. Louis consistently diverged from the amounts predicted by the statistical analysis, but in both cases the president of the team was also the president of the brewery that owned the rights to the team's broadcasts. It is not clear what contract "negotiations" mean for such teams. In addition, teams that package their own broadcasts normally derive greater broadcast revenues. When Detroit began packaging its own broadcasts in 1965, its revenues nearly doubled, but at least part of this increase simply reflected the additional costs of packaging the game itself.

Team performance also must have played an important role in some cases. After the Yankees finished last in 1966, their revenues fell by

42. The correlations of the profit-orientation variable with rights fees varied between a high of 0.53 in 1962, to a low of 0.11 in 1969. The correlations of the "sportsman" or nonprofit-orientation variable with rights fees varied between an (absolute) high of −0.48 in 1967 to an (absolute) low of −0.27 in 1968. In general, the absolute magnitudes of the latter were higher than those of the former.

Table 4. Coefficients for Local Broadcast Revenues of Selected Baseball Teams, Correlated with Profit Orientation of Owners and Hometown Population, 1962–71[a]

Year	Constant	Population	Sportsman owner	R^2
1962	492	0.046 (3.267)	−156 (1.661)	0.537
1963	495	0.056 (4.619)	−235 (2.816)	0.718
1964	501	0.054 (4.550)	−236 (2.819)	0.715
1965	563	0.051 (4.080)	−236 (2.665)	0.676
1966	599	0.067 (3.382)	−309 (2.178)	0.589
1967	654	0.052 (2.794)	−303 (2.248)	0.535
1968	521	0.096 (5.540)	−185 (1.460)	0.740
1969	581	0.098 (4.786)	−273 (1.816)	0.697
1970	992	0.096 (4.844)	−284 (1.948)	0.708
1971	716	0.084 (3.891)	−337 (2.085)	0.639

Sources: Population, same as Table 3; other data, compiled by author. Regression equation:

$$r_t = a + a_1 p_t + a_2 s_t + \text{error},$$

where t is time (in years), r is local revenues, a is a constant, p is population, and s is sportsman owner.

a. Includes the fifteen major-league teams operating in both 1962 and 1971. Numbers in parentheses are t-ratios; t-ratios of 1.782 and 2.179 are significant at the 10 and 5 percent confidence levels, respectively.

$250,000, and after the Reds won a pennant in 1970, their revenues increased by $400,000.[43]

These and other details, combined with the reported statistical analysis, lead to the following conclusions about the variables affecting broadcast revenues. (1) Local population is the key quantifiable factor in determining rights revenues. (2) Fan interest and, consequently, team performance can also be important, but because these are unstable and because clubs are often bound by long-term contracts, the impact of these variables is only occasionally felt. (3) Location in a two-team city is not necessarily harmful or helpful to broadcast revenues. (4) A large broad-

43. *Broadcasting*, Vol. 72 (Feb. 20, 1967), p. 36; Vol. 80 (Feb. 22, 1971), p. 19.

cast network can be very important, particularly when the network reaches populous areas. (5) The number of telecasts does not have any clearly discernible influence and, although every club's revenues tend to increase over time, most continue to televise the same number of games. (6) The profit orientation, bargaining ability, salesmanship, and imagination of management are all of considerable importance.

Broadcasting and Franchise Location

Although the magnitude of the effects of fan interest and team performance on broadcast revenues cannot be measured, they affect the size of the broadcast audience, which is of primary concern to sponsors. In view of the importance of broadcast revenues to the clubs, the potential broadcast audience can be a key influence in managerial decision making.

Several recent cases illustrate this influence. The Milwaukee Braves reached a high point of $0.5 million for their 1963 broadcast rights. This fell to $0.2 million in 1965, when the Braves were a lame-duck team attempting to move to Atlanta. An important consideration in the move was the vast Southeast broadcast audience that could be reached by Braves sponsors. Indeed, when the Braves moved in 1966, they were guaranteed $1.2 million in annual rights fees, and published reports in 1964 had alleged that a five-year, $7.5 million contract awaited their arrival. It was also claimed that Schlitz Brewing had countered with a three-year, $1.6 million offer for 1965 Braves rights in order to keep the team in Milwaukee. Thus, the decision to move (and the inability to do so immediately) cost the Braves $1.3 million in broadcast revenues in one year.

The 1961 shift of the original Washington franchise to Minnesota brought a three-year contract that tripled revenues to $600,000. Similarly, in 1967 the Kansas City Athletics, whose owner, Charles O. Finley, was searching for profit-generating changes in operations, received only $98,000 for TV rights and a total of $165,000 for broadcast rights. Oakland interests promised the Athletics a TV contract worth $705,000 annually, and the Athletics moved to California in 1968.

Football franchise shifts also have been affected by broadcast rights. Falstaff Brewing countered the ownership of the St. Louis Cardinals baseball team by Anheuser-Busch when, on March 12, 1960, its president, Joseph Griesedieck, bought a small interest in the Chicago Cardinals, an NFL club. In response to rumors of a shift of the Cardinals to St. Louis, their managing director Walter Wolfner stated: "It would cost the Cardinals too much money to move and I don't think it is necessary."[44] That evening the NFL approved the shift, effective for the 1960 season. Falstaff, which had held the rights in Chicago, continued to sponsor the football Cardinals in St. Louis, and owned the basic rights until 1968.

Broadcast potential has also played a role in major-league baseball expansion. The Mets entered the league in 1962 with a $1 million contract, and the Kansas City Royals began operations in 1969 with a $650,000 contract that surpassed by $250,000 the best contract that the nomadic Athletics had received while in Kansas City. Similarly, San Diego began operations in 1969 with a three-year, $700,000 per year contract. The Houston Astros (then called the Colt 45s) began operation in 1962 as the only team in the large Southwest broadcasting market. Although their broadcast revenue was initially only $500,000, by 1965 it had grown to $1.8 million, the highest in baseball. Including the $400,000 that each club received in 1969 from the network package, the San Diego and Seattle franchises both started with at least $1.0 million in assured revenues. At the time of the Atlanta and Oakland shifts, the network package payment was $300,000, so these clubs, too, were assured of over $1.0 million in revenues.

National Broadcast Rights

The distinguishing feature of a regular-season "national" broadcast is that a network carries the games of one or more clubs, either regionally or nationally, at approximately the same time and day for several weeks. Network radio broadcasts have not been regularly scheduled since 1961. Baseball and football games are televised throughout the season, whereas early-season (October to December) basketball and hockey games that would compete with football telecasts are ordinarily not televised (although NBC, until 1962, telecast Saturday afternoon NBA games in the fall). When only a few teams were included in a package, league schedules and blackout provisions made strict adherence to a regular program schedule impossible. Now, when entire leagues or conferences sign network contracts, sports programs are as regular as any other network broadcast.

In the network system, a network, acting as an agent for a set of individual stations, purchases the broadcast rights of one or more clubs. The

44. *New York Times,* March 13, 1960.

network then acquires, by purchase or gift, air time from its affiliates—some of which it may own—to carry the broadcasts. The network either resells time to sponsors at national or regional network rates, or permits the individual stations to sell time at what are generally lower local rates, or both. In sports broadcasts, the networks normally do both the packaging and the selling. CBS, NBC, ABC, and Hughes Sports Network on television, and Liberty and the Mutual Broadcasting System on radio have all been involved in regular network broadcasts. In addition, The Fourth Network, Vic Piano Associates, Tele-Sports Network, Mizlou Productions, and Black Associated Sports Enterprises have televised occasional professional and collegiate events. But only the three largest networks are serious contenders for national rights to an entire major-league schedule.[45]

The Determinants of National Rights Fees

Network sports telecasts are generally confined to weekend afternoons. Until recently, the exceptions have been holiday telecasts and an occasional prime-time special. The first extensive incursion of professional sports into prime evening time came in 1970, when the NFL scheduled thirteen Monday evening football games on ABC.

From a sponsor's standpoint, a league package has several advantages and is likely to command a higher fee. First, it assures the sponsor of an advertising monopoly for the league. Second, it permits the telecasting of either the most attractive game available, or else a game of regional interest. The former reduces dependency on local appeal; the latter takes advantage of it. Third, home territory need not be blacked out when the home club is scheduled to appear on the network. Rather, an alternate game that is not as attractive locally as the home club's game can be substituted in home territory. This procedure, successfully employed in all sports but hockey, appeals to the clubs because it reduces the potentially adverse effects of telecasts on gate receipts, while assuring sponsors that every telecast will not be blacked out in one large urban area.[46] The main disadvantage to advertisers of a league package is that unsuccessful

---

45. In 1969, Hughes Sports Network was rumored (*Broadcasting*, Vol. 76 [June 2, 1969], p. 66) to have outbid ABC for the NFL Monday evening telecasts, but sufficient outlets could not be arranged.

46. It is conceivable that a single sponsor could accomplish this by dealing with the individual clubs, but probably not as efficiently or cheaply.

bidders and firms too small even to consider sponsorship may well find themselves at a competitive disadvantage. Thus, network broadcasts will tend to be sponsored by the largest national firms. These firms are likely to be in the best position to reap the potential rewards of a nationwide advertising campaign.

Networks find two attractions in a league package. First, network programming demands that a particular program be presented at a fixed time, on a fixed day, over a given period of time—generally a thirteen-week sequence. This procedure simplifies scheduling and helps to condition audience viewing habits. Second, because the league package is attractive to sponsors, it increases advertising revenues and network profits—provided that the cost of setting up the package does not rise commensurately.

The cost of a given package will depend upon how effectively the member clubs bargain. From the league's standpoint, national exposure can be very important in generating fan interest. But individual clubs will ordinarily have little to gain from participating in a network program, beyond the direct monetary remuneration. In exceptional cases, such as the Yankees in the late 1950s, a club's road gate receipts may be improved by fans lured to the stadium by a team's televised performance, but this effect could easily work in the opposite direction. Still, national telecasts are unlikely to affect the gate receipts of most teams, so that an individual club ordinarily takes what is offered for its national broadcast rights unless its management can bargain more effectively.

Clubs have always considered themselves entitled to a stronger bargaining position. In 1958, Paul A. Porter, counsel to major-league baseball, tried to justify the legalized cartelization of the clubs with the argument that "in the absence of a rule, it has proved possible for broadcasters and sponsors to break down the desire and policy of an individual major league club to protect national association clubs from its broadcasts by representing to the major league club that 'We have the promise of rights from some of the clubs so your club might as well get on the bandwagon.' "[47] As Tigers President John Fetzer pointed out to the Senate in 1965, the bandwagon would be boarded at the broadcaster's price. Fetzer noted that "for many, many years NBC and CBS would go to three, four, five, or six clubs and enter into a contract . . . pretty well distributed amongst the four, five, or six that were lucky enough to have a contract. . . . But as time went on, as they renewed these contracts and were taking

47. *Organized Professional Team Sports*, Senate Hearings (1958), pp. 686–87.

more and more out of Yankee Stadium, the other clubs were being cut back. . . . And then gradually the price began to go down. So that clubs were offered as little as $10,000 a ball game, which was a little insulting to the intelligence of the participants."[48] Insulting, perhaps, but not necessarily less than the competitive price.

In the absence of a league-wide package, a club's bargaining position for national rights is weaker than for local rights in one crucial aspect. While the club usually has a monopoly in local rights, in the national rights market it is only one of many owners of a similar, if differentiated, resource, and faces only a few competing buyers (broadcast networks). The most desirable attractions can capture more revenues, but even these are limited by the fact that at some price differential the rights of a less desirable attraction are worth acquiring. A network that has the "best" teams in its package will, of course, have some advantage over competing networks in selling commercial time, but this advantage is limited. It takes two teams to play a game, and the best teams sometimes will be playing road games that could appear on a competing broadcast. In 1964 and 1965, the Yankees were the prime attraction in the CBS package, but in 1964, NBC televised five of the eight Saturday Yankee road games from four cities. In 1965, ABC scheduled eight Yankee road games—representing more appearances than any other club. On all these occasions the Yankees in fact competed with CBS.

Sharing of National Rights

Since 1966, national rights payments to all leagues have been evenly split by the members. But as recently as 1964, the CBS baseball package gave its members $25,000 for each home telecast; the visiting team and other members received nothing. The Yankees were the biggest draw in the package, and had the advantage of a New York location. With New York being a center for CBS transmissions, from a production standpoint it was advantageous for CBS, which owned the Yankees, to telecast out of New York. Consequently, the CBS contract provided for telecasts of all Yankee weekend home games, except for the last three in September. As a result, the Yankees received half of the $1 million paid by CBS, and the other four clubs in the package split the remaining $500,000.

48. *Professional Sports Antitrust Bill—1965,* Hearings before the Subcommittee on Antitrust and Monopoly of the Senate Committee on the Judiciary, 89 Cong. 1 sess. (1965), p. 62.

With the advent of the league package, equal sharing became the rule. There is very little economic justification for shares being other than equal. Broadcasting a game does not ordinarily generate any costs to the teams that are playing, so that a club's remuneration does not have to cover any costs that are related to the number of its home or road broadcasts. Only to the extent that some clubs have greater drawing power might there be a reason for unequal division of revenues, but this effect is mitigated by the fact that it takes two teams to play a game, and because success is to some extent unpredictable and temporary. An even split is appealing to the teams for several reasons. First, the run-of-the-mill clubs that would prefer an even split outnumber the clubs that star a Koufax, an Abdul-Jabbar, or a Namath. Second, absolute profits, not interteam profit disparities, are the prime concern of a club, so that if it earns at least as much from an even split as it would on its own, it has no reason not to accept the league package. Finally, since success in sports is usually transitory, accepting a constant, average income is often a small sacrifice for avoiding the risks of declining playing success.

An equal division of broadcast revenues will ordinarily tend to balance the economic strength of the members. The wealthier clubs may not favor this, particularly if their wealth can be used to advantage, as in the case of the former Yankee dynasty.[49] Nonetheless, an equal split that strengthens some of the clubs financially without hurting others will presumably tend to equalize competition, and thereby enhance the profits of all clubs. Thus, even the strong clubs could prefer pooling, unless, of course, the will to win overwhelms economic rationality.

The Development of the League Package

With large firms willing to pay the price, and the networks and clubs lured by higher profits, the league package is likely to evolve unless legally forbidden. Its evolution began with the agreement between the NBA and NBC in 1954, and Congress legalized it in 1961. The immediate effect was to increase broadcast revenues and to reduce the number of competing telecasts.

BASEBALL. In 1956, CBS started carrying a Saturday baseball "Game

49. If stadium rental fees and other costs associated with a franchise are unequal, then an equal division of revenues simply works to the advantage of the low-cost clubs, at least when the latter cannot do as well on their own, or lack the bargaining power to extract more than an equal share.

of the Week." NBC joined in on Saturday afternoons in 1957, each network telecasting on twenty-six dates, with league home territories blacked out. When CBS added a Sunday telecast in 1958, a total of sixty-nine games were televised nationally. By 1959 there were ninety-six network games, with NBC joining CBS on Sundays, an arrangement that continued through 1964. In addition, in 1960 the Mutual Broadcasting System concluded a ten-year series in which it had presented a daily radio broadcast.

The number of broadcasts dropped sharply with the advent of the national contract. From a 1960 total of about one hundred telecasts, the number of network games dropped to fewer than fifty in 1965 in the first eighteen-team package, and then to twenty-eight in the nineteen-team package of 1966. The number of competing network telecasts dropped from almost fifty in 1960 to fewer than fifteen in 1965, and to zero in 1966.

The allegedly declining popularity of baseball does not explain the reduced coverage. Between 1966 and 1969, with twenty-eight telecasts each season, the average number of households tuned into the NBC game rose from 4.71 million to 4.97 million, with a peak in 1967 of 5.31 million. By comparison NBA basketball, including playoffs and the all-star game, averaged 3.98 million households in 1966 and 5.02 million in 1969; AFL football averaged 4.34 million in 1966 and 5.15 million in 1969. Thus, network baseball telecasts have not declined in popularity, and the size of the audience is equivalent to that of the NBA and AFL.

Moreover, local baseball telecasts, which are traditionally more popular than the network games, actually increased in number during the same period. Fifteen cities had baseball franchises in both 1960 and 1970, with Chicago having two franchises. Between 1960 and 1970, the average number of telecasts for these sixteen clubs increased from forty-three to fifty-seven,[50] while their average home attendance increased by 30,000.

Finally, if declining popularity were the explanation for the decrease in national telecasts, an accompanying decline—or at least no increase—in the post-1965 rights payments should emerge, since only the number of teams in the leagues changed; the coverage was unaltered. Another reason for expecting a decline in baseball rights fees is that ABC reportedly lost $1 million in 1965 and did not exercise its option to renew

---

50. In 1957 the average was fifty-five games, but the New York Giants and Brooklyn Dodgers accounted for 20 percent of the telecasts; in 1960 the San Francisco Giants and Los Angeles Dodgers accounted for less than 2 percent of the telecasts.

in 1966; and in 1971 the "lagging economy, the departure of tobacco money and the tendency of other major sports to further overlap the baseball season" meant that "both stations and networks [were] having a hard time selling [to sponsors]."[51] In fact, the 1969 contract between NBC and major-league baseball increased each club's share from $300,000 to $400,000, and two new clubs received shares. Neither these increases nor an increase in prime-time games is consistent with the idea of a decline in baseball's popularity.

The disappearance of Sunday network telecasts is particularly interesting. The unit contract, and the fact that most of the baseball season does not overlap with other sports, assures that renewed Sunday telecasts would not encounter TV competition from other leagues. The Sunday telecasting of the other major-league sports and the consistent audience ratings of Saturday baseball indicate that TV sports fans would probably welcome Sunday games. Furthermore, the networks' Sunday programming alternatives are not more attractive in the summer than at other times. A plausible explanation for the disappearance of Sunday telecasts is the enhanced bargaining position and flexibility that baseball obtained through collective bargaining. Negotiations are not just for dollar amounts, but for the type of coverage given the games. The only current blackout areas for network baseball telecasts are the home territories of the participants. An alternate game is telecast in these areas, which gives sponsors access to all of the largest urban markets. Teams can always avoid conflict with the TV game by playing on Saturday evening, as many do.

Adding Sunday games creates several problems. First, fans do not have to pay to see a game, although the magnitude of this effect is debatable. Second, avoiding competition to home attendance by scheduling an evening game when a daytime game is televised would not only break a long-standing tradition, but would be illegal in some cities. Third, Sunday afternoon games are the minor leagues' greatest draw, and without blacking out minor-league cities, which would be unacceptable to sponsors, the effects on the minor leagues could be disastrous. Fourth, Sunday telecasts set up the possibility of competition with local telecasts. By eroding a club's local monopoly, this could reduce the value of local rights. Thus, individual clubs certainly prefer the least national coverage for a given payment. This is not to say that the club owners would not be interested in a Sunday "Game of the Week." In fact, they have not concealed this

51. *Broadcasting*, Vol. 80 (Feb. 22, 1971), p. 19.

interest. But the price that the networks might be willing to pay for a second game is not as great as the price that baseball would require. The result is a single "Game of the Week."

FOOTBALL. Football broadcast revenues have grown even more dramatically than baseball's. In 1960 and 1961, ABC (AFL games), NBC (Baltimore and Pittsburgh of the NFL), Sports Network (Cleveland of the NFL), and CBS (the rest of the NFL) had network broadcasts. The 1961 CBS-NFL contract that was ruled illegal would have given each NFL club $332,000. Without this contract, the Western Conference champions, the Green Bay Packers, received $75,000 for their 1960 TV rights, while the mediocre Steelers (with a record of 6–5–1 in 1959 and 5–6–1 in 1960) received $225,000. By 1962, the CBS-NFL contract was legal, and two of the four network broadcasts disappeared. This did not cause revenues to fall—on the contrary, revenues increased by one-third between 1961 and 1962 and by tenfold between 1960 and 1970.

As in baseball, the pooling of rights and collective bargaining would seem to be the most important factors in revenue growth. Between 1960 and 1970, the number of TV households increased by one-third, which, allowing for a 6 percent inflationary factor, would produce only a doubling in the total rights fees. Allowing for the heightened fan interest that probably accompanied the 25 percent increase in the number of football teams still produces no more than a tripling in the rights fees. The increased popularity of professional football is also important, but offers only a partial explanation.

At least three other factors have contributed to the growth of broadcast revenues in football: the end of blackouts in cities in which a game is being played, the increased number of double-headers on a single network, and the scheduling of games in prime-time slots. In the negotiations between CBS and the NFL during late 1965, the network expressed a desire for a less stringent blackout rule and more double-headers. Under the blackout rule, sponsors were denied access to each major urban area during half the season. During the negotiations, the NFL expressed an interest in early-season prime-time telecasts as a means of promoting fan interest.[52] In the contract that was eventually signed, CBS won the modified blackout proviso, but had to agree to seven prime-time games: four Friday evening exhibitions, one Thanksgiving evening game, the Friday evening league opener, and a mid-season Monday evening game. Based on preseason

52. *Broadcasting,* Vol. 70 (Jan. 3, 1966), p. 124.

forecasts, the three regular-season games would involve strong teams. Eight double-headers would also be televised during the last eight weeks of the season, but only one game would be telecast in the territory of a club playing at home. The price of the package was $37.6 million for two years, with CBS having an option for a third year. The NFL had sought $96 million for four years.

Although the NFL won neither its price nor the four-year contract, it did win prime-time exposure. The NFL's bargaining position lacked some strength, since both NBC and ABC had firm football commitments, to the AFL and the National Collegiate Athletic Association, respectively, and had indicated disinterest in bidding for the NFL package. Indeed, in the fall of 1965 the NFL was not discouraging the rumor that it might set up its own TV network.

As a result of network demands for more games and fewer blackout areas, and the leagues' interest in more prime-time exposure, the total number of telecasts in most areas of the country, including the thirteen Monday evening games, now exceeds the 1960 total. In 1960 and 1961, viewers who were offered all four football networks had the choice of perhaps fifty games, although both NBC and CBS practiced a blackout rule for the other's home cities as well as their own. In 1961, twelve AFL telecasts began after 3:30 P.M. EST in order to avoid direct competition with NFL telecasts. But in 1964 CBS introduced double-headers. Thomas Moore, ABC's president, testified in 1965 that "the televising of two National Football League games materially affected our television audience level of the American Football League. The American Football League plan had been devised on the basis of feeding an eastern game West and a western game East in order to avoid head-and-head competition on the air with the National Football League, and that plan was somewhat obviated when the National Football League went into the televising of more than a single game to any given market."[53]

As seen in Table 5, the total number of telecasts fell to thirty-two in 1962, with the CBS-NFL package, and then gradually edged its way up above sixty, although, with the exceptions of the thirteen Monday evening games and the several "specials" (Thanksgiving and Saturday), in most areas two games were shown simultaneously. Further, with the lifting of the blackout restriction, fans in the league cities had considerably more choice.

53. *Professional Sports Antitrust Bill—1965*, pp. 77–78.

Table 5. Number of Professional Football Network Telecasts and Viewing Households, 1962–69

	Number of telecasts[a]			Average number of viewing households (thousands)	
Year	NFL	AFL	Total	NFL	AFL
1962	16	16	32	7,320	3,590
1963	16	16	32	8,770	3,880
1964	22	16	38	7,840	3,260
1965	22	18	40	8,340	4,410
1966	29	19	48	8,670	4,340
1967	26	30	56	9,350	4,030
1968	28	33	61	9,120	4,390
1969	30	30	60	9,540	5,150

Sources: A. C. Nielsen Company, *A Look at Sports, 1969–'70 Season* (Nielsen, 1971), and relevant preceding issues. (A. C. Nielsen Co. cautions that "data are estimates subject to qualifications.")
a. Regular-season games only.

For example, in Indianapolis there were fifty different games televised on eighteen dates in 1960. In five instances the same game was carried on two different networks. On six of the dates there were four different games—but the three NFL games were ordinarily shown simultaneously. Only one NFL game was televised on four days, and NFL games did not conflict with the first two games of the AFL season. Although about one-fourth of the AFL games had a "late" starting time, only six games clearly had no TV competition. Allowing for the later AFL starting time, the total was approximately twelve noncompeting telecasts. In 1970, sixty-two different games were telecast in Indianapolis on thirty-one dates. Never more than two games were on at one time, and thirty telecasts had no TV competition.

Similarly, of twenty-five telecasts in New York on seventeen dates in 1960, eleven were essentially noncompetitive. In 1970, fifty-one games were telecast on thirty-one dates. Virtually all were noncompetitive, as CBS and NBC were forced into different starting times by the modified blackout rule. On seven Sundays in 1960, TV spectators in New York were restricted to one game.

In sum, one could indeed see more football on television in 1970 than in 1960, by watching two games on Sunday, and by tuning in on Monday evening, an option not available in 1969. But, fans content with one Sunday game had less choice in 1970 than in 1960. The networks now largely avoid dividing the Sunday audience.

The growth in the number of noncompeting telecasts offers a partial explanation for the growth in broadcast rights. The figures given in Table 5 for the average number of households viewing the games show that the growth in the number of viewers is of somewhat lesser importance. Between 1962 and 1969, the AFL's average household audience figure increased by 43 percent, while the NFL's increased by 30 percent. During this period, the number of telecasts in each league increased by 88 percent. Together these effects explain most, but not all, of the 334 percent increase in NFL network revenues and the 369 percent increase in AFL revenues.

In 1970, after the leagues merged and reorganized into conferences, NBC's payment for American Football Conference (AFC) telecasts increased by $6 million to $15 million. The merger shifted Baltimore, Cleveland, and Pittsburgh into the AFC and some 2.8 million TV homes onto NBC, so that the potential audience was 15.6 million TV households for the AFC and 21.7 million TV households for the National Football Conference (NFC), a difference that was almost perfectly mirrored in the NBC and CBS contracts. Thus, CBS paid the same amount for fewer home cities, but was getting the NFC championship game as part of its package. To an extent, the NBC increase is attributable to the occasional appearance of NFC teams in some areas, as well as to the regular appearance of the Colts, Browns, and Steelers. The American Conference's success in signing such stars as Joe Namath and O. J. Simpson and the Jets victory in the 1969 Super Bowl, with their effects on the NBC audience size, cannot be dismissed. Indeed, following the Jets 1969 Super Bowl victory, NBC raised its 1969 price to AFL sponsors by 40 percent; the CBS rate was unchanged. When O. J. Simpson was negotiating with Buffalo, *Broadcasting* speculated that his signing with the AFC rather than the NFC could mean as much as a $1.5 million difference in the final NBC bill.[54]

BASKETBALL AND HOCKEY. Since both the NBA and NHL have always had league contracts, the impact of Public Law 87-331 is not clearly demonstrable. One can only speculate that rights fees would be less were such contracts outlawed. Moreover, because of such contracts, there have never been competing NHL or NBA games. Rather, the NBA and NHL games compete with each other on Sunday afternoons from January through April or May. To avoid such competition, each network might consider shifting its games to Saturday, but this would mean competing with local and network college basketball through March, and network baseball starting in April. Competing Sunday telecasts probably entail as few difficulties as any other arrangement either NBC or CBS could conveniently make, given the presence of the other's telecasts.

INTERLEAGUE COMPARISONS. Network fees for league packages generally reflect the audience ratings, although other factors are also important. The ratio of the NFL's audience to that of the AFL has been nearly equal to the ratio of their broadcast revenues since 1963. The small differences that have appeared can be explained by differing expiration dates of network contracts. Similarly, the AFL and baseball have about the same audience ratings and national broadcast revenues.

Basketball and hockey receive much less revenue per viewer than football and baseball. The average NHL audience in 1969 (including playoffs) was 46 percent of the average AFL rating, while the NHL received only 13 percent as much revenue. Although the AFL telecast almost twice as many games as the NHL, the NHL still would appear to have struck a poor bargain. The NHL contract, its first in almost a decade, was a three-year contract given to a league whose previously televised playoff games had not drawn well, and the league had just doubled in size through the addition of six new teams that could surely benefit from television exposure of the sport. The NHL was not in a very good bargaining position. Similarly, although the AFL only slightly outdrew the NBA in 1969, the annual payment to the NBA was a little more than half that to the AFL, for about the same number of games (although the games are normally shorter). Again, the NBA's bargaining position does not appear to have been strong.

In sum, national fees reflect in part the size of the audience, but bargaining power is a critical factor. The huge growth in national rights fees during the 1960s is clearly ascribable in large measure to Public Law 87-331, which gave the clubs the right to bargain collectively and to offer the buyer a league-wide package containing a greater number of noncompeting telecasts.

Implications of Sports Broadcasts for Sponsors

The restrictions that limit competitive broadcasts give a sports sponsor a monopoly right to address the broadcast audience. Indeed, this is a readily acknowledged purpose of league broadcast restrictions. Testifying in the 1953 NFL case, New York Giants President John V. Mara stated: "The sponsor is entitled to an undivided audience for his advertising"; and Chicago radio executive John T. Carey supported him with the argument that radio restrictions protect sponsors against a divided sports audience.[55]

In some instances a club's local broadcasts are sponsored by competing companies, with one firm sponsoring telecasts and the other radio broadcasts. With respect to network telecasts, competitors sometimes sponsor different games of football double-headers, and one firm sometimes sponsors a game in one section of the country while a competitor sponsors it in another section. Customarily, several sponsors of basically noncompeting, or perhaps even complementary, products, share a sponsorship.[56] Network telecasts are generally shared by major regional or national firms. In 1968, the lineup for the NBC baseball "Game of the Week" was representative: Chrysler, Gillette, Phillips Petroleum, R. J. Reynolds, and Schlitz (automobiles, toiletries, petroleum products, tobacco, and beer).[57] With the ban on cigarette commercials, Sears (retailing) replaced R. J. Reynolds.

Table 6 shows the number of clubs in football and baseball sponsored locally by firms in the seven major sponsoring categories on either radio or TV, from 1960 to 1971. These are the primary sponsors, and do not include spot announcements. Until the early 1960s, broadcasts were typically cosponsored by a brewery, a tobacco company, and an oil company. The 1971 ban on cigarette advertising culminated a decade during which cigarette manufacturers gradually extricated themselves from local sponsorships, especially of football. The most frequent replacements have been automobile manufacturers, banks, and finance companies.

The major sponsors now are firms in a few oligopolistic industries that produce consumer-oriented products and services. Such firms usually rely heavily on advertising as a competitive weapon. By sponsoring sports telecasts, firms are able to direct their advertising toward the specific audiences they wish to reach. As one regional brewing company executive stated: "Dominant sports programming is helpful in maintaining entrenched markets as well as developing new or relatively weaker mar-

55. Reported in the *New York Times,* March 4, 1953.
56. In Los Angeles, for example, the Dodgers' 1971 radio broadcasts were cosponsored by Union Oil, Schlitz, Farmer John, and Pacific Telephone, each of which had one-quarter time; Toyota dealers replaced Pacific Telephone on the telecasts (*Broadcasting,* Vol. 80 [Feb. 22, 1971], pp. 20, 21).
57. *Broadcasting,* Vol. 74 (Feb. 19, 1968), p. 42; Vol. 78 (Feb. 9, 1970), p. 27.

Table 6. Number of Professional Baseball and Football Teams Sponsored on Local TV or Radio, by Type of Sponsoring Industry, 1960–71

Sport and type of industry[a]	Number of teams											
	1960	1961[b]	1962	1963	1964	1965	1966	1967	1968	1969	1970	1971
Baseball[c]												
Brewing	15	17	15	16	18	19	19	18	19	20	17	16
Tobacco	8	13	17	17	11	10	12	14	12	11	9	1
Petroleum	12	8	10	14	15	15	16	18	17	19	18	14
Banking and finance	1	2	4	6	6	8	9	11	10	9	9	10
Insurance	0	0	0	0	3	2	5	9	10	8	4	6
Automobile	2	2	1	2	4	3	6	5	8	12	5	9
Beverage other than brewing	0	2	3	3	0	3	4	3	3	5	4	5
Teams surveyed	16	18	20	20	20	20	20	20	20	23	23	23
Football												
Brewing	n.a.	14	n.a.	16	18	18	20	18	22	19	21	22
Tobacco	n.a.	12	n.a.	6	9	3	6	3	3	0	0	0
Petroleum	n.a.	9	n.a.	8	9	12	17	18	17	19	17	20
Banking and finance	n.a.	0	n.a.	8	17	15	15	20	21	21	21	20
Insurance	n.a.	0	n.a.	4	6	2	9	4	7	4	3	4
Automobile	n.a.	14	n.a.	7	15	17	19	20	20	21	20	22
Beverage other than brewing	n.a.	0	n.a.	2	3	3	7	3	2	6	7	7
Teams surveyed	0	14	0	22	22	22	24	25	26	26	26	26

Sources: Compiled from surveys by *Broadcasting*, various February and March 1960–71 issues (baseball), and July and August 1961–71 issues (football), and *Professional Sports Antitrust Bill—1965*, Hearings before the Subcommittee on Antitrust and Monopoly of the Senate Committee on the Judiciary, 89 Cong. 1 sess. (1965), pp. 188–89.

n.a. Not available.

a. Primary sponsor only.

b. Telecasts only for the NFL in football.

c. Excludes Montreal.

kets."[58] As for Gillette, which traditionally spends 90 percent of its advertising budget on sports: "The exact relationship of programming to sales is difficult to determine, but we feel that sports broadcasts are an ideal medium for our advertising messages. Network sports attract the large male audience we want and some of them . . . also attract a good share of women viewers for our women's and family products."[59] More specifically, approximately one-third of the audience for a network sports broadcast is composed of males between twenty-one and fifty. The list of sponsors reflects the products and services that this audience buys.

The market structure in the industries in question is oligopolistic, although the nature and "tightness" of the oligopoly differ considerably among them. The tobacco, automobile, and tire manufacturing industries are all highly concentrated, with a few dominant firms selling in the national market. In cigarettes and autos, four firms account for virtually all domestic production, while in cigars and tires, eight firms produce more than 80 percent of the output.

The brewing and petroleum products industries, which sponsor local as well as network broadcasts, have a similar structure, although the petroleum industry is much larger. In each, over half the output is accounted for by the eight largest firms. Both industries operate in a set of regional marketing areas in which the few large firms that market nationally compete with each other and with several smaller firms that market regionally. The result is a complex of oligopolistic markets, each of which is vulnerable to the threat of new competition, from either new firms or established producers selling in other markets.

The airlines form a cartel of national and regional firms, regulated by the government, in which fewer than four companies compete for passengers on most routes. Although there can be substantial differences in the cost of flying from one location to another depending upon the routing, the interairline competition that does exist is essentially in service and promotion. A small number of oligopolists compete in any one market, and price competition is expressly disallowed by government.

The financial-service industries are all subject to federal or state regulation, and their structures differ from state to state. Whether in banking, insurance, or credit, the customer can in principle choose from among a large number of competitors. Citizens of Indiana, say, can bank in Cali-

58. *Sponsor,* Vol. 13 (Aug. 22, 1959), p. 36.
59. *Broadcasting,* Vol. 68 (June 7, 1965), p. 48.

fornia, insure with a company in Rhode Island, and borrow money from a firm based in Illinois. Nevertheless, a given area rarely has more than a few banks. Credit and insurance companies, though more numerous, offer a relatively sophisticated product. The average customer will find it neither costless nor easy to determine either the service options available to him, or their costs. Advertising, whether to inform, to persuade, or to mislead, can thus be an important competitive weapon.

Network sports sponsorships are expensive undertakings. Between 1966 and 1971, the NBC rate for a commercial minute on the baseball "Game of the Week" increased from $28,500 to $32,000. NBC charged $35,000 to $37,000 per minute for AFL football in 1966, including the two postseason games. CBS charged $70,000 per minute for a similar package for the NFL.[60] These costs can only be borne by large firms. This is reflected in the list of 1970 sponsors of NFL games given in Table 7. These firms are among the leaders within their industries and in the nation, and they usually maintain a sponsorship for a period of years. Of the thirty-three corporations that sponsored NFL or AFL regular-season telecasts in 1969, only twelve did not return for any telecasts in 1970 (three others discontinued regular-season telecasts but sponsored preseason or championship games).

A similar situation exists in local sponsorships. Since a smaller audience is involved, smaller regional firms have an opportunity to secure a sponsorship. Nonetheless, the charges to sponsors will be perhaps triple the cost of local rights, depending upon the city and regional network arrangements. The importance of major breweries and petroleum refiners is shown in Table 8. Assuredly, some comparatively small firms do sponsor local broadcasts. But network sponsorships generally go to the giant corporations of a few industries, and, assisted by the national giants, the heaviest burdens for local rights tend to be borne by the large regional firms in a few industries.

60. *Broadcasting,* Vol. 71 (Aug. 8, 1966), p. 40. Although the total cost of television sponsorship is high, the cost of reaching a single household with a one-minute network commercial is very low. The all-sport average was $0.00524 in 1967–68 and $0.00521 in 1969–70. Football costs are the highest, but they are falling: in the 1967–68 and 1969–70 seasons they were $0.00727 and $0.00604 for the NFL, and $0.00620 and $0.00491 for the AFL. Baseball costs were $0.00361 and $0.00431; the NBA costs were $0.00329 and $0.00410; and the NHL costs were $0.00502 (playoffs only) and $0.00565, respectively. Despite these low costs per household, only large firms can take advantage of them because of the large number of households that are reached. The average audience size for all sports broadcasts increased from 4.98 million to 5.38 million during this period.

The role that advertising plays in helping a firm maintain or improve its competitive standing, thus possibly contributing to oligopolistic abuses, is often debated. To the extent that advertising is effective, it can accomplish two things. First, it can enhance the advertiser's position in the industry to the detriment of those firms that do not have equally effective advertising programs. Second, it can erect a barrier to entry to the market, either locally or nationally. When there are, in fact, few equally effective advertising media, and when by virtue of their high costs these media are not practical options for the smaller firms, advertising becomes a competitive weapon to benefit the strong at the expense of the weak. At the very least, heavy advertising by large firms could be expected to help maintain the existing industry structure, if not to "tighten" the oligopoly.

To illustrate the effect of advertising, consider the impact on the beer market in New York of the rise of the Mets. From the standpoint of the sponsor, Rheingold, the Mets provided a means of promoting beer sales in its home territory, where its local rival Ballantine sponsored the Yankees until 1967. And, indeed, while Ballantine sales fell from 4.5 million barrels in 1965 to 2.2 million in 1969, Rheingold sales increased from 3.0 million barrels in 1965 to 3.5 million in 1969. Similarly, Schaefer Brewing of New York, which sponsored the Giants, Knicks, and Rangers, increased sales from 4.6 million barrels to 5.4 million during this same period.

Another example is the use Schlitz made of the movement of major-league sports to Texas. In the mid-1960s, Schlitz built a $15-million, 1.4-million-barrel brewery in Longview, Texas—a single plant that produced more beer than all but nineteen brewers in the nation. Texas represented an untapped market to Schlitz, and, with its new brewery, Schlitz was in need of an appropriate advertising medium. In 1965, Schlitz outbid Texas-based Pearl Brewing for the rights to sponsor the Astros, paying $5.3 million for three years.[61] Schlitz then turned to football, replacing Texas-based Lone Star Brewing as the sponsor for Dallas in 1967 and Houston in 1969. Meanwhile, production at the Longview plant grew from 433,000 barrels in 1966, its first year of production, to 1,360,000 barrels in 1967, and to full capacity in 1968.[62]

Assuredly, if sports programs were not available to these firms they would find other programs or media through which to advertise. Nonethe-

61. *Broadcasting,* Vol. 67 (Dec. 7, 1964), p. 34.
62. Research Company of America, *Brewing Industry Survey, 1971,* 30th Annual Edition (RCA, 1971), p. 24.

Table 7. Selected Sponsors of Network Telecasts of National Football League Games, by Type and Rank of Industry, 1970 Season

Type of industry and company	Company rank within industry, 1970[a]	Company rank among all industrials, 1970[b]
Airlines		
United	1	...
Trans World	2	...
American	3	...
Qantas	...[c]	...
Insurance		
Equitable Life Assurance	3	...
New York Life	4	...
Employers Insurance of Wausau[d]	n.a.	...
National Association of Insurance Agencies	n.a.	...
Allstate	43	...
Petroleum		
Standard Oil	1	2
Phillips	11	39
Sun Oil	13	48
Union Oil of California	14	57
Marathon Oil	21	118
ADA Oil[e]	n.a.	n.a.
British Petroleum	...[c]	...
STP	n.a.	143
Automobile		
Ford Motor	2	3
Chrysler	3	7
Spark plug		
AC	n.a.	1
Champion	n.a.	347
Tire[f]		
Goodyear Tire and Rubber	1	22
Firestone Tire and Rubber	2	38
Car rental		
Hertz	1	21
Retailing		
Sears, Roebuck	1	...
Tobacco		
R. J. Reynolds	1	58
Philip Morris	3	123

Table 7. Continued

Type of industry and company	Company rank within industry, 1970[a]	Company rank among all industrials, 1970[b]
Brewing		
Schlitz	2	235
Pabst	3	367
Associated	10	722
Olympia	12	706
Stroh	13	...[g]
Lucky	22	...[c]
Jackson	25	...[g]
Electric shaver[h]		
Remington-Rand	n.a.	59
Norelco	n.a.	207
Sunbeam	n.a.	261

Sources: *Fortune*, Vol. 83 (May and June 1971); *Broadcasting*, Vol. 79 (Feb. 9 and July 20, 1970); Research Company of America, *Brewing Industry Survey, 1971*, 30th Annual Edition (RCA, 1971), p. 24; various industry reports.

n.a. Not available.

a. Airlines ranked by operating revenues, insurance companies by assets, all others by sales (barrel sales for breweries).

b. Ranked by sales—for the company itself if independent, for its parent company if not.

c. Foreign.

d. Part of the Employers Mutual Liability Insurance Company of Wisconsin, which has over $600 million in assets.

e. Affiliated with the Houston Oilers.

f. The third-ranked tire manufacturer, Uniroyal (industrial rank, 72), sponsored major-league baseball telecasts.

g. Privately owned.

h. Of safety-razor manufacturers, the leader, Gillette (industrial rank, 176), sponsored major-league baseball telecasts, while Schick, a division of Warner-Lambert (industrial rank, 89) sponsored NFL games. Other toiletry products manufacturers represented were Beecham (rank, 790) and Carter Wallace (rank, 613).

less, sports sponsorship offers unique attractions. The firms and industries that dominate sports sponsorships (the toiletries industry notwithstanding) are not in general the firms and industries that are the heaviest TV sponsors generally. Of the fifty-five parent corporations that sponsored NFL telecasts in 1970, only sixteen were among the leading one hundred network TV sponsors in 1970, and just six were among the leading fifty.

Economists have not reached a professional consensus on the effects of advertising on competition for the economy as a whole.[63] But sports

63. In particular, see the conflicting conclusions drawn by Lester G. Telser, "Advertising and Competition," *Journal of Political Economy,* Vol. 72 (December 1964), pp. 537–62, and by William S. Comanor and Thomas A. Wilson, "Advertising

Table 8. Selected Sponsors of Local Major-League Baseball Telecasts, by Type and Rank of Industry, 1970 Season[a]

Type of industry and company	Company rank within industry, 1970[b]	Company rank among all industrials, 1970[c]
Petroleum		
Texaco	3	9
Standard Oil of California	5	14
Atlantic Richfield	8	30
Sun Oil	13	48
Union Oil of California	14	57
Marathon Oil	21	118
Martin Oil	n.a.	n.a.
Skelly Oil	n.a.	n.a.
Brewing		
Anheuser-Busch	1	153
Schlitz	2	235
Pabst	3	367
Schaefer	5	467
Associated	10	722
Rheingold	11	468
Stroh	13	...[d]
Heileman	15	784
Ballantine	16	...[d]
National	17	...[d]
Meister Brau	20	988
Pittsburgh	24	n.a.
Hudepohl	n.a.	n.a.

Sources: Same as Table 7, and various additional issues of *Broadcasting*.
n.a. Not available.
a. Banks and finance companies comprised the third major category of sponsoring industry, sponsoring a total of nine clubs: six were commercial banks (including BankAmerica, the national leader, and three banks among the top fifty nation-wide), three were local savings and loan institutions, and two were national finance companies (Central Finance and Household Finance).
b. Ranked by sales (barrel sales for breweries).
c. Ranked by sales—for the company itself if independent, for its parent company if not.
d. Privately owned.

broadcasts offer an especially attractive opportunity for an oligopolist to erect a barrier to competition. Their effectiveness stems from the overt and tacit collusion among the clubs, the popularity of the local club's broadcasts, and the league broadcast package arrangements made possible

Market Structure and Performance," *Review of Economics and Statistics,* Vol. 49 (November 1967), pp. 423–40. See also Joe S. Bain, *Barriers to New Competition: Their Character and Consequences in Manufacturing Industries* (Harvard University Press, 1956), chap. 4 and pp. 201–03.

by Public Law 87-331. These give a few advertisers—the major national and regional firms—monopoly control of a unique resource. The oligopolies existed before sports broadcasts attained major economic significance, and would exist in their absence. But the present advertising situation can only serve to increase the advantage of the giant firms.

Myths and Folklore

Since sports broadcasting, as an aspect of sports, is a subject on which every fan, politician, and sports personality considers himself an authority, a repertoire of myths and folk wisdom has grown up around the subject. Two points must be kept in mind when considering this store of "information." First, the strictly objective sports fan is a rarity, and this lack of objectivity has helped to foster myths, some of which conflict with one another. Second, reliable data that could dispel a myth before it becomes part of the accepted doctrine are scarce indeed, so that statistical analysis is difficult. In fact, to assess the validity of the folklore, it is necessary to draw inferences based on a detailed consideration of the broad array of historical experience summarized in the preceding pages.

Nine common fallacies and contradictions, past and present, are presented below.

1. *Broadcasting is really a sports by-product: for most clubs the primary concern is with providing local fans with a winning team and getting fans out to the stadium.* This attitude was expressed by NFL Commissioner Bert Bell: "I don't believe—and this is simply a matter of opinion—that the television and radio will increase very much, for the simple reason that today the price of cables and pickups and the price of line charges and the price of time at the stations have increased so much that the sponsors, in my opinion, will not be able to pay much more in rights fees than they do today. Our policy is such that we would rather have 12 or 15 sponsors trying to get our games to a bigger audience and giving the public from Maine to Seattle, Wash., football every Sunday than we would our love for money."[64]

By-product though it may be, and the club owners' concern with gate receipts notwithstanding, broadcasting is clearly of major importance to sports, and the revenues certainly play a role in corporate planning.

---

64. *Organized Professional Team Sports,* House Hearings (1957), Pt. 3, p. 2524.

2. *The purpose of the league package is to equalize the incomes of clubs.* As AFL Commissioner Foss testified, ". . . one of the major factors in our being able to bring a second major football league into being was the kind of television arrangements which we set up. . . . Essentially these arrangements provided for a pooling of TV rights and an equal division of income among the teams."[65]

Collective bargaining does lead to an equal division of network broadcast revenues. Assuming that the clubs with higher local revenues would also command higher network revenues in the absence of collective bargaining, total incomes also tend to be equalized. In fact, relative incomes have tended to be equalized; the revenues of the Yankees certainly moved closer to those of the other clubs after 1965. But collective bargaining has not removed substantial differences in revenues from all sources among teams. The primary purpose and achievement of collective bargaining remains a higher income for all teams.

3. *In the absence of collective bargaining, only the wealthiest clubs, which would ultimately also become the strongest, would get contracts.* As NFL Commissioner Rozelle testified: ". . . unless the league is permitted to exercise some control over its television programming, only a limited number of teams . . . will have access to television facilities in 1962. Only those fans in the large metropolitan centers and favored by their geographical location—such as New York, Los Angeles, and Chicago—will be assured of seeing the games of their home team on television."[66]

This, of course, was not true before collective bargaining; distinct regional preferences have always assured local telecasts irrespective of the teams involved. Baseball Commissioner Ford Frick unwittingly supplied the raison d'être for Public Law 87-331 and the counter to the myth: "The agency may approach a club which it knows desperately needs funds and starts its program by dangling an offer which the club cannot afford to refuse. . . . The only effective way to get all clubs to follow a definite baseball policy is to have a rule or agreement which they are bound to follow. . . . If only a few clubs deviate from the desired line, the damage will be done."[67] The facts are that in 1961 all NFL clubs appeared on network TV, and so did most baseball clubs.

4. *Local broadcast rights are influenced by performance.* Although in several instances this has been the case, because of long-term contracts

---

65. *Telecasting of Professional Sports Contests,* House Hearing, p. 43.
66. Ibid., p. 5.
67. *Organized Professional Team Sports,* Senate Hearings (1958), p. 203.

and the team's and sponsor's long-run outlook, in the main, performance is not a very important determinant of rights fees. Broadcasters holding long-term contracts may find difficulty in selling to sponsors, but the clubs themselves rarely benefit or suffer from performance. The size of the potential broadcast audience simply overwhelms performance as a rights determinant.

5. *Sports broadcasts are free to the public.* In 1957, New York City Council President Abe Stark stated: "Under our system of free television, major league baseball can be seen in the home without any cost to the public. This year alone private sponsors will spend $32 million on broadcasting these baseball games. If these and other advertising channels are to be closed through the inroads of pay television, many industries that sell their goods directly to the consumer might suffer great damage. There would be a resultant loss to our national economy, since 12 percent of the $10 million spent on all forms of advertising is now carried over free television."[68] Matthew M. Fox, president of Skiatron TV, which developed toll-television programming, demolished this argument. "Now, it is an illusion to describe the existing network-television service as a free television service. The public pays for television programming today, and pays heavily. The fact that such payments are cloaked, so that currently they assume the form of hidden charges added to the basic cost of finished goods, does not alter the fact . . . the costs of so-called free television are felt by all purchasers of the products thus advertised."[69]

6. *Sports broadcasting is akin to news reporting, although, perhaps, a little more colorful.* In fact, sportscasters work for the leagues, teams, and networks. Part of their job is to sell the sport, the team, the league, and the sponsor's product. As Bert Bell stated when questioned about his censorship power over telecasts: "I only exercise that in the best interests of the public and professional football and the players. I do not want any kid criticized. . . . I also do not want any fellow talking about officials doing this and doing that." And elsewhere: "I select the man I think is in the best interest of professional football and of the public; not somebody who is going to criticize the officials and the game, and talk about players having bad days, and so forth."[70] Or, as Yankee President Dan Topping succinctly put it, "We own our announcers."[71]

68. *Organized Professional Team Sports,* House Hearings (1957), Pt. 2, p. 1816.
69. Ibid., pp. 2111–12.
70. Ibid., pp. 2607, 2741.
71. *Professional Sports Antitrust Bill—1965,* p. 28.

7. *Only the networks are capable of bearing the extensive production costs involved in telecasting professional football.* Rozelle in 1961: "Independent stations are precluded from competing in this market because of the distances between league cities and the production and line expense involved which put costs out of reach of local sponsors except when network affiliations reduce carrying costs per station."[72]

In 1970, virtually all NFL clubs planned live local telecasts of their exhibition games. Baltimore telecasts included games at Denver and Miami, and the often pitied Packers, whose small broadcast area was alleged to destroy their ability to get television coverage, had a five-station regional network for a five-exhibition-game package. As Rozelle predicted, the independent stations have indeed been precluded from competing for regular-season telecasts, but not for the reasons he gave.

8. *The professional football leagues have voluntarily decided not to telecast Saturday games so as not to damage college football gate receipts.* George T. Gareff, commissioner of the minor leagues' United Football League, testified that "the reason we play on Sunday night is that we don't want to interfere with high school ball and we don't want to interfere with college ball."[73] Rozelle said: "We do intend to protect the colleges and not schedule televised games against them on Saturday afternoon. . . . We have always had the right legally to televise on Saturday afternoons against the colleges during the regular season. But we have never exercised that right."[74]

Until the mid-1950s, the NFL was reluctant to risk competing with college football. Sunday games avoided this competition, and they still do. But now that professional football is so popular, the NFL's traditional "concern" for college and high school football is rapidly eroding, as Friday evening exhibition games, an occasional Saturday game, and Thanksgiving Day games (wherever the law permits) attest.

9. *Collective bargaining and blackout rules do not seriously impair the viewer's choice, but instead introduce a necessary order into the system.* The Congress in 1958 received Frick's assurance that "any rule that baseball adopts will protect only the home games of clubs and will permit broadcasting and telecasting of major league games on hundreds of sta-

72. *Telecasting of Professional Sports Contests,* House Hearing, p. 40.
73. *Professional Sports Antitrust Bill—1964,* Hearings before the Subcommittee on Antitrust and Monopoly of the Senate Committee on the Judiciary, 88 Cong. 2 sess. (1964), p. 83.
74. *Telecasting of Professional Sports Contests,* House Hearing, p. 38.

tions throughout the country. The local fans in all communities will have an opportunity to have their baseball both ways—at the local ball park and on their home sets."[75]

As previously indicated, network baseball telecasts have declined by 70 percent since the adoption of the sports broadcasting act in 1961. Upon conclusion of the Yankees-CBS broadcast agreement, the number of network telecasts immediately dropped by 50 percent; and with the signing of the first ABC baseball package, the number of games telecast by the independent Sports Network Inc., fell by 33 percent—all refutation of Frick's assurances.

Conclusions

The major-league clubs in the four major professional sports tacitly and overtly collude to impose profit-maximizing restrictions on their broadcasting activities. The resulting cartel arrangement, like other cartels, benefits the participants to the detriment of the consumer. The experience of the past decade suggests that the major-league broadcast cartels, in particular, produce higher rights fees for all their members and higher sponsor's fees paid either directly to the clubs for local rights, or to the networks for commercial time. Whether this leads to higher prices of products is debatable, but a distinct possibility.

The cartel certainly eliminates competition among the clubs in the sale of network and local broadcasting rights, and reduces or eliminates potential competition in the sale of regional rights. The secondary effect of this is to lessen competition among broadcasters, and to enhance the position of the three major networks. The tertiary effect, insofar as advertising can be used as an effective barrier to entry, is to help maintain or tighten the oligopolistic structure in several consumer-oriented industries. In the process, the cartel ultimately leads to a reduction in the public's viewing choice, and to an enhancement of the economic positions of already powerful sponsors.

Each club should have the right to regulate its own broadcast activities. There may be some justification for permitting each club to restrict local telecasts of games that would compete with its home games, but, beyond this, there is little justification for broadcasting collusion among the cartel members, or for Public Law 87-331 that legalizes it.

75. *Organized Professional Team Sports,* Senate Hearings (1958), p. 203.

CHAPTER NINE

Subsidies of Stadiums and Arenas

BENJAMIN A. OKNER

If you are going to build a major sports stadium today, you start out by digging a hole. That is where you are going to put the stadium. And that is probably where the stadium is going to put you.[1]

LOCAL GOVERNMENTS that own sports facilities subsidize professional sports teams both directly, by pricing stadium and arena rents below the economic value of such facilities, and indirectly, by forgoing taxes on such property. In this chapter the economic effect of these subsidies is examined and their magnitude estimated.

In 1970–71, there were ninety-two professional major-league baseball, football, basketball, and hockey teams in the United States.[2] These teams used seventy-six different stadiums, ballparks, and arenas as their home facilities. Of the seventy-six, twenty-three were privately owned and operated (including five university stadiums) and fifty-three were publicly owned. The distribution of these facilities by form of ownership and sport is shown in Table 1.

Although the actual arrangements for ownership and operation vary tremendously from place to place, a facility is herein considered publicly

1. Charles Maher, "Major Sports Stadiums: They Keep Going Up," *Los Angeles Times*, Nov. 14, 1971.
2. In addition, there were 110 professional minor-league teams in the United States, plus 4 Canadian professional teams that participated in U.S. league play. The playing facilities used by these teams are excluded from explicit consideration in this study, although much of what is presented also applies to them.

Table 1. Distribution of Sports Facilities, by Ownership and Sport, 1970–71 Season

	Number of facilities				
Ownership	Baseball	Football	Basketball	Hockey	Total[a]
Public	16	20	32	4	53
Private	7	6	7	8	18
University	0	·1	4	0	5
Total	23	27	43	12	76

Source: Author's compilation from public records.
a. Sum of individual rows may exceed total because some facilities are used for more than one sport.

owned if the ultimate responsibility for its financial obligations is borne by a city, county, or state government or by some authority created by one or more of these governmental units. (In the case of Washington, D.C., Robert F. Kennedy Memorial Stadium is regarded as a public facility because the federal government is ultimately liable for it.) Responsibility for the stadiums can be shared in numerous ways. In some places, the stadium is run directly by the city (for example, in Cleveland by the Department of Public Properties, or in Baltimore by the Department of Recreation and Parks), or by the county, as is the Milwaukee County Stadium. In other places, the stadium is a joint city-county venture, as in Atlanta, where the stadium is owned by the City of Atlanta and the Fulton County Recreation Authority. In addition, there are several very complicated arrangements, such as those in San Diego, Houston, and Pittsburgh.[3]

Public ownership of 70 percent of all professional sports facilities raises a number of important policy questions. Why are local governments in the stadium rental business at all? How should these facilities be priced?

---

3. In San Diego, the stadium is owned by the San Diego Stadium Authority, a joint body of the city and county of San Diego; the city leases the stadium from the authority and in turn subleases it to the Padres and the Chargers. In Houston, the Astrodome is owned by Harris County, which leases it to the Houston Sports Association; the Association, owner of the Astros, subleases the stadium to the Oilers and other users. A similar situation exists in Pittsburgh, where the stadium is leased by the city to the Three Rivers Management Corporation and the Alco Parking Corporation. The Three Rivers Management Corporation was created by the Pirates as a management and operating company and it subleases the stadium to the Pirates and the Steelers.

What pricing policies are actually used? What subsidies result from pre-vailing rental arrangements? Who benefits from stadium subsidies? And, finally, what is the magnitude of existing subsidies?

Public Ownership of Sport Facilities

A widely accepted argument for public provision of particular goods and services is that private production often results in external costs or benefits that are not taken into consideration by the producer. For such goods there is a divergence between the net private and total social bene-fits. This is well illustrated by the classic example of a private manufac-turing concern that emits smoke and other pollutants which greatly in-crease the clothes-cleaning costs of people who live in the surrounding area. Since the manufacturer includes only his private costs in making his production decisions—that is, he does not take into account the costs he imposes on others—he underestimates the total social cost of his pro-duction and operates at a level of production that is greater than socially optimum. Conversely, when the social benefits of production are greater than the private benefits, production in the private sector will be less than socially optimal. Thus, public ownership of ballparks and arenas could be justified if extensive social benefits arise from public provision of sports facilities.

Is it possible to demonstrate objectively that the social benefits to a community are sufficient to justify government provision of athletic facili-ties? As is often the case in public policy decisions, those in favor will unequivocally answer "yes," while those against will say "no." The fact that so many of the benefits a city derives from the existence of a sports facility are intangible makes it difficult to achieve a consensus about them because their value cannot be measured in monetary terms. In essence, proponents of such facilities place a very high subjective value on the external benefits derived from the facility, while opponents do not.

Many people believe that the mere presence of a professional sports team in their city enhances the community's prestige. As one person put it, "No place really can be considered to be a 'big town' if it doesn't have a professional baseball or football team." Since no community can attract such a team if it lacks adequate playing facilities, it follows that a big-league stadium is required to be considered a "big town." And, if private interests are unwilling or unable to provide such a facility and the community wants to acquire the big-town image and attendant prestige, it must provide the sports facility through public funding.[4]

In addition to the civic pride that a professional sports team fosters, a city derives benefits through increased publicity. This results from the fact that the regular and prominent mention of major-league sports contests in the news media publicizes the community, since virtually every team name includes the name of the city in which it is located. Such publicity (especially if the team is doing well) enhances the city's image and may well lead to the same kind of increased economic activity as that generated by the location of new industry in the area.

Other external benefits created by the presence of a professional sports team may include: (1) the possible generation of additional employment, consumer sales, and tax collections resulting from sporting events; (2) additional recreational opportunities for community residents, especially if attendance at sporting events replaces other activities that are socially destructive; (3) beneficial effects on the morale of the citizens resulting from the presence of a (successful) sports team in the city; and (4) the encouragement of an interest in sports among the young.

It is appropriate to count as external benefits the revenues generated by sports facilities only if they are truly additional. Based on data collected from spectators in 1954, the Baltimore Orioles estimated that about one-fourth of the fans attending their home games were out-of-towners.[5] This represented more than 276,000 out-of-town spectators who came to Orioles games and spent an average of $20 to $30 while in Baltimore, according to the survey responses. In the aggregate, out-of-town Orioles fans were estimated to have spent between $5.5 and $8.3 million in Baltimore during the season. The report indicates that "no claim is made that all of this money was 'brought in' by baseball,"[6] and goes on to say that

4. Alternatively, the community could subsidize private interests (which might include the sports team) to build the stadium. In terms of aggregate outlays, a direct subsidy equal to the annual cost of providing a publicly owned stadium could be a more efficient method of subsidization for a community. If a direct subsidy were structured to operate only so long as the team used the facility, it would relieve the community of a long-term, fixed obligation should the club decide to move the location of the franchise.

5. Baltimore Orioles, *Baltimore Baseball Club Survey, 1954* (1955), p. 7. In the survey, "out-of-town" was defined as being beyond Baltimore and its immediate vicinity by drawing a line arbitrarily dividing the outlying communities into local and out-of-town areas. The minimum driving time to the Memorial Stadium from the closest out-of-town place was about forty-five minutes.

6. Ibid., p. 8.

it is impossible to estimate what proportion of the total might be counted as truly additional revenue for the city. While it is not emphasized in the report, the definition of out-of-towner used in the study includes both spectators whose sole purpose in coming to Baltimore was to attend an Orioles game and persons who came to Baltimore for other reasons and decided to attend a ball game while there. To compute the additional revenue baseball brought to Baltimore, only the expenditures made by those who came solely to see the Orioles should be counted. Unfortunately, the Baltimore survey is now almost twenty years old and there is no way of knowing whether it is still valid for that city. And, of course, one cannot infer that the results could have been extended to other cities even in the mid-fifties.

A more recent analysis[7] purported to demonstrate that Shea Stadium in New York, which sustains a $300,000 annual operating loss, is actually "a financial plus, not a minus for [the] city."[8] In the Shea example, the loss was purportedly converted to a "profit" of almost $1.7 million by crediting $1.2 million spent by spectators and stadium employees in sub-way fares each year, more than $400,000 in city sales tax collected on tickets and concessions sold at the stadium, and about $66,000 in city income tax paid by stadium employees. To the extent that those employed at the stadium would not be employed elsewhere, that people who rode the subway to Shea would not ride it otherwise, and that none of the money spent for admissions or concessions at the ballpark would have been spent for any other taxable commodities, this "profit analysis" is correct. But people can and do substitute other leisure-time activities for attending ball games in New York, and while doing so they make other expenditures that also produce revenue for the city. In assessing the indirect revenues generated by a stadium, therefore, one should take account only of the marginal or extra revenue that would not be collected by the city in the absence of the facility.

The intangible benefits noted above cannot be disregarded just because it is not possible to put a price tag on most of them. Their perceived value to various communities is illustrated by the large number of cities that now provide publicly supported sports facilities. Despite the financial difficulties faced by most local governments during the 1960s, twelve new facilities were completed between 1965 and 1970, and at least five publicly

7. *New York Times,* May 30, 1971.
8. The $300,000 loss was for 1969–70. Primarily because of an increase in the number of nonsports events, the 1970–71 loss was down to $95,000.

owned stadiums and arenas were planned or under construction at the end of the period.[9]

The arguments for and against public ownership of professional sports facilities are not evaluated here. It should simply be noted that there is not unanimous agreement concerning their value to a city. For example, the following two statements were taken from correspondence with two public officials, each of whom is in a city that has recently constructed a large stadium to house its local ball club:

Official A. These professional teams, however, are a true asset to the City in attracting and entertaining tourists from the metropolitan area and adjoining states. This is reflected indirectly in the City's revenue from earnings taxes, sales taxes and merchants licenses and taxes. In addition, the City has a ___% amusement tax on gross receipts from admissions.

Official B. Proponents of these facilities argue that they generate business and commerce for the City and are on balance a benefit. A hard nosed analysis does not indicate that the business and traffic generated equal the subsidies and real estate tax loss.

Theory of Facility Pricing[10]

The determination of the "proper price" to charge a professional team for use of a publicly owned stadium or arena is both an interesting and a difficult economic problem. The question is important, since it is impossible to discuss subsidies without some notion of what a fair rental payment would be.[11] Although much has been written on the pricing of government-operated enterprises,[12] the usual conclusion—that in order to maximize social welfare, price should be set equal to the marginal cost of providing the good or service—cannot be immediately accepted in this situation. In the model usually underlying the marginal-cost pricing conclusion, the particular good is provided by a monopolist in a competitive market of buyers. A typical example is a city-owned public utility pro-

9. These are in Kansas City, Missouri; New Orleans; New Jersey; Nassau County, New York; and Buffalo.

10. The following discussion considers rational pricing of a facility that already exists and not the decision of whether it should be (or should have been) built; the capital investment decision is different from the pricing decision.

11. "Rent" here refers to the total package of agreements that provide the local government with revenue from a stadium operation. In most instances, this will include income from concessions and parking as well as the rent actually collected from a team for using the stadium.

12. For example, see A. M. Henderson, "The Pricing of Public Utility Undertakings," *Manchester School*, Vol. 15 (September 1947), pp. 223–50, for a compact summary on the subject.

viding hydroelectric power to its residents, where the cost of providing power increases as production rises;[13] at the same time, the demand curve for hydroelectric power will be downward-sloping, which means that consumers will purchase greater amounts of power at a lower price. The typical model does not, however, describe the situation existing between a city and a team. The difference is not in the supply, since a given stadium or arena operation can be considered a monopoly provider of such services; it is rather in the demand.

All but six U.S. cities[14] have only a single major-league professional team in any sport, and even in the cities with two teams, game scheduling and other constraints (including fan loyalty) produce a situation in which there are effectively no alternate users available for a particular facility. Instead of facing a market consisting of large numbers of buyers whose individual desires to purchase will result in a downward-sloping demand curve for the product or service, the city-monopolist faces a single (monopsonistic) purchaser who wishes to buy a fixed quantity of services. For a baseball team this would be approximately eighty days (and/or nights) of stadium services a season; for a football team, seven to ten days of service a season.

Since the marginal cost of operating a stadium up to its level of capacity is relatively low, both supply and demand are fixed—that is, both the marginal cost curve and the demand curve for the stadium services by the team are perfectly inelastic. In such a situation, there is no way to determine an equilibrium price or one that is socially optimal in terms of the allocation of stadium services. The final price agreed upon will be the result of negotiations between the team and the city, and there are few guidelines for what the resulting price will or should be.

The total cost of a facility involves two components: the annual fixed costs, such as interest and debt amortization, and the variable costs of operation, such as utilities and refuse collection. If the stadium is not used at all, the total cost is just the fixed cost, which by definition excludes costs directly related to usage. The total variable and fixed operating costs for a selected group of publicly owned facilities are shown in Table 2. Total operating costs for these stadiums ranged from $1.3 million to $2.3

13. The cost curves may also be perfectly inelastic, indicating that the plant must operate at a given fixed capacity and that the marginal cost for any output below capacity is zero. This particular situation will not change the nature of socially optimum pricing.

14. Boston, Chicago, New York, Los Angeles, Minneapolis–St. Paul, and the San Francisco–Oakland metropolitan area.

Table 2. Variable and Fixed Annual Operating Costs of Selected Publicly Owned Stadiums, 1970–71 Season

Thousands of dollars

| | | Fixed costs | | |
Stadium	Variable costs	Interest and depreciation	Other	Total costs
Anaheim Stadium	262	1,068	165	1,496
Atlanta Stadium	221	1,320	265	1,806ᵃ
Candlestick Park (San Francisco)	260	900	150	1,310
Cincinnati Riverfront Stadium	255	1,750	250	2,255
Astrodome (Houston)	255	1,500	260	2,015
RFK Stadium (Washington, D.C.)	265	1,285	284	1,834
San Diego Stadium	244	1,506	198	1,948
Shea Stadium (New York)	300	1,500	285	2,085

Sources: Annual financial statements of the respective stadiums. Figures are rounded.
a. Excludes extraordinary item of $335,000.

million in 1970–71. The estimated variable costs of operation, however, amounted to only 10 to 20 percent of the total. The remainder—the fixed costs of operation—clearly accounted for the lion's share of the annual operating costs.

As a first approximation, the city should seek a minimum rental that will cover the variable costs of operating the facility. Of course, any receipts that exceed the variable costs would be welcomed, as these would be available to help meet the fixed costs. And if the rental could be set high enough to meet (or exceed) the total cost of operation—that is, both the fixed and variable costs—the city would be the victor in the rental bargaining.

The team will naturally try to minimize its rental payment for the use of the playing facility since the lower the rental, the better its own financial position will be. In rental negotiations the team is in a bargaining position slightly superior to that of the city, which cannot move the stadium; the city can either rent it to the team, allow it to remain unused, or demolish it and use the site for some other purpose. The team has a somewhat better set of choices: play in the city at the public facility, perhaps play in another facility in the same city,[15] or move its franchise to another

15. Although it is unusual for a team to move between facilities in the same city, it is not unknown; in the 1971 playing season, the Chicago Bears moved from their long-time home of Wrigley Field to Soldier Field.

(presumably more receptive and understanding) locality. Moving the franchise is not costless for the owners, but the possibility exists and should give the team an edge in bargaining over the rental agreement.

So far, the city's bargaining strategy has been discussed as if the city were a private owner whose only goal was to maximize the profits (or at least minimize the losses) on the stadium operation. Since the city's justification for owning the stadium presumably rests on the external benefits generated, it should take account of such benefits (as well as any external costs) in making its pricing decision. To the extent that the benefits can be quantified (additional taxes generated, for example), the variable costs of operation should be reduced to take these into account. Likewise, variable costs should be increased to reflect marginal external costs associated with the facility.[16] These would include such things as the *additional* city police required to handle traffic congestion at the stadium.

Ideally, intangible external costs and benefits should also be included in the pricing calculus. Since civic pride resulting from the team's presence in the city cannot be expressed monetarily, however, such items cannot enter into the calculation explicitly. Probably the most practical suggestion is that in studying a given stadium operation, consideration always should be given to whether the direct financial losses might be offset somewhat or balanced by the presence of net intangible benefits.

Given the previous considerations, how should a city attempt to set the price for using its sports facility? First, the direct variable cost of the facility for each event should be computed (or estimated). From this should be subtracted an estimate of the marginal net intangible benefits to be derived.[17] The calculated variable cost per event times the number of events will then set the minimum amount for which the facility should be rented.[18] Of course, the city would also like to recover all, or at least part, of the fixed cost of operating the facility. This probably can be best achieved through bargaining with the team for some share of the team's

16. In addition, the total financial assessment should take account of any implicit fixed costs that result from the sports facility. The major item in this category is the local property tax forgone because the publicly owned facility occupies the site. Effects on property values of sites near the stadium also should be considered.

17. Since it is obviously very difficult to estimate even those intangible benefits and costs that are measurable, the city may well decide to omit them from the calculation. If this practice is followed, the city will be erring on the conservative side in pricing the facility.

18. As the number of home games to be played each season for each sport is known, computing a minimum rental rate for each season for each team should not be difficult.

gate receipts. A percentage cut, if one can be agreed upon between the city and the lessee, should be acceptable to both parties, for each will be better off if the team prospers. The final sharing agreement will take into account that both the team and the city want the sports club to be a viable financial undertaking. Thus, major sharing of receipts probably should not start until the club's attendance exceeds some break-even level of operation.[19] And it would seem reasonable to set the rate so that at high attendance levels the total revenue received from all teams using the facility plus external revenue generated because of the facility is sufficient to cover the total costs of operation.

Actual Pricing Policies

Since data on facility pricing are not readily available, the information presented here was solicited from local officials in all cities with a publicly owned stadium or arena in 1970–71. Even though these are public facilities for which one should be able to obtain information easily, most of the cities either do not keep separate accounting records for their stadiums and arenas or are extremely reluctant to release such information. It is impossible to know the extent to which such reluctance is the result of not having the information or an attempt to keep it out of the public spotlight. In many cases the information was supplied on a confidential basis; for that reason, individual facilities are not identified.[20] Information was received for twenty of the twenty-five publicly owned facilities used for major-league baseball and/or football, and for sixteen of the thirty-two publicly owned arenas used for professional basketball. Since information was provided for only one of the four publicly owned arenas used for professional hockey games, hockey is omitted from the data in this section.

19. In order to avoid large rewards to inefficiently managed clubs, the break-even level should be based on the average break-even attendance in the sports league. This should not be difficult to determine, since rules of thumb already exist for most sports. For example, the twenty-four major-league team owners use an annual attendance of 850,000 spectators as the break-even level for baseball; in professional basketball, the break-even level is estimated to be about 8,000 fans a game.

20. A large number of local officials and stadium managers cooperated in providing the data presented. Although they cannot be identified, their aid in this endeavor is gratefully acknowledged. In addition, Madeline B. Burgess kindly provided a large amount of stadium lease information that she had assembled for the National League of Cities.

The major lease provisions for baseball and football stadiums are summarized in Table 3. Stadium size and year of completion are not given in order to avoid precise identifications. As the compilation makes clear, lease provisions vary tremendously. In baseball, nine of the fifteen stadiums for which information was received charge a minimum annual rental payment that ranges between $25,000 and $461,500. The typical lease provides for payment of a specified percentage of the gate receipts (after deduction of sales or amusement tax and shares paid to the visiting team and the league) or an annual minimum, whichever is greater. The minimum rent guarantee is presumably intended to minimize the effect of variations in attendance (and, therefore, total income) on stadium revenue. In baseball, the minimum gate percentage specified ranges between 3.5 percent and 15.0 percent. The median minimum is 7.0 percent of the gate receipts, and twelve of the fifteen facilities receive between 5 and 8 percent of the gate. In six of the facilities, the gate percentage increases as total attendance rises, but the specified increase is not large. The median maximum share of the gate paid is 7.5 percent.

The baseball lease provisions indicate a rough trade-off among the different parts of the total lease package. For example, at stadium P, which has the highest fixed minimum amount and a high percentage of the gate, the city receives no cut of the parking or concessions revenue. At F, where the percent of the gate paid does not rise with attendance, the city gets 10 percent of concessions revenue and shares parking revenue equally with the team.

Table 3 also shows a wide variation in lease provisions for football facilities. Fewer than half the leases require a minimum annual payment, and for the eight that do the minimum ranges between $22,500 and $170,000 a season. In football, the gate-cut percentages paid to the city are generally higher than in baseball. The minimum annual percentage varies between zero and 17.5 percent, with a median of 9 percent. The practice of raising the percentage as attendance increases is much less prevalent in football leases: a sliding rent scale exists in only three of the football leases. This lack of an upward adjustment is not surprising, since professional football games are almost always sold out. As in baseball, it is necessary to look at the total rental package in comparing different football leases. At stadium H, for example, with no minimum annual payment, the city gets a 10 to 12 percent cut on gate receipts, all the parking revenue, and a third of the concessions revenue. On the other hand, at S the city gets no cut of gate receipts but receives the highest fixed annual

Table 3. Major Lease Provisions and Revenue of Selected Publicly Owned Stadiums Used for Major-League Baseball and Football, 1970–71 Season

Sta-dium[a]	Baseball lease provisions						Football lease provisions					
	Minimum season rent (thousands of dollars)	Rent as percent of gate receipts[b]		Percent of concessions revenue paid to city	Percent of parking revenue paid to city	Estimated gross revenue[c] (thousands of dollars)	Minimum season rent (thousands of dollars)	Rent as percent of gate receipts[b]		Percent of concessions revenue paid to city	Percent of parking revenue paid to city	Estimated gross revenue[c] (thousands of dollars)
		Minimum	Maximum					Minimum	Maximum			
A	0	7.5	7.5	...	100.0	1,685	45.0	9.0	9.0	...	...	86
B	n.a.	3.5	7.0	10.0	100.0	738	n.a.	10.0	10.0	n.a.	100.0	346
C	n.a.	15.0	25.0	...	...	852	n.a.	17.5	17.5	100.0	...	644
D	0	5.0	10.0	10.0-16.5	87.0	490	0	10.0	10.0	...	87.0	326
E	160.0	7.5	10.0	11.0	50.0	607	...	...	...	...	...	...
F	75.0	7.0	7.0	10.0	50.0	341	...	8.0	8.0	20.0	20.0	227
G	n.a.	5.0	10.0	67.0	100.0	55	94.4	10.0	10.0	100.0	100.0	226
H	65.0	7.0	7.0	80.0	100.0	632	0	10.0	12.0	33.0	100.0	669
I	125.0	5.0	5.0	...	93.0	353	...	...	...	...	...	...
J	60.0	6.0	6.0	33.0	...	387	32.4	6.0	6.0	50.0	50.0	592
K	25.0	5.0	10.0	16.5	...	193	0	5.0	5.0	16.5	...	167
L	0	8.0	8.0	...	88.0	393	0	8.0	8.0	30.0	88.0	403
M	125.0	5.0	5.0	10.0	64.0	452	0	7.5	10.0	35.0	92.5	701
N	150.0	7.5	7.5	10.0	100.0	1,831	100.0	10.0	10.0	10.0	100.0	477
O	...	...	...	...	...	...	150.0	10.0	10.0	15.0	100.0	749
P	461.5	10.0	10.0	0	0	995	70.0	10.0	10.0	...	24.0	402
Q	...	...	...	...	...	...	22.5	9.0	10.0	28.3	...	329
R	...	...	...	...	...	...	...	8.0	8.0	30.0	...	470
S	...	...	...	...	...	...	170.0	...	...	30.5	$1/car	535
T	...	...	...	...	...	...	n.a.	4.0	4.0	18.5	...	108

Source: Survey conducted by author in 1971.

n.a. Not available.

a. To preserve confidentiality, stadium names are omitted. Twenty of the twenty-three publicly owned stadiums are included.

b. Net of sales or amusements tax and shares paid to visiting team and league.

c. Based on average attendance figures and ticket prices and estimated average concessions and parking revenues generated by spectators, excluding possible revenues from non-sport events.

payment plus 30.5 percent of the concessions revenue and some of the parking revenue.

In addition to the provisions shown in Table 3, most baseball and football leases also cover items such as fees for World Series or special exhibition games, scoreboard advertising, and pay-TV revenues (in anticipation of future transmissions through this medium). Of special interest is the provision for stadium use charges, which are not now prevalent but are beginning to be levied on admissions in the newest stadiums. For example, in the lease for Riverfront Stadium in Cincinnati the city was given the right to impose a 25-cent stadium use charge on each admission. The revenue obtained goes into a special sinking fund for stadium operating expenses and debt service on outstanding stadium bonds. Similar provisions are included in the leases of the Denver Broncos and of the teams playing at Pittsburgh's Three Rivers Stadium.

Lease provisions for sixteen of the thirty-two publicly owned basketball facilities are summarized in Table 4. Almost all the arenas have a minimum rental of between $500 and $1,000 a game (which is equivalent to $20,000 to $40,000 for the season). In basketball, the range in the percentage of the gate paid to the facility is quite small: for seven of the sixteen arenas it is a straight 10 percent of receipts, and for four others it is 11 or 12 percent. In two of the other five arenas, the facility gets no cut of the gate: in one of these the arena has a high fixed minimum rental and it keeps all revenue from concessions and parking; in the other the facility receives all the concessions revenue and 30 percent of parking revenue.

The only immediate conclusion to be drawn from the compilation of existing leases is that the actual policies for pricing sports facilities are extremely varied. The four major components in the lease agreement—the annual minimum, the gate cut, the concessions cut, and the parking cut—can be, and are, combined in numerous ways. In order to make comparisons more meaningful, expected total income for each facility was estimated using average attendance figures during the past five years,[21] average ticket prices, and estimated average concessions and parking revenues generated by the spectators (see Tables 3 and 4). The variation in expected revenue per facility is due to differences in attendance

---

21. If the facility had not been in existence for five years, the average attendance over the actual life of the stadium was used, after adjusting it to take account of the "newness factor," which tends to draw additional spectators during the first year a stadium is open.

Table 4. Major Lease Provisions and Revenue of Selected Publicly Owned Arenas Used for Professional Basketball, 1970–71 Season

		Lease provisions				Estimated
	Minimum rent per game	Rent as percent o gate receipts[b]		Percent of concessions revenue paid	Percent of parking revenue paid	gross revenue[c] (thousands
Arena[a]	(dollars)	Minimum	Maximum	to city	to city	of dollars)
A	1,000	10.0	10.0	50.0	...	136
B	600	12.0	12.0	60.0	100.0	144
C	500	10.0	10.0	27.5	...	17
D	900	11.0	11.0	23.1	...	122
E	1,000	12.0	12.0	35.0	...	40
F	500	10.0	10.0	20.0	...	14
G	500	10.0	10.0	100.0	100.0	30
H	2,100	6.0	6.0	30.0	...	170
I	800	10.0	10.0	100.0	...	39
J	1,558	0	0	100.0	100.0	240
K	1,250	17.5	17.5	100.0	100.0	110
L	0	15.0	17.0	42.0	82.5	n.a.
M	500	10.0	10.0	38.0	...	6
N	1,000	10.0	10.0	...	...	116
O	800	12.0	12.0	100.0	...	92
P	1,000	0	0	100.0	30.0	78

Source: Survey conducted by author in 1971.
n.a. Not available.
a. To preserve confidentiality, arena names are omitted. Sixteen of the thirty-two publicly owned arenas are included.
b. Net of sales or amusement tax and shares paid to visiting team and league.
c. Based on average attendance figures and ticket prices and estimated average concessions and parking revenues generated by spectators, excluding possible revenues from nonsport events.

(and average ticket prices) and in the lease provisions regarding the allocation of total revenue at the various facilities.[22] The estimates of expected revenue based on lease provisions suggest that team performance and ability to attract spectators are far more important than actual percentages agreed upon in the rental package. In baseball, for example, at A there is no provision for an annual minimum payment, no city revenue from concessions, and a roughly average percentage cut of admissions; yet the expected revenue from the facility is the second highest in the group and

22. The estimates are based on the following assumptions: equal average expenditures per spectator for concessions, an average of three spectators per car, and equal parking fees per automobile. To some extent, the differences shown also reflect the variation in parking spaces available at the facilities.

is nearly twice the amount expected at P, which has the highest annual minimum and a minimum ticket cut of up to 10 percent of the gate. Similar situations exist in football.

Since the annual expected rental payments vary so much among facilities, it is difficult to see how revenue can bear a fixed relationship to the variable cost of operating a facility. In most places, the city and team seem to have entered a revenue-sharing arrangement by which the city can come out even or ahead only if the team draws large numbers of spectators to its contests. And since leases are drawn up in advance for long-term periods, cities enter contractual agreements whereby the relative playing success or failure of the team will largely determine how the city will fare financially over a long period of time.

Amount of Stadium Subsidies

As noted above, total revenue derived from a facility is primarily a function of attendance at sporting events.[23] On the other hand, total costs depend on the stadium size and age, whether it is used for both baseball and football, the method of financing, whether the costs of improvements are treated as current expenses or capital investments, and a host of other factors. At the facilities for which operating statements were obtained, there is considerable variation in the accounting treatment of many of these items.

Direct Subsidies

Rough benchmarks have been developed for various operating costs for a typical stadium (with approximately 50,000 seats) that is used for both professional baseball and football. Using data from the operating statements received, the total variable costs of operation for such a facility range between $225,000 and $250,000 annually.[24] Where a stadium is used for only one sport, the variable operating costs would be lower than the above figures. One benchmark that can be used for such

23. While stadium officials are eager to have their facilities used for purposes other than football and baseball, "other events" do not in fact contribute very much to total stadium revenues.

24. These figures include the variable costs for both sports, since the operating statements do not indicate them separately.

an estimate is the $115,000 annual direct cost of baseball operations reported for RFK Stadium in Washington.[25] Since the number of football games per season is only about one-tenth the number of baseball games, the variable cost of providing only football might appear to be much lower than $100,000. On the other hand, football is much harder on the playing field, so the costs of field preparation would boost the total variable operating costs. In addition, per-game attendance for football is generally five to six times the average for baseball, requiring additional cleanup costs as well as increased expenses for utilities and ushering, custodial, and protective services. On balance, the variable cost of providing only football games is probably just slightly lower than that of providing only baseball.

If the expenses related to bond amortization and interest as well as extraordinary expense items are excluded, the total fixed costs of operating a stadium used for both baseball and football amount to about $250,000 a year. This covers such items as office and administrative expenses, routine maintenance not directly related to games, insurance, and so forth. In older stadiums, such costs would probably be higher because routine maintenance costs are greater, but as an average this amount appears reasonable.

The expense that differs greatly among the various stadiums is that for amortization of the principal and interest on an outstanding debt. For very old stadiums, this amount is relatively small, either because the debt is extinguished or because the bonds were initially sold at low interest rates. For most stadiums built during the 1960s, the rule of thumb on initial cost was about $500 a seat, or $25 million for a 50,000-seat facility. To service the interest and retire a debt of this magnitude requires an annual expenditure of roughly $1.5 million. For the newest stadiums, the old rule of thumb no longer appears to be applicable owing to rising construction and land costs as well as to a trend toward "fancier" facilities. For example, the Three Rivers Stadium in Pittsburgh (completed in 1970) cost almost $35 million,[26] or about $700 a seat. With a higher principal and interest rate than was prevalent during the mid-1960s, this will involve annual debt service payments of around $2 million.

25. *Washington Post,* Aug. 20, 1971. This is lower than the estimated figure for RFK Stadium shown in Table 2; the difference presumably reflects the fact that the figure cited in the *Post* was for baseball only.

26. "Report of the Mayor's Stadium Advisory Committee" (Pittsburgh: The Committee, 1971; processed), p. 8.

While the estimated gross revenues shown in Table 3 are typically sufficient to cover the estimated variable operating costs and the fixed costs other than debt service for most stadiums, revenue from stadium rentals is generally insufficient to meet full costs of operation. Estimates developed for this study, shown in Table 5, indicate that the total annual subsidy to twenty of the twenty-five publicly owned facilities used for baseball and/or football is over $8 million. Although the estimates omit any offsetting effect of additional revenue generated for the city by the presence of the facility, the $8 million figure is still probably a conservative one. If the average subsidy to the remaining five facilities not included in Table 5 is equal to the average amount for older dual-purpose stadiums, the total amount of subsidies rises to $12 million. The data indicate that almost three-quarters of the total subsidy goes to the thirteen facilities used for both baseball and football, and of this, the majority of the loss is on facilities that have been built since 1960.

If, as the figures in Table 5 suggest, rent payments are not keeping pace with rising construction and financing costs, total subsidies to professional baseball and football teams will rise substantially in the future. Many cities are currently planning to build new sports facilities, in many cases to replace the existing relatively low-cost ones, and unless the new lease agreements include provisions that are more favorable to cities than those that

Table 5. Estimated Revenue and Costs of Selected Publicly Owned Stadiums Used for Major-League Baseball and Football, 1970–71 Season

Dollar amounts in thousands

Use of stadium	Number of stadiums	Revenue[a]	Costs	Operating loss
Baseball and football	13	$16,600	$22,475	$5,875
Stadium opened before 1960	5	5,240	5,742	502
Stadium opened 1960–69	6	7,654	11,973	4,319
Stadium opened 1970 and after	2	3,705	4,760	1,055
Baseball only	2	1,246	2,806	1,560
Football only	5	2,245	2,870	625
Total	20	20,090	28,151	8,061

Source: Author's estimates, derived from financial statements of respective stadiums. Includes data for twenty of the twenty-five stadiums used for baseball and football.
a. Includes estimated revenue from nonsport events.

now exist, the aggregate local government subsidy to professional baseball and football will be at least $10 to $12 million annually within a few years. Even at the present (conservative) $8 million level, these subsidies amount to about 3 percent of the estimated $270 million gross revenue of professional baseball and football clubs.

Direct subsidies to facilities used by professional basketball and hockey teams are probably quite small. The limited financial data available on the operations of these arenas indicate variable operating costs of about $1,500 a game. The lease provisions shown in Table 4 indicate that most basketball arenas have a minimum rental of $500 to $1,000 per game, but in most cases additional sources of revenue are sufficient to cover the variable costs of operating an arena for a basketball game. Since more than half of the publicly owned arenas were built before 1960, the fixed costs associated with heavy bond-debt service do not figure as prominently here as they do in the case of baseball and football stadiums. Even for the newer arenas, where substantial debt costs do exist, the fact that they are usually used for many events other than sports[27] means that the fixed cost to be allocated to the sporting events would be small. Undoubtedly, some of the newer arenas that have no minimum rental charge and house a poor team that draws few spectators are suffering losses; but such places are few. The relatively low fixed costs associated with presenting basketball and hockey games and the reasonable lease provisions for facilities in these sports probably result in few losses on publicly owned arenas.

Indirect Subsidies

In addition to the direct subsidies, indirect costs to local governments result from property taxes forgone on tax-exempt sports facilities. In order to assess the magnitude of this indirect subsidy, information was solicited from local tax assessors on the assessed valuation and local property taxes that would pertain to the publicly owned facilities in the absence of exemption. The following discussion is based on the information supplied for forty-four of the fifty-three publicly owned facilities used for professional sports in 1970–71.

Total property taxes forgone on stadiums used for baseball and/or football amounted to approximately $8.7 million annually. For publicly

27. For example, the Seattle Coliseum used by the Supersonics housed 260 different events during 1970. The 37 Supersonics games played there accounted for only 14 percent of the total usage.

owned basketball or hockey arenas, annual property taxes forgone were about $4.7 million. Thus, local-government revenue lost because of the tax-exempt status of existing sports facilities totaled about $13.4 million. That this figure represents the "true loss," however, is not clear, since it depends on the assumption that taxable structures of equal assessed value would occupy sites now used for sports facilities. Taxes on the sites themselves can be estimated to account for one-third of the total loss,[28] or $4.4 million. There are no grounds for assuming that if the land were used for other purposes, the structures occupying the sites would be more or less valuable than the sports facilities. As a conservative estimate, alternative structures and improvements are assumed to be, on the average, only half as valuable as the sports facilities, giving a figure of about $4.4 million for tax loss on improvements. Thus, a conservative estimate of the actual annual loss of property tax revenue for publicly owned sports facilities is approximately $8.8 million.

The Incidence of Subsidies on Sports Facilities

All subsidies involve a grant or transfer of real income from the government to the private economy. Whatever the precise form it takes, and there are many, any subsidy increases the recipient's money income or reduces the prices paid in some sector of the private economy, thereby increasing real purchasing power. In the case of publicly owned sports facilities, a subsidy exists whenever the government provides the services of these facilities to professional sports teams at a price below total cost. Since, by definition, a public subsidy causes some segment of the private economy to benefit from an increase in real income, a change in the overall distribution of income in the community will be effected.[29] Such a change in income distribution resulting from some public policy is what economists refer to as the "incidence of the action." While this concept is generally used in connection with the analysis of taxes, it is equally applicable to the analysis of subsidies.

28. The estimate of one-third seems reasonable in view of data showing that, for 1966, land was estimated to equal 31.3 percent of the total value of all urban property and 33.9 percent of the value of commercial and industrial property (Allen D. Manvel, "Trends in the Value of Real Estate and Land, 1956 to 1966," in *Three Land Research Studies,* Prepared for the Consideration of the National Commission on Urban Problems [1968]).

29. This discussion assumes that the most important distributional effects will be felt in the local community.

The immediate impact of the sports subsidy is to transfer income from the local treasury to the team or teams using the facility. Given the fact that cities derive most of their revenue from property taxes, the subsidy can be thought of as being paid by the property owners in the taxing jurisdiction. If local taxes are not raised to finance the subsidy, the real cost of the subsidy to the city involves the reduction of expenditures that otherwise would have been made with these funds. In specific terms, there will be lower expenditures on education, health, police and fire protection, and all the other services generally provided by local governments. This reduction is probably regressive, as low-income families will be most adversely affected by the curtailment of such services.

For the recipient of the subsidy, the initial impact of the payment is to reduce costs and thereby increase income. This does not necessarily mean that owners of sports clubs retain the subsidy benefit as an increase in profits (although this is a possibility). While the subsidy does reduce the club's operating costs, a precise determination of whose real income is increased would require knowledge of the owner's pricing policy and general objectives.[30] Undoubtedly, these policies differ from team to team within each sport, and also from city to city. The final outcome will depend upon the club's performance and the consumers' price elasticity of demand for sporting events. In general terms, it can probably be said that the subsidy will be split (not necessarily evenly) among the consumers, who will pay somewhat lower admission prices; the players, who will receive somewhat higher salaries; and the owners, who will receive somewhat higher profits.

Even if the entire subsidy amount is passed on to spectators in the form of reduced admissions to sporting events, the benefits to the total community are not uniformly distributed. Although there is little information available on the economic status of sports fans, some inferences can be drawn from typical ticket prices.[31] In the early 1970s, admission to games averaged about $3 per seat for baseball, $7 for professional football, and

30. For example, some owners may be pure profit maximizers, while others may strive merely for a profit (of any size) rather than a loss. Indeed, a few "sportsmen-owners" may be unconcerned with profits at all and will spend whatever is necessary to field a winning club.

31. The 1954 Baltimore Orioles survey found that 46 percent of the spectators had annual incomes of $5,000 and over (*Baltimore Baseball Club Survey, 1954*, p. 18). The U.S. Bureau of the Census estimated that about 35 percent of all wage earners earned more than $5,000 in 1954. Thus, the Orioles in 1954 were drawing spectators disproportionately from the middle- and upper-income groups.

$4 for basketball. Since spectator sporting events are discretionary purchases, preceded by expenditures for such things as food, clothing, and shelter, it is reasonable to assume that these events are not frequented by the poorest people in the community.[32] Thus, there is probably a regressive impact on the distribution of income in the community from the benefit side of the stadium subsidy as well as from the cost side.

The foregoing includes only rough estimates of the distributional effects of the direct monetary cost to the community and excludes any consideration of indirect or external benefits. It does not seem unreasonable to assume that any benefits from such intangible assets as community prestige and image are distributed more or less equally among all the residents, so that they are distributionally neutral. In addition to the intangible benefits, indirect financial benefits accrue to a city from having a professional sports team. Hotel, restaurant, and other business stimulated by out-of-town visitors who come to watch ball games generate private income as well as city tax revenue. There may also be revenue from transit fares, sales taxes on admissions and concessions purchased at the stadium, and city taxes on income earned there. To the extent that indirect financial benefits are present, their incidence on city residents is probably just the opposite of the subsidy incidence—that is, progressive.

Except in the rare instances where the financial indirect benefits are very large, the net incidence of direct and indirect costs and benefits attributable to publicly owned sports facilities is likely to be regressive. The regressive curtailment of public services to the poor is probably somewhat offset by the incidence of the direct benefits. But, other than in the case of a World Series, for example, it seems unlikely that such direct benefits would even approach a level sufficient to offset the general regressiveness of stadium subsidies.

Summary and Conclusions

In 1970–71, local government subsidies to professional sports probably totaled close to $23 million per year. Although this gives an average of about $425,000 for each of the localities with sports facilities, such a figure is not very meaningful, since in a few areas the direct stadium or arena operating profits are sufficient to cover the property tax forgone,

32. This inference seems valid despite various promotional devices, such as Ladies' Day, which attract many persons with free or very low-priced admissions.

while in others the total subsidy is quite large. Furthermore, the amount of subsidy is growing.[33]

Table 6 shows the distribution of localities for which both operating cost and property tax data were available by the amount of local government net gain or loss (that is, the algebraic sum of the facility profit or loss plus property tax revenue forgone). About 17 percent of the places had a net gain on their facilities. One-fifth sustained annual losses in excess of $1 million, while another 17 percent had losses of $500,000 to $1 million. In general, the "gainers" have an old arena that is used only for basketball games. The biggest "losers" are places with large new stadiums used for baseball and/or football. Since such facilities are most frequently located in large cities, the net loss tends to rise as city size increases. There is no consistent pattern of size of loss by region of the country.

For the twenty-five localities with losses, the per capita direct loss on stadium operations ranges from 10 cents to $6.80 per year, with an average of about 65 cents. While these amounts appear quite small when compared with the average 1970–71 per capita expenditures of $39.71 for education and $26.29 for police protection,[34] the direct benefits of having a local sports team are probably highly concentrated among a small proportion of the total population. In the 1954 Baltimore survey, for example, it was estimated that only 5 percent of the total population had attended an Orioles home game. And the prevalence of season tickets for professional football games suggests that it is roughly the same 50,000 fans that attend each game.

On the basis of the data and analysis presented, it is impossible to generalize about whether the local subsidy of a sports facility is "worth it" to any particular community. Although the question has never been posed in this manner, if asked to vote an additional $2.60 in annual taxes (for a four-person family) to support a sports stadium versus a similar tax hike for increased police protection or education, there are undoubtedly many communities where a referendum for the sports stadium would pass easily. What does seem obvious from the analysis is that a locality

33. In 1972, for example, ground was broken for a new $125-million Superdome and exposition center in New Orleans. The prospectus report on the economic viability of this undertaking estimated that it will involve public operating subsidies of $2.0 to $2.5 million *annually* during its first few years of operation. And in the past, such projections have proven to be overoptimistic.

34. U.S. Bureau of the Census, *City Government Finances in 1970–71*, Series GF71–No. 4 (1972), Table 4, p. 8.

Table 6. Distribution of Publicly Owned Facilities by Amount of Net Gain or Loss to Local Government, 1970–71 Season

Net gain or loss to local government	Number of facilities	Percent distribution
Net gain	5	17
Net loss	25	83
Under $50,000	2	7
$50,000–100,000	3	10
$100,000–500,000	9	30
$500,000–1,000,000	5	17
$1,000,000 and over	6	20
All facilities	30	100

Source: Estimated from Tables 3, 4, and 5, and from property taxes forgone by the governments. Percentages are rounded.

can provide a substantial subsidy to local sports by building a fancy new stadium; putting it on valuable property in the middle of a large city; and financing it by issuing general obligation stadium construction bonds that will saddle the city with large fixed costs for the next forty years.

In summary: (1) the rentals charged for use of publicly owned sports facilities vary considerably and any rationale for actual practices followed is difficult to discern; (2) in general, the benefits from publicly owned sports facilities probably accrue disproportionately to the moderate-income or well-to-do citizens in the community at the expense of the poor; and (3) to the extent that subsidized rentals are not passed on to consumers in the form of lower prices or to players in the form of higher salaries, the prime beneficiaries of the local government subsidies are the owners of sports teams—most of whom are extremely wealthy.

CHAPTER TEN

Self-Regulation in Baseball, 1909-71

LANCE E. DAVIS

ORGANIZED BASEBALL presents an interesting subject for academic scrutiny because it is one of the few cartels[1] on the American scene whose operating procedures are codified and available for public examination. Exemption from the antitrust laws has allowed the owners of major-league teams to draw explicit rules for the conduct of interteam business. In fact, the proclivity of members of almost any cartel, including this one, to cheat tends to produce an ever-growing list of business rules. A study of the original code and its amendments reveals the cartel's response to changes in the external economic environment and the stability of its structure under the continued assaults of members seeking to increase their profits. Since 1909, the National Agreement or, since 1921, its replacement, the Major League Agreement (with its supplement, the Major League Rules), has been reproduced in the *Baseball Blue Book*.[2] This series is the source for the cartel rule changes examined in this chapter.

The National Agreement for the Government of Professional Baseball was signed by the owners of the sixteen major-league baseball clubs in 1903, at the end of the American League territorial and player "war." It was designed to insure that the eight National League and eight American League teams would constitute major-league baseball in the United States, and to reduce competition for players among those teams and between the majors and the minors. Protected from the threat of competition both from without (new leagues) and from within (each other), the major-

1. The term "cartel," as used in this chapter, refers only to an organization in an industry, such as the organization of baseball teams, that limits competition and divides markets, and it has no moral or legal connotations.
2. Published annually by Baseball Blue Book, Inc., St. Petersburg, Fla.

league clubs, acting in concert, should have been able to adjust ticket prices and salary structures in a way that would lead to industry profit maximization. Achievement of this goal would, however, require that the cartel overcome many problems, some endemic to all cartels and some peculiar to baseball.

The Theory of Cartel Behavior

The literature of economics contains few systematic studies of cartel behavior. Consequently, cartel theory has not been very completely developed. Two hundred years ago, Adam Smith noted the penchant of businessmen for colluding to try to capture monopoly profits. But theory and history suggest that the mere existence of potential monopoly profits does not guarantee that attempts at collusion will succeed.

Both a monopoly and a competitive firm maximize their profits if their managers choose a level of output that equates the cost of the last item produced with the additional revenue it generates. Since a monopolist recognizes that extra items can be sold only if the price of all items is allowed to decline, the profit-maximizing decision will yield a level of output different from that in a competitive industry, even if the presence or absence of competition is the only difference between the two. In particular, the monopolist will choose a lower level of output and sell at a higher price than the competitive industry will. Moreover, the monopolist, because he recognizes the effect of output decisions on price, will earn a higher rate of profit than competitive firms, even though both use the same rules for decisions and attempt to make their profits as large as possible. In the case of a monopsonist firm (a monopolist in the market for inputs), its recognition of the rising supply price of inputs differentiates it from the competitive firm and leads to a higher rate of profit. This higher rate is achieved because the monopsonist employs fewer of the inputs and is therefore required to pay less for them than a competitive firm.

If an industry is neither monopolistic (monopsonistic) nor competitive, the search for maximum profits does not lead to a predetermined set of output and price decisions. In such oligopolistic (oligopsonistic) industries, the profits that any firm can earn depend not only on demand and cost conditions but also on the actions of other firms in the industry. If all firms act in collusion they can maximize the industry profits; if they compete fiercely they can reduce the industry's profits to the competitive level; and if they act in some other way they can produce a set of price-output decisions that will yield almost any other intermediate level of profits. Economists use the term cartel to refer to the organization and structure adopted by the firms in an oligopolistic industry in an attempt to effect a collusive (monopolistic) set of price-output decisions.

Cooperative behavior among the firms, while assuring greater profits to the industry than competitive behavior, will not necessarily maximize the profits of any particular firm. A firm could always earn even larger profits if it could convince all other firms to abide by the cartel rules and then itself cut prices, employ more resources, pay higher wages, and increase sales. Consequently, if a firm can avoid detection or if detection carries only a small penalty, it pays to cheat on the cartel rules. Cartels without strong provisions for detecting and punishing violations of their rules are, therefore, highly unstable.[3]

The instability of cartels was especially apparent in the nineteenth century. The agreement regulating New York–Chicago rail rates, for example, broke down in the 1870s and was not reestablished until the Interstate Commerce Commission became the enforcement mechanism for the cartel's decisions.[4] Charles M. Schwab commented on his experience of the durability of cartel and other collusive arrangements: "Many of them lasted a day, some of them lasted until the gentlemen could go to the telephone from the room in which they were made. . . ."[5]

In the absence of an exemption from the antitrust laws, a cartel that attempts to adopt strong measures to prevent cheating becomes an easy mark for legal prosecution. In any comparison of cartel behavior, therefore, one would expect "protected" cartels to be more stable since they can put some bite in their enforcement procedures.

In addition to questions of stability and efficiency in enforcing output-price decisions, cartelization may substantially affect the way in which an industry responds to changes in its economic environment. It has been argued that cartels are less able to innovate in response to external stimuli

3. For a discussion of the theoretical problems of cartel stability, see Daniel Orr and Paul W. MacAvoy, "Price Strategies to Promote Cartel Stability," *Economica*, N.S., Vol. 32 (May 1965), pp. 186–97.

4. Paul W. MacAvoy, *The Economic Effects of Regulation: The Trunk-Line Railroad Cartels and the Interstate Commerce Commission before 1900* (M.I.T. Press, 1965). Since cartel arrangements were declared illegal by the Sherman Antitrust Act, our knowledge of them in the twentieth century is much less complete.

5. Quoted in Burton J. Hendrick, *The Life of Andrew Carnegie* (Doubleday, Doran, 1932), Vol. 2, p. 50.

than competitive (and perhaps monopolistic) industries. Consider the case in which the potential benefits from the innovation are equally distributed among the members of the cartel. In a competitive milieu, the firm that is able to devise the best response to a change in the industry's environment dictates the pace of productivity increase. Other firms must follow its lead out of economic necessity for, if they fail to keep pace, losses will soon force them out of business. On the other hand, some innovations will not succeed, and firms that make them will suffer economic loss. In a cartel, a majority of the members must be convinced that a change is worthwhile before any firm can adopt it. The responsiveness of the cartel to opportunities for profitable innovation will thus be determined by entrepreneurs whose innovative vision is at or below the industry average. As a result, some potentially profitable innovations will be delayed or rejected, while some potentially unsuccessful innovations will not be made. Some profits are thus forgone and some losses not incurred.

While the net effect of these two tendencies is uncertain, there are reasons to believe that productivity growth will be slower in a cartelized industry than in a noncartelized oligopoly. First, if the innovation process requires investment in research and development and if the cartel is effective in that area, expenditure on that input will be reduced just as expenditures on other inputs are; other things being equal, lesser amounts of research and development expenditure should lead to a lower rate of innovation. Second, given that the average person is averse to risk but that some entrepreneurs are not, the cartel should display a much lower rate of risky innovations. In a competitive industry, if only one firm undertakes a risky but successful innovation, the rest of the industry will be forced to follow along. But in the cartel, unless the majority are risk takers, there will be a strong bias against risky innovations.

A cartel is also likely to resist any change that involves some income redistribution among its members. In principle, the firms that would suffer could be compensated by those that would benefit, as long as the innovation increased total profits; but in practice, it is extremely difficult to reach an agreement on a scheme to compensate the losers. Each firm has a strong incentive to create the impression that it would be injured by any change, and such a claim is nearly impossible to verify. A majority of firms may act to block a change that threatens the profits of any, some because they think the change will harm them, some because they want the others to reach that conclusion.

To a significant degree, the efficiency, stability, and innovative response of the cartel depend on its decision-making rules and the procedure for amending them. The higher the proportion of members that must give their assent to any cartel action, the greater the chance that no action will be taken. Moreover, if the gains from cartel membership accrue unequally to the members but members have equal votes, the survival of the cartel will be placed in jeopardy. In such cases, the penalty for withdrawal from the cartel must be so high that firms adversely affected by the income redistribution will not withdraw. Under these conditions one would expect that the financially stronger firms would demand voting rules that would allow them to block unfavorable income redistributions before they agree to join the organization.

Because of its inability to cope adequately with change, the extent to which a cartel succeeds in increasing the profits of the industry will tend to decline over time. If membership is involuntary or if withdrawal costs are high, the cartel can become so inefficient that industry profits will fall below what they would be in a competitive environment. Some firms in the cartel may fail financially, even though they would succeed without the cartel arrangement.[6]

A cartel also has important effects on those who provide its resources or buy its product. First, it introduces monopoly and monopsony into markets that would otherwise experience some degree of competition. This affects not only income distribution—by transferring income from owners of specialized resources used only in the industry and from consumers of the industry's product to the members of the cartel—but also economic efficiency. Because the cartel creates a scarcity in its product, the cost to society of producing additional units of output in the industry, as measured by the payments to the industry's resources, is significantly less than the benefit of additional output, as measured by the price consumers are willing to pay. In the absence of other social consequences of production or consumption, society would benefit from an expansion of the industry's output.[7]

6. It has been suggested that many regulatory agencies are essentially involuntary cartels, and that the financial problems in the railroad and airline industries reflect especially ineffective cartel operations. On railroads, see, for example, George W. Hilton, *The Transportation Act of 1958: A Decade of Experience* (Indiana University Press, 1969); Gabriel Kolko, *Railroads and Regulation, 1877–1916* (Princeton University Press, 1965); and MacAvoy, *The Economic Effects of Regulation.*

7. Chapter 3 argues that some such effects are present in sports, so that some method of restricting industry output below what a competitive industry would produce is justified.

A second cost to society is engendered by the cartel's resistance to change. To the extent that the cartel shuns potentially profitable innovations, it prevents changes that would increase consumer satisfaction in the industry's product. In this case, the consumer's loss may not be associated with any gain by the industry, but may simply derive from the difficulties in getting most or all of the firms to perceive that everyone—producers, consumers, and suppliers of specialized industry resources—could benefit from change.[8]

Applications to Baseball

Baseball operations illustrate most of the features of cartel behavior. The rules limiting output are those that establish the number of teams in the sport and the territorial rights accorded to each team. These rules prevent new teams from locating in another team's territory and significantly limit the amount of broadcast competition that can take place.[9] The rules governing the acquisition of players prevent competition for the industry's most important input.

Between the 1880s and 1903, the major-league owners came to realize that second teams in a city reduce the gate for the established club, and that competitive bidding for players transfers at least a part of the player's economic value from the team owner to the player. The National Agreement was designed to avoid both problems,[10] as the cartel itself was originally intended to minimize competition in both the product and labor markets. The major leagues separated themselves from the rest of professional baseball and established stringent rules to prevent the encroachment of new teams on established franchises. (That there were still five multiteam cities was a historical accident.) No further encroachment would be allowed without the written consent of the existing team. All contracts were to contain a reserve clause to eliminate competitive bidding between major-league clubs for established players. The minor-league draft was established to prevent minor-league clubs from sharing the major leagues' monopoly profits, although the minors were still allowed to sell players until the draft date.

8. For an account of how the behavior of the railroad industry may fit this pattern, see Aaron J. Gellman, "Surface Freight Transportation," in William M. Capron (ed.), *Technological Change in Regulated Industries* (Brookings Institution, 1971).

9. See Chapters 1 and 8.

10. *Sporting News,* Vol. 34 (Dec. 27, 1902), p. 6, reports: "Both want peace: Major Leagues are tired of expensive war."

Like firms in any cartel, baseball teams have a strong incentive to cheat on the anticompetitive rules. Each team would like to compete with the other teams for players, as long as the others abided by the rules; and each team would benefit if it could invade the territory of other teams, as long as the others did not reciprocate. In many cases, detection of cheating is easy. Club activities are closely scrutinized by the press, and at least rough estimates of most of the relevant information (attendance figures, player salaries, broadcast revenues, ticket prices, and so forth) are largely in the public domain. The prohibitions against competition for players, however, raise enormous enforcement problems, since negotiations with individual players can easily be carried out in secret. Again, like any cartel, baseball must invoke heavy penalties to dissuade members from violating rules that are difficult to enforce. There are thus serious penalties for "tampering"—that is, contacting a player whose rights are held by another team.

For most of sports history, temptations to engage in business competition were limited to the player market, but recently, because of televised games, teams have become competitive in the product market as well. One would expect that a profit-maximizing cartel would be designed primarily to reduce competition in these two areas, and that coercive regulations would be aimed at holding down players' salaries and choosing an "optimal" broadcasting policy.

Organized baseball has been relatively free to develop strict enforcement rules, because it has enjoyed exemption from the antitrust laws through much of its history. The exemption was not official until the early 1920s, but the leagues appear to have had a de facto exemption even in the earlier period.[11] But baseball has had difficulty in taking full advantage of its antitrust exemption. In addition to the features that tend to destabilize all cartels, baseball has several special characteristics that intensify this problem. The voting rules for cartel members in baseball make it difficult for the sport to adjust to changes in the economic and legal environment. At present, three-quarters of the members of a league must agree to a change on most matters. For league matters, such as the decision to expand or to relocate a franchise, only the members of the league vote,

11. The Federal League, organized in 1913, filed antitrust charges in 1915, asking the court to declare the National Agreement illegal, but Judge Kenesaw Mountain Landis pocket vetoed the case until after the dissolution of the league. The suit was the culmination of war between the leagues over contract jumping and the desire of the Federal League to become a major league.

but for issues involving both major leagues, the three-quarters rule must be satisfied in each league. Thus, it is possible for four of the twenty-four member clubs to prevent a change in the major-league rules.[12] Nearly all the most profitable teams are in the National League, making it especially difficult to effect a change that benefits weaker teams. In fact, the two financial giants of baseball—the Mets and the Dodgers—need find only two more National League members to form a coalition that can block a rule change.

This rules structure reflects in part the long-standing split between the two leagues. Although the National Agreement was intended as an instrument of peace in the American League war, the cartel is still divided into the National and American Leagues. And, while alliances across leagues are sometimes formed, there is still a distinct animosity between the two sub-groups, and frequently one will act to take advantage of the other. This characteristic was demonstrated in the period following the Black Sox scandal and was still obvious some thirty years later at the time of the major-league expansion.

Agreement within the cartel is also hampered by the fact that not all members are profit maximizers. Some owners view baseball as largely a sporting activity, with profitability at most a secondary concern. Even today, teams like the Red Sox and the Cubs behave quite differently from teams like the Dodgers. Given the relatively small size of the cartel and the protected positions of its members, this divergence in goals tends to produce instability.

A final destabilizing factor is the wide range in the size of the market, which produces great differences in the average attendance of the teams and, therefore, in income. Since visiting clubs receive a portion of the gate receipts, teams with large home market areas possess a great deal of bargaining strength within the cartel, which they often use to effect policies that serve the interests of the richer clubs but not of the entire industry. For example, the original American League agreement of 1901 called for a sharing of revenues as a league-balancing innovation. Under this plan, the visiting team was to receive 30 cents from each grandstand admission and 20 cents from each bleacher ticket sold, amounting to a total of 40

12. In the earlier period, the rules were different but the effect was much the same. For example, before 1921, decisions were made by the National Commission. The commission had three members—two elected by the National and American Leagues and the third chosen by the two elected members. Since a majority was necessary to choose a league representative, any five votes in one league could form a blocking coalition.

percent of revenues. Gradually increasing ticket prices eroded the visiting club's income, until by 1953 it amounted to only 21 percent of revenues. In that year, Bill Veeck argued for a return to the old percentage but was voted down. In his words, "Five clubs voted for the change I suggested and three voted against it. Since it takes six to make a change, I was licked. And who do you suppose lined up against me? You're right—the rich ones. The Yankees, Tigers and Red Sox. Cleveland went along with us on this one because, though the Indians are a going concern, they don't have the financial backing of the other three clubs."[13] In 1965, the league voted to give 20 percent of the gate to the visiting clubs, and this was considered a move toward greater financial equality.[14]

An examination of the institutional characteristics of baseball will make it possible to test the conjectures economists have made about cartels against the observed behavior of that industry and may ultimately help in the development of a better theory. Given freedom from the threat of antitrust prosecution, a strong cartel organization capable of punishing "cheaters" quickly and severely should emerge. Moreover, since the potential profits to be gained from keeping salaries down are great, one would expect that team owners would strongly support the cartel's attempts to act as a monopsonist in the market for players. However, since to some extent effective action in the area of broadcasting means a transfer of income within the cartel, one would expect less unanimity on the appropriate rules for regulating these activities. Finally, since cartel members have equal voting rights but unequal profits, other actions that might redistribute income among the members can be expected to put the organization under severe stress as well.

The history of organized baseball under the National and Major League Agreements is a history of innovative cheating on the system, of resistance to rules changes that would prevent such cheating, and of, at best, only slow adjustment to external changes that were eroding the industry's profitability. In fact, only under extreme external pressure has the cartel ever been able to adjust at all. If the cartel's decisions have been economically rational, the owners must have discounted future profits at an extremely high rate.

THE PLAYER MARKET. The cartel has largely succeeded in preventing competition for players already under professional contract. It has grad-

13. Quoted in *Sporting News*, Vol. 135 (Feb. 11, 1953), pp. 5–6.
14. See Leonard Koppett, *A Thinking Man's Guide to Baseball* (E. P. Dutton, 1967), p. 161.

ually evolved a set of rules that make it all but impossible for a minor-league club to capture any significant financial benefit from the lack of competition for players. It has permitted new teams to be formed without creating much additional competition for players. It has used its exclusive rights on player contracts to charge new teams a price for a specified minimum number of players that certainly exceeds the players' market value. It has been unable to eliminate competitive bidding for players from other sports, but since most athletes cannot play more than one sport at the highest professional level, this failure is of little economic consequence.[15]

The cartel's major failure has been in preventing competition for new players. Only in the mid-1960s did baseball finally adopt a drafting system for amateurs, and even then the procedure that was adopted was weaker than that in other sports.

THE PRODUCT MARKET. The cartel has worked much less efficiently in preventing interteam competition for revenues. Pressure from new leagues has been resisted, but in almost every other area the cartel's failure has been massive. It has not fared well in the competition with other sports (both professional and amateur) for audiences. Although major-league baseball attendance has managed some growth since the Second World War, its share of the total sports dollar continues to decline, and the day has long passed when one could unambiguously speak of baseball as *the* "national pastime." Even as its preeminent position was disintegrating, baseball steadfastly refused to adopt the innovations proposed by its leading entrepreneurs.

Baseball has not responded to the growth of broadcasting in a completely successful way. What had been isolated and monopolistic markets for baseball teams have now been thrown into direct competition because of technical changes in the communications industry. Beginning with radio in the late twenties and escalating rapidly with the innovation of television in the forties, major-league teams in New York and Boston have been placed in direct competition with teams in Chicago and Cincinnati. Moreover, the competition between televised major-league and live minor-league games has all but destroyed the minors, at a significant cost to the majors. Finally, the revenues from radio and television have further un-

15. Gene Conley and Dave DeBusschere both pitched in the major leagues and played forward in the National Basketball Association, but they are certainly exceptions. In bidding wars with other sports, baseball has not fared badly in the past. (The Giants, for example, signed Paul Giel despite competition from football.)

balanced the financial structure of the leagues, making the rich much richer but the poor only a little less poor. The cartel has proven itself almost completely unable to adjust to the impact of these changes on industry profits.[16]

Competition in the Player Market

The American League war caused salaries to rise sharply, so that the most important sections of the ensuing peace treaty were those ruling that competition for established players should cease. A National Agreement amendment of 1907 called for a standard contract for all players, the form of which was to be decided by the National Commission (the body charged with effecting cartel decisions). Moreover, contracts without a reserve clause were specifically banned, except where waivers were granted by the commission. This rule, although gradually expanded and more carefully specified, has remained a foundation stone of baseball's administrative organization. Only once have any exceptions to the rule been made (when the Giants, Yankees, and Superbas issued some multiyear contracts during the Federal League war), but the commission ruled these contracts void even though they had been signed by both parties. Here the cartel has been efficient in punishing "cheaters."

Between the demise of the Federal League and the 1950s, the major challenge to baseball's organization structure came from the attempts of Don Jorge Pasquel, millionaire president of the Mexican League, to make this league a major circuit. In that instance, the punishments levied against players who jumped their contracts to play in Mexico were so severe that, despite a great deal of talk, little emigration to Mexico actually took place. Although there was ultimately some recanting (to say nothing of an out-of-court settlement), Commissioner Albert B. Chandler's initial response was that those who did not return by opening day were out, and that they could not even petition to return to American organized baseball for five years.[17] And Cardinals owner Sam Breadon was fined $5,000 for not reporting his meeting with officials of the outlaw league.[18]

---

16. In 1952, the total television and radio income of the major leagues was about $4.0 million; by 1966, it was up to $27.5 million (Koppett, *A Thinking Man's Guide to Baseball*, p. 163).

17. *New York Times,* April 27, 1946.

18. Ibid., July 27, 1946.

Competition for New Players

In its attempt to prevent competition for new players, the cartel has been considerably less efficient. For years it was unable to prevent minor-league teams from capturing a significant share of the value of star players, and only in the very recent past has it finally found a way to reduce the ability of a few clubs to hoard baseball talent. A reading of the cartel's administrative history suggests that when a rule was adopted to prevent such practices, it was either repealed, emasculated, or ignored.

By the 1940s, a rule had been added that prohibited the signing of high school players until after their classes had graduated. The tendency has been to tighten this rule, particularly by making it more difficult to induce a player to drop out of school. Similar rules prevent the signing of American Legion ballplayers. In the case of college students, the object is similar but the actual constraints are weaker and were developed more slowly. The signing prohibition came a decade later; it was dropped for a time in the early sixties, and even today it is not without substantial loopholes.[19] Moreover, the evidence suggests that the rule itself was a product of cheating within the cartel in the clubs' search for player talent. As late as the 1940s, it was common for a team to secretly sign a college athlete and allow him to complete his college eligibility (although if the contract had been recognized he would have lost that eligibility). In such a world, a team faced substantial costs if it did not attempt to tamper with a potential star. In the Anthony Ravich case, Landis held that such contracts, although not valid (not being filed in the commissioner's office), succeeded in "deluding many of the players signing into an erroneous belief that they [were] obligated and . . . establishing a moral obligation to go through with the agreement."[20]

THE MINOR-LEAGUE AND FARM SYSTEMS. Most of the competition for players is for high school graduates who are not enrolled in a college and who are expected to develop their skills while playing in the minor leagues. In the early years of the National Agreement, the majors spent relatively little money on scouting and depended upon the minor leagues for most of the player talent. By the mid-1920s, some major-league executives

19. It is, for example, not illegal to sign a college player who has dropped out of school because of scholastic difficulties—certainly an inducement to tamper with prospective major leaguers.

20. *New York Times,* March 8, 1942. He made the Yankees give up Ravich.

recognized that this system allowed a fraction of the value of players to accrue to the minors, a fraction that increased substantially when the more successful minor leagues refused to participate in the annual player draft. These executives recognized the potential profitability of an investment in scouting, if the rules could be changed to permit a major-league club to control minor-league players. Over the objections of the commissioner (who thought such changes would unbalance the league), they began to buy minor-league franchises, and the farm system was born. Begun by Branch Rickey at St. Louis in the 1920s, the idea spread rapidly, and by the early 1930s almost every major-league club had at least one farm club, and some had many. Rickey saw the farm system as a device that would permit a team in a small market area to compete with its richer peers.

The minors resisted the expansion of the farm system because it reduced the profits they could earn on the sale of their players to the majors. In 1927, in fact, one minor league, the American Association, prohibited the sale of any more of its franchises to a major-league club. Because new leagues could always be formed and because selling franchises to the majors was profitable, these efforts were largely in vain. By the late 1930s, few independent minor-league teams were left, except in the lowest classifications. The proportion of independents in the early fifties is shown in Table 1.[21]

Given the minor leagues' opposition and his personal feelings about the effect of the system on relative club strengths, Commissioner Landis attempted to dismantle the "chain store" system.[22] To Landis, the farm system was an ideal camouflage for hidden option transactions, and for years he construed every sale from a major to its farm club as involving an option. In 1928 he ordered Ray Thompson to be returned to Louisville rather than sold to the Browns' Tulsa farm, and in 1930 he ruled that no team could draft a player from its own farm club.[23]

Landis was thwarted by the owners. In 1932, Philip Ball, owner of the Browns, threatened a court fight to overrule a decision by the commis-

---

21. In his testimony before the Celler Committee in 1952, Bonneau Peters, president of the Shreveport, Louisiana, team, reported that of the 364 minor-league teams, the majors owned or controlled 195. Of the 70 teams in Class A and above, there were only 13 independents.

22. *Organized Baseball,* Report of the Subcommittee on Study of Monopoly Power of the House Committee on the Judiciary, H. Rept. 2002, 82 Cong. 2 sess. (1952), p. 66.

23. *New York Times,* May 31, 1928.

Table 1. Percentage of Minor-League Baseball Clubs Controlled by the Major Leagues, by Classification, 1952

Classification of minor-league club[a]	Owned by major leagues	Controlled by working contracts with major leagues	Independent
AAA	50	29	21
AA	44	44	12
A	47	33	20
B	21	35	44
C	11	34	56
D	14	31	56
All clubs	21	33	46

Source: *Study of Monopoly Power*, Pt. 6, *Organized Baseball*, Hearings before the Subcommittee on Study of Monopoly Power of the House Committee on the Judiciary, 82 Cong. 1 sess. (1952), p. 765. Figures are rounded.

a. Classification is based on the minimum aggregate population of the cities comprising a league, as follows: AAA, 3 million; AA, 1.75 million; A, 1 million; B, 0.25 million; C, 0.15 million; D, up to 0.15 million.

sioner that caused the Browns to lose player Herschel Bennet. To appease Ball, and in an amazing display of anti-Landis feeling, the owners amended the cartel's rules to include the following: "All assignments, whether optional or otherwise, of players' contracts and all agreements and/or other transactions involving players' contracts mentioned in or provided for by the major league agreement and the major league rules shall be given, and shall have, the same force and effect for all and every purpose notwithstanding the stock ownership or control either directly or indirectly of any one club or by a stockholder or stockholders of any one or more other clubs."[24]

It is difficult to understand why the clubs voted to override the commissioner, in one of the very few such acts during Landis's tenure. The rule change set the stage for unrestricted farm operations; it forced all clubs to invest in some prototype system; and it resulted in an unbalancing of the leagues. There were to be many pennants for the Yankees and Dodgers and extra profits from player sales for the Cardinals, but little advantage for the other clubs.[25] Landis continued to oppose the system

24. Ibid., Dec. 16, 1932.

25. While the Cardinals profited most from the sale of farm players (see *Organized Baseball*, H. Rept. 2002, p. 65), even the teams that used their farm systems to upgrade their own rosters did occasionally sell players, thus adding to their profits. *Sporting News*, Vol. 134 (Jan. 28, 1953), p. 6, reported: ". . . since the 1952 season ended, the Brooklyn organization has quietly added about $200,000 to its bank ac-

as best he could. In 1938, he released some one hundred St. Louis farm-club players and fined both the Dodgers and the Tigers for concealing player contracts. In 1944, he freed ninety-two Detroit players whose value was estimated at $500,000.[26] But he could not put an end to the system, and by 1960, when the rules were again changed to achieve more equal balance, the majors owned or controlled 3,084 farm players (the Dodgers alone having 275).

Why did the cartel choose to support the farm-club owners, a definite minority, rather than the commissioner, whose opinions must have coincided with the interests of the majority of owners? The answer to this question probably lies in the lack of business acumen of the owners. At first, the owners felt the farm system was doomed to failure because it was economically shaky. Both Barney Dreyfuss and Frank Navin argued that the commissioner need take no action because the system would soon collapse. When, instead of failing, Rickey's experiment succeeded, the owners, failing to see that what was profitable for one could not be profitable for all, wanted no restrictions on jumping aboard the farm-team bandwagon. By the late 1920s, Barney Dreyfuss himself argued "you have to have them [farm clubs] yourself in order to put your ball players out on option."[27] Even if the owners did not know where their own best interests lay, why did Landis not take action in the name of the "best interests of baseball"? His failure to do so suggests that no cartel can effect decisions against the wishes, no matter how ill conceived, of the majority of its members, and that any such action by the commissioner might have caused another reorganization.

THE MINOR-LEAGUE DRAFT. The expressed cartel goal of maintaining some semblance of league balance goes back to the earliest days of the National Agreement. Some limitation was always placed on the total number of players a club could have on its roster, and originally the number of players a club could control through option agreements was as severely limited. The farm system undercut the effect of these limits. It is inter-

---

count from the sale of players and, in addition to the cash, received half a dozen players. . . . Bill Hunter, the brilliant young shortstop, went to Bill Veeck and the Browns for approximately $100,000, Clyde King, who might be called a youthful veteran, brought $25,000 from the Reds, and Pafko's purchase nicked Lou Perini for $75,000."

26. *New York Times,* Nov. 26, 1944.

27. Quoted in Harold Seymour, *Baseball: The Golden Age* (New York: Oxford University Press, 1971), p. 419. For a discussion of the growth of farm clubs, see pp. 413–19.

esting to note, however, that the cartel responded to the Federal League's threat by removal of the player limit. In 1914, some clubs were carrying as many as forty players on their rosters, to the marked advantage of the financially sounder clubs.[28]

At the heart of the strength equalization strategy was the annual player draft. Until the First World War, the draft was the chief source of player talent, and the majors made extensive use of it (in 1913, for example, drafting over one hundred players). Some minors welcomed the draft, but others saw it merely as a method of transferring player rent to the majors. As early as 1914, the Pacific Coast League had called for an end to the draft. This demand was muted during the Federal League troubles and the player shortage of the war, but it reemerged in 1919. In that year, the minors broke off relations with the majors, and even though the latter agreed to respect the minors' territorial rights and player contracts, there was no draft.[29] In an attempt to reestablish the older procedures, the majors agreed to a substantial increase in draft prices, and, to make the draft a more effective tool for equalizing strengths, began to draft in reverse order of standings. The price concession was insufficient to tempt the best minor clubs, who continued to sell players outside of the draft system. The price of player talent drawn from the International, Pacific Coast, American Association, Western, and Three-I Leagues rose markedly.

If the cartel had been effective, surely it could have moved against the recalcitrant minors, but cartel response was very slow indeed. In 1921, John A. Heydler, president of the National League, proposed a rule amendment that would have banned player purchases from the five minor leagues; though the plan was widely hailed, it could never muster enough votes to become a part of the agreement.[30] Once again, the owners indicated a willingness to leave loopholes that permitted cheating, and this failure to come to terms with the minors must have given added impetus to the innovation of the farm system: the majors were allowed to draft only players who had been assigned to the minors by major-league teams; they were not allowed to draft players signed by an independent club.

In 1930, the cartel finally acted, but the result could hardly be deemed a victory for league balance or for the reduction of player acquisition

28. *New York Times,* Nov. 6, 1914.
29. Ibid., July 11, 1919, and Feb. 14, 1920; *Organized Baseball,* H. Rept. 2002, p. 58.
30. *New York Times,* Dec. 14, 1921.

costs.[31] Not only did the compromise involve a substantial increase in the draft price (from $2,500 to $5,000 for a player from a class AA club, for example), but it also prohibited drafting of players who had not completed some minimum service in the minors (as much as four years for AA players). Thus, a minor-league team could sign a player and protect him from the draft for up to four years, which would often be enough time to determine if he had major-league potential and to capitalize on that knowledge by selling his contract before he was eligible for the draft.

This rule change, coupled with the farm system, drastically changed the baseball recruiting process. The independent minors could capture a portion of the value of good players, as happened in the cases of Joe DiMaggio and Fred Hutchinson. Moreover, the teams with an investment in scouting and a substantial farm system could protect their investment in a player until they could be fairly certain of his potential. In fact, if the old draft system had been allowed to continue, the farm system could not have operated so well. With the rule changes, it was possible for the Yankees to win eighteen American League pennants between 1935 and 1960, for the Dodgers to win eight in the National League, and for the Cardinals to become the most profitable franchise in either league by selling players to teams with less well developed farm systems. In this instance, the cartel did not act in its own best interest, since the majority of members voted for a rule that effectively transferred income to a minority. Perhaps, again, the owners' short-sightedness kept them from understanding that the farms that were profitable to some could never be profitable to all and that the long-run costs of scouting and farming could not be offset by the short-run gains from recapturing some rent from the minors.

THE BONUS WAR AND THE AMATEUR DRAFT. Once the major leagues had assumed the burden of scouting, they found themselves in direct competition with each other for player talent. The competition had been less obvious when scouting was a minor-league function, since the minors generally limited their search to their own geographic areas. Moreover, since a player could be drafted at the end of his first season, it did not pay to invest great amounts either in scouting or in bonus payments. With the rule change and the emergence of the farm system, the payoff from signing potential major-league players rose substantially, and, with competitive bargaining, that payoff could be transferred from club to player through the signing bonuses.

31. Ibid., July 10, 1930; Jan. 18 and Jan. 21, 1931.

Although the first bonus players appeared in the 1930s, the depression, followed by the manpower shortage during the Second World War, delayed the escalation of bonus warfare until the postwar decade. By that time, baseball was a very profitable business, and owners began to compete for new players by offering larger and larger bonuses. The cartel made some effort to prevent this transfer of value from club to player, but, once again, its response was at best ineffectual. In 1948, the minor-league draft rules were changed to state that a bonus player was subject to an unrestricted draft at the end of his first year of play if he was not retained on the roster of a major-league club.[32] Since it was difficult, if not impossible, to detect violations, and since the incentive to cheat was great, the rule proved largely unworkable. In fact, no bonus players were ever drafted, the bonus war did not stop, and the rule was repealed in 1950. Another attempt to curb competitive bidding was made in 1952. Under a supposedly more stringent rule, a bonus player was forced to remain with his major-league club for two years or be subject to an unrestricted draft.[33] The rule did place such strong restrictions on bonus players that, in the words of Commissioner Ford Frick, "club owners will be awfully careful in signing such players unless they are certain to deliver."[34] If this rule made owners more careful, it certainly did not stop the bidding. Clubs were willing to retain the bonus players for the required two years, and the consequence was a deterioration in the quality of baseball. As a result, this rule was scrapped in 1957, although the twenty-one bonus players on major-league rosters (including Sandy Koufax) were required to serve out their terms.

A rule passed in 1957 served to break up the larger farm systems but did little to stop the bonus war. The draft price was raised to $25,000; any minor leaguer with four years' service was made subject to the draft; and the limit on the number of players that could be drafted from a single team was removed. Since it was no longer possible to protect farm hands by loading up the roster of a single minor-league club with all the best players, the distribution of player talent became less uneven.

Finally, in 1961, over twenty years after it had begun, the first significant steps to curb the bonus war were made. At that time, bonuses had

32. A bonus player was defined as anyone having received $6,000 or more for signing.
33. This time a bonus player was defined as anyone having received more than $4,000 for signing.
34. *New York Times*, Nov. 6, 1952.

cost the major-league clubs an estimated $12 million.[35] The 1961 rule made it possible for each club to protect one bonus player, but all others were subject to an unrestricted draft unless they were on a major-league roster.[36] In 1964, the adoption of an unrestricted free-agent draft restored conditions to something like those that prevailed before 1920. That year fifty-nine first-year bonus players (and four veterans) were drafted, and the chaos was so complete that, despite the opposition of the Dodgers, Yankees, Cardinals, and Mets (normally a strong enough coalition to veto any change), a new rule was adopted.[37] The rule permitted the clubs, in reverse order of their standings, to draft the negotiation rights to any unsigned player. Once drafted, a player could sign only with the team that had drafted him. If he failed to sign after six months, his name was returned to the draft pool. The results were impressive. In the 1965 draft 814 players were chosen.[38] Where a year before Rick Reichardt had signed for $200,000, Rick Monday (at least as promising a prospect) received only about half that amount. Although bonuses were still paid, the day of the large bonus for the untried prospect was largely past.[39]

After twenty-five years, the cartel had finally found a partial solution to the problem of high player bonuses, but it was certainly a less efficient solution from the cartel's point of view than the draft that had long been practiced by the National Football League and even by the National Basketball Association. In those sports, draft rights were granted to the club in perpetuity, so there was, and is, little incentive for a player to refuse to sign. In baseball, a player could always wait six months, have his name returned to the pool, and hope to get a better offer from another club. As a result, baseball players continue to draw substantial bonuses, although the incidence of huge bonuses has declined.

In this case, the theoretical explanation of cartel behavior breaks down,

35. An estimate made by the *New York Times,* Dec. 1, 1961.

36. The results were immediate, and the nearly moribund minor-league draft was revitalized. At the 1962 selection meeting, fifty-six players (forty-five first-year and eleven regular) were drafted at a cost of $695,000. The next year saw eleven regulars drafted at the price of $25,000, plus fifty-two first-year men (*Official Baseball Guide for 1963* [Sporting News, 1963], p. 225, and *1965,* p. 254).

37. *New York Times,* Dec. 3, 1964. See also *Official Baseball Guide for 1965,* p. 254.

38. *Official Baseball Guide for 1966,* pp. 167–70.

39. The effects of the change were immediate. In the 1965 minor-league draft, for example, only twenty-three players were chosen, and of this number seventeen were veterans. By 1969, the total number was nineteen, all veterans (*Official Baseball Guide for 1966,* pp. 263–64; *Official Baseball Guide for 1970,* p. 367).

and the special characteristics of baseball must be taken into account. It would appear reasonable to conclude that the baseball cartel, with its antitrust exemption, would be more efficient at extracting monopoly rents than the football cartel that does not have the same exemption; but, in fact, the baseball cartel is the weaker of the two. The explanation probably rests in part on the history of the two sports. The wealthy baseball clubs have long resisted any rule change that undercuts their competitive advantage. In contrast, the football owners can remember the not too distant past, when it was careful cartel management that turned them from a marginally profitable into a very profitable industry. Moreover, the football cartel consists of twenty-six more or less equally profitable franchises—a result in part of cartel decisions and in part of the nature of the sport—so there is not the same rich-poor division within the cartel that exists in baseball.

Competition for Veteran Players

While the baseball cartel has not been very effective in containing competition for new players, it has been more successful with regard to veterans.[40] The legal protection of the reserve clause, upheld by three Supreme Court decisions that exempted baseball from antitrust action,[41] has contributed to this success. Also important was the attitude of Commissioner Kenesaw Mountain Landis, who did not favor allowing players to bargain for higher salaries. This was well expressed in his 1921 decision in the Heine Groh case. Groh, a Cincinnati third baseman, had held out for a higher salary, and the club management, unwilling to meet his demands, prepared to trade him to a team that would. Landis ruled that the Reds could not trade him, and that he would play for Cincinnati or nowhere.[42] This ruling, in making it difficult for one club to tamper with the players of another, also made it difficult for a player to bargain.[43]

Despite the support of the courts and the commissioner, the cartel has

40. So successful, in fact, that in 1921 Dickie Kerr, the star of the White Sox pitching staff, found an offer from a Texas semipro team attractive enough for him to quit organized baseball (Bill Veeck, *The Hustler's Handbook* [Putnam, 1965], p. 296).

41. *Federal Baseball Club of Baltimore* v. *National League*, 259 U.S. 200 (1922); *Toolson* v. *New York Yankees, Inc.*, 346 U.S. 356 (1953); *Curtis C. Flood* v. *Bowie K. Kuhn et al.*, 407 U.S. 258 (1972).

42. Seymour, *Baseball: The Golden Age*, pp. 391–92.

43. In June 1921, Landis banned for life pitcher Ray Fisher of Cincinnati because he took a position as coach at the University of Michigan, a case in which tampering was hardly a possibility (Seymour, *Baseball: The Golden Age*, p. 373).

not always been victorious in its dealings with players. At the time of the Federal League war, for instance, the players were able to squeeze some major concessions out of the owners. And at the end of the war, the National Commission was powerless to prevent substantial bidding for players released by the clubs of the moribund league. Pronouncements were made that such players should not be allowed back into organized baseball, and attempts were made to agree on uniform salary cuts to reduce the war-swollen payrolls, but no cartel action was taken.[44] At the end of the hostilities, despite attempts by the National Commission to find some other mechanism for allocating the released players, there was vigorous bargaining for the services of the best of the Federal League players.[45]

The depression, too, provided an opportunity for joint action to reduce wage costs, but here again the cartel was unable to move effectively. No team wanted to take the lead in reducing salaries, for to do so would undermine the morale of its players and its attractiveness to free agents. The rules were changed to reduce the player limits from twenty-five to twenty-three, but attempts to legislate an across-the-broad pay cut came to nothing. Although the owners were willing to give lip service to the doctrine that "by reason of prevailing conditions and the decrease in attendance at our games, it becomes necessary that the general operating expense, including salary lists of ball players of both major leagues be substantially reduced," the wealthier clubs, led by Jacob Ruppert of the Yankees, induced the cartel to leave the players' salaries up to each club owner.[46] One month later, the Yankee club secretary was able to announce that Lou Gehrig and Vernon ("Lefty") Gomez had already accepted terms and that the Yankees "contemplated no serious salary controversies with their players this spring."[47] Such was not the case for the less solvent teams; once again, the rich clubs were given an edge on signing new talent.

THE RISE OF PLAYER UNIONS. As long as Landis remained commissioner, collective bargaining was never mentioned. After his death that, too, changed. With Chandler as commissioner, with the threat of competition from the Mexican League providing the players with a little bargaining power, and with Robert Murphy's players union standing in the wings,[48]

44. *New York Times,* Nov. 21, 1914.
45. Ibid., Dec. 23, 1915.
46. Ibid., Dec. 8 and 11, 1931.
47. Ibid., Jan. 13, 1932.
48. By June of 1946, Murphy claimed to have enrolled the majority of the players on six major-league teams (*New York Times,* June 5, 1946).

the players were able to wring some substantial concessions from the cartel—almost the first since 1914. The majors' first minimum salary schedule was added to rule 17 of the Major League Rules, and rule 26 was amended to read: "In all matters which concern the standard form of player's contract or its provisions or regulations, the players shall be represented on the Executive Council by two (2) active players, one (1) to be elected annually by the players of each league."[49] Moreover, for the first time, the idea of management-union negotiations was legitimatized, the club owners admitted the possibility of collective bargaining, and the players received direct benefits in terms of owner contributions to the player pension fund.[50]

From the point of view of the cartel, the first concessions marked the beginning of a trend, at first slow but gradually accelerating, toward a diminution of its unilateral monopoly vis-à-vis its players. The players as a group sought professional representation: at first, a part-time lawyer to negotiate and generally look after their interests, and ultimately a full-time representative whose previous experience had been not in baseball but in the trade union movement. The owners responded by establishing a player relations committee separate from the commissioner's office, and by employing a full-time labor negotiator of their own. Clearly, the position of the cartel as supreme arbiter of player contracts had been subverted.[51] Why did the cartel allow its powers to be diluted in the one area where most owners might be expected to agree about joint action? Neither the theory nor the special conditions of baseball contribute to an explanation; our knowledge of cartel behavior is still far from complete.

Although economic theory does not allow us to predict with certainty the result of bargaining between two monopolies, it is clear that it will be different from the product of bargaining between a monopolist and a number of competing sellers of services—the situation that existed in baseball before the growth of the players' union—and that the difference does not favor the baseball owners' cartel. Football, which does not have an antitrust exemption, has been far more successful in thwarting union activity. Perhaps the explanation lies in the composition of the cartel members. Certainly the football owners are more unified, less tradition bound,

49. For a history of the negotiations, see the *New York Times* for May 3, May 16, June 5, July 19, and Oct. 22, 1946.

50. Ibid., Jan. 26 and Feb. 17, 1954.

51. Chapter 6 documents the concessions that owners have made to player associations, especially since the mid-1960s.

and probably more uniformly profit motivated. For these reasons they may be more able to provide nearly unanimous support for cartel decisions, support that was clearly lacking in recent player-cartel negotiations in baseball.

Competition in the Product Market

In the product market, the success of the cartel has been mixed, with difficulties arising when the owners are split on an issue. The first threat to the cartel's monopoly position in the local baseball market came from the Federal League. The new league had opened competing franchises in Chicago, St. Louis, and Brooklyn. The treaty that ended the Federal League war abolished the Brooklyn club and allowed the Federal League owners to assume the existing franchises—the Cubs and the Browns—in the other two cities. In the case of the Cubs, the old National League owners were forced to accept a bargain they did not want. Among the other terms of the agreement were the reinstatement of Federal League players and the dropping of the Federal League's antitrust suit against organized baseball.[52] Although the treaty involved some sacrifices for individual cartel members, the industry as a whole suffered no long-term ill effects.

Competition from the Mexican League had some effect on the player market but not on the market for baseball games. The competing teams were located thousands of miles away from existing franchises, and there was still no viable television to introduce the outlaw league to potential spectators. Recognition was given to the Cuban Professional Baseball League and some rules were changed to protect Mexican nationals, but neither represented any serious loss to the cartel.

In the case of the Continental League, the changes wrought in the cartel structure were permanent and costly. The league was well financed, backed by considerable political clout (including the support of Emanuel Celler), and included several cities that were large enough to support major-league teams (the original franchises were New York, Toronto, Atlanta, St. Paul–Minneapolis, Dallas–Fort Worth, Denver, Houston, and Buffalo). The league had agreed to pool radio and TV receipts, so it was apt to be both balanced and strong. While only the Yankees were to be faced with direct competition, a number of minor-league franchises owned

52. *New York Times,* Dec. 23, 1915. See also *Sporting News,* Vol. 60 (Dec. 23 and 30, 1915).

by the majors were threatened. More important, the league would compete with the cartel for national television revenues and with some cartel members for local radio-TV revenues. Faced by this threat, the cartel moved to accommodate. The rules were changed to require only a three-fourths vote on the question of expansion, and National League clubs were placed in New York and Houston, and American League franchises in Minneapolis–St. Paul and Los Angeles. The National League had voted to expand without conferring with either the minor leagues or the commissioner; the American League responded with a unilateral plan of its own. The cartel was almost torn apart by the ensuing conflict. While New York was almost open territory after the departure of the Giants and Dodgers, the Yankees could hardly have welcomed new competition. More important, the move of a new franchise into Los Angeles was in direct conflict with a major-league rule. Ultimately an accommodation was reached between the leagues, but not before it became apparent that the American League was ready to go ahead alone, despite a threatened veto by the commissioner. More clearly than ever before, the chance for an increase in short-term profits (from franchise and player sales) for a few owners was shown to be sufficient to push the cartel almost to the breaking point. Television coverage increased competition not only in the new two-club cities (New York and Los Angeles), but throughout the league. Some clubs lost good regional network markets to the expansion clubs,[53] and the national television receipts had to be divided among a greater number of teams. In the long run, the windfalls from franchise and player sales probably could not offset these losses, especially when they are compounded by the increased player costs that go with the need to stock four more teams. Once again, the effect of the American and National League blocs and the political power of the rich clubs proved sufficient to undercut the cartel's authority.

Responding to the Growth of Broadcasting

In a similar situation, less obvious but more fundamental, the behavior of the owners also reflected a willingness—nay, eagerness—to abandon long-term cartel profits for the short-term dollar returns to individual teams. The inability of the cartel to respond to forces that threaten the

53. The greatest loser here was Milwaukee. Minnesota had previously been part of its market, and suddenly it was squeezed between Chicago 100 miles to the south and Minneapolis 300 miles to the west.

very life of the industry was clearly demonstrated by its response to the question of radio and television rights. As early as 1931, radio had begun to present severe problems to organized baseball. In that year, the minors complained about the effect of major-league broadcasts on their attendance, and the Western Union Company demanded some action to protect its monopoly on baseball press wires (a monopoly for which the company paid a substantial sum). Even at that time, when some clubs gave broadcasting privileges away, it was impossible for the owners to agree on a uniform policy.[54] The question was raised year after year, but, while the majority of the owners always admitted something should be done, specific rules changes were invariably postponed.

As radio became more important and television broadcasts were introduced, the problem was compounded, and the effects of this new form of competition on minor-league attendance escalated. Even the majors began to be directly affected, as the teams with large video and radio markets prospered at the expense of those less favored.[55] Major-league clubs found their attendance affected by the television policies of neighboring clubs that had never before competed in the same market. Within the cartel, some owners pressed for a sharing of radio-TV receipts in a manner similar to the division of gate receipts, but the clubs with the largest video markets resisted. Fred Saigh of the Cardinals was able to work out a sharing agreement with the Cubs, but that was the exception rather than the rule. More typical was Bill Veeck's experience at St. Louis. Since the visiting club had to agree to the telecast of a game, Veeck attempted to bargain for some division of video receipts. The Yankees responded by scheduling all their games with the Browns in the afternoon, thus denying them a share of the lucrative night games at Yankee Stadium.[65] Despite

54. *New York Times,* Dec. 8, 1931.

55. "New York, with a 15,000,000 potential reaching into southern New England, is the prime TV area; Houston, which has constructed a radio network, with relatively little television, over an area of hundreds of miles, because no other major-league team is geographically close, commands a million-dollar fee; but Kansas City, with St. Louis to the east, Minnesota to the north, Houston to the southeast and sparsely settled plains and mountains to the west, can get only a couple of hundred thousand. The Los Angeles Dodgers, in car-bound California, get as much for radio as Eastern teams do for television" (Koppett, *Thinking Man's Guide to Baseball,* p. 161).

56. *New York Times,* Dec. 6, 1952. *Sporting News* (Jan. 28, 1953) reported that Bill Veeck estimated that he would be deprived "of 'between $15,000 and $20,000' by this enforced loss [of eight night games] placed upon him by the Red Sox, Indians and Yankees in retaliation for his refusal to allow them to televise his games in their parks in 1953" (p. 12).

the example of the nascent Continental League, no provision was ever made for sharing broadcast receipts or for limiting broadcasts, and it was 1964 before eighteen of the twenty teams could agree on a single national television contract.[57]

To the majors, the problems raised by radio and television may have been serious, but to the minors, the ensuing major-league competition was fatal. While the major-league owners may or may not have recognized the problem, it was obvious to an informed layman. The first national telecast of a World Series game moved a Los Angeles sports writer to report this conversation:

"I'll wager that the series telecast killed baseball on the Coast. . . . By your standards Bobby Brown is just an average third baseman. By our standards he pulled fielding plays such as we on the Pacific Coast had never seen before. Do you think we'll stay satisfied if we get much more of that sort of stuff?"

"Wait until you see a miracle worker like Billy Cox," was the response. "He'll finish off the Pacific Coast League all by himself."[58]

For a few years in the mid-forties, the cartel adopted a rule prohibiting major-league broadcasts in minor-league territory.[59] The owners were never committed to the rule, and, as weak as it was, it was emasculated in 1951 and scrapped shortly thereafter. The reaction may have been due in part to a threat of antitrust action by the Justice Department, but it also reflected a desire to increase the majors' revenues from sales of television rights.

While Commissioner Ford Frick might argue that "baseball cannot survive without the minor leagues," the owners did not share his views. And, just as the Los Angeles sportswriter had predicted, the minors were all but killed. In 1949 (before nationally televised games), there had been fifty-nine minor leagues; that number had been reduced to thirty-six by 1954 and, by 1970, to twenty (including three rookie leagues and three located in Mexico). Despite desperate pleas by minor-league owners and executives, to say nothing of a number of suits brought against the cartel by the minors, no action was taken.[60] When Frick resigned in 1965, he was still

57. *New York Times,* Dec. 16, 1964.

58. Quoted by Arthur Daley, *New York Times,* Dec. 9, 1952.

59. Minor-league territory even then was not very large: it was defined as the area within a radius of fifty miles from the home park.

60. In 1959, the Portsmouth, Virginia, club sued the majors for $250,000, and later the same year the Portland, Oregon, club sued for $1,800,000 (*New York Times,* Feb. 10 and July 31, 1959).

saying that the need for a television policy was one of the major problems facing organized baseball. In the meantime, the minor-league problem had taken care of itself—there were no minors left. The problems that remained were ones of financial imbalance within the majors and the direct attendance effects of broadcasts in cities with more than a single franchise. Again, it is difficult to believe that the cartel acted effectively from the point of view of long-term industry profits.

The Cartel Organization

Why did the cartel fail to act effectively in both major market areas? To understand the sources of its weakness an examination of the cartel's structure is useful. The cartel was established by the National Agreement in 1903. A national commission was to be the supreme tribunal of baseball, and all clubs agreed to abide by its decisions. The commission had three members. The presidents of the National and American Leagues were to be permanent members and together they were to elect annually a third member, who would serve as chairman. The first and only chairman was August Herrmann, the president of the National League Cincinnati Reds, though a long-time friend of the American League. The commission was never very important, nor was it held in very high regard by the majority of club owners. Most of its decisions involved disputes between minor-league clubs, and the chairman's penchant to support the American League was a source of continued unhappiness in the National League. The commission's prestige was so low, in fact, that in 1915 the owners seriously considered abolishing it in order to save the $40,000 that was spent annually on its maintenance. In the words of one critic, "The commission gets little or no trouble from the major leagues and any controversy which they do adjudicate could be settled by compromise among the leagues themselves."[61]

By 1916, the National League was regularly calling for the replacement of Herrmann as chairman, but even the support of three American League clubs was insufficient to oust him. Byron Bancroft (Ban) Johnson was able to retain his American League presidency with the votes of five member clubs, and thus to retain the right to veto any nominee for commission chairman.

61. *New York Times,* Feb. 13, 1915.

The bankruptcy of the commission was well known, but it was particularly well demonstrated in the 1918 dispute over Scott Perry, a player claimed by both the Philadelphia A's of the American League and the Boston Braves of the National. The commission awarded Perry to Boston, but Ban Johnson took strong exception. With the league president's support, the A's enjoined the commission from putting its decision into effect, despite the rule that all commission decisions were final and that each club in signing the agreement gave up its right of appeal to the courts. The inability of the commission to function or to force the American League to accept its decisions caused John K. Tener, the National League president, to resign.[62]

The depth of the schism within the cartel is evident in Johnson's response to the suggestion that Tener might resign: "From advice I have received from several sources, that course is absolutely necessary for the welfare of baseball. . . ."[63] In 1919 even August Herrmann recognized that the commission had to be strengthened, and in the best interests of baseball he resigned as chairman. But his resignation did not solve the problem. Johnson and his five American League allies continued to veto every proposed chairman. As a result, for two years—years that saw the Black Sox scandal—the commission was totally paralyzed. For example, in 1919, Carl Mays, a Boston pitcher, walked off the field in Chicago and said he would never play for the team again. Ultimately the Red Sox traded him to the Yankees. Johnson, incensed at a player's refusal to play, suspended Mays, but the Yankees still used him in a number of ball games. At the end of the season, the Tigers claimed that the New York club should be forced to forfeit its victories because of its illegal behavior. With those wins the Yanks were third in the league; without them they would have finished below the Detroit club. Neither the league nor the commission could arbitrate the dispute, and it was months before the third-place winner in the American League race was determined.[64] The post–First World War period thus saw a return to a situation not unlike the war that existed before 1903. Individual clubs openly signed players in violation of the cartel rules, the American League again moved to capitalize on the weakness of the National League, and even the once solid American

62. Ibid., July 10 and Aug. 7, 1918.
63. Ibid., July 10, 1918.
64. Ibid., Nov. 6, Nov. 7, and Dec. 17, 1919; Feb. 11, 1920. Carl Mays may be the sole example of a player who, once signed to a contract, was still able to bargain his way onto another team.

League was divided into squabbling camps, with clubs willing to take advantage of each other despite the reduction of industry profits. Baseball was hardly an example of an effectively run cartel.

The Pressures for a Strong Commissioner

The National League owners had already gone on record as favoring a single impartial commissioner with arbitrary power to rule the sport.[65] Despite the strong opposition of Ban Johnson, they were joined by the owners of the New York, Boston, and Chicago franchises in the American League (all having at one time or another experienced Johnson's wrath). It is hard to predict what would have happened had it not been for the Chicago Black Sox scandal (when eight players confessed to accepting bribes to throw the 1919 World Series), but that event encouraged the three dissident teams to threaten to withdraw from the American League and join the eight National League clubs in a single new major league. It was this nascent league that first offered Kenesaw Mountain Landis, a federal judge in Chicago, the position of commissioner. With public opinion focused on gambling and with his teams in revolt, Johnson and the five American League owners were coerced into supporting the restructuring of professional baseball. The administrative rules of the game were rewritten and most of the cartel decision-making authority lodged in the hands of a single czar.[66] Landis was appointed to that position, and he opened his offices in Chicago early in 1921.

The public reaction to the Black Sox scandal was powerful enough to scare the owners and force them into surrendering much of their power to Landis, but even Landis was certainly on the owners' team. Despite the extreme pressures of the time, the owners chafed against the restraints put upon them, and it was only the threat of public reaction to his resignation that kept them from withdrawing some of his powers. The new organizational rules (contained in the Major League Agreement and implemented in the Major League Rules) granted the commissioner very broad powers indeed. He could rule on any practice suspected of being "detrimental to baseball," and from his decision there was no appeal (the owners agreeing never to appeal any decision to the courts). The rules provided for an advisory council, but the commissioner was not required to solicit their advice and there is no record that Landis ever did.

65. Ibid., Jan. 3, 1919.
66. *Organized Baseball*, H. Rept. 2002, p. 59.

By 1926, the owners had already begun to chafe under Landis's "arbitrary" rules. They argued that he should at least meet with his advisory board, which until then he had never done.[67] The next year they gave expression to their discontent by electing Landis's old enemy Ban Johnson to the board. Moreover, for the first time there was open talk of revising the commissioner's job, and Jacob Ruppert of the Yankees went so far as to announce that he was in favor of restricting the commissioner's powers.

Still, during most of Landis's tenure, the owners, while discontented, were not in open revolt. With the exception of the farm-system case, they seldom moved openly against his decisions. In the 1940s, they again attempted to revitalize the executive council (previously the advisory board) by increasing its membership, officially empowering it to advise the commissioner, and requiring that it meet at least once each quarter. Although there is little evidence that it did much to alter the commissioner's decisions, at least for the first time there was an official institutional structure that paralleled the commissioner's office.

With Landis's death, the owners moved quickly to reassert control. First, they made it more difficult to elect a commissioner. Where before a simple majority vote was sufficient, the agreement was amended in 1945 to require twelve (out of sixteen) affirmative votes, and in the early sixties that was changed to three-quarters of the votes in each league. Second, the owners released themselves from their pledge not to appeal the commissioner's decisions to the courts, and they emasculated the "detrimental-to-baseball" clause, which had provided the basis for many of Landis's most unpopular decisions. While it remained in the agreement, it was amended to read that nothing that was passed by both major leagues could be deemed detrimental. All the commissioner could do was to note his objections and require the teams to vote again at the next joint meeting.[68] With these safeguards the owners felt secure in electing A. B. ("Happy") Chandler to be baseball's second commissioner.

So amended, the Major League Agreement provided the official structure of the cartel in the immediate postwar period. The rules had been rewritten and the owners had shown that they intended to resume control of the sport. Chandler, however, acted as if he still had Landis's supreme powers, and he was less of an "owners' man" than the first commissioner had been. His attitude is suggested by this comment: "I told them (the

67. *New York Times,* Dec. 15, 1926.
68. Ibid., Feb. 3, 1945.

club-owners) that if I ever made an issue of a matter that I said was detrimental to baseball that I would win or they would have a new Commissioner."[69] What he failed to realize was that the owners no longer feared a public reaction to a commissioner's resignation. So confident had they become that they surprised even themselves by firing their second commissioner in 1950.[70] It took almost another year to agree on a third czar. Their choice was Ford C. Frick, long a close associate of the baseball owners, and a man who never doubted that the commissionership was not the job it had been in the days of the Chicago judge.

Frick held the post until his retirement in 1964. During that period he served as an able public relations man and a competent executive. He successfully negotiated for major TV contracts and blunted the congressional attacks of the fifties, but he never attempted autocratic rule. Although he accepted his role, he was not happy with it, and his 1964 retirement statement makes very interesting reading. In it he argued that baseball was in danger of losing its public image, and that the sport had to look no farther than itself to find the causes of its problems. In Frick's words, "So long as the owners and operators refuse to look beyond the day and hour; so long as clubs and individuals persist in gaining personal headlines through public criticism of their associates; so long as baseball people are unwilling to abide by the rules which they themselves make; so long as expediency is permitted to replace sound judgment, there can be no satisfactory solution."[71] To solve these problems, he called on the owners to restore Landis's autocratic powers to his own successor. Frick understood the cartel's failure and he should have understood the character and nature of the owners, but if he thought that his suggestions would be effectively implemented, he clearly misunderstood their goals and desires. Given the publicity attached to his statement, the owners felt compelled to adopt some of his recommendations, but their actions proved that they did not take the reforms seriously.

On paper the owners were willing to make whatever concessions the public demanded, but they had already learned that they could dispose of a commissioner. The 1945 amendments were repealed, but the commissioner was given five deputies to handle specific areas. Lee MacPhail (the former president of the Orioles) was put in charge of top-level administration, and other deputies were authorized for public relations, radio

69. Ibid., July 13, 1945.
70. Ibid., Dec. 12, 1950.
71. Ibid., Nov. 6, 1964.

and television, players' pensions and other matters involving working conditions, and liaison with the amateur leagues, including the Little League.[72]

In theory, the commissioner was now free to concentrate on judicial matters, although these were not specified. With these changes, the owners selected William D. Eckert, a retired Air Force lieutenant general, as their fourth commissioner.[73] Eckert was not, in fact, an adequate spokesman even for the owners. He served three years, and almost his only noteworthy action was his announcement that the majors would not be ready to expand for at least ten years, an announcement he made only weeks before the owners voted to expand. During his tenure, player relations were turned over to a professional negotiator, supervised not by the commissioner but by an expanded player relations committee that did not include the commissioner among its members.[74] Although Eckert had been hired on a seven-year contract, the owners dismissed him in 1968 after only three years. The office of commissioner had become completely a creature of the owners.

It took the owners three months to find a fifth commissioner, and six months to make his appointment permanent. They reduced his term from seven to four years, thinking, perhaps, of the wasted money in buying up the contract of a commissioner who displeased them. During his term of office, the new commissioner, Bowie Kuhn, has been stripped of his authority in disputes between players and clubs. Moreover, it is a tenure that has seen the owners, against the commissioner's advice, vote to transfer the Washington, D.C., franchise to Arlington, Texas, a move made to accommodate a single owner at a time when the political cost of such a move must be almost immeasurable. The move was sanctioned at a time when the Curt Flood case had still to be reviewed by the Supreme Court and when the reserve clause was still very much in the public eye. It was also a time when Senator Warren Magnuson, the chairman of the Senate Commerce Committee, was still smarting under the treatment his native

72. Ibid., Nov. 18, 1965.
73. Ibid.
74. The committee was made up of Joseph Cronin, president of the American League; Warren Giles, president of the National League; Bowie Kuhn, attorney for baseball; Bing Devine, president of the Mets; Dick Myer, president of the Cardinals; Thomas A. Yawkey, president of the Red Sox; and Jerry Hoffberger, president of the Baltimore Orioles. All in all, it was not a group likely to turn to Eckert for advice (*New York Times,* Aug. 11, 1967).

Seattle had been given. Finally, the move was announced on the day that the Senate Antitrust Subcommittee began hearings on professional basketball owners' petition to extend certain antitrust exemptions of baseball and football to their sport. The baseball owners apparently did not consider it important that the hearings might be widened to include baseball and that they could lose their antitrust exemption. Kenesaw Landis, always attuned to the social and political environment, would have turned over in his grave.

Clearly, the organizational structure adopted by the cartel has not been the most efficient possible for maximizing long-term industry profits. The history of the evolution of the cartel's structure provides some explanation for this deficiency. In 1903, the first cartel was a part of the peace treaty between two warring leagues. There is no way to predict whether a cartel established under conditions of extreme animosity will be very strong (since both sides probably expect that one would try to benefit from the arrangement at the other's expense) or very weak (so that when one side cheats the other will be able to respond by cheating itself), but it is likely that the organization will be at one extreme or another. The baseball cartel was a weak one, and it was as inefficient in dealing with disputes between its members as its authors must have intended. By the early 1920s, when the organization was reconstituted, history had shown that the members had a proclivity to cheat, but that an efficient cartel was potentially very profitable. As a result, it is reasonable to expect that the owners would choose a very strong organizational form, one capable of preventing cheating and accruing those profits. The arrangement actually made was fairly strong, but, given the external pressures that brought about the change (in particular the Black Sox scandal) and the evidence of internal strife within the cartel, it may have been less strong than could be expected. More important, as the scandal receded into the past there was continual pressure to weaken the structure, and the three decades after the death of Landis saw return to an organization hardly stronger than the one that existed in the Black Sox era.

The explanation for this weakening of the cartel probably lies in the peculiar nature of the industry itself. It is, after all, an industry that is characterized by a high degree of income inequality and by a minority of owners who are not particularly profit motivated. Since the rich determine in part the profits of the poor (as Bill Veeck discovered) and friendship is often as important as profits to some owners, it should perhaps not be surprising that the cartel does not operate effectively to redistribute profits.[75] Moreover, since some firms can earn substantial profits even when they give in to the pressures of the players' association, there is considerable internal pressure for settlement of player disputes (when the alternative is loss of game revenues), even though the profits of the majority are substantially reduced by the settlement. When it is the rich who want to settle, they can call upon both friends and those who want favors for support. They can live without a strong commissioner who takes the industry's point of view. It would be interesting to examine the behavior of other cartels to see if income inequality alone leads to weak cartel structure.

Conclusions

Because of the antitrust exemption, the economic decisions of baseball teams are never completely tested in the marketplace. In contrast to its posture toward most other industries not subject to antitrust prosecution, government has not chosen to regulate the sport, and the industry has been left to regulate itself. The Black Sox scandal, as well as the paralysis that characterized the National Commission in those crucial years, suggests that self-regulation left something to be desired in the period before 1920, from the point of view of fans, players, and owners. There is a general presumption that under the aegis of Kenesaw Mountain Landis self-regulation was fairly effective: profits were reasonable and not too inequitably distributed; the fans were convinced that the sport was honest and that their team had a shot at a title, held back only by incompetence on the field and in the front-office management; and the players, if not happy, were at least not in open revolt. Since 1945, however, there has been a gradually increasing public uneasiness, a feeling that something has gone wrong with the national pastime. Congressmen investigate, franchise shifts begin to resemble a vast game of musical chairs, a player strike causes the opening games of a season to be canceled, and teams in one league make major policy decisions without consulting either their peers in the other league or the commissioner.

This chapter has attempted to examine the history of the cartel, to determine how closely the public's view of the sport conforms to reality,

75. How but in terms of friendship can the move of the New York Giants to San Francisco be explained? For a humorous but probably correct version of this story, see Veeck, *The Hustler's Handbook,* pp. 304–07.

and to assess how effective the industry's attempts at self-regulation have been. In general, it appears that the commonly held opinion that the pre-1920 cartel was ineffective is probably correct, that the post-1945 behavior has been even less effective than was supposed, and that the performance during the Landis regime, while better than what preceded and followed it, was not as effective as is generally believed.[76]

As one might expect, the cartel has been most effective when it has pursued policies aimed at transferring income from outside the cartel to a member. At the same time, it has been least effective in dealing with policies that mean gains for some and losses for other members of the cartel. In addition, the owners have proved easily seduced by the vision of short-term profits, and they have opted time and time again for policies that sacrifice long-term for immediate rewards. In practice, this tendency has led to continued cheating on cartel decisions, to the innovation of structures that permit members to circumvent cartel decisions when cheating is difficult, and to continued opposition to rules changes that would effect more equitable distribution of players and revenues.

The areas of most noticeable cartel success (in terms of industry profit maximization) have included players' salaries, relations with the minor leagues, and, to a lesser extent, broadcasting rights. History suggests that the cartel has managed to hold player salaries substantially below the levels that would have prevailed under competitive bargaining. (Recently, however, their effectiveness in this area has been limited by the rise of a militant players' association.) Before the reorganization of the 1920s, minor-league teams accrued a fraction of the value of a player through signing players and then selling them to the majors. This fraction almost certainly increased during the 1920s as the leading minors refused to participate in the draft. Here, the cartel moved efficiently, if not swiftly. In the case of broadcasting rights, joint cartel bargaining has led to some lucrative contracts, but the refusal of some clubs to surrender control over their own games certainly delayed successful negotiations and probably produced prices below what could have been extracted by a united front.

The areas of cartel failure have also been substantial. First, the organization did not begin to move toward equalization of player strengths until the early 1960s, and it was another three years before a free-agent draft was undertaken. The system that existed in 1909, characterized by free minor-league drafting, coupled with a stringent limit on the number of

76. The conclusions reached in this chapter on the regime of Commissioner Landis are similar to those reached by Seymour in *Baseball: The Golden Age*.

minor-league players a major-league team could have under option, must have tended to produce more balanced playing strengths. However, the development of the farm system (pushed through over the opposition of Commissioner Landis) and changes in the draft rules designed to permit the loading of good players on a single minor-league team clearly meant the end of the possibility of balance. Second, in the competition for new players, the cartel acted with almost unbelievable slowness in halting the bonus wars that cost the majors an estimated $12 million between the end of the Second World War and the mid-1960s. Since some cartel members felt they could gain at the expense of the others, they resisted any changes in the rules aimed at banning bonus payments, and they emasculated such rules as were passed. Third, the cartel has done little to produce a more equal distribution of profits. The result is not only unprofitable franchises but also noncompetitive teams, and such teams must be a drag on the long-run profits of even the most profitable franchises. A national television contract was a move in the direction of more equality, but the failure to give visiting teams a share of local broadcasting receipts leaves teams with small network areas at the mercy of those with large ones, and may account for a significant proportion of the franchise shifts that have occurred in the past two decades.[77] Fourth, the very high rate at which owners appear to discount future income has produced a broadcasting policy—or nonpolicy—that has killed the minor leagues, the source of future major-league playing talent. The average major-league team now pays more than $1 million a year—almost as much as it receives for the broadcasts that necessitated subsidies of this magnitude—to support the remnants of the minor leagues so that the training of players can continue. Finally, the incessant franchise shuffling of the past few years has reduced fan interest, almost split the cartel apart, and produced an immeasurable amount of political ill will on Capitol Hill (where a quick end could be put to baseball's antitrust exemption if the sport should lose congressional support). It is difficult to imagine, for example, what economic calculus could have produced the recent move of the Washington Senators to Arlington, Texas.

Turning for a moment from the industry itself, what can be said about the nature of cartels in general? First, it appears that cartels whose members do not share equally in the earnings of the industry behave considerably differently than cartels in which they do. Since almost all change is likely to involve some income redistribution among the cartel members,

77. A division of such receipts would not guarantee equality of playing strengths any more than a sharing of gate receipts does, but it would reduce the differentials.

there is a great reluctance to make any changes. Moreover, there appears to be a tendency in this situation to create a loose cartel structure to protect the income of the rich from the deliberate attempts by the poor to redistribute it or from attempts by the cartel itself to adopt measures that, while increasing cartel income, reduce the income of the wealthy.

Second, not only does potential income redistribution appear to interfere with the ability of the cartel to innovate, but also there appear to be forces at work that tend to produce slow innovation even when income is nearly equally shared. Only when all the members of the winning coalition within the cartel are not averse to risk will there be an attempt to make risky innovations. In contrast, only one firm in a noncartelized industry must be willing to innovate to insure that, if the change is successful, the remainder will be forced to follow. The successful cartel has no incentive to take risks, while voluntary associations that are trying to cartelize an industry or to make the industry they have cartelized more profitable may be willing to assume such risks. Thus, the American League in 1900–03 moved quickly into potentially profitable geographical areas not served by the National League and innovated long-term player contracts that aided them in recruiting from the established leagues. The National Football League, while attempting to establish a profitable market for its sport, adopted both interleague play and divisional playoffs— schemes that had been suggested for baseball at the turn of the century but never adopted. It was the American Football League that adopted two-point conversions and the American Basketball Association that adopted the three-point long shot, each attempting to capture a share of the market from the established leagues in their sports. The lagging National League in the late 1940s and early 1950s first brought up numerous black ballplayers, and, more recently, the badly suffering American League has finally taken a step toward two-platoon baseball (introduced in football by the NFL thirty years before).

The cartel's antitrust exemption has not produced the behavior that was predicted. One would expect that immunity from antitrust prosecution would have led to a strong cartel, able to move swiftly and effectively against owners attempting to undercut industry profits. Such has not been the case. In fact, the football cartel, which has a very limited exemption, has been far more efficient even in areas not covered by its exemption than has the baseball organization. Moreover, one would assume that exemption should be an asset highly valued by the cartel, but baseball has behaved as if its exemption had no value at all. Whether this attitude is typical of all cartels whose owners have long exercised monopoly power without external threat, or whether it is an aberration produced by the peculiar nature of the baseball industry itself, remains to be discovered.

Clearly, the industry's attempts at self-regulation cannot be given very high marks, but what are the alternatives? A judicial or legislative repeal of the antitrust exemption would certainly result in an increase in players' salaries and force the teams to behave in a more economically efficient manner. What effect it would have on entry is less clear, but there might be another major league before adjustment was complete. On the other hand, professional football has shown that a partial antitrust exemption produces relatively few benefits for players or fans if the cartel is an effective one. In the case of baseball, if the shock of such a legal change turned the cartel into one that resembled that of professional football, the only gainers might well be the club owners.

Government regulation has been suggested, although there is no theory that predicts what the results of such direct regulation would be. However, judging from the effects of regulation on railroads, trucking, and the airlines, it is hard to believe that either the players or the fans are apt to benefit. The cartel's major problem has been the unwillingness of certain members to go along with joint decisions, and government regulatory bodies do have legal powers to enforce such decisions.

Finally, it has been suggested that all franchises be owned by local nonprofit corporations, but it is difficult to see how this change would make any substantial difference. There is no reason to believe that public bodies are interested in effecting a redistribution of power and income in favor of the players or that maximizing directors' salaries is not a major goal. Here again, theory is not very useful, but the performance of the Amateur Athletic Union and the U.S. Olympic Committee in running amateur athletics does not inspire confidence in the ability of a similar organizational structure to solve the problems of professional sports.

In sum, then, it appears that a total repeal of the antitrust exemption might—from the point of view of public and players—produce the most desirable results. Failing that, letting the present fractured and relatively ineffective cartel continue to operate may be as much in the public interest as any of the alternative policy suggestions.

Kenesaw Mountain Landis, like Pete Rozelle in football, recognized how a cartel should operate if it was to effectively maximize industry profits. Unlike Rozelle, he was not always successful in pushing the owners along that path, but for a quarter of a century he did manage to save those owners from themselves. Lately they have not been so lucky.

CHAPTER ELEVEN

Sports Leagues and the Federal Antitrust Laws

STEVEN R. RIVKIN

APPLYING the antitrust laws to professional sports, like any attempt to push a square peg through a round hole, is bound to be troublesome. When the act to protect trade and commerce—the Sherman Antitrust Act— became law in 1890,[1] there was no hint that its expansive terms might have a diminished reach. The broad aims of the act were summed up by the Supreme Court in later years:

The Sherman Act was designed to be a comprehensive charter of economic liberty aimed at preserving free and unfettered competition as the rule of trade. It rests on the premise that the unrestrained interaction of competitive forces will yield the best allocation of our economic resources, the lowest prices, the highest quality and the greatest material progress, while at the same time producing an environment conducive to the preservation of our democratic political and social institutions. But even were that premise open to question, the policy unequivocally laid down by the Act is competition.[2]

1. The principal substantive provisions of the Sherman Act (26 Stat. 209; 15 U.S.C. secs. 1–7) are now as follows:

Sec. 1. Every contract, combination in the form of trust or otherwise, or conspiracy, in restraint of trade or commerce among the several States, or with foreign nations, is declared to be illegal. . . . Every person who shall make any contract or engage in any combination or conspiracy declared . . . to be illegal shall be deemed guilty of a misdemeanor. . . .

Sec. 2. Every person who shall monopolize, or attempt to monopolize, or combine or conspire with any other person or persons, to monopolize any part of the trade or commerce among the several States, or with foreign nations, shall be deemed guilty of a misdemeanor. . . .

Other statutes considered to fall within the body of antitrust laws (the Clayton Act [38 Stat. 735], the Federal Trade Commission Act [38 Stat. 717], the Lanham Act [69 Stat. 427], the Robinson-Patman Act [49 Stat. 1526]) are not pertinent to professional sports.

2. *Northern Pacific Railway Co.* v. *United States,* 356 U.S. 1, 4 (1958).

Despite its comprehensive sweep, the Sherman Act's application as a standard of control over the economy has regularly turned on an exercise of judicial judgment as to the practical meaning to be given to the act's unequivocal words. In *Northern Pacific,* the Court recognized that, though the statute's prohibition "is literally all encompassing, the courts have construed it as precluding only those contracts or combinations which 'unreasonably' restrain competition."[3]

Determining the elusive standard of "reasonableness" for a practice being challenged under the antitrust laws has become the central function of the courts. With respect to competition in professional sports, the courts have long recognized that the structural conditions of sports are unique. A district court, in a case that struck down certain restrictive practices on the part of the National Football League (NFL) in pooled radio and television sales, verbalized this uniqueness as follows:

Professional football is a unique type of business. Like other professional sports which are organized on a league basis it has problems which no other business has. The ordinary business makes every effort to sell as much of its product or services as it can. In the course of doing this it may and often does put many of its competitors out of business. The ordinary businessman is not troubled by the knowledge that he is doing so well that his competitors are being driven out of business.

Professional teams in a league, however, must not compete too well with each other in a business way. On the playing field, of course, they must compete as hard as they can all the time. But it is not necessary and indeed it is unwise for all the teams to compete as hard as they can against each other in a business way. If all the teams should compete as hard as they can in a business way, the stronger teams would be likely to drive the weaker ones into financial failure. If this should happen not only would the weaker teams fail, but eventually the whole league, both the weaker and the stronger teams, would fail, because without a league no team can operate profitably.[4]

These conflicting principles—the Sherman Act's hostility to private restraints on free competition and the practical desirability of joint action to achieve balanced, sustained, and geographically dispersed athletic activity—complicate the relevance of antitrust laws to professional sports and thus undermine their usefulness as a "charter of economic liberty" in this area.

The resulting pattern of application of the laws has by no means been rational. Glaring inconsistencies have emerged, ranging from total exemp-

3. Ibid. at 5.
4. *United States* v. *National Football League,* 116 F. Supp. 319 at 323 (E.D. Pa. 1953).

tion in one sport (baseball)[5] to guarded intrusions where other professional sports are concerned. In some instances, legislative measures have been invoked to achieve relief from the application of the antitrust laws in politically potent areas. A consequence of the unevenness with which the antitrust laws have been applied has been an uncertainty in their relationship to other federal statutes, notably the National Labor Relations Act. This chapter surveys the field of judicial and legislative activity affecting professional sports and, in a concluding section, sets forth some lines of possible future development.

The Baseball Exemption

Despite the illogic of a definition that starts with a negative, the exemption of baseball from the antitrust laws is a useful and timely point of departure for examining all professional sports. This is so not only for historic reasons—baseball being the professional sport where the first effort was made to apply the antitrust laws—but also because the enduring exemption of the "national pastime" conveys a sense of the intense controversy surrounding the issue. Curt Flood's unsuccessful effort to overturn baseball's antitrust immunity has given fresh life to an anomaly of long standing.

Beginning with *Federal Baseball Club* v. *National League,* professional baseball has enjoyed a total exemption from the antitrust laws, though not without recurring efforts to reverse the situation. In *Federal Baseball,* the Baltimore club of the Federal League sued the American and National Leagues for the treble damages enunciated in the Sherman Act as recompense for "any person . . . injured in his business or property by reason of anything forbidden in the antitrust laws. . . ."[6] Baltimore claimed that the defendants had caused the Federal League to collapse by deliberate efforts to buy out its other members. In an opinion by Justice Oliver Wendell Holmes, the Supreme Court construed baseball exhibitions to be beyond the reach of the antitrust law since they were "purely state affairs" not within federal jurisdiction over interstate commerce. The movement of players across state lines was viewed as "a mere incident, not the essen-

5. Recently reaffirmed by the Supreme Court in *Curtis C. Flood* v. *Bowie K. Kuhn et al.,* 407 U.S. 258 (1972), *aff'g* and 443 F.2d 264 (2d Cir., 1971), 316 F. Supp. 271 (S.D.N.Y. 1970).
6. 15 U.S.C. sec. 15.

tial thing."[7] The opinion came to rest on a homely analogy of baseball competition to "a firm of lawyers sending out a member to argue a case, or the Chautauqua lecture bureau sending out lecturers."[8] Thus, baseball was originally removed from antitrust coverage by a constitutional rationale quite characteristic of that conservative era, but one whose limited reach was soon read out of the mainstream of Supreme Court jurisprudence during the New Deal struggles over control of the economy.

While the decision in *Federal Baseball* has been roundly damned— Judge Henry J. Friendly more recently called it "not one of Mr. Justice Holmes' happiest days"[9]—it has never been overruled. Despite the breakdown of the jurisdictional limits upon the reach of federal power over commerce in other fields of economic activity,[10] the Court has not followed suit with respect to baseball.

It would be logical that the Supreme Court might have found occasion to reverse itself or quietly to sanction a reversal in lower courts. A reexamination of *Federal Baseball* was actually begun in *Gardella* v. *Chandler*,[11] which overturned a district court's refusal to hear the plaintiff's antitrust claims when the reserve clause was invoked to bar his return to organized baseball after he had spent a season playing professionally in Mexico. One appellate judge, Learned Hand, thought the district court should weigh the effect on commerce of radio and television coverage of baseball, which had vastly increased the economic role of the sport. Another, Jerome Frank, thought the Supreme Court decisions on the expanded scope of the commerce power had already dictated reversal, that the reserve clause was an "illegality," and that "no court should strive ingeniously to legalize a private (even if benevolent) dictatorship."[12]

Before the trial, Gardella's suspension was lifted by agreement and the litigation was terminated. Judge Frank's confidence notwithstanding, the parties' decision to avoid further litigation turned out to be a fortunate choice for Gardella, since the Supreme Court soon confounded its ob-

7. 259 U.S. 200 at 208–09 (1922).

8. Ibid. at 209.

9. *Salerno* v. *American League of Professional Baseball Clubs,* 429 F.2d 1003 at 1005 (2d Cir. 1970).

10. For example, in *Wickard, Secretary of Agriculture* v. *Filburn,* 317 U.S. 111 (1942), produce grown and consumed on the farm was held to fall under federal crop controls, and in *United States* v. *South-Eastern Underwriters Association,* 322 U.S. 533 (1944), the Sherman Act was applied to fire insurance companies despite repeated early assertions that "insurance is not commerce."

11. 172 F.2d 402 (2d Cir. 1949).

12. 172 F.2d at 415.

servers by bluntly reaffirming *Federal Baseball* in its next review of a challenge to the reserve clause, *Toolson* v. *New York Yankees*.[13] The Court gave short shrift to the arguments that the changing nature of the game and the Court's prior opinions about interstate commerce made it time for *Federal Baseball* to be reversed:

> ... Congress has had the ruling [in *Federal Baseball*] under consideration but has not seen fit to bring such business under these laws by legislation having prospective effect. The business has thus been left for thirty years to develop, on the understanding that it was not subject to existing antitrust legislation. The present cases ask us to overrule the prior decision and, with retrospective effect, hold the legislation applicable. We think that if there are evils in this field which now warrant application to it of the antitrust laws it should be by legislation. Without re-examination of the underlying issues, the judgments ... are affirmed on the authority of *Federal Baseball* ... so far as that decision determined that Congress had no intention of including the business of baseball within the scope of the federal antitrust laws.[14]

On the failure of Congress to challenge its earlier opinion for a generation the Court built a renewed justification for exemption, based on a construction of Congress's presumed intent rather than on any requirements of the Constitution or the wording of the law. In the Court's reasoning, the growth of the game over the years, proposed by the plaintiff as grounds for the extension of federal power, became a sufficient reason for curbing its exercise. The Court merely sought to avoid an unjust retroactive impact on the web of valuable relationships that had grown up assuming antitrust exemption. From a distance, the Court's concern seems overdrawn, since retroactive application could easily have been avoided, had the Court taken pains to do so. Instead, the Court sidestepped any prospect that it might itself have to fashion the rules to govern organized baseball, and passed the buck to Congress, whose indifference to the baseball exemption was already patently obvious.

Further explanation of this strained but expedient logic was given in *Radovich* v. *National Football League*,[15] which placed professional football within the antitrust laws and thus made it necessary that the existing exemption of baseball be distinguished. To meet the claim that bringing football under the antitrust laws might seem "unrealistic, inconsistent, or illogical" in the light of *Toolson*'s holding—about which it was, at last, freely confessed that "were we considering the question of baseball for

13. 346 U.S. 356 (1953).
14. Ibid. at 357.
15. 352 U.S. 445 (1957).

the first time upon a clean slate we would have no doubts"[16]—the Court offered the following justification for its continued deference to a legislative course of reversal:

We, therefore, conclude that the orderly way to eliminate error or discrimination, if any there be, is by legislation and not by court decision. Congressional processes are more accommodative, affording the whole industry hearings and an opportunity to assist in the formulation of new legislation. The resulting product is therefore more likely to protect the industry and the public alike. The whole scope of congressional action would be known long in advance and effective dates for the legislation could be set in the future without the injustices of retroactivity and surprise which might follow court action.[17]

Whether or not one is disposed to join with the critics of the Court in faulting it for inaction, the outcome of the Court's *Toolson* decision has not been overturned by the Congress. It is clear that, since 1953, Congress has been reluctant to close the loophole, despite more than forty days of testimony in at least five separate sets of hearings prior to the Ninety-second Congress[18] and consideration of more than fifty separate bills.[19] In fact, the only two pieces of relevant legislation that have passed either house both provided for continuing exemptions of professional league sports with respect to "the employment, selection, or eligibility of players, or the reservation, selection, or assignment of player contracts."[20] A con-

16. Ibid. at 452.
17. Ibid.
18. Cited in Post-Trial Memorandum of All Defendants Other Than Bowie K. Kuhn, in *Flood* v. *Kuhn,* reported at 316 F. Supp. 271 (S.D.N.Y. 1970).
19. In the *Flood* decision, the Supreme Court cites the following parade of inconclusive legislative deliberation (407 U.S. at 281, note 17): "Hearings on H.R. 5307 et al. before the Antitrust Subcommittee of the House Committee on the Judiciary, 85th Cong., 1st Sess. (1957); Hearings on H.R. 10378 and S. 4070 before the Subcommittee on Antitrust and Monopoly of the Senate Committee on the Judiciary, 85th Cong., 2d Sess. (1958); Hearings on H.R. 2370 et al. before the Antitrust Subcommittee of the House Committee on the Judiciary, 86th Cong., 1st Sess. (1959) (not printed); Hearings on S. 616 and S. 886 before the Subcommittee on Antitrust and Monopoly of the Senate Committee on the Judiciary, 86th Cong., 1st Sess. (1959); Hearings on S. 3483 before the Subcommittee on Antitrust and Monopoly of the Senate Committee on the Judiciary, 86th Cong., 2d Sess. (1960); Hearings on S. 2391 before the Subcommittee on Antitrust and Monopoly of the Senate Committee on the Judiciary, 88th Cong., 2d Sess. (1964); S. Rep. No. 1303, 88th Cong., 2d Sess. (1964); Hearings on S. 950 before the Subcommittee on Antitrust and Monopoly of the Senate Committee on the Judiciary, 89th Cong., 1st Sess. (1965); S. Rep. No. 462, 89th Cong., 1st Sess. (1965). Bills introduced in the 92d Cong., 1st Sess., and bearing on the subject are S. 2599, S. 2616, H.R. 2305, H.R. 11033, and H.R. 10825."
20. H.R. 10378, 85 Cong. 2 sess. (1958), and S. 950, 89 Cong. 1 sess. (1965).

gressional consensus for exemption from the antitrust laws, at least concerning the reserve clause issue in *Toolson,* thus could still be inferred.

Construing Congress's intent is an exercise that often skates on the edge of reality. This has been particularly so with respect to baseball's exemption from the federal antitrust laws. The Supreme Court as much as acknowledged in *Toolson* that it "got off on the wrong foot" in *Federal Baseball* but that, if the course were now reversed, economic interests with a powerful hold on the public imagination and evident congressional support would have to be displaced. Indeed, the perturbations caused by *Federal Baseball* and *Toolson* are now so pronounced that bizarre ramifications have followed at the state level: in *Wisconsin* v. *Milwaukee Braves, Inc.*,[21] for example, a state court narrowly held that Wisconsin's antitrust statute could not be used to bar a franchise movement. The court reasoned that uniform national regulation is required, so that Congress's silence must therefore express a federal determination that the business of baseball should not be regulated at any level.[22] Thus, while the intended implication of *Federal Baseball* was probably that baseball, as an intrastate sport, could only be regulated locally, the growth of the sport since 1922 has become the basis on which the possibility of state control was entirely eliminated as a means of restraint against competitive abuse.

With the Congress unyielding as a source of redress, those who would bring baseball under antitrust controls could only turn again to the courts to try to show that baseball's exemption had become an ever-increasing anomaly that could and should be eliminated. The *Flood* case was the maximum effort in this regard, starring Curt Flood (universally acknowledged to be "a grand little center fielder," according to Red Smith's description) as plaintiff,[23] and Arthur J. Goldberg (the former colleague on the Supreme Court of four sitting justices) as attorney. A 2,000-page record of testimony was submitted. Yet, despite the strength of the effort

21. 31 Wis. 2d 699, 144 N.W.2d 1 (Wis. 1966), *cert. denied,* 385 U.S. 990 (1966), *rehearing denied,* ibid. at 1044.

22. In denying relief sought by Curt Flood, the Supreme Court quoted with favor the following appeals court holding, again putting the prospect of state jurisdiction to rest: "[A]s the burden on interstate commerce outweighs the states' interest in regulating baseball's reserve system, the Commerce Clause precludes the application here of state antitrust law" (407 U.S. at 284, citing 433 F.2d at 268). Two months earlier, the Court of Appeals for the Ninth Circuit refused to bar a suit brought by a state in a state court under state law (*Washington* v. *American League of Professional Baseball Clubs,* 460 F.2d 654 [9th Cir. 1972])—a result *Flood* would appear to have undermined.

23. *New York Times,* June 21, 1972.

and some advance judicial encouragement capable of wishful interpretation,[24] the weight of the status quo proved too heavy to move.

The Supreme Court's grant of certiorari (an undertaking to review that does not require a majority vote) in the *Flood* case appeared to give the advocates of antitrust coverage new hope, but the eventual repudiation of Flood's challenge, in a five-to-three loss, was no less decisive for having been close. Once again, five decades of self-imposed restraint were continued for the future, a result wholly in accordance with a conservative view of judicial prerogative. For the Supreme Court to have done otherwise would, indeed, have placed the Court deep within the controversy over conditions and terms of employment in organized baseball—an area where the burdens on the Court would have been all the more severe for having been so long postponed.

In this context, the majority holding by Justice Harry A. Blackmun should have surprised no one with its conclusion: "We continue to be loath, 50 years after *Federal Baseball* and almost two decades after *Toolson,* to overturn those cases judicially when Congress, by its positive inaction, has allowed those decisions to stand for so long and, far beyond mere inference and implication, has clearly evinced a desire not to disapprove them legislatively."[25] The Court based its holding on a finding of "positive inaction" by the Congress—a semantic contradiction, which Justice Thurgood Marshall challenged in dissent,[26] but one whose factual correctness cannot be denied. Underneath some verbal ornamentation by Justice Blackmun, this premise is now the rock on which baseball's legal status has come to rest.

Emphasizing the Court's adamant refusal to reverse its abstention from the baseball controversy, Justice Blackmun indicated that the court was

24. In *Salerno* v. *American League,* 429 F.2d 1003 (2d Cir. 1970), *cert. denied,* 400 U.S. 1001 (1970), the court affirmed the dismissal of an antitrust claim brought by discharged umpires. The court—about to become embroiled in the *Flood* case— echoed the criticism of the baseball exemption but declined to anticipate, at an intermediate level, Supreme Court reversal. It said:

. . . We continue to believe that the Supreme Court should retain the exclusive privilege of overruling its own decisions, save perhaps when opinions already delivered have created a near certainty that only the occasion is needed for pronouncement of the doom. While we should not fall out of our chairs with surprise at the news that *Federal Baseball* and *Toolson* had been overruled, we are not at all certain the Court is ready to give them a happy dispatch (429 F.2d at 1005).

25. 407 U.S. at 283–84.

26. Justice Marshall thought that congressional acquiescence in judicial application of the antitrust laws to other sports could be read as an invitation to the courts to apply consistent treatment to baseball (407 U.S. 288 at 292).

continuing to adhere to the doctrines of *International Boxing* and *Rado-vich* (discussed below), which apply antitrust standards to other sports. Whatever "inconsistency and illogic" there is in this approach, he said, is of such "long standing that [it] is to be remedied by the Congress and not by this Court," and is, indeed, balanced by consistency in the Court's own position over time.[27] From this position, the Court has thus reiterated its refusal to budge, repudiating once again the availability of antitrust remedies in the baseball field.

Antitrust Restraints in Other Sports

The principal efforts to impose federal antitrust restraints on professional sports clubs have centered on the role of individual players in organized competition. This issue is discussed first, while the next section considers the antitrust problems involved in relationships among competitive teams.

Antitrust and Player-Team Relations

Deliberate cooperation among teams in acquiring, training, and utilizing players is to some extent an essential aspect of organized athletics. In the absence of artificial barriers (such as baseball's jurisdictional exemption[28]), professional sports are fully subject to statutory prohibitions against contracts, combinations, and conspiracies that restrain trade. Specifically, three aspects of team control of individuals have been brought under antitrust scrutiny: systems for the recruitment and entry of players

27. 407 U.S. at 284.

28. The requirement of establishing that an activity has a prohibited effect on interstate commerce has virtually dropped out of antitrust cases involving organized sports. In the 1950s, the original jurisdictional exemption for baseball was confined to that sport by the Supreme Court's rulings in *United States* v. *International Boxing Club of New York,* 348 U.S. 236 (1955), and *Radovich* v. *National Football League.* Today, even in cases where a valid question might be raised, the involvement of interstate commerce is beyond contention: see, for example, *Bridge Corporation of America* v. *American Contract Bridge League, Inc.,* 428 F.2d 1365 (9th Cir. 1970), *cert. denied,* 401 U.S. 940 (1971) (defendant refused to permit use of a scoring computer), and *STP Corporation* v. *U.S. Auto Club, Inc.,* 286 F. Supp. 146 (S.D. Ind. 1968) (entry barred by defendant's safety standards). Incidentally, in *Flood* the Supreme Court gave a decent burial to the commerce rationale by holding professional baseball to be a business engaged in interstate commerce (407 U.S. at 283–84).

of team sports (the "draft"), controls governing player mobility ("reserve" and "option" contract clauses), and rules on individual eligibility and participation in other activities.

All three areas reflect forms of organized control over individual players that are intended to be responsive to the economic conditions unique to particular sports. As such, however, they resemble the kinds of group economic activity—contracts, combinations, and conspiracies—roundly condemned by the courts when they are shown to be in restraint of trade. The restrictions written into player contracts are effective because of the agreement among teams not to compete for players and to use a uniform contract. This collective agreement by teams closely resembles restrictions placed by trade associations on the conduct of competitors, such as the agreement of filmmakers to act jointly vis-à-vis motion picture exhibitors that was condemned in *Paramount Famous Lasky Corporation* v. *United States*,[29] and the division of markets among competitors with the aim of fixing prices, struck down in *United States* v. *Socony-Vacuum Oil Co.*[30]

To the extent that the accomplishment of group purposes involves collective action to enforce compliance, sanctions imposed against individual players closely resemble a group boycott, which has been condemned as a restraint of trade in *Fashion Originators' Guild* and *Klor's, Inc.*[31] The Supreme Court has found group boycotts to be violations of the Sherman Act because of the damage joint action does to competition. In fact, in the *Fashion Originators'* and *Klor's* cases, where boycotts were established, the Court expressly discarded the need to establish "unreasonableness" with respect to the impact on competition (the standard derived from *Northern Pacific*), finding a "per se" violation in any concerted refusal to deal. Such practices, the Court has held, cannot be justified by *any* motive or ultimate goal, however reasonable.

Whether a case can qualify under this per se rule has come to mean the difference between a viable antitrust claim and a lawsuit that, even if it can be won, is so protracted and expensive that it is usually not worth pursuing. This is because the elimination of the need to uncover the busi-

---

29. 282 U.S. 30 (1930).

30. 310 U.S. 150 (1940) .

31. *Fashion Originators' Guild of America* v. *Federal Trade Commission*, 312 U.S. 457 (1941), found a boycott by sellers against buyers purchasing competing brands to be illegal; *Klor's, Inc.* v. *Broadway-Hale Stores, Inc.*, 359 U.S. 207 (1959), produced a similar ruling on a boycott by buyers against sellers dealing with competing buyers.

ness justification offered by every challenged practice—the question of reasonableness—radically simplifies the problem of proving that the practice is, in fact, a "contract, combination . . . or conspiracy, in restraint of trade."[32] *Klor's* turned on the defendant's effort to require proof that its acts had the purpose of influencing prices, quality, or quantity of goods available to the public. The Supreme Court felt that a group boycott was beyond the pale of justification, simply because

[it] interferes with the natural flow of interstate commerce. It clearly has, by its "nature" and "character," a monopolistic tendency. As such it is not to be tolerated merely because the victim is just one merchant whose business is so small that his destruction makes little difference to the economy. Monopoly can as surely thrive by the elimination of such small businessmen, one at a time, as it can by driving them out in large groups. In recognition of this fact the Sherman Act has consistently been read to forbid all contracts and combinations which tend to create a monopoly, whether the tendency is a creeping one or one that proceeds at full gallop.[33]

In that case, a retailer used its purchasing power to extract commitments from equipment manufacturers that they would not sell to a competing retailer, or would sell only on less advantageous terms. When a player of an organized professional sport is faced with a similar requirement, similarly enforced by a concerted refusal to deal, that he abide by league-imposed restraints or be barred from participation, the outlines of what is commonly called a group boycott are plain.

Thus, many of the cooperative structural arrangements that make professional sports activity possible are presumably in per se violation of antitrust laws because of the coercive combinations that give them power. Even the office of league commissioner, though instituted to guarantee fair application of restrictive rules, does not remove such joint boycotts from the list of prohibited practices.

Again, however, the literal force of the antitrust laws has been tempered by judicial restrictions. The process of qualification reached its peak in *Silver, Doing Business as Municipal Securities Co. v. New York Stock*

---

32. In *Northern Pacific*, the Supreme Court gave this catalogue of the limited number of situations that have been deemed so harmful to competition as to justify the application of a per se rule: "Among the practices which the courts have heretofore deemed to be unlawful in and of themselves are price fixing, *United States* v. *Socony-Vacuum Oil Co.*, 310 U.S. 150, 210; division of markets, *United States* v. *Addyston Pipe & Steel Co.*, 85 F. 271, *aff'd.*, 175 U.S. 211; group boycotts, *Fashion Originators' Guild* v. *Federal Trade Comm'n*, 312 U.S. 457; and tying arrangements, *International Salt Co.* v. *United States*, 332 U.S. 392" (356 U.S. at 5).

33. 359 U.S. at 213–14.

Exchange,[34] where the Supreme Court retreated from a full application of the per se prohibition in fields where "public policy" has introduced conflicting considerations outside of the mandate of the antitrust laws. *Silver* involved the action of the New York Stock Exchange (essentially an association of competing dealers) in cutting off the private-wire connections of a nonmember securities dealer, allegedly on an arbitrary basis. The Court held that, though the Securities Exchange Act of 1934 granted securities exchanges a limited exemption from antitrust rules for the purpose of managing their own affairs, the denial of a telephone connection without notice or hearing was an arbitrary use of that power, beyond the reach of the exemption, and hence a group boycott in violation of the antitrust laws.

While the *Silver* case concerned the impact of another federal statute on the coverage of the antitrust laws, the Court made clear that its task of reconciling principles of public policy was not limited to situations where two statutes might clash. Upon the initial finding that the Sherman Act would have barred the Exchange's conduct, Justice Goldberg's opinion mandates a further inquiry: "Hence, absent any justification derived from the policy of another statute *or otherwise,* the Exchange acted in violation of the Sherman Act. In this case, however, the presence of another statutory scheme, that of the Securities Exchange Act of 1934, means that such a conclusion is only the beginning, not the end, of inquiry"[35] (emphasis added). The inquiry on which the court thereupon embarked—into "any justification derived from the policy of another statute *or otherwise*"— proceeded to analyze the requirement for self-regulation dictated by the structure of securities markets. Had the reasonableness of the Exchange's action been established, there would have been no antitrust violation, but the way in which the Exchange conducted itself brought it within the statute's reach.

While no similar statute permits self-regulation for professional sports, a powerful case can be made that the structural requirements of organized competition do just that—do, in other words, what Justice Goldberg meant when he said justification for self-regulation could be found "otherwise" than by statute. That is precisely how at least one court has read his meaning.[36] Thus, the *Silver* case now establishes a framework in which

34. 373 U.S. 341 (1963).
35. Ibid. at 348–49.
36. The Court of Appeals for the Second Circuit, the intermediate court that has heard by far the greatest volume of sports antitrust litigation, drew precisely this

courts are enabled to evaluate the reasonableness of restraints placed upon players. Although the inquiry with respect to reasonableness covers much of the same ground as the examinations that would be required in the absence of a per se rule, the recognition that concerted action represents a group boycott has shifted the burden of justification to the defendant sports association or league. In the context of the practicalities of antitrust litigation, by which the need to discover and shape facts for the court imposes enormous burdens of effort and expense, this shifting of the burden of justification has great significance in making resort to the antitrust courts a useful tool of economic restraint.

Though there have been few occasions thus far to measure the effects of *Silver* on relationships between professional athletes and organized sports, there is no reason, other than the availability of resources and willingness of potential litigants to go to court, why the involvement of courts in player-management disputes should not now increase. Though early cases left no doubt that outright exemption was confined strictly to baseball—both *United States* v. *International Boxing Club of New York, Inc.,*[37] and *Radovich* v. *National Football League* attempted to open up new fields of applicability—these cases were wound up without actually determining the reasonableness of the controls on athletes' activities that were being challenged under the Sherman Act. Since the 1950s, the issue of reasonableness has been proposed in several cases, establishing broad patterns that others will doubtless follow. The principal mileposts are:

• *Molinas* v. *National Basketball Association.*[38] The suspension of a professional basketball player for wagering on the "point spread" of his team's games, imposed through the provisions of the National Basketball Association's reserve clause, was upheld as a reasonable exercise of the Association's inherent powers of self-preservation: "A rule, and a corresponding contract clause, providing for the suspension of those who place

---

inference in deciding a follow-up securities case to *Silver, Cowen* v. *New York Stock Exchange:* "Indeed, even absent a statutory duty of self-regulation such as that under the Securities Exchange Act, similar self-regulatory activities involving refusals to deal have been held not to violate the antitrust laws. See *Deesen* v. *Professional Golfers' Ass'n,* 358 F.2d 165 (9th Cir.), *cert. denied* 385 U.S. 846. . . . (1966)" (371 F.2d 661 at 664 [2d Cir. 1967]). In *Deesen,* discussed below, the need of an association to set criteria for competition was held to justify league restriction on the plaintiff's ability to play.

37. 348 U.S. 236 (1955).
38. 190 F. Supp. 241 (S.D.N.Y. 1961).

wagers on games in which they are participating seems not only reasonable, but necessary for the survival of the league."[39]

• *Washington State Bowling Proprietors Association, Inc.* v. *Pacific Lanes, Inc.*[40] A bowling alley sued a bowling alley association of which it was not a member, claiming that the association's eligibility rules limiting tournament play to bowlers who had qualified in its lanes were unreasonable: "Even assuming that abuses in the sport existed it has been established . . . that such circumstances do not justify a private association passing regulations to deal with the problem when their effect is to restrain or regulate interstate commerce."[41]

• *Deesen* v. *Professional Golfers' Association of America.*[42] The same court held, on the other hand, that the Professional Golfers' Association eligibility requirements for tournaments did not violate the antitrust laws. Deesen's eligibility was terminated after a committee had assessed his performance against objective standards, and opportunities were accorded to prove he was qualified for tournament play. The court found that the eligibility standards were required by the industry structure, that the standards in question were intended to serve this goal flexibly and with reasonable limitations, and that adequate procedural safeguards were present.

• *Denver Rockets* v. *All-Pro Management, Inc.*[43] Basketball superstar Spencer Haywood succeeded in invalidating the draft rules of the National Basketball Association by which basketball players were ineligible for all league play until college graduation or four years after the date they would have graduated from high school. The issue, as framed by the court, was the legality of the Association's rules that prevent "Haywood, a qualified professional basketball player, from contracting with any NBA team, even though he does not desire to, or may not be eligible to, attend college and even though he does not desire to, and is ineligible to, participate in collegiate athletics."[44] The court applied strictly the method and holding of *Silver,* viewing the absence of a requirement or opportunity for a hearing as fatal to the reasonableness of the rule. (The court explained the difference between *Deesen* and *Washington Bowling* by finding a hearing requirement in the former and none in the latter.) It said: "It is clear from the constitution and by-laws of the NBA that there is no provision for even

39. Ibid. at 243.
40. 356 F.2d 371 (9th Cir. 1966), *cert. denied* 384 U.S. 963 (1966).
41. 356 F.2d at 376.
42. 358 F.2d 165 (9th Cir. 1966), *cert. denied* 385 U.S. 846 (1966), *rehearing denied* 385 U.S. 1032.
43. 325 F. Supp. 1049 (C.D. Cal. 1971).
44. Ibid. at 1060–61.

the most rudimentary hearings before the four-year college rule is applied to exclude an individual player. Nor is there any provision whereby an individual player might petition for consideration of his specific case."[45] Though the court was mindful that the four-year requirement played a useful player-development role, it was also moved by the fact that "the rules in question are absolute and prohibit the signing of not only college basketball players but also those who do not desire to attend college and even those who lack the mental and financial ability to do so. As such they are overly broad and thus improper under *Silver*."[46] Both procedural and substantive considerations thus played an important role in the determination that the rules were unreasonable.

Hence, over the years, it is apparent that courts have become willing to examine in detail the justification for challenged practices, finding them reasonable where required by the "economic structure" of organized competition and unreasonable where applied through unfair procedures or with greater breadth than necessary.[47] It may fairly be said that many more cases of judicial intervention will be required before limits to the deliberation will be set, though it is also clear that the path is now open.

An orderly approach to the process of evaluation has been suggested by Justice William J. Brennan, Jr., in his concurring opinion in *White Motor Co.* v. *United States*,[48] a case where territorial restrictions placed by the manufacturers on its distributors were attacked as per se unlawful. The issue was a novel one before the Supreme Court and was not resolved, but Justice Brennan suggested a method of analysis of testimony to be taken at trial, which has recently been applied by the district court in the Spencer Haywood case. Justice Brennan suggested examining whether the challenged restraints are "reasonably related to the needs which brought them into being" and "whether . . . the restraint . . . is more restrictive than necessary, or excessively anticompetitive, when viewed in light of the extenuating interests." In addition, the Court should "explore the availability of less restrictive alternatives."[49] Together, these considerations suggest a rule that may well emerge as the principal touchstones of antitrust law with respect to restraints on players. Hence it becomes crucial in assessing the future application of antitrust restraints

45. Ibid. at 1066.
46. Ibid. at 1066.
47. In two recent cases—*Bridge Corporation* v. *Contract Bridge League* and *STP Corporation* v. *U.S. Auto Club*—the joint setting of technical criteria for participation was held reasonable.
48. 372 U.S. 253, 264 (1963).
49. Ibid. at 270, 271.

to weigh the practical effectiveness of existing controls on players and to determine whether viable alternative measures exist that might be less restrictive of individual economic freedom.

Antitrust and Interteam Relations

Sam Rayburn's oft-quoted remark that "those who want to get along have to go along" is a practical rule, if not a legal one, that applies to businessmen as well as politicians. It is probably characteristic of any law such as the Sherman Act that its most visible applications are to extreme deviations from accepted behavior, and its literal prohibitions are often far removed from the reality of most business transactions. Only when disregard for the law becomes too obvious does a consensus emerge for cracking down on lawbreakers, and this is especially so for laws that depend heavily, as the Sherman Act does, on the cooperation of aggrieved businessmen for successful enforcement.

These considerations may well explain why the act has been so infrequently applied to the relationships between competing teams, which are seldom likely to challenge the bases for their own existence. (By similar logic, antitrust challenges by players are more common precisely because they have little investment in the system.) The adoption of the institution of league commissioners responsive to the "best interests" of a sport "as a whole," on the other hand, suggests the much greater reliance placed by team owners on the mechanics of material self-interest in an unregulated economy.

According to one district court: "The successful operation of a major league professional . . . team requires (1) membership in a league in which the several clubs are reasonably well matched in playing strength and are located in areas which can and will support the teams by attendance throughout the season sufficient to provide adequate revenues for both the home and visiting clubs, (2) the acquisition of a group of capable players, and (3) the sale of television rights."[50] The antitrust laws are relevant to each of these areas, but with respect to each there has been only limited antitrust activity.

The terms and conditions on which franchises are granted to professional teams might well be subject to antitrust action, since they reflect deliberate efforts to curb competition in any geographical market and to control conditions of entry, sale, and movement. But no decisions have

50. *American Football League* v. *National Football League,* 205 F. Supp. 60 at 62 (D.C. Md. 1962), *aff'd.* 323 F.2d 124 (4th Cir. 1963).

been reported in cases brought against leagues by thwarted franchise applicants.[51] On the other hand, a recent decision of the Court of Appeals for the District of Columbia, *Pro-Football, Inc.* v. *Hecht*,[52] could presage considerable future litigation by would-be applicants. The court ordered an inquiry into the allegations of three businessmen who had sought franchises to compete with the Washington Redskins that the team's lease to use Robert F. Kennedy Memorial Stadium on an exclusive basis violated the antitrust laws by blocking competitive access to a scarce monopoly resource.[53] If the plaintiffs prevail in challenging the exclusivity of the Redskins' stadium lease—threshold efforts to shelter the stadium as a governmental instrumentality having now failed—further litigation of at least two significant sorts can be expected to follow. First, exclusive leases of stadiums can be challenged thereafter. Aside from *Hecht* itself, *Shayne* v. *National Hockey League*,[54] where the NHL won a lease to the new Nassau Coliseum over the competing World Hockey Association, is a precursor of such highly destabilizing developments. Second, if the definition of the monopoly "facility" is expanded beyond the arena itself, it would be but a very short step to attempt to attack grants of territorial exclusivity from organized leagues to member teams.

In the latter connection, specific practices affecting competition in certain sports have been attacked also under the provisions of section 2 of the Sherman Act, which bars monopolization, attempts to monopolize, or combinations or conspiracies to monopolize any part of interstate trade. Such litigation does not follow paths as simple as the per se rule under section 1, but requires full-scale inquiries into the economic conditions

51. No opinion is reported in the $12 million suit against the American Football League (mentioned in congressional hearings on the proposed NFL-AFL merger bill in 1966) claiming that, in the absence of the merger agreement, the plaintiff would have been granted a new AFL franchise in Chicago to compete with the NFL Chicago team. *See Professional Football League Merger,* Hearings before the Antitrust Subcommittee of the House Committee on the Judiciary, 89 Cong. 2 sess. (1966), pp. 70–72.

52. 444 F.2d 931 (1971), *reversing* 312 F. Supp. 472, *cert. denied,* 404 U.S. 1047 (1972).

53. A long series of cases proclaim requirements for openness and nondiscrimination in access among users of what have been called "natural monopoly" resources, commencing with *United States* v. *Terminal Railroad Association of St. Louis,* 224 U.S. 383 (1912) (railway company controlled a vital landing for river barges) and extending to the Supreme Court's important recent holding in *United States* v. *Otter Tail Power Co.,* 409 U.S. 820 (1973) (dominant power company in area refused to "wheel" power for competing municipal utilities).

54. See Bureau of National Affairs, *Antitrust and Trade Regulation Report,* No. 541 (Dec. 7, 1971), p. A-17.

of the industry in question to ascertain whether the defendant possesses "monopoly power" in the industry (the "relevant market"), and whether the defendant's conduct has aimed at acquiring or maintaining such monopoly power. Tests are normally subjective and at best imprecise. Thus, the economic burden of such litigation tends to be prohibitive for private litigants, who have seldom prevailed in cases of this type.

The leading case in this area is *United States* v. *International Boxing Club of New York, Inc.*,[55] in which the Justice Department successfully mounted a lengthy attack on a conspiracy to monopolize the market for championship boxing (in the aftermath of the retirement of heavyweight Joe Louis) by virtue of exclusive contracts with all contenders, control over key stadiums, preferential agreements with the Columbia Broadcasting System, and the organizational medium of the International Boxing Club. The courts ordered divestiture of stadiums and dissolution of the IBC, prohibited exclusive contracts with boxers, and ordered compulsory leasing of stadiums on reasonable terms. Inasmuch as the offense of monopolization banned by section 2 can derive from a set of practices considerably more pervasive than any particular restraint of trade, the *International Boxing* case reflects the equally pervasive remedies—including divestiture of ownership—available to successful plaintiffs in a section 2 case.

Less effective was litigation brought by the American Football League against the National Football League, claiming that the NFL had undertaken to expand in an effort to exclude the newer AFL from key cities.[56] Despite the coincidence of NFL expansion with the launching of the new league, the court found that the "relevant market" for major-league football competition was a national one, not local or regional, so that the NFL did not have the requisite degree of market power to exclude another league from competition.[57]

In a more recent case, the same issues arose regarding the emergence of a new league in hockey, wherein an established league was temporarily enjoined from enforcing its reserve clause.[58] The court found that the

55. 358 U.S. 242 (1959).

56. *American Football League* v. *National Football League,* 205 F. Supp. 60 (D.C. Md. 1962), *aff'd.* 323 F.2d 124 (5th Cir. 1963).

57. Similar issues are posed in the context of the local New York City market by *Shayne* v. *National Hockey League,* cited above.

58. *Philadelphia World Hockey Club* v. *Philadelphia Hockey Club,* reported in Bureau of National Affairs, *Antitrust and Trade Regulation Report,* No. 588 (Nov.

NHL possessed and exercised unreasonable monopoly power, because it controlled essentially all the hockey players available for major-league play. NHL control was an unreasonable restraint because it made it impossible for a new league, such as the WHA, to compete successfully with it.

The court's decision opened the door for competitive leagues, but its intent was clearly not to reverse the *AFL* decision. The court made several distinctions between hockey and football to justify different treatments of the two sports. First, it noted that the NHL's reserve clause granted a team exclusive bargaining rights with a player for three years after the termination of the contract, a provision substantially stronger than the NFL's one-year option clause. Second, the court saw an important distinction between the sports in the supply of new players. Whereas football obtains most of its players from colleges, hockey uses an extensive minor-league system, in which a player is bound to his minor-league team by a reserve clause, unless he can make an NHL team. The court concluded that these two factors produced in football a "picture of relative openness and availability of players."[59] The court rejected the NHL claim that it resembled a vertically integrated steel producer that also owned an iron ore mine on the grounds that it had monopolized the counterpart to iron ore—the ranks of professional hockey players. The NHL had claimed that the relevant resource was the amateur hockey system, but the court disagreed, defining the relevant market as the market for major-league players, rather than for professional players generally. According to the court: "The . . . 50,000 amateur hockey players allegedly available to the WHA are not the 'iron ore' from which viable competition can be built. If the WHA is to compete effectively for attendance and television rights with commensurate payments, the WHA must have a 'show' which is equal or nearly equal to that of the NHL today."[60]

14, 1972), p. A-3. This case was one of several that arose from the signing of former NHL players by the WHA just before the latter began its first year of operation. Four other cases were consolidated for argument with *WHA* v. *NHL,* including suits against players John McKenzie and Bobby Hull that were entered by their former teams.

59. *WHA* v. *NHL* (E.D. Pa., No. 1995), p. 104 of the Opinion.

60. Ibid., p. 100. A later case in another federal judicial district has enforced the same reserve clause on breach-of-contract grounds under state law, without reversing or resolving antitrust issues. See *Nassau Sports* v. *Peters,* reported in Bureau of National Affairs, *Antitrust and Trade Regulation Report,* No. 594 (Jan. 2, 1973), p. A-10.

Drawing an inference from the *International Boxing, American Football League,* and *World Hockey Association* cases that might be relevant to other sports is not likely to be particularly productive with respect to the central issue in all three cases, the alleged monopolization of franchises and players, because of the unique circumstances of each sport cited by the courts. Nonetheless, speculation about the contribution of public support for the practices to the ultimate resolution of each case is inevitable, and probably of some pertinence as well.

For football, public acceptance of league autonomy has been so strong that, after litigation failed to resolve the differences between the two football leagues, oblique public sanction was given for an otherwise questionable merger to divide a larger pie, thus sparing the owners from having to try to outbid each other for players and franchises. The leagues' joint agreement—centering on the creation of a championship game (the Super Bowl), a common draft of college players, full integration of playing schedules, equal division of television income, and controlled expansion —was itself exempted in 1966 from antitrust attack by a statutory rider attached by the House Ways and Means Committee to an investment credit bill. Thus, a provision expressly tailored to exempt the NFL-AFL merger from the antitrust laws enables two or more professional football leagues to combine through a joint agreement in a single league "if such agreement increases rather than decreases the number of football clubs so operating."[61]

The football merger exemption was only the most recent congressional statement on the antitrust aspects of interteam relationships. Joint agreements for obtaining sponsored telecasts of professional football, baseball, hockey, and basketball events have also been exempted. Thus, the ever-increasing interrelationship between sports and advertising in mass communications, which lies at the economic foundation of professional sports, is removed from antitrust coverage.

Public Law 87-331[62] was enacted in 1961 to lift the prohibitions laid down by Judge Allen K. Grim of the U.S. District Court for the Eastern

61. 15 U.S.C. sec. 1291.

62. Its key provisions are as follows: "That the antitrust laws . . . shall not apply to any joint agreement by or among persons engaging in or conducting the organized professional team sports of football, baseball, basketball, or hockey, by which any league of clubs participating in professional football, baseball, basketball, or hockey contests sells or otherwise transfers all or any part of the rights of such league's member clubs in the sponsored telecasting of the games of football, baseball, basketball, or hockey, as the case may be, engaged in or conducted by such clubs" (75 Stat. 732).

District of Pennsylvania in 1953 in *United States* v. *National Football League*.[63] In that case, the Justice Department succeeded in attacking the provisions of article 10 of the NFL's bylaws, which, inter alia, prohibited telecasts of competing professional games in home territories of other teams as being territorial restrictions unlawful under section 1 of the Sherman Act. Specifically, the court invalidated the provisions of article 10 that blocked telecasts competing with telecasts of away games, while upholding as reasonable (to protect the league structure) a similar prohibition on days when home games are played and striking down the football commissioner's powers to control all television and radio broadcasts. Since the ability of the commissioner to maximize radio and television revenue was thus judicially impeded, the subsequent enactment of P.L. 87-331 represented an important step in the growth of a political consensus that permits professional sports to become a primary television commodity.[64]

Thus, another key aspect of the activities of professional sports teams and leagues was legislatively exempted from the antitrust laws. Meanwhile, within the coverage of these laws there lies much ground as yet unplowed but capable of sustaining a bumper crop of antitrust litigation. Whether Congress now maintains a hands-off attitude, permitting litigation to flourish in the courts, or takes some initiative to legislate solutions that can avoid continuing antitrust confrontations is the key question for the future.

The Antitrust Future

To speculate about the future importance of antitrust principles to professional sports requires making assumptions about the public's desire to bring sports commercialism under firm external control. From this review of applications to organized sports of the Sherman Act's "charter

---

63. 116 F. Supp. 319.

64. In the process of permitting the expansion of television coverage of professional sports, Congress was conscious of the possible impact of such growth on attendance and gate receipts of collegiate and high school athletics, as well. The effort to protect such activities, expressed in P.L. 87-331 as a limitation of the antitrust exemption of league telecasts to times other than those at which high school and college football is normally played (Friday nights and Saturday afternoons), has not stopped "dropout" games, in which individual professional teams make their own arrangements for telecasts on those days, presumably at the risk of violating any applicable antitrust laws.

of economic liberty," it appears that much of the past unevenness of this pattern can be explained in terms of the strength of public sentiment toward activities that sometimes approach national mania. To the extent that organized athletics can maintain public respect, there will be little incentive on the part of either courts or Congress to force professional sports to conform to norms of behavior somewhat arbitrarily drawn from less noble realms of economic activity. On the other hand, whenever abuse of public confidence is clearly perceived and unambiguously substantiated, the barrier to external regulation will tend to fall away.

This formulation may illuminate the reasons why Curt Flood's challenge to baseball's antitrust exemption proved ultimately impotent. Flood's chances for success rested on the hope that a demonstration of changing attitudes toward the sport—pitting the vulnerability of individual players against the deepening commercialism of their profession—could sway the Supreme Court to undertake a thorough-going reexamination of the grounds for its judicial restraint. It is perhaps significant that the section of the Court's opinion which presents its stone-faced denial of relief is preceded by somewhat anomalous snatches of verse and history in the tradition of the sport's most romantic bards. All of this was in bold relief to the claim of peonage that Flood had unsuccessfully sought to advance.

By any measure, it is an uphill fight to apply and extend the dead seriousness of the antitrust laws to the mythological kingdom of professional sports. This is especially so with regard to legislative changes. The economic and sentimental influence of organized sports has produced, if anything, two legislative *exemptions* during the past decade (for televised sports and for the AFL-NFL merger), and an exemption for mergers in all sports has been proposed.[65] It may be that the high-water mark of outright exemption, both legislatively and judicially defined, has now been reached and that the future will see Congress making a deliberate effort to reconcile the public's interest in free competition with the need for structured interaction between professional teams.

The possible approaches to external controls, ranging from full application of the antitrust laws to outright exemption, are as numerous as the questionable practices themselves.[66] One possibility with respect to

65. First introduced as S. 2373, 92 Cong. 1 sess. (1971). The intent was to permit the merger of the two professional basketball leagues, but its language was general.

66. Indeed, this review would not be complete without reference to the separate body of federal legislation centered on the National Labor Relations Act, under

the proposed basketball merger is to legislate restrictions on specific key aspects of league activity, such as player retention. Another may be to impose legislative guidelines upon judicial disposition of antitrust suits, although this device poses the considerable risk that a statute will not mean exactly what it appears to say.[67] Another approach would be to place professional sports under a structure of regulation by commission more or less comparable to the regulation imposed on particular segments of industry.[68]

How soon a consensus on any one approach can be reached by the entire Congress is debatable. Indeed, given increasing antagonisms be-

---

which the Supreme Court has indicated that controversies between employers and organized employees are immune from antitrust sanctions. See *Amalgamated Meat Cutters* v. *Jewel Tea,* 381 U.S. 676 (1965), a case urged upon the Supreme Court by the major leagues in the *Flood* case. The issue, however, was not touched on by the Court in its decision, 407 U.S. at 285, and hence remains an open question. See Michael S. Jacobs and Ralph K. Winter, Jr., "Antitrust Principles and Collective Bargaining by Athletes: Of Superstars in Peonage," *Yale Law Journal,* Vol. 81 (November 1971), pp. 1–29. Practically speaking, collective bargaining (supported by the threat, and in the 1972 baseball season by the fact, of strikes) has already proved to be a tool of maximum utility for players, complementing and supporting interrelated strategies of antitrust litigation and legislative pressure. By financing players' suits—typified by the Flood case itself and *Oscar Robertson* v. *National Basketball Association* (S.D.N.Y. 1970, No. 1526), which enjoined the basketball merger and forced the merger question before the Congress—collective action in the broadest sense has already begun to equalize power between owners and players.

67. One such compromise measure introduced in the House in 1972, H.R. 2305, would apply the antitrust laws to organized professional team sports, but would exempt application to measures bearing on "(1) the acquisition of competitive playing strengths; (2) the employment, selection, or eligibility of players, or the reservation, selection, or assignment of player contracts; (3) the right to operate within specific geographic areas; or (4) the preservation of public confidence in the honesty in sports contests."

68. One measure suggested in 1972, S. 3445, entitled the Federal Sports Act of 1972, would have created a Federal Sports Commission within the Department of Commerce. The substantive powers of this commission were limited to issuance of rules concerning:

(a) the procedures for imposing territorial restrictions on the broadcast of professional sports events on commercial television (said rules shall be promulgated only after consultation with the Federal Communications Commission);

(b) the sale and/or transfer of professional team franchises;

(c) the mechanisms or procedures for transferring amateur athletes into professional sports;

(d) the form of player contracts (but not the terms of those contracts), in order to best assure adequate disclosure of the terms of such contracts to the contracting parties (S. 3445, 92 Cong. 2 sess., introduced March 30, 1972, p. 7).

Other powers and lines of authority for commission regulation are, of course, conceivable.

tween the key participants—witness the 1972 baseball strike—it might seem altogether improbable that any clear direction could emerge from the legislative process. In the eventuality of continuing conflict, it might be preferable for Congress to delegate resolution of conflict to a separate advisory body, a National Sports Commission. Such a group would be a *study* commission, not a *regulatory* commission, and would in its composition attempt to bring together experts holding the confidence of the public, the Congress, and effected interests. Certain aspects of its activities, however, must be mandatory. It must have a definite charge from Congress to make clear-cut recommendations for national policy within a definite time period. It must have subpoena powers and powers of confidentiality, so that it can extract the information needed for accurate and informed economic judgments. It must have ample financial resources to retain staff and consultants and ensure high-quality personnel. Under such circumstances, and—above all—if vigorously led, an independent National Sports Commission could itself serve as the vehicle for the long-overdue compromises that the health of professional sports now so clearly requires.

In the meantime, of course, there may not yet be the occasion for compromise. Hence, despite the burdens and the costs of continued confrontation, a growing volume of antitrust litigation of the sort outlined in this chapter must be anticipated. In this regard, the federal courts have been more and more utilized as a check against competitive abuses throughout organized sports—with the continuing exception of baseball. The path suggested by Justice Brennan in *White Motor* is becoming a promising avenue for relief. Diligent efforts are required to demonstrate that particular team practices are excessively harsh in their effects upon individuals and that reasonable alternatives exist to ensure the effective organization of professional sports. Whatever the legislative outcome, therefore, the patient mining of the factual contexts in which professional sports operate will continue. Through this process of substantiating for both courts and Congress that better ways exist—the kind of effort pioneered in this book—it may well be that our legal institutions stand the greatest chance of being able to play a constructive role.

CHAPTER TWELVE

Alternatives in Sports Policy

ROGER G. NOLL

THE PRINCIPAL CONCERN of the sports fan is about matters that affect him clearly and directly: the availability of contests (live and broadcast) and the quality and evenness of athletic competition. The effects on these matters of the operating rules of professional sports are not easily perceived, even by those most intimately connected with the game. But at least some aspects of these effects emerge from the analysis of various aspects of the industry developed in this book. This chapter brings these strands together in a discussion of the policy alternatives available in dealing with the concerns of the fan. The first section deals with the problem of predicting how the performance of the industry would be altered by changes in its operating procedures. The second section discusses the institutional means—such as the proposed federal sports commission—for making the operating rules of sports more consistent with the public interest.

Policy Issues and Sports Operations

The concerns of fans are related to many other subsidiary issues of sports operations and government policy. This section connects the more important operating procedures of sports—franchise location decisions, the player reservation system, and broadcasting policy—with the interests of fans, owners, and players, and proposes some alternatives to the current rules and policies that leagues have voluntarily adopted or that have been imposed by government.

Franchise Locations

Citizens and sportswriters are quick to express outrage when their home city loses a sports franchise. The public policy issue that usually arises is whether the government ought to prevent, or at least control, the

411

movement of teams. But this is a highly superficial response to the problem. One must first ask why citizens become so concerned over losing a team. The answer is simply that it is very difficult to find a replacement, even if one could be profitable, because the leagues carefully control both the number and the location of franchises. A city can spend literally decades convincing the management of sports that it should have a team.

It does not make sense to force the owner of a business to continue to sustain financial losses operating in one location when he believes he could do much better elsewhere, so it is unlikely that the government will ever decide to prevent the transfer of franchises. But that does not mean that it should continue to be next to impossible for a city to gain a franchise. The central issue of public policy—and the one that seems most likely to result in government action—is whether existing teams should be permitted to maintain a scarcity of franchises.

The scarcity of franchises accomplishes two ends. First, it enhances the value of existing teams. This occurs because it reduces competition for fans; causes revenues from national broadcasting rights to be divided among fewer teams; allows the market price of both existing and expansion teams to be higher; preserves a few potentially lucrative franchise sites so that an existing team that begins to fail financially has an attractive alternative site; and, because of the threat of moving, gives a team additional bargaining power when negotiating stadium agreements or local broadcasting rights. The last point is illustrated by the attempts of the operators of Robert F. Kennedy Memorial Stadium in Washington, D.C., to keep the Senators, and later to lure the Padres, by promising a better rental agreement. Second, with fewer teams, and, consequently, fewer openings for major-league players, the average quality of play is probably higher—how much higher, and whether fans care about absolute quality of teams (rather than close competition or the presence of a few superior players), is uncertain.

Another important question related to the transfer of franchises is why a team would suffer financial losses in the first place. The reason usually given is that the team does not receive adequate support from its hometown fans, but it must be small comfort to a city the size of Seattle that it lost a baseball team because its team did not draw as well as teams in New York or Los Angeles. If each team must depend largely upon the revenues it can generate from admissions and broadcasting in its home territory, the charge of inadequate hometown support will persistently recur in all but the largest cities. The financial success of teams in smaller cities depends critically on the arrangements within its league for dividing revenues.

The effect of tax policies on franchise locations is also important. The practice of allowing owners to capitalize and depreciate most of the purchase price of a franchise has created a significant incentive for fairly rapid turnover of franchises. If a team is resold every few years, it is likely that occasionally the highest bidder will be someone from another geographical area who wishes to acquire the team. Furthermore, since only rich people with diverse business interests can take full advantage of the tax benefits of ownership, an owner is less likely to be interested in building a durable market for his team. His main concern is that he have a salable asset when his depreciation runs out, and as long as the number of franchises is scarce, businessmen in other cities will continue to be willing to purchase his team no matter how bad the team's local operation.

Finally, the instability of franchise locations is further magnified by the competition among local governments to promise ever lower rents for increasingly expensive facilities in order to attract teams. Since these subsidized rents bear no relation to true costs, a city that holds out for a cost-based rental agreement can lose its team to a city in which the true economic value of the team, measured by the excess of revenues over true costs, is actually lower.

Both forms of public subsidy of sports—tax breaks and stadium rents below cost—can have an effect on the number of financially viable teams. Several teams benefit from these subsidies by more than $1 million annually. In baseball, this is roughly the net gain to a team from attracting an additional 500,000 fans during a season,[1] which represents nearly half the average attendance of major-league baseball teams. These indirect subsidies are also about two-thirds the size of the average baseball team's total revenues from broadcasting. Thus, it is reasonable to conclude that many teams are financially viable only because of the subsidies they receive.

Whether subsidies of sports enterprises are socially desirable depends upon one's view of several related issues. The first is the overall equity of

---

1. With an average price of $3 per ticket, a team captures $1.5 million in gross revenues from 500,000 fans. But about 20 percent of this goes to the visiting team, and about a third more goes to rent, admissions taxes, and the other costs to the team that depend upon attendance (such as ushers, ticket sellers, and maintenance). Each fan generates about 50 cents in concession profits to the team, so that 500,000 fans produce a net gain of about $1 million.

the system of taxes and expenditures. The tax provisions used by sports teams are a small part of the much larger issue of tax reform, and the expenditures of local governments on sports facilities are rarely more than a small part of the debate over local government priorities. Second is the social merit of subsidizing sports as a means of increasing the number of economically viable sports enterprises. Third is the effectiveness of indirect subsidization through taxes and low rent as compared to other methods of increasing the profitability of sports enterprises. Among the alternatives are direct subsidies, more liberal rules governing league expansion, and more even revenue-sharing arrangements among the teams in a league.

The principal disadvantage of tax subsidies as compared with these alternatives is that they apply to all teams, regardless of the amount of subsidization the franchise requires in order to survive. In fact, since the more remunerative franchises sell for higher prices and therefore have a larger basis for calculating player depreciation expense, the subsidy provided to them through the tax system is actually somewhat larger than for the less successful teams.

With these thoughts in mind, several other possibilities for dealing with the franchise problem emerge. All appear to make more sense than either the present system or direct government prohibition of or restriction on the relocation of teams.

• Government could require some minimum degree of revenue sharing among teams in a league. This would at least partially alleviate the wide disparities in the economic potential of franchise sites that contribute to the instability of franchises.

• Government could eliminate or severely restrict the extent to which franchise costs could be allocated to players and depreciated. The upper limit should be the reasonable profit expectations of teams in a sport. This would eliminate the present incentive to use ownership of a sports enterprise as a shelter from income taxation revenues earned in other business activities. It would also tend to return sports ownership to individuals whose primary motivation for owning a team is to operate the team successfully, and who are thus less interested in selling the team within a few years. But to preserve many of the existing teams, this measure would have to be accompanied by more even revenue sharing.

• Government could insist that leagues expand whenever someone is willing to put up a reasonable amount of money for a franchise. What would be "reasonable" is, of course, debatable. Existing owners have some claim to compensation, to the extent that expansion reduces the income of existing teams. This will happen if more teams share in a fixed national broadcasting contract, if attendance at games in the expansion city is below the league average (the existing teams then receive a diminished visitor's share for games in the new city), or if the new team goes bankrupt, forcing the league to operate the franchise until a new owner can be found or the team can be disbanded in an orderly fashion (certainly not in the middle of a season). To the extent that the new arrangements continued to permit reserve or option clauses in player contracts, owners would have a financial stake in the contracts they controlled. New teams would still be required to purchase these contracts. In order to forestall the possibility that owners might thwart a relatively open expansion policy by setting player prices unrealistically high, limits could be set on the price of a contract: two or three times the player's salary might be a reasonable limit, and would establish at least a rough correlation between the price of a contract and the quality of the player, a characteristic that current expansion prices do not have.

Player Reservation and Comparative Team Strengths

Sports officials argue that without limitations on the competition for players, playing talent would tend to be concentrated in the biggest cities and in the teams whose owners are willing to spend the most money. The greater earning potential of the big cities and the economically irrational drive to win regardless of the cost that is said to motivate some owners would give a few teams an enormous advantage in bidding for players. Other teams would then be left with weak players and poor playing records, which would further erode their revenues and cause them to fail financially.

None of the empirical or theoretical analysis in this book, even by authors who favor maintaining some form of reservation system, lends any support to the view that player reservation has a significant effect on the balance of competition. The theoretical conclusion is that the reserve clause could balance competition only if player trades and sales were prohibited—certainly an undesirable and unenforceable proposition. Empirical investigations find no discernible relation between the closeness of competition on the field and the degree of competition in the market for players. They also find no evidence that the prime motivation of the vast majority of owners is any consideration other than profits.

Support for the reserve clause, or a similar measure, can be based on two grounds. First, it improves the financial position of teams in the less lucrative markets by lowering their costs and by giving them assets—exclusive rights to their players—that can be sold to richer teams. Second, it offsets to some degree the tendency in the competitive market to pay a player in relation to his contribution to team revenues rather than to revenues for the entire league. Since some of the revenues a player generates for a team arise because he improves the relative standing of his team, the net contribution of the player to his sport must reflect the declining revenues his performance causes for other teams whose relative quality he causes to decline. Thus, the reserve clause does operate to increase the number of financially viable teams and compensates for an inherent inefficiency in the player market.

Perhaps more important than the debate over the exact effects of the reserve clause is the fact that all three of its alleged benefits—more balanced competition, greater financial security for weaker teams, player salaries more in line with a player's value to a league—could be obtained by mechanisms other than the reserve clause.

All three objectives would be served if teams divided income more evenly. In order to preserve an owner's incentive to maintain the quality of a team, a team's financial success must depend heavily on its ability to attract fans. But the dependence need not be total, as it is in most sports. At the minimum, other sports might be required to copy football's lead, by sharing gate receipts relatively evenly between home and visiting teams. For sports that are heavily dependent on local broadcasting fees, similar sharing arrangements could be required for these revenues. Even more effective than splitting revenues between the home and visiting teams would be to divide a share of the revenues equally among all teams. For example, the home team might receive 50 percent of gate and broadcast receipts, the visiting team 25 percent, and a league-wide fund, to be divided equally among all teams, the remaining 25 percent. This would reduce the financial disparities among teams and would also result in lower player salaries than would a competitive system with less even revenue sharing. Since a team would receive half of the increase in revenues attributable to a player (the rest being shared), the maximum it would be willing to pay to a player is less than if it received all the hometown revenue he generates.

Interteam financial disparities could also be reduced by increasing competition among teams for revenues. More teams could be placed in the most lucrative markets, and prohibitions on broadcast competition could be removed. Competition in a single market cannot be expected to result in a roughly equal division of revenues among all the teams in each year. Since some fans will give their loyalties to the more successful team, in a given year wide disparities in attendance and revenues would result. But over a long period of time, a capable owner should field the most attractive team in his city a reasonable fraction of the time, so that long-run revenues would be more evenly balanced. In any event, it is difficult to see the justification for preventing an owner from attempting to capture a share of a big-city market should he want to try. If he fails, the team can always move back to a smaller market. If he succeeds, the effect on league financial and playing balance can only be beneficial.

An effective mechanism for preventing an overzealous owner from monopolizing playing talent is to place a ceiling on a team's total budget for player salaries. Suppose that no team could spend more for player salaries than 150 percent of the league average expenditure in the previous year, and that each year every player was free to play for any team that offered him a job. The limit on total salaries would prevent a single team from signing a large number of superior players, would still permit substantial annual growth in the average compensation of players, and would substantially narrow the spread among teams in total player salaries (and, presumably, playing quality). An argument against the proposal might be that it is difficult to enforce: how would the league prevent illegal extra payments to players? The best protection against this is competition. The previous contracts of each player would be available for inspection, as would all the other offers that a player rejected. If a team persistently succeeded in signing players at salaries lower than other teams were offering, it would arouse suspicion that it was violating the rule. Furthermore, detection would be aided by the fact that if a team were substantially exceeding the league salary limit, either several players would have to be receiving payments on the side or a few players would have to receive much more than called for by their contracts. Investigations of the records of the teams and players, together with the information on past and rejected salary offers, should make enforcement of this rule feasible.

Broadcasting Rights

For most fans, televised sports are the most important source of sports entertainment. And fans, sportswriters, and even the President of the

United States have spoken out against various aspects of current broadcasting policy, particularly the local blackout of games.

The proposal to make local blackouts illegal raises knotty economic issues. First, the broadcasting rights to a performance by two teams are clearly the property of the teams. Some teams do not now sell rights to televise their home games locally because they believe, rightly or wrongly, that the revenues they would receive from local telecasts would be more than offset by a decline in gate receipts. A requirement that these rights be given or sold to a local station is a rather arbitrary confiscation of personal property.

Second, to force a local team to allow a local station to carry a local game that was being televised elsewhere is to provide an economic boon to the station. A home game of the local team will draw larger audiences than another game, and thereby increase the advertising revenues of the station that carries it. Some of this increase in audience and advertising revenues will come at the expense of other stations in the same locality.

Third, the value of local broadcasting rights is likely to increase significantly in the near future with the development of pay-TV or, as it is more politely known, subscription television (STV).[2] Many cable television systems have already begun to offer STV channels that, for some charge in addition to the monthly subscription fee for cable television, give viewers access to programs not normally televised—principally recent movies and sports events. In addition, over-the-air STV is likely to develop in several of the largest cities during the mid-1970s. The regulatory rules established by the Federal Communications Commission to control STV provide that no sports event that appears locally on free TV can switch to STV until it has been off the free TV airwaves for two years. Thus, to require teams to televise their home games locally would be to deny them access to the potentially lucrative STV market, and to deny the emerging STV industry what is likely to be one of its more attractive offerings. In smaller cities, revenues from local sports events on STV might be the determining factor in whether the area could support a major-league team, or whether STV would be financially viable. Even in the biggest cities, the viable number of teams and competing STV channels on cable systems will be affected by whether home games are allowed to be shown on STV.

2. For a more complete analysis of the prospects for STV, see Roger G. Noll, Merton J. Peck, and John J. McGowan, *Economic Aspects of Television Regulation* (Brookings Institution, 1973).

The preceding arguments are not necessarily definitive ones against a rule to lift blackouts, but they do show that the issue has important financial consequences for the sports industry, broadcasters, and the emerging STV industry, in addition to its obvious relation to the welfare of sports fans. Lifting blackouts would clearly benefit some fans and some broadcasters; would clearly harm some teams, some broadcasters, and STV; and might harm some sports fans, to the extent that it prevented the emergence of new teams.

Another complicated issue is the restriction on broadcast competition. The principal effect of the current arrangements—pooled national rights, exclusive local markets—is to create a series of broadcast monopolies that increase broadcast revenues for sports and advertising costs for sponsors, while reducing the number of broadcasts available to the fan. Although national broadcast revenues are evenly split among the teams in a league, the overall effect of broadcast practices probably contributes to disparities in the financial health of teams. This is because a team's monopoly in broadcasting in its home territory is more important the larger the broadcasting market in which the team is located. The wide variance among teams in local broadcasting revenues, which reflects market sizes, also increases financial disparities, particularly since the visiting team does not receive a share of the revenues from local broadcasts.

Elimination of monopoly rights in broadcasting would, by itself, reduce the broadcast revenues of sports, and might reduce the revenues of every team, including those whose financial condition is weakest (although this is not certain). If a team in a small city could broadcast games into the home territory of a team in a larger city, two possibilities for additional revenue would arise. First, the current practice of granting a visiting team the right to broadcast games back home could be ended, and a team like Kansas City could broadcast its home games against the Yankees back to New York, thereby gaining access to the lucrative New York broadcast market. Second, one or a few teams might produce a package of games to be broadcast either nationally or in nearby major-league cities, in competition with the games and broadcasts of the home teams in the latter area. Thus, San Diego might broadcast games into Los Angeles, or Milwaukee might broadcast into Chicago, or Baltimore might broadcast into Philadelphia. These practices would probably reduce the revenues of teams in big cities, but the benefit to teams in smaller areas could more than offset the losses they would suffer from losing national and local monopoly positions. In any event, the net effect would be to narrow the spread in financial resources among teams. An ancillary benefit would be the added possibilities for competition in broadcasting. Stations that currently cannot broadcast games because of present restrictions, particularly independent stations, would be free to enter the field.

The preceding discussion suggests the following arrangement as a reasonable alternative to the present system, or to the present system modified by a prohibition of blackouts.

• Relatively even sharing of broadcast revenues, along the lines recommended above for gate receipts: either a 60–40 split between home and visiting teams, or a 50–25–25 split among the home team, the visiting team, and a fund to be divided equally among all teams.

• Repeal of the 1961 sports broadcasting act, which exempts leagues from antitrust laws when they pool broadcasting rights to form a single national package, the 1973 bill that lifts the blackouts of sold-out home games, and the rules that inhibit placing home games on STV.

• Prohibition of league rules that grant each team the right to exclude the broadcasts of other teams from its home territory.

Institutional Alternatives in Sports

All sports have essentially the same governing structure. Baseball, football, and both leagues in basketball and hockey each have a single commissioner who, together with a committee of owners, decides upon the operating rules of the sport. Occasionally, governmental institutions exercise some influence: Congress has passed a few laws defining the legal boundaries of policies within sports, the Department of Justice has occasionally intervened in sports operations by invoking antitrust statutes, and the Federal Communications Commission has laid down a few rules that affect sports broadcasting. But, for the most part, serious attempts to change the operating procedures of sports have come from within the industry, when players or new leagues have used labor relations and antitrust laws as the basis for attacks on the restrictions on competition for players and on the number and location of franchises.

The major development in the institutional organization of sports over the past several decades has been the rise of militant, strong player associations. This has had a significant effect on the operating rules of sports. Before analyzing alternative institutional structures, it is worthwhile to examine how player associations are likely to affect the present system, in the absence of intervention by the federal government and assuming that mergers between competing leagues are allowed to proceed.

Where the Player Associations Are Taking Sports

The principal effect of the player associations has been to raise all salaries while narrowing salary differentials between the least and most able major-league athletes. In the short run, they have achieved this by raising minimum pay, increasing fringe benefits (such as pensions, per diem allowances on road trips, moving allowances, and health coverage), and obtaining greater job security (higher severance pay, arbitration of disputes between players and management, easing requirements for players to be placed on the disabled list, and so forth). In the longer run, they have attacked the player reservation system. Gains thus far include salary arbitration, the requirement that a veteran player approve an assignment of his contract to another team, and, in basketball, the delay of a merger, the terms of which would substantially reduce competition for players.

The attack on the player reservation system can be expected to continue, through new antitrust suits against teams and leagues and through periodic negotiations of the agreements between leagues and player associations. It is reasonable to predict that the current institutional structure of sports will produce a significant weakening of the player reservation system in all four major sports. The prediction will prove incorrect only if the internal strength of the player associations is not great enough to prevent management from destroying them before they achieve this goal. If the associations' strength is in doubt, there will probably be protracted labor disputes in at least some sports before the player reservation system is dismantled (as is most likely) or the associations are emasculated.

The effect of the player associations on the welfare of the fans is likely, in the long run, to be minimal. The dispute between players and management is over the profit in sports, much of which arises from monopolistic practices in the marketplace: broadcasting, home games, control over the number of franchises, concessions, and, in the future, subscription television. Practices that increase the total revenues of sports will be favored by players and owners alike. Thus, player associations will not try to change monopolistic practices that do not directly affect competition for players.

Even the part of the player reservation system that governs competition for new and minor-league players is unlikely to be changed through negotiations between leagues and player associations. Both owners and veteran players will have higher incomes if salaries for minor leaguers and new players are depressed. Since the player associations represent the veteran major-league players, they are likely to agree on the desirability of eliminating competition in the market for nonveteran players. In basketball, for example, owners and players have agreed that the draft system for players coming out of college should be retained, with the drafting team having exclusive negotiating rights to a drafted player for two years.

Increased player salaries would affect fans adversely if they led to increased ticket prices. This result seems unlikely, since the price-setting process in sports is not closely related to player salaries. If a team is maximizing its profits, ticket prices and team quality will be set so that the changes in the team's revenues and costs associated with attracting and serving one more fan are equal. The cost to the team of increasing attendance has two components. First is the direct cost of providing a seat, involving expenditures on ticket sales, ushers, and stadium rent and maintenance. These costs account for one-third to one-half the costs of a sports enterprise, and obviously are unrelated to the salaries of players. Second is the cost of attracting additional fans by improving the quality of the team, which is related to player salaries since, in general, better players receive higher salaries. But the cost of improved quality has other components as well—the cost of purchasing the contract of a player from another team, and the cost implicit in not taking advantage of the possibility of selling player contracts to other teams. Competition in the player market transfers the latter two costs to the player salary category, but does not change the total cost of improving quality. Consequently, it has no effect on the costs that enter into the price-setting mechanism.

The preceding argument rests on the assumption that outcomes in the player market are governed by the quest for profits by teams. The evidence suggests that this is an apt characterization of most sports operations but that some exceptions clearly exist. Where it holds true, profit orientation insulates fans from paying for higher player salaries. The relatively few teams that appear to be operated according to other motives, and that tend to set prices to cover costs but not to create maximum profits, will respond to higher costs of any kind by raising prices. An important consequence of the rise of player associations is that it will tend to make all teams set prices as if they were profit oriented, regardless of their actual motivation, with the increased revenues then going to the players.

Finally, player associations are not likely to try to reduce the financial disparities among teams. While players have an interest in keeping financially troubled franchises operating, they also have an interest in making the value of players as high as possible in the most financially lucrative markets. The greater the disparity in the markets of the members of a league, the higher player salaries will be. Thus, player associations are likely to try to preserve weak franchises by seeking governmental subsidies, by gaining pledges from owners that the league will continue to operate a failing franchise, or by increasing the monopoly power of teams in selling games and broadcasts, but not by adopting more equal sharing of revenues within the league.

One can only conclude from the preceding analysis that the present structure of sports is not likely to produce any material change in the procedures that most affect the welfare of fans. In most cases, the interests of the players coincide with the interests of the owners, and both tend to benefit from the restrictive practices that are costly to fans.

If player associations are unlikely to alter significantly sports operations outside the player market, the only remaining question is whether attempts to enter the industry by those now excluded could do so. But this, too, is not likely to be particularly effective. First, the cost of fighting court battles with established teams to break monopolistic practices is significant; only if entry promises exceptionally good returns is it worth attempting. Second, entrants, being astute businessmen, are not likely to want to make permanent changes in the operating rules of sports; instead, their interests lie in gaining membership in a restored cartel, which can then reinstitute its restrictive practices. Both baseball and football have survived periods of competition without making significant long-term changes in operating structure (other than in the number of teams), and basketball has tried to follow a similar path.

If new entrants into sports are unlikely to change sports operations, then the remaining alternative is governmental action.

Federal Regulation of Sports

One proposed response to the public concern about sports operations is to establish a federal agency to regulate sports, much as other regulatory agencies oversee such industries as transportation, telecommunications, broadcasting, drugs, and financial services. In 1972, Senator Marlow W. Cook introduced legislation that would create a federal commission within the Department of Commerce to regulate sports broadcasting arrangements, drafting procedures, the sale and movement of franchises, and the limitations on competition for players.[3]

One advantage of the proposal is that Congress could delegate to others the difficult task of writing detailed operating rules for sports. A second advantage is that the operations of sports would be subject to continual scrutiny, whereas reliance on congressional intervention would be likely to result in only intermittent investigations and actions. Ideally, a federal regulatory agency would be a highly expert body that would monitor day-to-day developments in sports, vigilantly protecting the public interest by adjusting the operating rules of sports as new policy issues arose.

Whether it is realistic to expect federal regulation of sports to achieve this ideal is debatable. Experience with public regulation in other agencies gives reason to doubt the wisdom of establishing a federal sports commission. In general, regulatory bodies tend to give most of their attention to the arguments and interests of groups that are effectively represented in the formal proceedings of the agency, while overlooking the interests of groups that are not effectively represented.[4] In the sports business, three groups are certain to be well represented: owners of teams, veteran major-league players (through player associations), and broadcasters. Two other groups are almost certain not to be effectively represented. One is sports fans. Only when a city loses a franchise and the city officials act to protect the interests of their constituents is a group of fans likely to have substantial resources available to argue its case. The other unrepresented group consists of players without major-league experience, including free agents and minor leaguers.

As argued above, on a surprisingly large number of issues regarding the operation of sports the interests of the three represented groups either coalesce or at least are not competitive. All three groups probably benefit from the limitations to competition in broadcasting, since scarcity increases the total income each earns from broadcasts. Similarly, the scarcity

3. S. 3445, 92 Cong. 2 sess., introduced March 30, 1972.
4. More elaborate statements of this characteristic of regulatory agencies are presented in Roger G. Noll, *Reforming Regulation: An Evaluation of the Ash Council Proposals* (Brookings Institution, 1971), and "The Behavior of Regulatory Agencies," *Review of Social Economy*, Vol. 29 (March 1971), pp. 15–19 (Brookings Reprint 219). For other views, see Marver H. Bernstein, *Regulating Business by Independent Commission* (Princeton University Press, 1955); Theodore J. Lowi, *The End of Liberalism: Ideology, Policy, and the Crisis of Public Authority* (Norton, 1969), and The President's Advisory Council on Executive Organization, *A New Regulatory Framework: Report on Selected Independent Regulatory Agencies* (U.S. Government Printing Office, 1971).

of franchises is probably in the interests of all three, for it reduces or eliminates competition in each local market and thereby increases the total profitability from admissions and broadcasts. Some of this increased profitability probably accrues to the veteran ball player as a higher salary.

The unrepresented groups are the only ones that might benefit from more competition in the selling of sports contests. If there were more teams, fans would have more choice in attending contests, and more jobs in major-league sports would be open to marginal players. More competition in broadcasting would probably have little effect on unrepresented players, but it would give fans more choice in viewing and listening.

Regardless of the merits of the case for increasing competition in the sale of sports contests, a federal regulatory authority is not likely to take significant steps in that direction, for it will be subject to little if any organized pressure to do so.

The principal source of disagreement among the well-represented groups are the reservation system (players versus owners) and the blackout rule (broadcasters versus owners). Experience indicates that a regulatory agency faced with adjudicating a conflict of interests between two well-represented groups will seek to strike a compromise, even if the merits of the case, based upon either arguments of justice or the consequences of decisions for the general public, indicate that one side should win a clear victory. One might expect that a regulatory agency would settle the issue of player reservation by easing, but not eliminating, the limitations to competition, such as by establishing in all sports an option-clause system that was applicable only to players with a few years' experience and that placed an upper limit on the compensation paid to the team losing a player. This is probably a less liberal outcome than would ultimately emerge from negotiations between players and owners without government interference. One might also expect that some, but not all, aspects of the blackout rule would be eliminated, such as by permitting telecasts of playoff games in the cities in which they are located even if they are not sold out, but maintaining blackouts for regular-season games for which tickets are still available.

These types of compromises will undoubtedly strike many as reasonable resolutions of sticky policy issues, and perhaps they are. But it is not on the basis of their merits that their adoption is predicted. In planning a regulatory agency for an industry, including sports, the nature of the decisions the agency is likely to make should be recognized. If the public interest would be reasonably well served by reaching compromises on the issues that divide the three major special interests in sports, while maintaining the status quo on practices that generate criticism only among groups that are not as well represented, then a regulatory authority for sports is a desirable instrument for making public policy. If, however, the interests of society dictate fundamental changes in the procedures by which franchises are granted and located and by which broadcasting rights are obtained, a regulatory authority for sports is not likely to be effective.

Legislation on Sports Operations

The alternative to regulation of sports is to pass legislation that specifically delimits the extent to which sports enterprises can engage in anticompetitive behavior. Instead of avoiding the responsibility either by inaction that implicitly ratifies continuation of the present system of self-regulation or by establishing a regulatory agency, Congress would undertake to identify the public interest in sports operations and then set forth operating rules for teams and leagues that served that interest.

Congress has engaged in several investigations of sports enterprises, but has succeeded in passing only bills that make matters worse, such as those that authorized league-wide pools of national broadcasting rights and the merger of the two football leagues in the 1960s. Congressman Emanuel Celler, in particular, carried out two exhaustive investigations in the 1950s, but never succeeded in obtaining the kind of comprehensive legislation he thought desirable.

Despite the rather sorry historical record, there is reason to believe that the performance of Congress in this area is improving, and that balanced, comprehensive sports legislation will eventually emerge. Congress did not rush to approve the proposed merger in professional basketball as it had done a few years earlier with the football merger. Many factors contributed to the change in attitude: football is a more popular sport and its owners are probably more influential (although, on the other hand, basketball was represented by Senator Thomas H. Kuchel, whose standing in Congress is high); and the NBA Basketball Players Association in the 1970s, led by Oscar Robertson and Lawrence Fleischer, was a far more potent force against merger than the NFL Players Association was in the mid-1960s, before John Mackey became president and Edward R. Garvey became executive director. But also important was the increasing public concern that had been brought about by franchise shifts, construction of several expensive stadiums, player strikes, and the self-destructive feud between the National Collegiate Athletic Association and the Amateur Athletic Union over control of American participation in international competition. All of these served to weaken the prestige of the individuals responsible for sports operations.

The Senate Subcommittee on Antitrust and Monopoly, at the conclusion of its hearings on the basketball merger in mid-1972, reported out a bill establishing several conditions under which the leagues could obtain an antitrust exemption for their merger.[5] The bill was not passed and eventually died, but its provisions were unique in the history of sports legislation and suggest an important direction that government sports policy might follow. The most important provisions of the bill were:

(1) The contracts of all veteran players were to have a fixed duration that was negotiated by the player and his team, with no limitation on the right of a player to switch teams after the expiration of his contract.

(2) The free-agent draft was to be retained, but a rookie was obligated to play for the team that drafted him for only two years, after which he would be free to negotiate with any team.

(3) National broadcasting revenues were to be shared equally (the merger agreement had stipulated that the American Basketball Association would not share until the expiration of the then current national contract held by the National Basketball Association), and gate receipts were to be split, 70 percent to the home team and 30 percent to the visitors.

The bill did not deal with the pooling of local broadcast revenues, which would more appropriately be dealt with in the context of all sports, nor did it establish rules governing expansion, sharing of local broadcasting rights, territorial rights, and the relocation of teams. Nevertheless, the bill was the first in the history of sports to establish conditions for granting sports an antitrust exemption, and thus may prove to be an important precedent.

In any event, the most likely source of significant changes in sports operations, other than in player relations, is Congress. Only Congress can undo the effects of past legislation, and only Congress is likely to take steps to reduce the financial disparities among teams and to ease the procedures controlling expansion. Finally, only Congress has the power and the resources to undertake a thorough examination of the financial aspects of sports. The information on which this book is based is incomplete in important respects because a great deal of the relevant data is not publicly

5. S. 2373, reported Sept. 18, 1972.

available. A necessary first step in reaching firm conclusions on what changes would be in the public interest is for Congress to conduct a definitive investigation of all aspects of sports operations. It could then write comprehensive legislation, covering all the restrictive business practices in sports, spelling out which practices, and with what modifications, should be given antitrust exemption. This would go a long way toward eliminating the present considerable uncertainty over the future of sports, would probably prevent several years of serious labor relations problems punctuated by strikes and lockouts, and would undoubtedly reduce significantly the number of expensive, protracted, and often inconclusive lawsuits that have become characteristic of sports.

Bibliography

Allen, Lee. *The American League Story.* New York: Hill and Wang, 1962.
————. *The National League Story.* New York: Hill and Wang, 1961.
————. *100 Years of Baseball: The Intimate and Dramatic Story of Modern Baseball from the Game's Beginning up to the Present Day.* New York: Bartholomew House, 1950.

Anderson, Mark F. "The Sherman Act and Professional Sports Associations' Use of Eligibility Rules," *Nebraska Law Review,* Vol. 47 (January 1968).

Andreano, Ralph. *No Joy in Mudville: The Dilemma of Major League Baseball.* Cambridge: Schenkman, 1965.

"The Balance of Power in Professional Sports," *Maine Law Review,* Vol. 22 (1970).

Brennan, James T. "Injunction against Professional Athletes Breaching Their Contracts," *Brooklyn Law Review,* Vol. 34 (Fall 1967).

Davenport, David S. "Collusive Competition in Major League Baseball: Its Theory and Institutional Development," *The American Economist,* Vol. 13 (Fall 1969).

Demmert, Henry G. *An Economic Analysis of the Professional Team Sports Industry in the United States.* Lexington, Mass.: Lexington Books, 1973.
————. *The Economics of Professional Team Sports.* Lexington, Mass.: Lexington Books, 1973.

"Discipline in Professional Sports: The Need for Player Protection," *Georgetown Law Journal,* Vol. 60 (February 1972).

Ducker, Bruce. "Pros Offside? The Antitrust Laws and Professional Sports," *Case and Comment,* Vol. 76 (September–October 1971).

Durso, Joseph. *The All-American Dollar: The Big Business of Sports.* Boston: Houghton Mifflin, 1971.

429

Eckler, John. "Baseball: Sport or Commerce?" *University of Chicago Law Review,* Vol. 17 (Autumn 1949).

Edwards, G. Franklin. *The Negro Professional Class.* Glencoe: The Free Press, 1959.

Edwards, Harry. *The Revolt of the Black Athlete.* Glencoe: The Free Press, 1970.

El Hodiri, Mohamed, and James Quirk. "An Economic Model of a Professional Sports League," *Journal of Political Economy,* Vol. 79 (November–December 1971).

Eppel, John P. "Professional Sports," *American Bar Association Section of Antitrust Law, Antitrust Law Journal (Proceedings),* Vol. 33 (1967).

Graham, Frank. *The New York Giants: An Informal History.* New York: Putnam, 1952.

Gregory, Paul. *The Baseball Player: An Economic Study.* Washington: Public Affairs Press, 1956.

Hoffman, Robert B. "Is the NLRB Going to Play the Ball Game?" *Labor Law Journal,* Vol. 20 (April 1, 1969).

Jacobs, Michael S., and Ralph K. Winter, Jr. "Antitrust Principles and Collective Bargaining by Athletes: Of Superstars in Peonage," *Yale Law Journal,* Vol. 81 (November 1971).

Johnson, Frederic A. "The Law of Sports: The Unique Performer's Contract and the Antitrust Laws," *The Antitrust Bulletin,* Vol. 2 (January 1957).

Johnson, William. "Television and Sport," *Sports Illustrated,* Vol. 32 (January 5, 19, 26, 1970).

Jones, J. C. H. "The Economics of the National Hockey League," *Canadian Journal of Economics,* Vol. 2 (February 1969).

Keith, Maxwell. "Developments in the Application of Antitrust Laws to Professional Team Sports," *Hastings Law Journal,* Vol. 10 (November 1958).

Koppett, Leonard. *A Thinking Man's Guide to Baseball.* New York: E. P. Dutton, 1967.

Krasnow, Erwin G., and Herman M. Levy. "Unionization and Professional Sports," *Georgetown Law Journal,* Vol. 51 (Winter 1963).

Law and Contemporary Problems, issue on "Athletics," Vol. 38 (Winter–Spring 1973), ed. John C. Weistart.

Maher, Charles. "Major Sports Stadiums: They Keep Going Up," *Los Angeles Times,* November 14, 1971.

Neale, Walter C. "The Peculiar Economics of Professional Sports," *Quarterly Journal of Economics,* Vol. 78 (February 1964).

Olsen, Jack. "The Cruel Deception," *Sports Illustrated,* Vol. 29 (July 1, 1968).

Parrish, Bernie. *They Call It a Game.* New York: Dial, 1971.

Pascal, Anthony H., and Leonard A. Rapping. "The Economics of Racial Discrimination in Organized Baseball," in Anthony H. Pascal (ed.), *Racial Discrimination in Economic Life.* Lexington, Mass.: Heath, 1972.

Peterson, Robert. *Only the Ball Was White.* Englewood Cliffs: Prentice-Hall, 1970.

Pierce, Samuel R., Jr. "Organized Professional Team Sports and the Antitrust Laws," *Cornell Law Quarterly,* Vol. 43 (Summer 1958).

Rooney, John F., Jr. "Up from the Mines and Out from the Prairies: Some Geographical Implications of Football in the United States," *Geographical Review,* Vol. 59 (October 1969).

Rosenblatt, Aaron. "Negroes in Baseball: The Failure of Success," *Transaction,* Vol. 4 (September 1967).

Rottenberg, Simon. "The Baseball Players' Labor Market," *Journal of Political Economy,* Vol. 64 (June 1956).

Rowan, Carl T. with Jackie Robinson. *Wait Till Next Year: The Life Story of Jackie Robinson.* New York: Random House, 1960.

Scully, Gerald W. "Economic Discrimination in Professional Sports," *Law and Contemporary Problems,* Vol. 38 (Winter–Spring 1973).

———. "Pay and Performance in Major League Baseball," *American Economic Review,* in press.

Seymour, Harold. *Baseball: The Early Years.* New York: Oxford University Press, 1960.

———. *Baseball: The Golden Age.* New York: Oxford University Press, 1971.

Sharnik, Morton. "The Buckeyes Don't Have It," *Sports Illustrated,* Vol. 35 (July 5, 1971).

Shecter, Leonard. *The Jocks.* New York: Warner Paperback Library, 1970.

Shulman, Daniel S., and Bernard M. Baum. "Collective Bargaining in Professional Athletics: The NFL Money Bowl," *Chicago Bar Record,* Vol. 50 (January 1969).

Sloane, Peter J. "The Labour Market in Professional Football," *British Journal of Industrial Relations,* Vol. 7 (July 1969).

————. "The Economics of Professional Football: The Football Club as a Utility Maximiser," *Scottish Journal of Political Economy,* Vol. 18 (June 1971).

"The Super Bowl and the Sherman Act: Professional Team Sports and the Antitrust Laws," *Harvard Law Review,* Vol. 81 (December 1967).

Topkis, Jay H. "Monopoly in Professional Sports," *Yale Law Journal,* Vol. 58 (April 1949).

U.S. Congress. House. Committee on the Judiciary. Subcommittee on Study of Monopoly Power. *Study of Monopoly Power,* Pt. 6, *Organized Baseball.* Hearings. 82 Cong. 1 sess. Washington: Government Printing Office, 1952.

————. *Organized Baseball.* Report of the Subcommittee on Study of Monopoly Power. House Report 2002. 82 Cong. 2 sess. Washington: Government Printing Office, 1952.

————. Antitrust Subcommittee. *Organized Professional Team Sports.* Hearings. 85 Cong. 1 sess. Washington: Government Printing Office, 1957.

————. *Telecasting of Professional Sports Contests.* Hearing. 87 Cong. 1 sess. Washington: Government Printing Office, 1961.

————. Senate. Committee on the Judiciary. Subcommittee on Antitrust and Monopoly. *Organized Professional Team Sports.* Hearings. 85 Cong. 2 sess. Washington: Government Printing Office, 1958. Hearings. 86 Cong. 1 sess. (1959).

————. *Professional Sports Antitrust Bill—1964.* Hearings. 88 Cong. 2 sess. Washington: Government Printing Office, 1964.

————. *Professional Sports Antitrust Bill—1965.* Hearings. 89 Cong. 1 sess. Washington: Government Printing Office, 1965.

————. *Professional Basketball.* Hearing. 92 Cong. 1 sess. (Pt. 1) and 2 sess. (Pt. 2). Washington: Government Printing Office, 1972.

Veeck, Bill. *The Hustler's Handbook.* New York: Putnam, 1965.

————, with Ed Linn. *Veeck—as in Wreck: The Autobiography of Bill Veeck.* New York: Putnam, 1962.

Voigt, David Q. *American Baseball.* Vol. 1: *From Gentlemen's Sport to the Commissioner System.* Vol. 2: *From Commissioners to Continental Expansion.* Norman: University of Oklahoma Press, 1966 and 1969.

Young, A. S. ("Doc"). *Negro Firsts in Sports.* Chicago: Johnson, 1963.

Conference Participants

GEORGE BURMAN *Washington Redskins*
MICHAEL E. CANES *Center for Naval Analyses*
JOHN CLARK *Arthur D. Little, Inc.*
SHELDON S. COHEN *Cohen and Uretz*
PETER S. CRAIG *Southern Railway System*
JAMES D. CULLEN *St. Louis Blues* and *Thomas, Busse, Weiss, Cullen & Godfrey*
LANCE E. DAVIS *California Institute of Technology*
DONALD DE JARDIN *Philadelphia 76ers*
EDWARD F. DENISON *Brookings Institution*
MOHAMED EL HODIRI *University of Kansas*
LAWRENCE FLEISCHER *National Basketball Players Association*
JAMES GARNER *American Baseball League*
EDWARD R. GARVEY *National Football League Players Association*
KERMIT GORDON *Brookings Institution*
JAMES HANNAN *Milwaukee Brewers* and *Reynolds Securities, Inc.*
GEORGE W. HILTON *University of California at Los Angeles*
PHILIP R. HOCHBERG *Daly, Joyce and Bosari*
IRA HOROWITZ *Indiana University*
LEWIS HOYNES *National Baseball League*
MACLAY R. HYDE *Lindquist and Vennum*
THOMAS H. KUCHEL *Wyman, Bautzer, Rothman & Kuchel*
JOHN J. MCGOWAN *Yale University*
MARVIN MILLER *Major League Baseball Players Association*
ROBERT R. NATHAN *Robert R. Nathan Associates, Inc.*
WALTER C. NEALE *University of Tennessee*
ROGER G. NOLL *Brookings Institution*
BENJAMIN A. OKNER *Brookings Institution*

433

WALTER Y. OI *University of Rochester*

BRYAN O'NEAL *National Hockey League*

ANTHONY H. PASCAL *RAND Corporation*

JOSEPH A. PECHMAN *Brookings Institution*

MERTON J. PECK *Yale University*

JAMES P. QUIRK *California Institute of Technology*

LEONARD A. RAPPING *Carnegie-Mellon University*

DONALD J. REGAN *Nagel, Regan & Davidson*

STEVEN R. RIVKIN *Nicholson & Carter*

SIMON ROTTENBERG *University of Massachusetts*

FRANK B. RYAN *Committee on House Administration, U.S. House of Representatives*

IRVING SALEM *Caplin and Drysdale*

JAMES G. SCOVILLE *University of Illinois*

GERALD W. SCULLY *Southern Illinois University*

PETER SLOANE *University of Nottingham*

BILL VEECK *Tranquillity Farms*

EDWARD WEINBERG *Wyman, Bautzer, Rothman & Kuchel*

Note: The affiliations given for the participants listed above are those of December 1971, when the conference was held. As of March 1974, the following participants had changed their affiliations: Michael E. Canes, University of Rochester; Philip R. Hochberg, O'Connor & Hannan; Ira Horowitz, University of Florida; John J. McGowan, Charles Riner Associates; Roger G. Noll, California Institute of Technology; Gerald W. Scully, Southern Methodist University.

Index of Cases Cited

General Index

Aaron, Hank, 250
Adelman, M. A., 269n
Abdul-Jabbar, Kareem, 13–14
Accounting practices, 160–61, 164–65; effects of, 180–83; and investment evaluation, 176–80; and tax write-offs, 166–70, 173–76. *See also* Capitalization; Depreciation
Acme Colored Giants, 226
Advertising. *See* Sponsorship, broadcast
Akena, Lang, 226
Alco Parking Corp., 326n
All-America Conference, 10
Allen, George, 209
Allen, Lee, 225n, 226n
Amateur Athletic Union, 427
American Association, 224, 361, 364
American Baseball Guild, 206–07
American Basketball Association: bonuses in, 170n; and broadcasting, 291. *See also* Basketball; specific franchises (by city and name)
American Broadcasting Company, 283, 289, 292, 300, 302, 304, 306, 307, 323
American Football League: antitrust suit by, 404; and broadcasting, 283, 285, 292, 304, 307–09, 310, 314; and NFL merger, 10, 145, 403n. *See also* Football; specific franchises (by city and name)
American League (baseball): expansion, 372; hiring of blacks by, 233; "war," 10, 349, 356, 359. *See also* Baseball; specific franchises (by city and name)
American League (basketball), 10
Andreano, Ralph, 123n, 186n, 239n, 251n, 252n
Anheuser-Busch Brewing, 298
Anson, Adrian ("Cap"), 225, 226
Antitrust laws, 387–410; areas of application of, 395–407; and Congress, 391–95, 406–07, 408–10, 426–28; exemptions from, 9, 31, 213–14, 275, 279–81, 283, 351, 355, 382, 385–86, 389–95; future of, 385–86, 407–10. *See also* Government,

federal, monopoly studies by, regulation of sports by
Antitrust suits, 211, 213, 215, 279–83, 371, 374, 389–410
Arbitration, 207–09, 212–13; of salary disputes, 216–17
Arenas. *See* Stadiums
Assets, sports: defined, 161–62; exchange of, 175–76; sales of, 173–75. *See also* Contracts, player, sale of; Franchises
Association of Major League Umpires, 208
Atlanta Braves, 19n, 166, 172, 298
Attendance: break-even points in, 130, 133–34, 152; and broadcasting, 281, 284–86, 290n, 292–93, 294–95, 301; and championship races, 119, 139–40, 148–50, 156–57; and competing entertainment, 117, 124; factors affecting, 115–57, 231n, 422; and league model, 35, 37–38, 43, 44, 58; in minor leagues, 284, 305; and player costs, 82; and profits, 130, 422; and race, 119, 128–30, 140, 229, 230, 231–32; and salaries, 200, 422; and stadium rentals, 333–34; and team quality, 92–93, 96–99, 117, 122–23, 127–28, 139–40, 141, 144–45, 148–50, 152, 155–56, 422

Bain, Joe S., 318n
Ball, Philip, 361–62
Ballantine Brewing, 315
Baltimore Colts, 176, 286, 293, 309, 322
Baltimore Orioles, 171, 172, 236, 296, 328–29, 344n
Barker, Donald G., 252n
Baseball: attendance, 96–99, 120–31; and broadcasting, 279–81, 284, 286–91, 293–99, 301–06, 314n, 371–75; costs, 354–86; finances of franchises in, 17–22, 162; franchise costs in, 162–64; industrial self-regulation in, 349–86; interleague animosity in, 356, 372, 375–77; and player markets, 359–71; population-success correlations in, 45–48; and

437